"十三五"江苏省高等学校重点教材（2016-2-098）

普通高等教育国际经济与贸易专业规划教材

# International Settlement
# 国际结算（双语）

尤宏兵　许立帆　林大燕　编

机械工业出版社

本书秉承新颖性、实务性、可操作性原则，主要依据 URC522、UCP600 及 URDG758 等最新、目前正式使用的国际结算规则为指南，以国际结算工具、汇款、托收、信用证业务等常用国际结算方式为主线，系统分析了国际结算的基本原理及实务操作流程，同时增加了国际结算单证制作及国际结算风险管理的内容。本书还对银行保函、备用信用证及国际保理等国际结算方式进行了简要阐述。

本书可供高等院校经管类专业教学使用，也可作为相关业务培训用书。

### 图书在版编目（CIP）数据

国际结算：双语/尤宏兵，许立帆，林大燕编．—北京：机械工业出版社，2018.8（2024.2 重印）

"十三五"江苏省高等学校重点教材 普通高等教育国际经济与贸易专业规划教材

ISBN 978-7-111-60664-2

Ⅰ．①国… Ⅱ．①尤… ②许… ③林… Ⅲ．①国际结算 – 双语教学 – 高等学校 – 教材　Ⅳ．①F830.73

中国版本图书馆 CIP 数据核字（2018）第 183822 号

机械工业出版社（北京市百万庄大街 22 号　邮政编码 100037）

策划编辑：常爱艳　责任编辑：常爱艳　刘鑫佳
责任校对：王明欣　封面设计：鞠　杨
责任印制：李　昂
北京捷迅佳彩印刷有限公司印刷
2024 年 2 月第 1 版第 4 次印刷
184mm×260mm・18 印张・440 千字
标准书号：ISBN 978-7-111-60664-2
定价：49.00 元

凡购本书，如有缺页、倒页、脱页，由本社发行部调换

| 电话服务 | 网络服务 |
| --- | --- |
| 服务咨询热线：010-88379833 | 机 工 官 网：www.cmpbook.com |
| 读者购书热线：010-88379649 | 机 工 官 博：weibo.com/cmp1952 |
|  | 教育服务网：www.cmpedu.com |
| 封面无防伪标均为盗版 | 金 书 网：www.golden-book.com |

# 前言

目前,中国开放型经济已进入新的发展阶段。自加入世界贸易组织(WTO)以来,中国对外贸易发展迅猛,2009年成为世界第一大出口国,2013年成为世界第一大贸易国。2016年贸易额则提高到了1701亿美元,同比增长44.1%;根据海关统计,2017年我国进出口总额27.79万亿元人民币,同比增长14.2%,其中出口15.33万亿元,同比增长10.8%,进口12.46万亿元,同比增长18.7%,顺差2.87万亿元,收窄14.2%。在对外直接投资上,从20世纪90年代末开始,随着中国"走出去"战略的提出,中国企业对外直接投资规模迅速扩大。至2015年,对外直接投资达到1180亿美元的历史新高,全年对外承包工程业务完成营业额1541亿美元。与此同时,2016年对外承包工程业务完成营业额达到1594亿美元,比2015年的1541亿美元增长3.5%。随着开放型经济的深化发展,国际结算业务在中国迅速拓展,对既懂国际结算业务又懂相关国际惯例的专业人才的需求迅速增加。

英国《独立报》2016年9月14日的报道,2015年来华留学的学生接近40万人,人数超过2005年的两倍,且上述学生中有一大部分是为了攻读商科和涉外经济相关专业学位的。

针对上述形势,结合国际贸易和国际结算规则的发展与变化,借鉴同行经验,编写了这本《国际结算(双语)》(International Settlement)。

本书体系完整,英文部分、中文部分各10章。其中英文部分每章主要有学习目标、核心内容及章后思考题,个别章节附有案例专栏。同时,书末附有主要国际结算单据。

与同类书相比,本书具有以下三个方面的特色:

1. 编排上:英、中对照

与目前国内出版的《国际结算》相比,本书最大的特点是英、中文双语对照。

本书正文部分按先英文、后中文的模式编排。由于国际结算涉及很多专业词汇,此编排方式一方面可避免来华留学学生因汉语不熟练只能接受全英文教学的尴尬局面,使其有机会学习中文专业词汇;另一方面可避免实施双语乃至全英文教学导致部分英文基础功底不扎实的中国学生不能透彻理解书中内容特别是专业词汇的情况。

2. 内容上:全面性与前沿性相结合

(1)注重全面性。随着技术手段的变化及国际贸易的发展,国际结算方式也在不断升级。特别是,随着2008年金融危机的出现,国际结算的风险呈现出扩大和加深的趋势。因此,本书在内容上特别注重全面性,不仅对国际结算工具、国际结算方式等传统的国际结算内容进行了全面而精辟的分析,而且对国际结算单据的种类、内容与制作技巧也进行了分析,还特别增加了国际结算的风险与管理部分,以帮助读者增强风险意识、提高国际结算风险的预警与管理能力。与国内同类书相比较为领先,前瞻性突出。

（2）注重前沿性。本书关注国际结算的最新发展趋势，在内容上充分体现前沿性。具体而言，采取了以下做法：

第一，进一步丰富了对目前使用较频繁的银行保函、国际保理等方式的介绍，以帮助读者更为全面地了解这些方式，且能在实践中更好地操作与运用。

第二，以最新国际结算管理为指导。与其他国际贸易活动一样，在国际结算中，规则先行同样非常重要。为此，针对指导规则及政策始终不断调整和完善的现状，本书采取了与时俱进、当下为纲的原则，在分析问题时始终坚持内容的新颖性和前沿性，以最新且有效的国际结算惯例与规则作为分析问题的依据。

（3）体例上：理论性与实践性紧密结合。本书的编写始终坚持理论与实践的紧密结合，力求原理清晰、实务突出，全面培养学生的综合应用能力和实际操作能力。

具体表现在以下三个方面：

第一，穿插案例。在内容分析时，穿插大量相关真实案例的解析，以帮助读者及时巩固所学知识、熟悉分析问题的思路。

第二，章后附有思考题。本书英文部分每章之后均附有一定数量的判断、选择及案例分析题，部分章节还附有计算题和实际操作题，以供读者进行课后思考与联系，及时巩固所学知识。

第三，充实单证。"单据买卖"是国际贸易的一个重要特征，所以国际结算依据的往往是一系列国际结算单据。鉴于此，本书不仅向读者展示了国际结算主要单据样式，而且结合国际结算实践，介绍了国际结算主要单据的制作技巧。当然，为编排需要，大部分单据以附录的形式呈现给读者。

本书第1、5、6章及第10章中英文部分由尤宏兵编写，第2~4章中英文部分由林大燕编写，第7~9章中英文部分由许立帆编写。

本书为"十三五"江苏省高等学校重点教材（2016-2-098），在此感谢江苏省教育厅及南京理工大学教务处的大力支持。

本书在编写过程中，参考了大量国内外相关图书，在此对相关作者一并致谢。由于编者水平和能力有限，书中难免存在一些不足甚至错误之处，恳请读者批评指正，多提宝贵意见，以便再版时修改。

为方便教学，我们为选择本书作为授课教材的老师，免费提供配套电子课件（PPT）、课后习题答案、教学大纲。请联系责任编辑索取：changay@126.com。

编　者

# 目 录
# CONTENTS

前 言

**Chapter 1  Overview of International Settlement** ·············· 1
　Learning Objectives ················ 1
　1.1　Concept and Characteristics of International Settlement ········· 1
　1.2　The Evolution of International Settlement ··············· 4
　1.3　Banks for the International Settlement ··············· 8
　Questions ···················· 12

**Chapter 2  Payment Instruments in International Settlement** ········ 13
　Learning Objectives ················ 13
　2.1　Overview of Negotiable Instruments ··············· 13
　2.2　Bill of Exchange ············ 18
　2.3　Promissory Note and Cheque ······· 34
　Questions ···················· 37

**Chapter 3  Remittance** ············· 40
　Learning Objectives ················ 40
　3.1　Definition and Parties Concerned ················ 40
　3.2　Categories ··············· 41
　3.3　Reimbursement and Cancellation of Remittance ············ 44
　3.4　Application of Remittance in International Trade ············· 46
　Questions ···················· 48

**Chapter 4  Collection** ············· 49
　Learning Objectives ················ 49
　4.1　Definition of Collection and Parties Concerned ············ 49
　4.2　Characteristics of Collection and *URC 522* ·············· 54
　4.3　Categories and Procedures ······· 56
　4.4　Payment Clause under Collection in the International Sales Contract ··· 60
　Questions ···················· 61

**Chapter 5  Letter of Credit** ·········· 65
　Learning Objectives ················ 65
　5.1　Definition and Contents of L/C ······ 65
　5.2　Parties Concerned and Their Rights and Obligations ············ 67
　5.3　Characteristics of L/C ············ 73
　5.4　General Procedure ············ 74
　5.5　Categories of L/C ············ 84
　5.6　Payment Clause by L/C under Sales Contract ··············· 97
　Questions ···················· 98

**Chapter 6  Bank's Letter of Guarantee** ·············· 106
　Learning Objectives ················ 106
　6.1　An Overview of Bank's Letter of Guarantee ··············· 106
　6.2　The Functions and Contents of Bank's Letter of Guarantee ······ 109
　6.3　The Types of Bank's Letter of

|  | Guarantee ⋯⋯⋯⋯⋯⋯ 112 |
|---|---|
|  | Questions ⋯⋯⋯⋯⋯⋯⋯ 119 |

**Chapter 7   International Factoring** ⋯⋯⋯ 121
  Learning Objectives ⋯⋯⋯⋯⋯⋯ 121
  7.1  Concept and Characteristics of International Factoring ⋯⋯⋯⋯ 121
  7.2  Types of International Factoring ⋯⋯⋯⋯⋯⋯⋯⋯⋯ 123
  7.3  Procedure of Factoring Business ⋯⋯⋯⋯⋯⋯⋯⋯ 127
  Questions ⋯⋯⋯⋯⋯⋯⋯⋯⋯⋯ 128

**Chapter 8   Standby Letter of Credit** ⋯⋯⋯⋯⋯⋯⋯⋯⋯⋯ 131
  Learning Objectives ⋯⋯⋯⋯⋯⋯ 131
  8.1  The Connotation and Type of Standby Letter of Credit ⋯⋯ 131
  8.2  Types of Standby Letters of Credit ⋯⋯⋯⋯⋯⋯⋯⋯⋯ 135
  8.3  The Operating Principle of Standby Letters of Credit ⋯⋯ 138
  8.4  International Practice of Standby L/C ⋯⋯⋯⋯⋯⋯⋯⋯⋯⋯⋯ 139
  Questions ⋯⋯⋯⋯⋯⋯⋯⋯⋯⋯ 140

**Chapter 9   Documents for International Settlement** ⋯⋯⋯⋯⋯⋯⋯⋯⋯ 142
  Learning Objectives ⋯⋯⋯⋯⋯⋯ 142
  9.1  General Overview on Documents for International Settlement ⋯⋯⋯ 142
  9.2  Basic Requirements of Making Documents for International Settlement ⋯⋯⋯⋯⋯⋯⋯⋯ 144
  9.3  Commercial Documents: the Making of Invoice ⋯⋯⋯⋯⋯⋯ 146
  9.4  Business Documents: Transport Documents ⋯⋯⋯⋯⋯⋯ 149
  9.5  Commercial Documents: Insurance Documents ⋯⋯⋯⋯ 158
  9.6  Other Commercial Documents ⋯⋯ 163
  9.7  Official Documents ⋯⋯⋯⋯⋯⋯ 168
  Questions ⋯⋯⋯⋯⋯⋯⋯⋯⋯⋯ 173

**Chapter 10  International Settlement Risks & Management** ⋯⋯⋯ 175
  Learning Objectives ⋯⋯⋯⋯⋯⋯ 175
  10.1  An Overview of International Settlement Risk ⋯⋯⋯⋯⋯ 175
  10.2  Bill Risks and Prevention ⋯⋯⋯ 177
  10.3  Collection's Risk and Management ⋯⋯⋯⋯⋯⋯⋯ 178
  10.4  Risk Management Strategy under L/C ⋯⋯⋯⋯⋯⋯⋯ 183
  Questions ⋯⋯⋯⋯⋯⋯⋯⋯⋯⋯ 190

**第1章　国际结算概述** ⋯⋯⋯⋯⋯⋯⋯ 194
  1.1　国际结算的含义与特征 ⋯⋯⋯⋯ 194
  1.2　国际结算的演进 ⋯⋯⋯⋯⋯⋯ 196
  1.3　国际结算中的往来银行 ⋯⋯⋯ 198

**第2章　国际结算票据** ⋯⋯⋯⋯⋯⋯⋯ 201
  2.1　票据概述 ⋯⋯⋯⋯⋯⋯⋯⋯⋯ 201
  2.2　汇票 ⋯⋯⋯⋯⋯⋯⋯⋯⋯⋯⋯ 203
  2.3　本票与支票 ⋯⋯⋯⋯⋯⋯⋯⋯ 206

**第3章　汇款** ⋯⋯⋯⋯⋯⋯⋯⋯⋯⋯⋯ 208
  3.1　汇款的含义与当事人 ⋯⋯⋯⋯ 208
  3.2　汇款类型 ⋯⋯⋯⋯⋯⋯⋯⋯⋯ 208
  3.3　汇款的偿付与退汇 ⋯⋯⋯⋯⋯ 209
  3.4　汇款的使用 ⋯⋯⋯⋯⋯⋯⋯⋯ 210

**第4章　托收** ⋯⋯⋯⋯⋯⋯⋯⋯⋯⋯⋯ 211
  4.1　托收的概念与托收指示 ⋯⋯⋯ 211
  4.2　托收的当事人及其责任与义务 ⋯⋯⋯⋯⋯⋯⋯⋯⋯⋯⋯⋯ 211
  4.3　托收的种类与一般支付程序 ⋯ 213
  4.4　托收支付条款 ⋯⋯⋯⋯⋯⋯⋯ 214

**第5章　信用证** ⋯⋯⋯⋯⋯⋯⋯⋯⋯⋯ 216
  5.1　信用证的定义与基本内容 ⋯⋯ 216
  5.2　信用证的当事人及其权利与责任 ⋯⋯⋯⋯⋯⋯⋯⋯⋯⋯⋯ 217
  5.3　信用证的特点 ⋯⋯⋯⋯⋯⋯⋯ 218
  5.4　信用证的业务流程 ⋯⋯⋯⋯⋯ 218
  5.5　信用证的种类 ⋯⋯⋯⋯⋯⋯⋯ 219
  5.6　信用证支付条款 ⋯⋯⋯⋯⋯⋯ 222

## 第6章 银行保函 ……………… 224
6.1 银行保函概述 ………………… 224
6.2 银行保函的作用与内容 ……… 225
6.3 银行保函的类型 ……………… 227
6.4 银行保函的业务操作程序和业务处理 ……………………… 230

## 第7章 国际保理 ………………… 233
7.1 国际保理的概念与特点 ……… 233
7.2 国际保理的类型 ……………… 233
7.3 保理业务的程序 ……………… 235

## 第8章 备用信用证 ……………… 236
8.1 备用信用证的内涵与类型 …… 236
8.2 备用信用证的类型 …………… 237
8.3 备用信用证的运作原理 ……… 238
8.4 备用信用证国际惯例 ………… 239

## 第9章 国际结算单据 …………… 240
9.1 国际结算单据概述 …………… 240
9.2 国际贸易结算单据制作的基本要求 ………………………… 241
9.3 商业单据——发票 …………… 242
9.4 商业单据——运输单据 ……… 244
9.5 商业单据——保险单据 ……… 248
9.6 其他商业单据 ………………… 250
9.7 官方单据 ……………………… 251

## 第10章 国际结算中的风险与防范 …… 254
10.1 国际结算风险概述 …………… 254
10.2 票据风险与防范 ……………… 254
10.3 主要结算方式风险 …………… 255

## 附录 …………………………………… 260
附录A Bill of Exchange（汇票）…… 260
附录B Remittance Application（汇款申请书）……………………… 261
附录C Documentary Collection Application（托收申请书）…… 263
附录D Letter of Credit（信用证）… 264
附录E Application for the L/C（开证申请书）………………… 268
附录F Standby Letter of Credit（备用信用证）………………… 270
附录G Invoice（发票）……………… 273
附录H Bill of Lading（提单）……… 274
附录I Insurance Policy（保险单）…………………………… 275
附录J Packing List（装箱单）……… 276
附录K Weight Memo（重量单）…… 277
附录L Certificate of Origin（一般原产地证书）………………… 278

## 参考文献 …………………………… 279

# Chapter 1

# Overview of International Settlement

**Learning Objectives**

- To understand the concept, characteristics and the evolvement of international settlement.
- To understand the general contents of the course of international settlement.
- To understand the fund clearing systems in major international financial centers.

## 1.1 Concept and Characteristics of International Settlement

### 1.1.1 Concept and Categories of International Settlement

As a kind of economic activities, the settlement refers to those activities of the monetary payments and the liquidation of creditor's rights and debts originate from the trade of commodities, the supply of the labor, the mobility and allocation of the funds. While international settlement refers to the financial activities conducted among the parties who are located in different countries/regions, in which payments are effected or funds are transferred from one country to another in order to settle accounts, debts or claims emerged in the course of political, economic, cultural, diplomatic and military exchanges and communication among the states. In a word, the international settlement is the funds transfer via banks to settle accounts, debts and claims amount different entities.

Based on the causes of international settlement, it can be divided into two types: International trade settlement and International non-trade settlement. International trade settlement refers to the settlement of creditor's rights and debts because of the imports and exports of the physical commodities. It is also called the international visible trade settlement. It is the foundation and the main part of the international settlement. The international non-trade settlement means those financial activities across the borders generated in the course of political, cultural and economic activities other than import and export of commodities. Besides, the international non-trade settlement also reflects the breadth and depth of opening to the outside of a country/region to some certain extent.

In practice, the transfer of funds among countries/regions arisen from the need of governments or privates, such as the relief donation between the governments, overseas remittances, educational expenses, inheritance, etc.

The international trade settlement has dominated before the early of the 1980s, and the total amount has been more than that of the non-trade settlement. However, the international capital flow has accelerated and the total value of international non-trade settlement has risen sharply because of so large amount of capital. Nowadays, the scale of non-trade settlement has been hundreds of times of that of the international trade settlement. Because the international trade settlement is linked closely with international trade, its process is more complex than that of international non-trade settlement. Therefore this textbook focuses on the analysis of the international trade settlement.

### 1.1.2 Characteristics of International Settlement

Unlike the domestic settlement, international settlement features three basic characteristics as follows:

**(1) Different Sphere of the Currency Activities**

As to the domestic settlement, the monetary activities don't go beyond the national borders, while the international settlement is carried out across the national borders.

**(2) Different Currencies Are Used**

Both the payer and the payee use the same currency when they do business domestically. Generally, foreign exchange(s), especially international freely convertible currencies are used for international settlement. Thus, it often needs the currency exchange, which inevitably brings about the foreign exchange rate risk, especially the transaction risk.

**(3) Different Legal Systems and Laws**

When there is a settlement problem in domestic business, the relevant parties will follow the same laws or legal systems to settle the dispute. However, it is very difficult to choose the law(s) or rules to settle the international settlement dispute. In general, the dispute will be solved according to the international customs and practices or the law(s) or regulation(s) agreed upon by the parties concerned.

### 1.1.3 Contents

Generally speaking, the international settlement mainly analyze how to collect or make payment timely and safely for each international transaction. In practice, the international trade settlement is the main part, which is also called as terms of payment in a contract of international trade. The main contents of the international settlement are as follows:

**(1) International Settlement System**

The contemporary international settlement is realized through the interbank fund-transfer. In order to proceed business formalities concerned with the international settlement safely, quickly and effectively, one of the most important tasks is to establish the relationship between the branches, agents and the account banks among the banks concerned and then choose the most convenient routes and procedure from the cluster of the banks business network based on the needs of the actual business activities. Thus, we will briefly describe the international settlement system among banks in Chapter 1.

**(2) International Settlement Tools**

Before the 6th century B.C., barter trade, which is just the exchange of the commodities, was so popular. However, it is not so easy because one party may need the commodities supplied by the opposite side while he may not meet the requirements of the opposite side, or the total amount may not be the same. When gold, silver and other precious metals have begun to serve as the medium of exchange at the beginning of the 5th century B. C., it helped the development of international trade and later evolved into cash settlement.

However, the cash settlement also has its disadvantage, such as transportation risks, inventory inconvenient, difficulty in distinguishing the authenticity etc. With the establishments of foreign exchange banks at the end of the 18th century, international payments could be settled by the funds transferring among the banks. Then the non-cash settlement has been brought out and been universally adopted all over the world nowadays.

Under the non-cash settlement, bills are needed in order to show the relations of the fund-transfer. There are three kinds of bills as follows: bill of exchange, promissory note and cheque. The governments in almost all the countries/regions in the world have enacted the related laws or acts to regulate the form, contents and the actions concerned with the bills so that they can play their roles effectively and properly. We will analyze them in detail in Chapter 2.

(3) **International Settlement Methods**

The International settlement methods refer to the routes, ways and channels to collect or make payment. It mainly solves the problem as to how to transfer the money (foreign currency) from the importing countries/regions to the exporting countries/regions, which is the key content for international settlement. The international settlement methods have always been developed. Nowadays, there are six kinds of settlement such as remittance, collection, letter of credit, bank guarantee, international factoring and forfeiting. Among them, the L/C has been widely used and its business procedures are more complicated than the others. We will discuss them one by one from Chapter 3 to Chapter 8.

(4) **International Settlement Customs and Laws**

In order to specify the procedures of international settlement and settle the disputes originating from the international trade settlement, many international or regional non-governmental organizations or governments have been trying to make the rules and laws related to international settlement.

Those customs and practices, laws which are in force nowadays are as follows.

There are so many international laws and practices made by the ICC (International Chamber of Commerce) and some other organizations. The following are some key laws or practices of them:

1) Uniform Law for Bills of Exchange and Promissory Notes, singed at Geneva, 1930.

2) Uniform Law for Cheque, singed at Geneva, 1931.

3) Uniform Rules for Collection, ICC Publication No. 522.

4) Uniform Customs and Practice for Documentary Credit, ICC Publication No. 600.

5) UCP Supplement for Electronic Presentation (V.1.1).

6) International Standard Banking Practice for Examination of Documents under Documentary credits, ICC Publication No. 681.

7) Uniform Rules for Bank-to-Bank Reimbursements, ICC Publication No. 725.

8) International Standby Practice, 1998.

9) Uniform Rules for Demand Guarantees, ICC Publication No. 758.

Regional laws are as follows:

1) UK Bills of Exchange Act of 1882.

2) US Uniform Commercial Code of 1952.

**(5) International Settlement Documents**

Both commodities documentization and documents commercialization have been the basic operation mode for the contemporary international trade. All kinds of documents have become the most important content of the international settlement, which can make the funds transfer and the delivery and receipt of the goods smoothly, safeguard the lawful rights and interests of the parties concerned and facilitate the international trade.

There are many kinds of international settlement documents, which include commercial invoice, shipping documents, financial documents and insurance policy, etc. The Marine bill of lading and multimodal transport bill of lading represent the ownership of the goods, which are the most important documents in international trade. In addition, sometimes some other documents may be required. We will detail them in Chapter 9.

**(6) International Settlement Risks Management**

Since the financial crisis in the United States in 2008, the international trade has developed a little slower than before. However, the total amount has continuously increased. According to the WTO statistics, the total value of world trade of physical goods amounted to US $ 18.494 trillion in 2014. Not only there is fiercer competition in the international market because of so many factors, but also the international settlement methods have been prompted to change and develop more constantly than before. Therefore, the effective prevention of international settlement risks has become a more important topic. It is time for China, the Top one in terms of export value in the world, to strengthen the analysis of the prevention of the international settlement risks. We will pay our special attention to it in the last Chapter.

## 1.2  The Evolution of International Settlement

The Settlement System has been developed along with the change and development of the social economic system, the productivity, the international trade, the monetary and credit system. So far, it roughly experienced three modes such as Cash Settlement, Non-Cash Settlement and Electronic Settlement.

### 1.2.1  Cash Settlement

Along with the main western countries have entered into the capitalist period, the international trade has come into being, which has given rise to the development of the international settlement. However, in the early stages of international trade, cash or the gold, silver and other precious metals were often used. In ancient period, the trade among China, Japan, countries in South-east Asia and Middle Asia had long done by the gold, silver and copper coins etc. There were so large transport risks, so high transport cost, besides it is no easy to identify the authenticity and count the money.

Therefore, with the expansion of trade, the precious metals as settlement tools cannot meet the needs of the development of the international trade, which has provided a space for the development of the non-cash settlement.

### 1.2.2 Non-cash Settlement

In 11th century A. D., the international trade has developed alongside the Mediterranean coast and the businessmen there have begun to use written receipt instead of the cash. In 14th and 15th century A. D., the business has developed so fast in some important Italian cities, the banks have come into being and the bill of exchange has been used for the international settlement through the banks. In the 18th century, the concept of documentization has been generally accepted and the advantages of the settlement by the bills emerged continuously. Thus, the settlement way has transferred from the cash settlement to the non-cash settlement.

In the late 19th century and early 20th century, the payment methods against documents have been perfected, which marked that the banker's credit has begun to join the international settlement and the banks have been the center of the international settlement. The banks have turned the settlement between the importers and exporters into the banks among different countries through buying and selling all kinds of different currencies, different amount and the bills in different periods. And the international settlement has been characterized by both financing and settlement. The balance after the settlement will be deposited in the debtor's bank in the form of deposits by the creditor bank, while it does not need to be settled through the transport of the cash, the documents have evolved into the negotiable certificates from the general cargo receipt in the past.

There is a strong link between the international settlement and the banker's business, in turn, the development of the international settlement has promoted the development of international trade. As the international trade intermediaries, the banks have given their full play to their guarantee roles and financing ability, which has promoted the further development of international trade. In practice, a set of the inter-bank seal system differentiating the true and the false have been formed for the security. The banks have begun to open an account in the opposite side which has helped the formation of high efficient fund transfer network in the world. Safe and efficient capital settlement has brought both the expansion of international trade and social benefits.

### 1.2.3 Electronic Settlement

Since the Second World War, the banker's settlement business in the world has been growing so rapidly with the great change in the scale of international trade, the trade modes, the transportation modes and the change of the commodity structure. Thus, it has raised higher and newer requirements for the speeds and quality of international settlement's service. And with the rapid development of the electronic technology, the banks in the developed countries have begun to combine the modern communication technologies with electronic computer and constituted the inter-bank international settlement system. It has greatly improved the efficiency of international settlement. Nowadays, the popular electronic settlement systems are as follows:

(1) CHIPS

The full name of CHIPS is Clearing House Interbank Payment System. The Clearing House of the United States says "CHIPS is the largest private-sector U.S.-dollar funds-transfer system in the world, clearing and settling an average of USD1.5 trillion(by 2015) in cross-border and domestic payments daily."

The Clearing House was founded in 1853, and is the oldest, most innovative bank association and payments processor in the United States. Established to simplify the daily check exchanges in New York, The Clearing House later became a pioneer in the emerging field of electronic funds transfers and continues to be a leader in the payments arena, operating in addition to CHIPS, an automated clearinghouse (ACH) known as EPN (Electronic Payments Network), and a check-image clearing house.

CHIPS is a real-time system for transmitting and settling high-value U.S.-dollar payments among its participating banks. The Clearing House began operating CHIPS in 1970 to simplify and expedite interbank payments in New York City. Backed by more than 40 years of reliable operation, CHIPS serves 49 foreign and domestic banks, representing 21 countries, through a network of sending and receiving devices, which range from microcomputers to large-scale mainframe computers. Nowadays it contained about 140 member banks among which 2/3 are foreign banks from 43 countries.

(2) CHAPS

The Clearing House Automated Payment System (CHAPS) is the UK's same day high value payment system. CHAPS is the only UK payment system that guarantees real time finality, on any value, in "Central bank money" as each payment instruction settles.

Launched in February 1984, the CHAPS system guarantees same day settlement finality for payments of any value. Since 1996, CHAPS has used an enhanced Real Time Gross Settlement (RTGS) system where each individual payment is settled in real time across its Direct Participants' settlement accounts at the Bank of England.

CHAPS continues to be one of the largest RTGS systems in the world, offering efficient, risk-free and irrevocable same day payments to meet the sterling RTGS payment requirements of its 26 Direct Participants. In addition, over 5,000 financial institutions also make CHAPS payments and settle through agency arrangements with the Direct Participants. CHAPS is also a critical mechanism for ensuring liquidity in the financial markets.

Most of the daily value processed by CHAPS is from wholesale transactions where CHAPS acts as the portal through which international sterling flows take place. CHAPS is used by banks, building societies and other payment service providers to pay each other. However, it is most generally known within the UK as the payment method for house purchases, although this represents only a fraction of 1% of the daily value processed.

£76 trillion was processed through the system in 2016. As of July 2011, the total value processed since the start of CHAPS exceeded one quadrillion (£1,000,000,000,000,000) pounds.

This system has some specialty like high-automated computerized information transfer method, which makes it possible for those businesses that the payer is a bank outside London maintains the Two Ties Clearing System inter in the banks in London continuously.

(3) SWIFT

The full name of SWIFT is Society for Worldwide Interbank Financial Telecommunication. It is a non-profit and cooperative organization which was established in Brussels in 1973, led by CEO Carl Reuterskiold and gained support form 239 banks from 15 countries.

It started to establish common standards for financial transactions and a shared data processing system and worldwide communications network. Fundamental operating procedures, rules for liability, etc. , were established in 1975 and the first message was sent in 1977.

SWIFT provides a network that enables financial institutions worldwide to send and receive information about financial transactions in a secure, standardized and reliable environment. SWIFT also sells software and services to financial institutions, much of it for use on the SWIFT network.

The majority of international interbank messages use the SWIFT network. As of September 2010, SWIFT linked more than 9,000 financial institutions in 209 countries/regions, who were exchanging an average of over 15 million messages per day. SWIFT transports financial messages in a highly secure way but does not hold accounts for its members and does not perform any form of clearing or settlement.

SWIFT is headquartered in Brussels, Belgium. It has established three operation centers in Belgium, the Netherlands and the United States and has branches in its member countries/regions. It is a high-speed telecommunications network between Banks in the world. The system is characterized by the follows:

Firstly, extensive business coverage. It can be used for the transfers of funds among banks in the world, foreign exchange, foreign exchange dealing, letters of credit, collection and reconciliation, etc. .

Secondly, work efficiently around the clock. It operates 24 continuous hours a day, 7 days a week and can get the response from the receiver in about 2 minutes after the telecommunications has been sent.

Thirdly, good secrecy. It can store information automatically, add secret or check the password, process the message in cipher. It is responsible for all the telecommunications and will never lose something.

Fourthly, standardized format. It requires that to send and receive the telegraph in conformity with the unified standardized format so as to prevent the misunderstanding or mistake both in literal or translation.

(4) FEDWIRE

The full name of FEDWIRE is Federal Reserves Wire Transfer System. It was started in 1913. It is formally known as the Federal Reserve Wire Network. FEDWIRE is a real-time gross settlement funds transfer system operated by the United States Federal Reserve Banks that enables financial institutions to electronically transfer fund between its more than 9,289 participants as of March 19, 2009.

### (5) TARGET2

TARGET2 is the latest edition of TARGET, which full name is Trans-European Automated Real-time Gross Settlement Express Transfer System. It is the real-time gross settlement (RTGS) system for the Eurozone, and is available to non-Eurozone countries. It was developed by and is owned by the Eurosystem. TARGET2 is based on an integrated central technical infrastructure, called the Single Shared Platform (SSP). SSP is operated by three providing central banks: France (Banque de France), Germany (Deutsche Bundesbank) and Italy (Banca d'Italia). TARGET2 has begun to replace TARGET since November 2007.

TARGET2 is also an interbank RTGS payment system for the clearing of cross-border transfers in the Eurozone. Participants in the system are either direct or indirect. Direct participants hold an RTGS account and have access to real-time information and control tools. They are responsible for all payments sent from or received on their accounts by themselves or any indirect participants operating through them. Indirect participation means that payment orders are always sent to and received from the system via a direct participant, with only the relevant direct participant having a legal relationship with the Eurosystem. Finally, bank branches and subsidiaries can choose to participate in TARGET2 as multi-addressee access or addressable BICs (Bank Identifier Codes).

As of 2012, TARGET2 has settled the cash positions of 82 ancillary systems, processed a daily average of 354,185 payments, representing a daily average value of €2.477 billion, while the average value of a TARGET2 transaction was EUR 7.1 million and 99.94% of TARGET2 payments were processed in less than five minutes.

## 1.3 Banks for the International Settlement

### 1.3.1 Banker's Credit and International Settlement

The banks are the main indispensable parties for the international settlement. There are so many advantages when the banks handle the international settlement.

#### (1) Convenient

The establishment of the banks and their international agent network make it so easy to meet the needs of customers from all over the world without the restriction by the time or the place.

#### (2) Safe

The banks have more abundant funds and the banker's credit is better than that of commercial credit, which makes the international settlement be more safe and reliable.

#### (3) Economical

Banks can collect so much debtor-creditor relationship and offset them to a great extent, which helps to shorten the settlement path, and to save time, costs and the interest, and makes the international settlement more economical.

#### (4) Standard

So many kinds of international customs and practices, laws and rules related to the international settlement have been enacted, which let the banks have the unified regulations when they handle the international settlements. It makes the procedures of the international settlement be more rational and standard, and helps to reduce or avoid the international trade disputes.

(5) **Speedy**

With the application of high-tech, especially the computer technology and communication technology in banking, the operation process has been transferred from the artificial way to the electronic one. Thus, the international settlement has become more safe, reliable, economical, convenient and swift.

The settlement of the creditor's right and debts between different countries/regions can be handled through the banks because it is mainly based on the banker' credit. We can say, the appearance and the promotion of the banker's credit have been the foundation of the modern international settlement. It was due to the access of the bank's credit that makes the modern international settlement be the non-cash settlement system centered on the banks.

## 1.3.2 Functions of the Banks in International Settlement

Banks are the hub for the international settlement. International banking is effected through the cooperation of commercial banks all over the world. It is impossible to fulfill the international settlement without the cooperation of the commercial banks. As to the international settlement, the banks' functions are as follows.

(1) **International Exchange**

International Exchange refers to settle the international relations between the creditor's rights and the debts by converting one currency into the other currency and entrust the local bank to pay a certain amount to the payee or creditors at the request of the remitter or the debtor. In the international trade, the bank accepts the commission of the importers and/or exporters and provides the international remittance, collect and pay the payment and charges related, etc. It is a kind of intermediary business in a bank.

(2) **Credit Guarantee**

The international trade settlement risks mainly lie in that it is unable to deliver and acquire the payment simultaneously or vice versa for the seller and the buyer. In practice, neither the exporter nor the importer would like to transfer the payment, the goods or the documents of the title to goods to the opposite side. Thus, it needs a trusted third party who acts as a middleman and guarantor. It is obvious that the bank would be the best choice. Under the payment methods such as the letter of credit and the bank guarantee etc., the international trade may develop smoothly just because of the banker's credit.

(3) **Financing**

To obtain the finance from the bank(s) is one of the most important conditions to engage in the international trade for both the importers and the exporters. No matter what kind of enterprise you are, the capital of your company is always limited, which means to get the finance from the bank(s) is necessary for international trade. Generally speaking, banks cannot only provide general loans to the importer or the exporter, but also finance them, establish a line for confirmation of credits, discount the financial bills, etc. , which can promote the development of international trade.

(4) **Reducing Foreign Exchange Risk**

Because of the wide line and more parties concerned, it usually takes two or three months from the conclusion to the performance of the contract, that is to say, the period from the seller delivers the commodities and gets payment to the buyer takes delivery of the commodities and makes payment. It will surely bring out foreign exchange risk for both the seller and the buyer, while the banks can reduce or even eliminate the foreign exchange risk through forwarding foreign exchange transaction, future contract and options for the importers and exporters.

### 1.3.3 Correspondent Banks

A set of international banking network is the most fundamental of international settlement, because all of the receipts and payment are implemented through the inter-bank clearing. The wider the banking network, the greater range of international settlement and the more convenient fund settlement. Therefore, to establish the bank-to-bank contact is the base of smooth international settlement.

Bank-to-bank contact includes the exchanges between central Banks, commercial banks, corresponding bank and agents. Generally speaking, those commercial banks who operates foreign exchange have branches abroad, however, it is unlikely to establish in all the countries/regions where there are credits and debts. Therefore, it is necessary for the domestic and foreign banks to closely cooperate with each and form an efficient transfer network.

These overseas correspondent banks mainly are as follows:

(1) **Overseas Branches**

Overseas Branches are the branches abroad established by the commercial banks, who deal with the international financial business, with the approval of the government in the host country. They are the same legal person as the parent bank. All the assets, liabilities, related expenses and income of the branches are incorporated into the accounting statements of the headquarters. The headquarters shall bear the joint liability and share all the resources with the branches.

Overseas branches will be bound by two sets of banking regulation system. As part of the head office, it is governed by the financial supervision regulations from both the home country and the host country. Generally, overseas branches are allowed to carry out the deposits, loans and charging business in the host country. Overseas branch is one of the important organizational forms for multinational banks when they do business abroad. In the United States, the assets of the overseas branches occupy almost half of the total assets of all American banks.

(2) **Foreign Subsidiary**

Foreign subsidiary, which possesses independent legal personality, is registered and established in the host country by the head office according to the law of the host country. Most or even all the equity of the subsidiaries is owned by the headquarters. It can be divided into wholly owned subsidiaries and holding subsidiaries according to the source of the registered capital.

As an independent company, the overseas subsidiaries must abide by the regulations of the host country, however, its total loans are restricted just by their own capital instead of that of the headquarters. When they do those business related to the international trade, they cannot only provide international payment services for the customers from the head office, but also provide loans in local currency or other international hard currencies. Because the foreign branches and subsidiaries are controlled by foreign capital, the host country usually restricts their business fields to some extent, however, the international settlement business is of exception.

(3) Affiliate

Overseas affiliates refers to a bank registered but cannot be held by their headquarters in the host country. The other shareholders of the affiliates can be either the local institutions or other foreign banks. Sometimes, the affiliates were set up abroad by the headquarter itself, however, they were local banks while some of the stocks have been bought by the headquarters. Legally, overseas affiliates are those financial institutions supervised by the host country. Because the affiliates are allowed to handle normal banking business, they can provide services for the customers from their foreign shareholders.

(4) Overseas Office

A bank establishes overseas offices so that their customers can do business in the country where the overseas offices were established or its neighbors. The main function of the overseas office is to provide information and advisory services. Because the overseas office is not a commercial organization, it cannot accept deposits, provide loans and provide international trade payment services such as the draft, the L/C, etc.

(5) Associated Bank

Associated Bank is a bank jointly established by the bank both in the host country and the parent country. Sometimes, many foreign investors may participate in it. However, only the bank from the host country can control the associated bank. In no case the foreign bank can do so. Due to this reason, there are fewer restrictions on the business of the associated bank from the government of the host country than affiliates and overseas offices.

(6) Agent

Agent refers to a bank that has signed an agreement with a bank from the other countries and entrusted to handle the settlement business. A bank may operate the international settlement business from all over the world. However, it can only set up branches, subsidiaries and affiliates in those financial centers and some central cities due to its own business and the limits from the host country. Then, when the bank needs to handle the international settlement business from those areas where he has not established overseas institutions, he has to obtain the aids from the local banks. Considering this, the bank who operates the international settlement business should establish the correspondent banking relationship with those banks that have abundant capital, honest and steady operation style and high professional competence through friendly negotiation.

They must detail the business scope mutually entrusted and institutions who will participate(the headquarters and participants, etc.) in the agency agreement and exchange the control documents, which includes test key, the list of specimens of authorized signature, schedule of terms and the conditions and SWIFT authentic key etc.

## Questions:

### I. True or false.

1. The payments between the China mainland and China Hong Kong, China Macao and China Taiwan regions, because they belong to the same country, so it belongs to the domestic settlement.
2. Currently, the vast majority of international settlement used billing settlement.
3. The agency relationship between Banks, the bank's head office is directly set up by both parties, generally not an independent foreign branch agency relationship.

### II. Multiple choice.

1. Implement multilateral settlement to use (    ).
   A. bookkeeping currency
   B. foreign currency
   C. gold and silver
   D. convertible currencies
2. The following (    ) reflects the limitations of commercial bill of exchange and settlement.
   A. in business between, exporters, trust each other
   B. the party has the ability to pay money and exporters
   C. the amount of import and export of goods and payment time
   D. the exporter's account is not in the importer
3. The new content of contemporary international settlement credit management involves the (    ).
   A. credit and legal credit system
   B. employees credit and bank credit
   C. bank of credit and commercial credit
   D. company credit and commercial credit

# Chapter 2

# Payment Instruments in International Settlement

## Learning Objectives

- Grasp the concept, characteristics and the circulation procedure of the bills.
- Understand the legal systems related the bills.
- Grasp the essential elements bill of exchange, promissory note and cheque.

## 2.1 Overview of Negotiable Instruments

Negotiable instrument or bill is a kind of document in which the maker himself makes a promise or entrust the payer to pay a certain amount on demand or on the specified date. It is the main tool in the international settlement.

### 2.1.1 Characteristics of Negotiable Instruments

#### (1) Right-Setting

Right-setting means that the instrument itself and its right are inseparable, which means the right has come into being when the instrument was set up. The right of the instrument cannot be certified without the instrument.

The purpose of the issuance of the bills is to set the rights on a negotiable instrument, rather than the existing rights. The rights and obligations of the instrument may have existed when the instrument has been made or may not exist. However, when the instrument was made, the right was established. As a financial credit, or settlement tool, the purpose of the instrument is to pay, or act as a payment method instead of the cash.

#### (2) Requisite in Form

A negotiable instrument must be in the statutory form, which means it must contain the prerequisite items. The laws on the negotiable instrument in different countries have detailed the conditions and contents of the bills even though they are different from each other.

When the bills are transferred, the relationship between the rights and obligations of the parties is determined by the meaning of the phrase in the negotiable instrument. If the items recorded in the instrument is not unified, or some important records is not clear, then it will be difficult to determine the rights and obligations of the parties which will lower the acceptability of the bills.

#### (3) Negotiability

This is the basic characteristics of the instrument. The transferee of the instrument will obtain all the rights and can sue all the parties on it in his own name when he has acquired the instrument. Those people who are bona-fide and have paid the price will not be affected by the defect of the instrument.

The right of the transferee is conditional, which includes as follows:

Firstly, the transferee must have paid the price.

Secondly, the transferee shall obtain the instrument kindly.

Thirdly, the instrument is complete and eligible.

Fourthly, the instrument is convertible.

Negotiable instruments will be transferred through the delivery or endorsement.

However, the transfer of the rights on the instrument is quite different from the transfer of the creditor's in the civil law. It is characterized as follows:

Firstly, the holder is transferable by the delivery or endorsement after delivery to the others, without notification of the original obligor.

Secondly, when the transferee has accepted the instrument, he can acquire all the sights on the instrument and can file a suit in its own name when it has been dishonored or other problems have encountered.

Thirdly, the rights of the bona-fide transferee will not be affected due to the flaws of the priors.

(4) **Non-Causative**

It means that the instrument should be paid unconditionally. Whether the instrument is effective or not has no relations with the reason why the instrument was drawn or transferred. It is to say, the reasons to issue or to endorse need not to be written on the face of the bill. Only if it meets the legal form, the drawee shall pay unconditionally on its maturity. While the transferee does not need to investigate the reasons to issue or to transfer, he can acquire the rights as long as it is in a qualified form.

The reason for the transfer of a negotiable instrument is its basic relationship and it is also the cause of how the rights and duties in the instrument came into being. It includes the money relations between the drawer and the drawee, the consideration relationship between the drawer and the payee, the relationship between the endorser and the endorsee.

(5) **Monetary**

Monetary refers to that the right represented by the negotiable instrument. It is a kind of creditor's rights paid in money. So the debtor can only pay in money, not pay with goods.

(6) **Presentation**

Presentation means that the holder should present the negotiable instrument to the payer on its maturity when he wants it to be paid. Otherwise, the payer may neglect it. For example, the sight draft should be presented within one month to the payer for payment according to *the Negotiable Instrument Law of China.*

(7) **Returnability**

Returnability requires that the holder of the negotiable instrument should return it to the payer when he has acquired the payment. If he would not like to return it, the debtor may decline to make payment. Due to the characteristics of returnability, the negotiable instrument cannot flow indefinitely. It will end its circulation after the payment has been made when it is due. It also implies that the negotiable instrument has its limitation on the functionality of the currency. When the negotiable instrument is paid, it cannot further circulate.

(8) To recourse

To recourse means that the holder of the negotiable instrument has the right of recourse to all the debtors through the legal procedures and acquire the right on the negotiable instrument when the payer or the acceptor has refused to accept or pay for a qualified bill, which can help him go safeguard his right.

## 2.1.2 Function of Negotiable Instruments

(1) Settlement Instrument

To non-cash settlement is the basic method of the international settlement. Under this method, it is necessary to use a certain kind of payment tools to settle the international creditor's rights and debts, while the negotiable instrument can serve as a payment and settlement tool instead of the money.

(2) Credit Instrument

The negotiable instrument itself has no value because it is not a kind of commodity and does not contain the social labor. It is only a kind of written payment instrument established on the basis of credit. When the businessmen have done business and both have agreed to pay one month after the delivery, the buyer may make a promissory note to the seller at one month after sight, that is to say, the buyer's credit of payment in one month has been replaced by the promissory note.

(3) Circulation

Circulation means that the negotiable instrument is a kind of medium of circulation. The negotiable instrument can be transferred through the delivery of endorsement and it can be further transferred. The endorser of the negotiable instrument should be responsible for payment. So more the negotiable instrument is endorsed, the more people will be responsible for the payment and the higher of the value of the negotiable instrument. The negotiable instrument will be circulated widely by the endorsement, the transfer and be a kind of medium of circulation. Thus it not only saves the utilization of the cash, but also expands the mediums of circulation.

## 2.1.3 Law of Negotiable Instrument

While the negotiable instrument has played more and more important role in the international settlement and social economic activities, the governments have begun to attach tremendous importance on it and successively formulated the rules on the circulation of the negotiable instrument, and they have become the laws on the negotiable instrument. The negotiable instrument originated in the Europe, France was the first country that enacted the laws on the negotiable instrument, then Germany, and the UK subsequently followed. Because the laws on the negotiable instrument were enacted at a different time, and there are differences in the economic development, business practices and legal thought, thus multiple legal systems have been established. There exist two different bodies of laws on negotiable instruments: Continental legal system; British and US law system.

### (1) Overview of the Two Major Legal Systems

Continental legal system, or civil law system is based on a very detailed set of laws organized into codes. When law courts interpret civil law, they do so with regard to these codes. Over 80 countries, including Germany, France, Japan, and Russia, operate with a civil law system. A civil law system tends to be less adversarial that a common law system, since the judges rely upon detailed legal codes rather than tradition, precedent and custom which they interpret. Judges under a civil law system have less flexibility than those under a common law system.

British and US law system, or common law evolved in England over hundreds of years. It is now found in most of Great Britain's former colonies, including the United States. Common law is based on tradition, precedent, and custom. British and the United States were selected as the representative of Common Law or the British and US law system.

### (2) The Difference of the Two Major Legal Systems

Most participants of *the Negotiable Instrument Law Geneva* are continental European countries (continental legal system), while the UK and the United States have not participated in it and still insist their own point of view (British and US legal system).

Firstly, the classification. Geneva legal system treats the bill of exchange and promissory notes as the same category, while the check the other, and respectively made the *Uniform Law for Bills of Exchange and Promissory Notes* singed at Geneva and the *Uniform Law for Cheque* singed at Geneva.

While British acts on negotiable instruments treat bill of exchange is the basic negotiable instrument. They thought that the promissory note and cheque derived from the bill of exchange because the identity of the parties concerned are different, so the British legal system on the negotiable instrument has been divided into three kinds, the same as the United States.

Secondly, rights of the holder. British acts on negotiable instruments which emphasize the characteristics of the circulation and credit and differentiate the basic parties of the negotiable instrument and those derived from the circulation and entrust them different fights.

Thirdly, handling of a forged endorsement. According to British acts on negotiable instruments, the false endorsement is null and void and thus the right on the negotiable instrument cannot be transferred. While the Geneva laws argue that the risk of a forged endorsement shall be borne by the person who lost the instrument. Only if the holder has acquired the negotiable instrument legally, not collaborated with the perpetrator and not concerned with it, he will not bear the obligation.

Fourthly, prerequisites. According to British acts on negotiable instruments, the negotiable instrument does not need the prerequisites. Only if the form of the instrument complying with the definition, it will be an effective instrument. While Geneva law has set the conditions for the negotiable instrument, there are eight factors as follows: name of the negotiable instrument, unconditionally order to pay a certain amount, name of the drawee, time of payment, place of payment, name of beneficiary, date and place of issue, the signature of the issuer.

In order to promote the coordination and unification of the laws on the negotiable instruments, the United Nations Commission on International Trade Law has begun to enact to a uniform law on negotiable instruments adapted to the international trade regulation since 1971 and established the group on international negotiable instruments. The group reviewed and passed *the Draft on Convention of International Bill of Exchange and Promissory Note and Draft on Convention of International Cheque* in 1981, however, it is a pity that it was still in discussion among countries.

## 2.1.4 The Risks and Its Management

### (1) Risks of Negotiable Instrument

The risks of the negotiable instruments are caused by so many reasons, such as the counterfeit and forgery of the negotiable instruments; procuring improperly, obtaining out of malice or gross negligence; invalid or defect action; as well as lack of experience or lack of ability of the relevant personnel, etc.

**Forgery** refers to the action to make out the negotiable instruments in other's names, for example, to forge the signature and/or seal, or seal by stealing that of the other, etc. Forgery cannot easily be found in the process of circulation and the transfer. Only when the negotiable instrument expires and is presented for payment by the holder, it could be found. Because the debtors are unable to timely know the forgery, which lets so many parties accept the paper continually and be the direct or indirect victims. In principle, the forged negotiable instrument is invalid; it is the forger who bears the losses. However, in practice, most successful forgers are poor and they will hide and squander what he has cheated. When the negotiable instrument is due and found it was faked, it is difficult to compensate the losses of the holder because the forger has squandered even if he has been caught. Considering this, the provisions of the laws on negotiable instruments in many countries stipulate that the fake does not affect the validity of the true signatures. The forger and the receiver of the forgery are not liable for the payment, however, those people who signed or sealed the negotiable instrument authentically must bear the obligation according to it. So, the person who bears the obligation will fall in the first endorser, who received the forged bill. In this case, the receiver himself will bear the loss when he cannot chase up the payment from the forger.

**Alteration** refers to the action to alter or modify the contents in the legal form by the person who has neither been authorized nor has the right. There are so many kinds of alteration, for example, the actor altered the amount for USD110,000.00 to USD210,000.00; changed the expiry date and advanced or delayed the time for the payment; modified the interest so as to increase or decrease it etc. The alteration will affect the benefits of some parties concerned and bring out the instrument risks.

**Defects** of rights on the negotiable instruments refer to the defective ownership on its rights. For example, the holder acquires the negotiable instruments by means of fraud, intimidation, violence, or illegal consideration, or in violation of the principle of good faith in the process of transfer paper circulation, or the equivalent of fraud. Such kind of behaviour will damage the interests of the parties concerned and cause the instrument risks.

When the acquisition of the negotiable instruments due to malice or gross negligence, the risks will also generate. The malicious acquisition means to accept the negotiable instrument when the receiver has known his/her prior has no right to dispose or deliver the negotiable instrument. For example, if party A stole a cheque from party B and transferred it to party C, however party C has known the fact but still accepted the bill, it is a kind of malicious acquisition. Gross negligence means that the transferee may have known that the transfer has no right of disposition if he has been more careful. For example, Party A has known the tact the Party B was on a budget and could not have a cheque in a large amount, however, Party A still decided to accept the check stolen by Party B.

(2) The Risks Prevention

In order to prevent the risks of the negotiable instruments, the parties concerned should pay attention to the follows:

Firstly, it is necessary to understand the customer's credit standing from the start, especially for those unknown new customers as well as those customers who are located in those countries where the foreign exchange are limited, depreciating or uncertainty.

Secondly, it is necessary to entrust the bank concerned to investigate so as to ensure to get the payment safely.

Thirdly, it is necessary to sign the contract on the basis of equality and mutual benefit.

Fourthly, it is injudicious for the seller to deliver the commodities before the bank has helped him get the payment so as to avoid both the commodities and money are lost.

Fifthly, it is important to keep in mind that the exporter cannot get the payment even if he has received a check from the bank of the best reputation in the world. In recent years, the cases frequently occur that some foreign unscrupulous businessmen use forgery negotiable instruments and remittance voucher, it should be more careful than before.

In addition to the precautions mentioned above, it is important to strengthen the management of the accounting department in the bank and clarify the settlement discipline and responsibility.

The main contents for the settlement discipline and responsibility in a bank are as follows:
- To strictly abide by the provisions on the settlement no matter for personnel of legal person.
- Not allowed to lease or loan the account.
- Not allowed to issue rubber or time checks.
- Not allowed to elicit the banker's credit.

Let the party itself bear the bank's losses when he filled the settlement documents wrongly or brought out losses due to the loss of the negotiable instruments or seal.

Allow the holder of the negotiable instruments to recourse on the drawer, endorser and the other debtors when it was dishonored.

To punish those parties who have violated the provisions of bank settlement and discipline.

To pay the customers with compensation when the bank has handled the settlement wrongly or delayed the settlement etc.

## 2.2 Bill of Exchange

### 2.2.1 Definition

According to Article 3 of *UK Bills of Exchange Acts* of 1882, bill of exchange or draft is defined as follows.

A bill of exchange (See Appendix A), also called draft, is an unconditional order in writing, addressed by one person to another, signed by the person giving it, requiring the person to whom it is addressed to pay on demand, or at a fixed or determinable future time, a sum certain in money, to, or to the order of a specified person, or to bearer.

Besides, it says that the bill which does not meet the mentional-above conditions or requirements, payment instruments other than the completion of other acts, not the bills.

However, *Negotiable Instruments Law of China* specifies that draft is to be drawn and signed by the drawer and authorize the payer to pay a certain amount of money unconditionally to payee or bearer at sight or at the specified date.

## 2.2.2 Essential Contents of Bill of Exchange

As what we have discussed before, the bill of exchange should be in requisite in format. However, different laws on the negotiable instruments have a different specification.

(1) Negotiable Instruments Law of China

According to article 22 of *Negotiable Instruments Law of China*, the bill of exchange must specify the following seven elements:

- mark of "exchange".
- unconditional order for paying.
- a specific amount.
- name of the payer.
- name of the payee.
- date of issuance.
- signature of the drawer.

The bill of exchange will be invalid when it has not specified one of the above-mentioned.

Besides, Article 23 specifies: "The date of payment, place of payment, place of issuance elements should be clear and definite."

(2) **Convention Providing a Uniform Law for Bills of Exchange and Promissory Notes, Geneva**

According to Article 1 of *Convention Providing a Uniform Law for Bills of Exchange and Promissory Notes*, the bill of exchange should specify those factors as follows:

- The term "bill of exchange" inserted in the body of the instrument and expressed in the language employed in drawing the instrument.
- An unconditional order to pay a determinate sum of money.
- The name of the person who is to pay (drawee).
- A statement of the time of payment.
- A statement of the place where payment is to be made.
- The name of the person to whom or to whose order payment is to be made.
- A statement of the date and of the place where the bill is issued.

- The signature of the person who issues the bill(drawer).

### (3) UK Bills of Exchange Act

According to the *UK Bills of Exchange Act*, 1882 edition, a bill of exchange should contain at least eight compulsory factors as follows:

#### 1) Marking of "Exchange"

Usually the word "Exchange" is clearly indicated on the face of a bill of exchange. The purpose of indicating this word on a bill of exchange is to distinguish a bill from a promissory note or a check, and at the same time to help the relevant parties handle the relative business.

#### 2) An Unconditional Order for Paying in Writing

"Unconditional order" means the implementation or completion of an order cannot be attached to any condition or subject to any restriction, whether expressed or implied. Otherwise, the command is invalid or it is not a valid bill of exchange.

"To pay USD100,000.00 form ××× Account" is a conditional command; While "Pay to Company B one thousand US dollars after he has endorsed on the back of the draft" does not either to conform to the requirements of unconditional.

"In writing" means that the bill must be written by hand, or by type-written or printed and oral expressions cannot be allowed. In practice, drawing a bill in pencil is usually not encouraged by banks because of the easy opportunity for the fraudulent alteration.

The correct way of expressing an unconditional order is "Pay to...". Sentences like "If the quality of the goods meets the sales contract, please pay..." or "I should be pleased if you would kindly pay..." are not unconditional orders, but requests.

#### 3) Date and Place of Issue

The date of issue refers to the date when the bill is drawn. It performs three functions: to decide the date of presentation or the date of acceptance(if it is a usance bill); to make certain that the date of maturity date if the bill is payable after the date of issue; to determine the behavior ability of drawer.

The issuing place is very important, because, for an international draft, whether the draft is valid or not depends on the local law of the issuing place. When a discrepancy arises concerning the validity of a bill. If there is no indication of such a place, the place where the drawer resides is considered the place of issue.

#### 4) Time of Payment/Tenor

Tenor means the due date of a bill on which the drawee or the acceptor should effect payment. According to *the UK Bill of Exchange* of 1882, a bill of exchange may be payable on demand or at a fixed or determinable future time. Based on this, we can divide bills into two types: sight bills and usance bills. A sight bill is payable at sight while a usance bill payable at a determinable future time. The following are the different tenors a bill may be made:

**Firstly, payable on demand**

The words "at sight" or "on demand" or "on presentation" are indicated on the bill. For example, "Pay USD2,000.00 to the order of Bank of China at sight"; "Pay to David on demand"

## Chapter 2  Payment Instruments in International Settlement

or "Pay GBP2,000.00 to bearer on presentation", etc.

However, those drafts without the time of payment on the bill will be thought as sight bill. For example, "Pay to A Co. or order..." .

For a sight bill, when the holder duly presents the bill for payment, the drawee should immediately effect payment.

**Secondly, payable at a future time**

- Payable at a fixed time after sight.

When a bill is payable at a fixed time after sight, the holder should first present the bill to the drawee for acceptance and then on the due date for payment. Here "sight" in the "after sight" means the acceptance on. In the other words, the due date is calculated based on the accepting date. For example, "At 30 days after sight pay to Citi Bank or order." And "Pay to the order of Mr. Smith at one month after sight."

In practice, it can be divided into two situations as follows:

- Payable on a fixed date.

For example,

"On Dec. 20 2016 pay to Joan."

"Pay to the order of... at 30 days after issuance of B/L."

"Pay to the order of... at 60 days after the date of negotiation."

- Payable at a fixed time after the happening of a specified event.

For example,

"Pay to the order of... at 30 days after issuance of B/L"

"Pay to the order of... at 60 days after the date of negotiation."

For a bill of exchange, the payers should effect payment in the future, regardless of the payment terms expressed in any other forms, the holder needs to present the bill twice to the payer. So, how is the specific maturity date to be calculated?

In conformity with *the UK Bill of Exchange* of 1882 and the *Geneva's Uniform Law*, the rules for calculating the due date of a bill are as follows:

Firstly, one should note that if the paying date is a non-business day, the bill should be paid on the succeeding business day.

Secondly, where a bill is payable at a fixed period after date/sight/the happening of a specified event, the time of payment is determined by excluding the day from which the time is to begin to run and by including the date of payment.

Thirdly, if the bill for those who see the votes after the regular payments, while the bill has been acceptance, self-acceptance from the date; such as bills of exchange is refused acceptance or non-payment, as from the refusal to the date of the certificate.

Fourthly, the term "month" in a bill means a calendar month.

**Thirdly, payable at a fixed time after date(issuing date)**

When a bill is payable at a fixed time after date, the holder is also recommended to present for acceptance first and then for payment on the due date, for by acceptance the drawee becomes the acceptor, the principal obligor of the bill. The due date is calculated based on the date of issue.

### 5) Name of the Payee

The payee means the person to whom a bill of exchange is payable. Since a bill may be payable to a named person only, a named person or order, or bearer, there are three different ways of writing the payee of a draft.

- Restricted order.

A bill may be payable to a named person only or to a named person not transferable. For example, "Pay somebody only"; "Pay somebody not transferable" or "Pay to somebody not negotiable."

This kind of order implies that the bill is a non-negotiable instrument. It may not be transferred to another person.

- Demonstrative order.

A bill may be payable to the order of a particular person or to a particular person without any words indicating the prohibition of further transfer. For example,

"Pay to somebody or order".

"Pay to the order of somebody".

"Pay to somebody".

This kind of order means that the bill can be transferred after being endorsed by the named person.

- Payable to bearer.

A draft may be payable to bearer without a specific person as the payee. For example, "Pay to bearer or holder".

"Pay to".

"Pay to somebody or bearer."

This kind of order indicates that the bill can be transferred more freely, as no endorsement is needed.

### 6) Name and Address of Drawee

The name and address of the drawee must be fairly and definite. A bill of exchange addressed to two or more drawee jointly, such as named "Tom Barber and Joan Brown" is valid, but "Tom Barber or Joan Brown" is not proper.

If the drawer and drawee are the same people, or the drawee is fictitious, the bill can be considered either a promissory note or a bill of exchange at the holder's option.

The place of payment means the place where the holder should present the bill for payment. If there is no such indication on a bill, the location where the drawee resides should be considered the place of payment.

### 7) A Specific Sum

The amount must be "certain" that means the amount in money must be directly clearly expressed in both words and figures and the two amounts must be the same.

If the amount due the text and figures also said that while there are differences, should be the amount indicated in words shall prevail.

In addition, the amount payable may be paid with interest; by stated installments, or according to an indicated rate of exchange. In these, the interest rate, installment method and the exchange rate must be indicated clearly on the bill.

**8) Name and Signature of the Drawer**

A bill of exchange must be signed by the drawer who is the obligator of the instrument, or instrument invalid. The drawer of a bill of exchange may be an individual or a legal entity. If it is an individual, the person himself signs the bill, and if it is a legal entity, the authorized manager signs on behalf of the entity. When a natural person on behalf of legal persons when the issue of bills of exchange, bills of exchange must show that the principal-agent relationship. The words, showing the principal-agent relationship, may include "For", "Per pro", "On behalf of" or "For and on behalf of".

In addition to the above essential contents, bills of exchange may also have some additional or optional elements. These additional items may appear in a money order or do not appear, maybe one or a number of. These mainly include the following:

- A set of bills.
- Place of Payment.
- A Banker designated as Payer.
- Limit of time for presentation.
- Notice of Dishonor Excused or Protest Waived.
- Without Recourse.

Sample 2.1

**BILL OF EXCHANGE**

Drawn under _____ Irrevocable L/C No. _____

Payable with Interest _____%

No. _____ Exchange for ============= Nanjing _____

At _____ Sight of This FIRST of Exchange (Second of Exchange Being Unpaid)

Pay to the order of _____

the sum of ===============================================

To

## 2.2.3 Rights, Obligations and Responsibilities

There are three necessary parties concerned with the draft: the drawer, the payee and the drawee (or the payer), at the same time, they are also the basic parties before the bill of exchange enters into the circulation. In addition, bill of exchange sometimes involves the endorser, the endorsee and guarantor etc. The basic rights, obligations and responsibilities of the parties concerned are shown in table 2-1.

Table 2-1　The Rights, Obligations and Responsibilities of the Parties Concerned with the Bill of Exchange

| Parties concerned | Concept | Rights | Obligations and responsibilities |
|---|---|---|---|
| Drawer | The party who draw the draft | The principal creditor when the bill of exchange is drawn | To pay or accept when it was presented by the payee or the formal holder and is the principal debtor |
| Payee | The party who receives the payment | The main creditor | The payee will be the first endorser when it was endorsed and will bear the responsibilities that the draft will be paid or accepted just the same as the drawee; and he will pay back to the bona-fide holder when it was dishonored |
| Drawee | The party who is ordered to make payment | | Assume liability to be paid, however, assumes no obligation that the draft will be surely paid |

According to the parties when they participate in the activities of the draft, the parties can be divided into two groups: the basic parties and the non-basic parties.

(1) **Basic Parties**

These are the parties based on the original acts of the bill of exchange. They include the drawer, payee and payer, whose name or business name are recorded on the draft(s).

1) **Drawer**

It refers to the enterprise or bank that draws the bill of exchange. Article 20 of *Bill Law of China* stipulated: "The drawing is the act that the drawer issues the bill and deliver it to the payee." Now that the drawing is a kind of action of the bill of exchange, the qualification of the action shall comply with the provisions of the law. Therefore, to have the ability to conduct is necessary for the issuance of the bill and those with no ability of conduct should be done by his agent such as his legal representative or guardian.

2) **Payee**

It refers to the party who receives the payment on the bill of exchange.

3) **Drawee**

The drawee is also the payer who performs the payment of the bill of exchange.

4) **Acceptor**

It is the party who bears the obligation to pay on maturity. Generally, the acceptor is the drawee mentioned-above.

(2) **The Non-Basic Parties**

In practice, there are two non-basic parties.

1) **Endorsee**

It refers to the party who acquires the right of a negotiable instrument when it was transferred. He has nothing to do with the bill when the bill was drawn; however, he has become the holder of the bill of exchange when it was endorsed. The endorsement includes the transfer, pledge, and discount through the endorsement. The endorsee can be an endorser when he transfers the bill of exchange again.

**2) Guarantor**

This refers to the party who guarantee that the payee or bearer will get the payment and then assumes joint liability.

## 2.2.4　Categories

According to different characteristics, bills of exchange can be categorized into different types.

### 2.2.4.1　Drawer

**(1) Commercial Bill**

A commercial bill or trader's bill is usually drawn by a trader or natural person on another trader or on a bank. In the international trade settlement, the bill of exchange is issued on the importer by the exporter when he has delivered the goods according to the contract.

**(2) Banker's Bill**

A banker's bill or bank draft is the one issued by a bank and its payer is also the bank. That is to say, both the drawer and drawee of the banker's bill are banks. In practice, the banker's bill is used for remittance.

In the international trade, the former is more popular.

### 2.2.4.2　Payee

**(1) Bill with Restricted Payee**

It is also known as a straight bill of exchange. The payee can only be the specified party on the draft and it cannot be transferred through endorsement.

**(2) Order Draft**

When the payee of the bill of exchange is specified "Pay to somebody or order" or "Pay to the order of somebody", it is a kind of order draft. This kind of draft is most commonly used in business, it can be through the endorsement in the business.

**(3) Bearer's Draft**

The payee of the bearer's draft is the bearer of the holder of the bill of exchange. In practice, such kind of draft can be transferred without endorsement.

### 2.2.4.3　Tenor

**(1) Sight Bill or Demand Bill**

A sight bill or demand bill is payable at sight, on demand, or on presentation. Sight bills are most commonly used in the international trade. A sight bill does not need acceptance.

**(2) Time Bill or Usance Bill or Term Draft**

A time bill, or usance bill or term draft is payable at a fixed or determinable future time. A time bill needs to be presented twice by the bearer and has been accepted by the payer to determine the liability of the payer. The time for usance draft can be described as follows, for example:

- at 30 days after sight of...
- at 30 days after date of...

- at 30 days after date of B/L
- on Oct. 30, 2017

The last one is called the bill with a fixed date.

#### 2.2.4.4 Whether the Shipping Documents Are Attached Thereto

(1) **Documentary Bill**

A documentary bill is a bill to which shipping documents (generally, Bill of Lading) are attached thereto, which is most frequently used under the payment methods by letter of credit or documentary collection.

(2) **Clean Bill**

A clean bill is a bill without shipping documents attached thereto. It is usually adopted to collect a commission, interest, or sample fee etc.

#### 2.2.4.5 Acceptor

(1) **Trader's Acceptance Bill**

A trader's acceptance is an accepted bill drawn on a trader or natural person and accepted by the trader or natural person. Trader's Acceptance Bill is established on the commercial credit. If the acceptor went bankrupt or could not make payment because some accidents have happened, the holder cannot acquire the payment on its maturity.

(2) **Banker's Acceptance Bill**

A banker's acceptance bill refers to the usance bill drawn on a bank and accepted by the bank. Banker's acceptance bill is established on the basis of the banker's credit. When the bill of exchange has been accepted by the bank, the holder can commonly acquire the payment on its maturity.

#### 2.2.4.6 The Currency Used

(1) **Domestic Money Bill**

It means the bill used domestically.

(2) **Foreign Exchange Bill**

It means the bill issued in foreign currency.

#### 2.2.4.7 Whether the Places of Issue and Payment Are in the Same Country

(1) **Inland Bill or Domestic Bill**

If the places of issue and payment are the same, the bill is an inland bill.

(2) **Foreign Bill**

When the places of issuance and payment are in different countries, the bill will be a foreign bill.

According to *the UK Bills of Exchange Act* of 1882, if a bill is drawn and payable in the U.K., the bill is deemed to be an inland bill, while a bill that is drawn in the U.K. but payable in another country, it is called a foreign bill.

The mentioned-above is only part of the categories of the draft. To categorize the draft according to its characteristics does not itself mean that a draft only has one characteristic, however, it can have multiple characteristics at the same time. For example, a draft cannot only be a commercial draft but also a documentary draft and time draft.

## 2.2.5 The Acts of Bill of Exchange

The acts of bill of exchange refer to those activities in order to establish certain relations between the rights and obligations to the draft. Generally, it includes four stages for a bill of exchange respectively: to issue, to present, to accept and to pay. In the circumstances when it is transferred, it may also include the endorsement. Besides, there are protest and recourse. Most of the actions related to a draft may also be applied to a promissory note or a check.

### 2.2.5.1 Issue

To issue is the beginning of a bill of exchange. It comprises two acts by the drawer: to draw a draft and sign it and to deliver the draft to the payee. The bill can be issued by the drawer only on condition that the drawer completes these two acts.

Delivery means the transfer of possession actually or constructively from one person to another. Only writing a bill without delivering is invalid. In fact, whatever acts such issue, endorsement or acceptance without delivering would be invalid. Actual delivery means the handover of a bill. Constructive delivery, in contrast, it means the bill is not physically handed over, but the title control is transferred through any non-physical hand-over delivery.

After the draft is drawn and delivered to the payee, it becomes irrevocable and in meantime the liability of the bill is established. The payee becomes the creditor to the bill who obtains the rights of payment requests, the right of bill transfer and the right of recourse.

The drawer becomes the primary debtor to the bill who engages to the payee and related holders that the bill should be accepted and paid. If it is dishonored by non-acceptance or by non-payment, the drawer must pay off the debt by himself, while the holder has the right of recourse against the drawer thereon. As to the payer, he/she may decide to pay or not pay based on the capital relations between the drawer and himself/herself.

### 2.2.5.2 Presentation

When a bill of exchange is presented to the payer for acceptance or payment by the holder, it is called presentation. There are two types of presentation, presentation for payment and presentation for acceptance. A bill must be duly presented for payment(presentation for payment) if it is a sight bill or duly presented for acceptance (presentation for acceptance) first and then payment at maturity (presentation for payment) if it is a time bill.

Presentation is an act that the holder requests his/her whole rights of the instruments. That is to say, the presentation must be made within the reasonable time and also at the proper place specified on the bill. If the bill is duly presented and is dishonored by the drawer, the holder will immediately obtain a right of recourse against the prior parties till the drawer. Otherwise, he/she will lose this kind of right that the drawer and all other prior parties may be discharged of their liability on the bill.

(1) The Time for Presentation

A bill must be presented for payment or acceptance at the specified time. Different instrument laws have different stipulations on the time of presentation for payment or acceptance. It will be determined based on the law of the country where the event of acceptance occurs.

For presenting a sight bill for payment or a time bill for acceptance, *the UK Bills of Exchange Act* of 1882 requires that the presentation be done within a reasonable time and in business hours on a business day, whereas *the Geneva's Uniform Law* requires that the period for presentation be one year. For presenting an accepted bill for payment, the former requires that the presentation should be done on the due date, while the latter on the due date or within two days after the due date.

According to *the People's Republic of China Law on Negotiable Instruments*, the presentation of a sight bill for payment must be done within one month after its issuance, and the presentation of a time bill for payment within 10 days from the due date. For a bill payable at a fixed future time or at a fixed time after date, the holder must present for acceptance before the maturity. For a bill payable at a fixed time after sight, the holder should present it for acceptance within one month from the date of issue.

(2) The Place of Presentation

A bill must be also presented for payment or acceptance at the specified place.

If no place is indicated, the bill should be presented at the drawee's or acceptor's business office, and if no business office is specified, the bill should be presented at their residential house.

## 2.2.5.3 Acceptance

Acceptance is an act by which the drawee promises to make payment at the bill maturity through the signification of his assent to the order given by the drawer.

In general, a valid acceptance includes two acts:

Firstly, the word "accepted" must be written on the bill and followed by the signature of the acceptor and the date of acceptance. When there are two copies of the drafts, only one of them needs to be accepted.

Secondly, to deliver the accepted bill. It means that the payer delivers the bill to the holder when it has been accepted. (It can be delivered actually or constructively which means that the payer has notified the holder that the bill has been accepted someday.)

According to the international practice, those usance bills at 180 days after sight will not be returned back to the holder after it has been accepted in order to facilitate all the parties concerned, while it just need to notify him that the bill has been accepted by a written notice.

Acceptance can be classified into general acceptance and qualified acceptance.

(1) General Acceptance

ACCEPTED

Date: 1 Oct. 2016

Due: 20 Dec. 2016

For Bank of China, Jiangsu

Zhang Shan(signed)

A general acceptance is an acceptance by which the acceptor assents without qualification to the order given by the drawer. For example,

ACCEPTED

Date: 1 Sept. 2016

Due: 20 Dec. 2016

For Bank of China. Jiangsu

Joan(signed)

### (2) Qualified Acceptance

A qualified acceptance is an acceptance by which the acceptor agrees to pay a bill at maturity with qualification. In practice, there are four types of qualified acceptance as follows:

#### 1) Conditional Acceptance

ACCEPTED

5th July, 2016

Payable on the delivery of all documents

For ABC Bank Ltd, New York

Adam Smith(Signature)

A conditional acceptance is one by which the payment to be made by the acceptor will depend on the fulfillment of a certain condition as stated. For example,

ACCEPTED

5th July, 2017

Payable on the delivery of all documents

For ABC Bank Ltd, New York

Adam Smith(Signature)

#### 2) Partial Acceptance

ACCEPTED

28th July, 2016

Payable for the amountof GBP50, 000.00 only

For Bank of China, Beijing

Zhou Min(Signature)

A partial acceptance is one by which the acceptor will pay only part of the amount for which the bill is drawn, say, where the whole amount stated thereon is GBP100,000.00, a partial acceptance is written as:

ACCEPTED

28th July, 2016

Payable for the amount of GBP50,000.00 only

For Bank of China, Beijing

Zhou Min(Signature)

#### 3) Local Acceptance

A local acceptance is one by which the acceptor will make payment only at a particular specified place. For example,

ACCEPTED

26th Sept., 2017

Payable at Bank of China, Shanghai and there only

For ABC Bank Ltd, New York

David(Signature)

If there is no word "and there only" in the above acceptance, it will be a general acceptance.

**4) Qualified Acceptance As to Time**

ACCEPTED

1st Dec., 2016

Payable at 3 months after date of acceptance

For Citi Bank, New York

Dana(Signature)

This kind of qualification focuses on the time schedule. That is, when accepting, the drawee may change the payment schedule of the bill. The qualification is usually a longer period than that stated on the bill. For example, the maturity time that the bill shows is only one month, however, when accepted, the actual payment time may be 3 months. For example,

ACCEPTED

1st Dec., 2016

Payable at 1 months after date

For Citi Bank, New York

Dana(Signature)

The most fundamental characteristic of qualified acceptance at the time of acceptance is to change the text of the original draft. That is, to change the nature of paying par value unconditionally. According to *the Geneva's Uniform Law*, acceptance is unconditional, if in the acceptance the main conditions of the acceptance of draft are modified by the acceptor. This kind of acceptance is treated as refused to accept, but the acceptor still should express its acceptance conditions responsibility.

### 2.2.5.4 Payment

Payment means that the payer or the acceptor pays the amount stipulated in the bill to the holder of the bill at maturity.

Generally, the drawee requires the bearer to issue a payment receipt or mark "Received", sign his name on the back of the bill as a payment proof and return it to the drawee. As to partial payment, as long as the bearer accepts it, he can retain the bill and recourse the unpaid amount. In this case, the drawee must mark the prepaid amount on the draft and requires the bearer to issue a receipt.

### 2.2.5.5 Endorsement

Endorsement means that the payee or holder(endorser) of a bill signs his or her name on the back of the bill or together with the name of the transferee (endorsee) to transfer his or her rights in a bill of exchange to the transferee. The endorsement also contains two acts: the payee or holder signs on the back of a bill (to endorse) and delivers it to the endorsee.

The endorsement itself not only means the transfer of the rights on the bill, but also means the endorser ensures the endorsee that the draft will be accepted or/and paid. If it has been dishonored, the endorsee is entitled to recourse to the endorser.

Where a bill is payable to a specified person only or to a specified person not transferable, the bill cannot be negotiated. Where a bill is payable to bearer, it can be negotiated by mere delivery without endorsement. Where a bill is payable to the order of a specified person, it can be negotiated by endorsement.

*The UK Bills of Exchange Act* of 1882 prescribes the following requisites for a valid endorsement.

● It must be written on the bill itself and be signed by the endorser. A simple signature of the endorser on the bill, without additional words, is sufficient.

● It must be of the entire bill while not part, that is to say, an endorsement that purports to transfer to the endorsee only a part of the amount payable, or which purports to transfer the bill to two or more endorsee severally, does not operate as a negotiation of the bill.

● If there are two or more payees, all of them must endorse the bill before it's transferred unless one of them has the authority to endorse for all the others.

● If the payee or endorsee is wrongly designated, or his name is mis-spelt, in a bill payable to order, he may endorse the bill as therein described, add, if he thinks fit, his proper signature.

● If there are two or more endorsements on a bill, each endorsement is deemed to have been made in the order in which it appears on the bill, until the contrary are proved.

● An endorsement may be made in blank or special. It may also contain terms making it restrictive.

Generally, there were four kinds of endorsements as follows:

(1) **Blank Endorsement**

Blank endorsement, also referred to as "general endorsement", is where the transferor merely signs the bill on its back without writing the name of the endorsee.

A bill so endorsed becomes payable to bearer, that means a bill with a blank endorsement can be further transferred by the holder merely by delivery. Once again, the endorsement of a bill of exchange with a blank endorsement is just for the responsibility of endorser and the right of endorsee. On the other hand, the holder may fill in the blank one either with his own name as the endorser and with the name of some other person as the endorsee, transferring the blank endorsement into a special endorsement. Certainly, the holder may transfer the bill to another person without filling in the blank and without endorsing it, i. e., by mere delivery. In this, the bill is deemed to be payable to bearer.

In China, however, the blank endorsement is not allowed and only special endorsement can be used, just like what we have mentioned that one should note different laws have different stipulations or explanation on a certain item.

"Pay to the order or Bank A"

Or "pay to Y or order"

Or "pay to Y"

(signature)

(2) **Special Endorsement**

Special endorsement, also known as "order endorsement" or "endorsement in full", is where the transferor adds a direction to pay a particular person in addition to the signature of the endorser.

"Pay to Co. A or the order"

Or "pay to Y or order"

Or "pay to Y"

(signature)

### (3) Restrictive Endorsement

A restrictive endorsement is where the endorsement prohibits a further transfer of the bill, in other words, the transferee has the only right to present the instrument for payment and cannot transfer his right to payment to any other person.

For example, suppose Bank A is the endorser while Bank B is the endorsee. When Bank A transfers the bill by endorsing, he may write as follows:

"Pay to Bank B only"

Or

"Pay to Bank B not to order"

Or

"Pay to Bank B not transferable or not negotiable"

(signature)

When the bill has been endorsed restrictively, it cannot be transferred again according to *British Bill Acts* stipulates. However, it can be further transferred according to *Geneva Uniform Bill of Exchange and Promissory Note*.

### (4) Conditional Endorsement

A conditional endorsement is where the endorsement with some additional conditions or instructions, such as "Without Protest" or "Without Recourse".

### 2.2.5.6 Dishonor

The act of dishonor is a failure or refusal of acceptance on or payment of a bill of exchange when presented. In addition, the bill may be considered to be dishonored when: A. the drawee heeling or fabricating make holder unsuccessful when presenting for acceptance or payment; B. the drawee escaping, declaration of bankrupt according to the law, or death, or ordered to stop business activities, makes payment in fact impossibly executed.

Dishonor may include two kinds of situations: dishonor by non-acceptance and dishonor by non-payment. When a bill is duly presented for acceptance and is not accepted within reasonable or specified time, the person presenting it must treat it as dishonored by non-acceptance. Dishonored by non-acceptance is in usance drafts. When a bill is duly presented for payment and payment is refused or cannot be obtained, it is considered dishonor by non-payment. Dishonored by non-payment is in sight draft or in expired usance drafts.

When a bill is dishonored either by non-acceptance or non-payment, the right of recourse should be accrued to the holder at once. If he does not treat it as dishonored by non-acceptance or non-payment when actually refused, the holder shall lose his right of recourse against the drawer and his prior endorsers for payment. When the holder dishonored he may exercise his right of recourse against his prior endorsers and drawer for payment. When exercising the right of recourse, unless otherwise stipulated by the instrument, the holder must deal with the presentation, protest, and notice of dishonor based on the relative law.

(1) **Notice of Dishonor**

A notice of dishonor is a notice made by the holder to his all prior parties about the dishonor. The purpose of giving such notice is to inform the drawer and all the prior endorsers who remain liable on the bill the default of acceptance or payment by the drawee or the acceptor so that they should get ready to honor the payment. According to *UK Bills of Exchange Act* of 1882, if the notice of dishonor is not given, the holder shall be discharged of the right of recourse against the drawer and all the prior endorsers. For a holder in due course, however, his/her recourse claim shall not be prejudiced by such an omission. According to *the Geneva's Uniform Law*, the right of recourse of the holder shall remain unless the drawer and or the endorser do suffer loss due to his omission of giving the notice, in which case the holder must compensate for the loss.

The notice of dishonor may be given in writing or in words, but must be given by or on behalf of the holder or an endorsee on the next business day after the dishonor of the bill.

*Geneva's Uniform Law* stipulates that the holder must give the notice within four days after the consummation of protest; the endorser must be in two days. According to *UK Bills of Exchange Act* of 1882, the holder should give the notice to the prior party in another place at the next day after the consummation of protest, the endorser may do so to his prior party at the next day after receiving the notice. According to *the Law on Negotiable Instruments of People's Republic of China*, the holder should give the notice to his prior party within three days after receiving the relevant evidence of non-payment or non-acceptance; the prior party should notify his prior transferor within three days after receiving the notice of dishonor.

If the drawer or any endorser states besides his name on the bill such wordings as "Notice of Dishonor Excepted", it means that in the event of that the bill is dishonor; the holder doesn't give the notice to him.

(2) **Protest**

A protest is a written certificate under seal drawn up and signed by a notary public (legal) or court or banking associations or another authorized person in the dishonor place for the purpose to giving evidence that a bill of exchange has been presented by him for acceptance or for payment but dishonored.

Article 51 item 7 in *the British 1882 Law of Bills* stipulates that the protest should be accompanied by a draft copy and record the following:

1) the name of the applicant.

2) refuse the certificate made into a place and date; and the reason or reasons; proposed requirements, and the answers given (if any); or were unable to find the drawee or acceptor of the facts.

The protest fee paid to the notary public is to be borne by the drawer and will be charged to him at the time when compensation for the amount the bill is claimed. If the drawer is not willing to pay the protest fee, he must add such words "protest waived" or "please do not protest if dishonored" on the bill at the time of its issue. In that case, the protest fee may be for the account of the holder if he still requests the notary public to draw up a protest.

#### 2.2.5.7 Right of Recourse

Recourse refers to the right of the holder of a draft to compel his prior endorsers or the drawer to perform their legal obligation of payment if it is dishonored by the drawee or by the acceptor. In other words, in case of a bill of exchange being dishonored, the holder then has a right to claim compensation from the drawer or any endorser. The compensation should include the amount payable on the bill with interest, the fees for giving the notice of dishonor and protest and other actually incurred expenses.

The conditions for the holder performing his right of recourse:

- To present the bill to the drawee for payment or acceptance in the legally given period of time.
- To give *the Notice of Dishonor* to his prior party in the legally given period of time.
- To make a Protest in the legally given period of time.

In practice, if the drawer and/or any endorser of a bill of exchange is not willing to be claimed compensation by the holder in the event of the instrument being dishonor, he can write the words "without recourse" or "sans recourse", which will discharge the drawer and the endorser of their liability.

#### 2.2.5.8 Guarantee/Aval

The act of guarantee is performed by a third party called guarantor, who engages that the bill will be paid on presentation if it is a sight bill or accepted on presentation and paid at maturity if it is a time bill. That is to say, the guarantor stands surely for a debtor such as the drawer, the endorser, or the acceptor and assumes his/her indebtedness to the holder. If the bill is dishonored by non-payment or non-acceptance the guarantor shall pay it, hold it and have the right of recourse against the drawer or the acceptor.

In the form of guarantee:

Given for _____ (guarantee)

signed by _____ (guarantor)

dated on _____ (date)

(signature)

#### 2.2.5.9 Discounting

Discounting a bill of exchange is to sell a time bill that has been already accepted by the drawee but not yet fallen due to a financial institution such as a bank, investing corporation or discounting company at a price less than its face value.

## 2.3 Promissory Note and Cheque

### 2.3.1 Promissory Note

#### 2.3.1.1 Definition

According to *the Uniform Law for Bills of Exchange and Promissory Notes of Geneva* of 1930, a

promissory note must record the following factors:
- The term of Promissory Note.
- An unconditional promise to pay.
- The name of the person to whom or to whose order payment is to be made.
- A statement of the time of payment.
- A determinable sum of money.
- Statement of the place where payment is to be made.
- Statement of the date and of the place where the promissory note is issued.
- The signature of the maker.

But *China's Bill of Exchange Law* (the second version) specified that promissory note is to be drawn and signed by the drawer and promise to pay unconditionally a certain amount of money to payee or bearer at sight or at the specified date. Promissory note defined in this law is bank one.

From the definitions of the promissory note, it is easy to find, unlike a bill of exchange, that the promissory note is an unconditional promise to pay in writing. It has only two basic parties: the maker and the payee. In addition, there are no need to accept the promissory note if it is payable at a future time because the maker is always the primarily liable party.

#### 2.3.1.2 Essential Contents of a Promissory Note

Based on *the UK Bills of Exchange Act* of 1882, *the Uniform Law for Bills of Exchange and Promissory Notes of Geneva* of 1930, and other laws on negotiable instruments, a promissory note must have to be eight statutory:
- Marking of "promissory note".
- Unconditional promise for paying in writing.
- Date and place of issuing.
- Time of payment/Tenor.
- Name of the payee.
- Places of payment.
- A specific sum.
- Name and signature of the maker.

#### 2.3.1.3 Categories

The promissory note can be divided into two kinds: one is commercial promissory note; and the other is banker's promissory note.

### 2.3.2 Cheque/Check

#### 2.3.2.1 Definition

A check is an unconditional order in writing drawn on a bank signed by the drawer, requiring the bank to pay on demand a sum certain in money to or the order of a specified person or to bearer.

The person writing the cheque, the drawer, has a transaction banking account (often called a current, cheque, chequing account or checking account) where their money is held.

#### 2.3.2.2 Contents

- Marking of "check" or "cheque".
- Unconditional order for paying in writing.
- Name of the payer.
- Place of payment.
- Date and place of issue.
- Name and signature of the drawer.

#### 2.3.2.3 Categories

The check can be divided into several kinds from different characteristics.

**(1) Order Check**

Order check refers to a check which is payable to the order of a particular person.

**(2) Bearer Check**

Bearer check is a kind of check which is payable to the holder without a specific person as the payee. The bank bears no responsibility on whether the holder has acquired the check legally.

**(3) Certified Check**

A certified check is one that is certified by the drawee bank. When the cheque has been certified, it is more negotiable.

**(4) Crossed Check**

It is the cheque with two parallel lines across its face which implicate that the payee can collect the check proceeds only through a bank other than asking for payment in cash directly on the counter of the drawee bank. A crossed cheque can prevent it be being falsely paid when it has been lost so that safeguard the interests of the beneficiary.

**1) General Crossings**

It specified no name of the collecting bank and it means the check can be collected through any bank.

**2) Special Crossings**

It specified the name of the collecting bank on the check. (the name of the bank is shown between two bold parallel lines on the check.)

### 2.3.3 The Difference of Bill of Exchange, Promissory Note and Cheque

As to the difference of bill of exchange, promissory note and cheque, please see table 2-2.

Table 2-2 The Difference of Bill of Exchange, Promissory Note and Cheque

| Item | Bill of Exchange | Promissory Note | Cheque |
| --- | --- | --- | --- |
| Characteristics | Written debt certificate; Contain a certain amount, in a certain time, the holder can require the issuer or the specified payer to pay a certain money | | |
| Roles | Payment methods, circulation tools, financing tools (i.e., play to the role of the settlement, credit, circulation etc.) | | |

## Chapter 2  Payment Instruments in International Settlement

（续）

| Item | Bill of Exchange | Promissory Note | Cheque |
| --- | --- | --- | --- |
| Unconditional | An unconditional order addressed to another, requiring the person to whom it is addressed to pay to a third party | An unconditional promise made by one person to another and engage to pay to the latter | Issued by the bank's customer to the bank and authorize the bank to pay to a third party or pay by himself |
| Basic Parties Concerned | Payee<br>Drawee<br>Drawer | Payee<br>Maker | Payee<br>Paying bank<br>Customer |
| Main Debtor | For usance draft:<br>Before the drawing: the drawer<br>After accepted: the acceptor | Maker | Issuer |
| Creditor | The holder (payee; endorsee) | | |
| Obligation of the Issuer | To ensure that the drawee will accept and make payment | To be obligel to pay by himself | To guarantee that the payer must pay |
| Rights of the Holder | Can require the parties concerned to make payment and exercise the rights of recourse | | |
| Time for Payment | Sight and usance | Sight and usance | Pay at sight or on demand |

# Questions:

## Ⅰ. True or false.

1. A sight bill should be presented for acceptance.
2. Anytime, the holder has the right of recourse against the other parties.
3. An endorser of a bill is liable on it to subsequent endorsers and holders of the bill.
4. In the international trade, the most frequently used means of payment include bills only.
5. When a check is crossed, it can be pay into a bank account and be cashed over the counter.
6. When discounting, a time bill should already be accepted and not yet fallen due.
7. Promissory note is a written and signed promise to pay a stated amount of money to a particular person.
8. Drawer is the person who writes the order and gives directions to the person to make a specific payment of money.
9. A bill shows "Pay to ABC Co. providing the goods in compliance with contract No. 4. the sum of one thousand US dollars.", it is acceptable.
10. If a bill is payable "at 30 days after date", the date of payment is decided according to the date of acceptance.
11. If a bill shows "Pay to the order of A Co. the sum of five thousand US dollars plus interest.", the bill is acceptable but the clause is unacceptable.
12. Discounting means to sell a time bill already accepted by the drawee but not yet fallen due to a financial institution at price equal to its face value.

## Ⅱ. Multiple choice.

1. The payer of the promissory note is the (     ).
   A. drawer         B. drawee         C. payee         D. creditor
2. (     ) is a written order to a bank to pay a certain sum of money from one's bank account to another person.
   A. bill of exchange     B. promissory note     C. cheque(check)     D. draft
3. If the (     ) falls on a day when the bank is closed, then it should be extended to the first day following the day on which such bank is open.
   A. negotiation period                B. expiry date
   C. presentation period               D. date of shipment
4. If the drawer is a bank, the bill is called (     ). It is mainly used in remittance.
   A. banker's draft                    B. commercial draft
   C. commercial acceptance bill        D. banker's acceptance bill
5. In the transfer of the bill of exchange, if the bill of exchange is accompanied by shipping documents, it is a (     ).
   A. clean bill                        B. documentary bill
   C. sight draft                       D. usance bill or time bill
6. (     ) type of a draft requires endorsement when transferable.
   A. Restrictive payee     B. To holder     C. To order     D. To bearer
7. (     ) is the written signification by the drawee of his assent to the order of the drawer.
   A. To draw         B. Presentation     C. Acceptance     D. Endorsement
8. (     ) is the refusal to make payment or accept a bill by the payer when it is presented for payment or acceptance.
   A. Recourse        B. Dishonor         C. Acceptance     D. Endorsement
9. A promissory note is like a bill of exchange that has been accepted, and can only have (     ).
   A. one copy        B. two copy         C. three copy     D. four copy
10. A (     ) must be accepted by the drawee before payment.
    A. sight bill                        B. bill payable at… days after sight
    C. promissory note                   D. bill payable on demand
11. The effect of a blank endorsement is to make the check payable to the (     ).
    A. order of a specified person       B. specified person
    C. bearer                            D. named person.
12. A (     ) carries comparatively little risks and can be discounted at the finest rate of interest.
    A. sight bill      B. bank draft       C. commercial bill     D. trade bill

## Ⅲ. Case study.

In May of a year, Company A sold goods valued at US＄65,000 to Company B. On May 20, Company B, as the drawer, issued a bill of exchange payable at a fixed date with a demonstrative order to Company A with Bank C as the payer and Company A as the payee. The amount of the bill was US＄65,000 and the payment date was July 20. On June 10, the endorsement of the bill was transferred by the payee, Company A to Company D. On July 5, Company D transferred the endorsement to Company E and Company E was dishonored when presenting for payment to Bank C on the first day of the lunar month. Company E made a timely certified protest and notified all the prior endorses. After that, Company E exercised the right of recourse over Company B. But Company B refused to pay the bill with the reason that the goods received were not agreeable to those in the contract.

## Questions:

(1) Is Company B's practice reasonable? And why?

(2) What is the proper way of Company B?

# Chapter 3

# Remittance

**Learning Objectives**

- To understand the concept of forward and backward transfer.
- To grasp the definition, general procedures of different remittance.
- To understand the situation when the remittance is utilized.

The settlement methods or payment methods refer to the specific transfer routes of the payment from the payer to the payee.

According to whether the flow direction of both the capital and the negotiable instrument, we can divide the settlement methods into two groups: the forward transfer and the backward transfer. Under the remittance, the flow direction of both the capital and the payment tool are the same, which belongs to the forward transfer; while under collection and the letter of credit, they are in opposite direction, thus they are backward transfer.

We will focus on the discussion of remittance.

## 3.1 Definition and Parties Concerned

### 3.1.1 Definition

Remittance refers to the transferring of funds via a bank. It is one of the most simple, convenient and common terms of payment in international settlement, which is based on commercial credit.

Under remittance, neither the original payer nor the final payee is a bank. It completes the settlement between the payer and the payee through the inter-bank fund transfer channel. The certificate used for remittance is called as payment order(PO in short). Because the transfer direction of the PO and the direction of capital flow are the same, the remittance belongs to the forward transfer.

Among the international trade settlement methods, the remittance is the most convenient which only takes advantage of the convenience on the currency transfer among the banks. It is not concerned with the banker's credit. Whether the seller and the payer can execute the contract only depends on their own credits. Thus, the remittance is of commercial credits.

### 3.1.2 Parties Concerned

There are four parties concerned with the remittance, they are as follows respectively:

### (1) Remitter

The remitter, also known as the payer, is the person who applies to his bank to remit funds to the payee or beneficiary in a foreign country. Remittance application, which evidences the contract between the remitter and the remitting bank when the latter has accepted, is necessary for the remittance. Generally speaking, the remitter would be the importer in the international trade.

### (2) Payee or Beneficiary

The beneficiary or payee is the party who is addressed to receive the funds by remittance. In practice, the exporter would be the payee when remittance is used for the payment of goods in international trade.

### (3) Remitting Bank

Remitting bank is the bank that transfers the funds at the request of a remitter to its correspondent or its branch in another country and instructing the latter to pay to a certain amount of money to the payee or the beneficiary. The remitting bank is located in the same city as that of the remitter who is located in the importing country.

### (4) Paying Bank

Paying bank, also known as the receiving bank, is the bank that is entrusted by the remitting bank to pay a certain sum of money to the payee or beneficiary named in the remittance advice.

When handling the remittance, the remitter should fill in and submit the remittance application form to the remitting bank, while the remitting bank has the obligation to send the remittance payment advice according to the application. After the paying bank has got the payment order, he has the obligation to make payment to the beneficiary (usually the exporter). However, neither the remitting bank nor the paying bank would bear the losses caused by their own negligence (for example, the payee is impossible to get the payment or acquire it late because the loss or delay of the payment order). Besides, the remitting bank is not liable for the negligence of the paying bank.

## 3.2　Categories

There are three kinds of remittance, such as mail transfer, telegraph transfer and demand draft.

### 3.2.1　Mail Transfer

Under mail transfer (M/T in short), the remitting bank, at the request of the remitter, transfers the funds by mailing a payment order or advice to its correspondent bank, authorizing the latter to pay to the payee or beneficiary. Since the payment order is sent by mail, we call it as mail transfer. Because it is slow and the bank concerned may have a chance to utilize the funds to some extent, to pay by the M/T is cheap.

When the M/T is used, it should have been agreed by both the exporter and the importer in the contract. When the time for payment is coming, the general procedures of the M/T will be as follows (see Figure 3-1):

1) The remitter fills in the M/T application form (See Appendix B), presents the proceeds and

pay the commission for remittance to the remitting bank.

2) Upon receipt of the application form, the proceeds and the commission, the remitting bank offers a receipt to the remitter.

3) The remitting bank sends a payment order or advice to the paying bank by mail, entrusting the latter to pay to the payee or beneficiary.

4) Upon receipt of the PO and authenticating the signature, the paying bank notifies the payee in the PO.

5) The payee issues a receipt to the paying bank.

6) The paying bank makes payment to the payee.

7) The paying bank sends the debit advice and the payment receipt from the payee to the remitting bank.

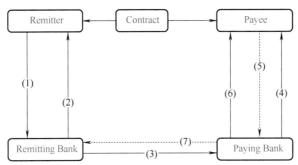

Figure 3-1 General Procedures for M/T

### 3.2.2 Telegraphic Transfer

Under telegraphic transfer(T/T in short), the PO is sent to the paying bank by cable, telex or SWIFT.

Because the bank can provide faster service than M/T and have no chance to use the money remitted, it will charge the remitter more than remitting by M/T.

The procedures are similar to M/T(see Case 3-1).

---

**Case 3-1   T/T**

**Background:**

Type of Remittance: T/T

Application: Law on Negotiable Instruments of the People's Republic of China, latest edition

Exporter: Firm A in China

Importer: Firm B in the USA

**Circumstances:**

Firm A: Firm A exported handicraft products to Firm B in 2008. They used to maintain a long-term business relationship with each other, so Firm B is credit worthy.

Firm B: For the first deal, Firm B required to settle the proceeds by the T/T for the purpose of so-called cost-saving and mutual benefits.

Firm A: Based on their long-established reliable business relationship, Firm A agreed to the use of the T/T for settlement. And after completing the shipment and acquiring the B/L. Firm A faxed it to Firm B to claim for payment.

Firm B: Firm B immediately made the payment by the T/T to the account of Firm A, which seemed to very smooth and successful.

Firm A: After a month, Firm A shipped the second lot of the same goods to Firm B, once again agreeing to use the payment method of the T/T. Within the following three months, there had been altogether four lots of the goods with the total amount of over USD200,000 having been shipped to the Port of New York on the same basis of the T/T. After the forth lot of the goods had been dispatched, firm A made claim to Firm B for T/T payment as the previous.

Firm B: Firm B refused to pay for the last shipment by finding all kinds of excuses. Half a year later, Firm B could no longer be located, and had proven to become out of business.

**Questions:**
1. What were the errors of Firm A that had led to its final loss in this case?
2. What lessons can be learned from this case of the T/T settlement?

**Answers:**
1. There were at least three errors which had resulted in Firm A's final loss. Firstly, in the very first deal as a new business relationship, Firm A agreed with Firm B's requirement of T/T (open account, O/A) payment method just based on its past impression or experience; Secondly, Firm A did not make all timely necessary efforts to collect the deferred payment from the importer such as taking a legal action or arbitration; Thirdly, Firm A was not alert enough to do some specific researches in the standing and business status of Firm B before agreeing to the use of the T/T(O/A) as an international payment term.

2. Open account (O/A) by T/T is the most dangerous method of the international settlement for the seller, so any exporter must be very cautious in the use of it. Unless in the relationship of subsidiary or affiliation in a large group or for a very small amount of trade, such a kind of a payment method should not be applied in any circumstances.

## 3.2.3 Demand Draft

Compared with M/T and T/T, demand draft (D/D in short) is a little special. Under D/D, the remitting bank will draw a sight draft or demand draft on its correspondent bank in the country where the payee or beneficiary locates, order him/her to pay to the payee at sight upon presentation.

It is similar to M/T and T/T, it should have been agreed to be paid through D/D by both the exporter and the importer in the contract. Its general payment procedures are as follows (see Figure 3-2):

1) The remitter fills in the D/D application form, presents the proceeds and pay the commission for remittance to the remitting bank.

2) Upon receipt of the form, the proceeds and the commission, the remitting bank draws a demand draft and gives it to the remitter.

3) The remitter sends the demand draft directly to the paying bank.

4) The remitting bank sends an advice of drawing to the paying bank.

5) Upon presentation of the demand draft by the beneficiary, the paying bank will make payment after he has made sure the authenticity of the draft.

6) The paying bank sends the debit advice to the remitting bank.

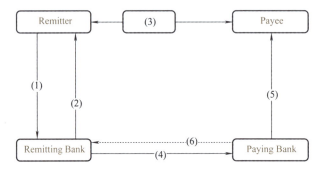

Figure 3-2   General Procedures for D/D

## 3.3   Reimbursement and Cancellation of Remittance

When the paying bank has made payment to the payee or the beneficiary according to the PO, the paying bank should be reimbursed the same amount from the remitting bank. Besides, the remittance may be cancelled at the request of the remitter or the payee decline the payment. So, it is also important to know the general procedure for both the reimbursement and cancellation of remittance.

### 3.3.1   Reimbursement of Remittance

Reimbursement of remittance refers to the act that the remitting bank pay back the same amount to the paying bank when the latter has made payment successfully.

How to reimburse depends on the currencies used and the establishment of the accounts between them. There are three categories as follows: direct accounting, accounting through a third bank and accounting under a payment agreement.

(1) **Direct Accounting**

When there is a vostro account or nostro account between the remitting bank and the paying bank, it is convenient for the remitting bank to reimburse by direct accounting. Vostro and nostro are the Italian languages, which the former means yours and the latter means ours. Vostro account is an account held by a bank on behalf of its correspondent bank, while nostro account is an account in foreign currency established by a bank in its correspondent bank abroad.

If the remitting bank pay in its own currency and have a vostro account, then the reimbursement procedure would be: ①The remitting bank marks in the PO as follows: "In cover, we have credited your a/c with us. "②The remitting bank gives notice to the paying bank that "Your a/c credited" (see Figure 3-3). After the paying bank has got the notice of "Your a/c credited." and confirm the cover has been transferred into his accounts, he she may release the payment to the payee with his/her own cover.

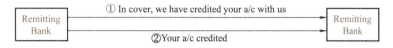

Figure 3-3 Reimbursement of Remittance When the Paying Bank Opens an a/c with the Remitting Bank(Vostro Account)

If the remitting bank pay in its foreign currency and have a nostro account, then the reimbursement would be in the following procedures:① The remitting bank marks in the PO as follows:"In cover, please debit our a/c with you."② The paying bank gives notice to the remitting bank that "Your a/c debited" (see Figure 3-4). After the paying bank has debited the a/c of the remitting bank, he may release the payment to the payee.

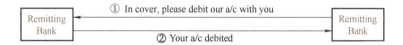

Figure 3-4 Reimbursement of Remittance When the Remitting Bank Opens an a/c with the Paying Bank(Nostro Account)

(2)Accounting Through a Third Bank

When there is neither vostro account nor nostro account between the remitting bank and the paying bank, the remitting bank will find a third bank, where both the remitting bank and the paying bank have opened a current account. Suppose both the remitting bank(Bank X) and the paying bank (Bank Y) have opened a current account in a third bank (Bank Z), then the reimbursement procedure through Bank Z would be that shown in Figure 3-5.

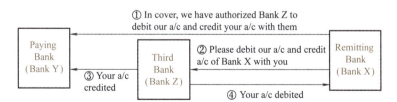

Figure 3-5 Reimbursement of Remittance Through a Third Bank

(3)Accounting Under a Payment Agreement

If there is a payment agreement between two countries where the remitting bank and paying bank are located respectively, the reimbursement procedures must comply with the terms of the agreement. In this case, the instructions concerned would be:

The instruction from the remitting bank would be: "In cover, you are authorized to debit our

Central Bank's clearing account with your Central Bank."

While the instruction from the paying bank would be: "In cover, we have requested our Central Bank to credit the sum to the clearing account of your Central Bank with them."

### 3.3.2 Cancellation of Remittance

(1) Cancellation of M/T and T/T

Under M/T and T/T, the paying bank may return the payment to the remitting bank by cable, telephone or airmail if the cancellation was put forward by the payee or beneficiary. While it is the remitter who requires cancelling the remittance, the remitting bank must advise the paying bank to stop the make payment by cable, telephone or airmail immediately and cancel the remittance. However, when the paying bank has effected the payment, the remitter has no right to cancel the remittance and can only negotiate with the payee to cancel it.

(2) Cancellation of D/D

When the D/D was chosen, the remitter in general cannot stop the payment. While the draft has been lost or stolen, the remitter may stop to pay or ask to return by reporting the loss. In this case, the remitter should issue a letter of guaranty, in which he makes a promise to bear the losses of the remitting bank because of the cancellation and return the draft to the remitting bank when he/she found it again.

(3) Procedures of Cancellation

The procedures of cancellation in the remitting bank are as follows: ①The remitter applies first and details the reason to cancel the remittance, provides guarantee if any; ②The remitting bank check the application; ③The remitting bank send a notice for the cancellation to the paying bank; ④The paying bank offsets when he agrees to it and change it to local currency and credit the a/c of the remitting bank.

The procedures of cancellation in the paying bank are as follows: ①Check the seal on the notice of cancellation and make sure whether the payment has been made or not; ②If he/she has made payment, he/she can send the receipt issued by the payee and tell the remitting bank that he has paid; ③If he/she has not made payment, then he/she will return the cover and return the PO or draft(s).

## 3.4 Application of Remittance in International Trade

Remittance can be used for both trade and non-trade settlement. Remittance is simple, flexible, cheap, timely and swift, however, it is less trustworthy because of its characteristics of commercial credit. Thus, it is widely used between those trade partners who are trustworthy and reliable. In practice, we often use it for the collection of incidental charges or non-trade settlement.

Generally, the remittance for the international trade settlement can be categorized into two groups: to collect first while delivering later and to deliver first while collect later.

## 3.4.1 Collect First while Deliver Later

It can also be subdivided into two types: pay in advance and pay with order.

(1) Pay in Advance

Payment in advance, aka cash in advance, under which, the importer pays part or even all the proceeds before the delivery or prior to the shipment of the goods. As to the importer, it means to pay in advance, while it means to collect or get the payment first, while delivering the commodities later.

(2) Pay with Order

Besides, the importer may make part of a one-time payment to the exporter when he/she has payed the order.

By insisting on payment in advance or pay with order, the exporter obviously has complete assurance of obtaining payment, which has most advantageous to the exporter while it has more risks to the importer. So the importer should only choose such kind of remittance when he/she does business with those exporters who are reliable and located in those countries where the political or economic environment are stable.

In practice, when the exporter and the importer are reliable and when the commodities are the best sellers, "collect first while deliver later" will be used. In order to decrease or escape the risks under this method, the importer may require the exporter to provide a letter of guarantee guaranteeing that he will delivering the goods after he has got the payment.

## 3.4.2 Deliver First while Collect Later

It can also be subdivided into two sections: open account trade and cash on delivery.

(1) Open Account Trade

Open account trade, aka O/A trade in short, is a kind of arrangement between the exporter and the importer, by which the exporter has manufactured the commodities in the sales contract and finished the delivery before the importer has made payment, that is to say, the importer will effect payment after he/she has received the goods. Under the O/A trade, it is unnecessary for the importer to issue any negotiable instrument evidencing his/her legal commitment, which is most beneficial for the importer. Before using this method, the seller must have absolute confidence that he/she will be paid at the agreed date.

(2) Cash on Delivery

Compared with the O/A trade, the buyer will make payment to the exporter upon taking delivery of the goods.

Under the O/A trade and cash on delivery, the exporter will deliver first, while getting the payment from the import later. Thus, it is the exporter who should use it cautiously and carefully.

Generally speaking, when we use remittance for the international trade settlement, the payment clause in the sales contract should contain the following information: the specific payment method (M/T, T/T or D/D); time for payment; the amount etc. For example.

The Buyers shall pay 100% of the sales proceeds in advance by M/T to reach the Sellers not later than Oct. 10th.

# Questions:

**Multiple choice.**

1. M/T stands for (　　) in import and export business.
   A. telegraph transfer　B. demand draft　　C. mail transfer　　D. collection
2. The method that takes the transfer of bank draft issued by remitting bank to complete payment is called (　　).
   A. telegraph transfer　B. mail transfer　　C. demand draft　　D. bank transfer
3. The bank that is entrusted by the remitting bank to do the solution pay to the payee is (　　).
   A. remitting bank　B. receiving bank　C. collecting bank　D. transmitting bank
4. The method of remittance that can provide financing convenience for the payee is called (　　).
   A. mail transfer　　B. demand draft　　C. wire transfer　　D. payment after sight

# Chapter 4

# Collection

## Learning Objectives

- To understand the definition of collection and the parties concerned.
- To grasp the general procedure for different collection methods.
- To understand the general information on the *URC522*.

## 4.1 Definition of Collection and Parties Concerned

### 4.1.1 Definition

As to the collection, International Chamber of Commerce (ICC) has enacted the relevant customs: *Uniform Rules for Collection* (URC in short). Nowadays, the latest edition was revised in 1995. Because it was just the $522^{nd}$ publication of the ICC, it is named *URC522* in short.

Article 2 item(a) of URC522 defined the collection as follows:

a. "Collection" means the handling by banks of documents as defined in sub-Article 2(b), in accordance received, in order to:

Ⅰ. obtain payment and/or acceptance, or

Ⅱ. deliver documents against payment and/or against acceptance, or

Ⅲ. deliver documents on other terms and conditions.

In practice, when the collection is used for the international trade settlement, it is called export collection, in which the exporter (the creditor) draws the draft(s) and present them with the shipping documents to the remitting bank after he/she has effected the shipment, entrust the remitting bank to collect the payment through its correspondent bank in the importing country.

### 4.1.2 Parties Concerned

According to the stipulation in *URC522*, there are four parties concerned with the collection: principal, remitting bank, collecting bank and drawee.

#### 4.1.2.1 Principal

Namely, the principal refers to the party who entrusts a bank to handle the collection. In the practice of the international trade, it is the exporter who entrusts a bank to collect the payment from the importer. The exporter often has to draw a draft, so it can also be called as the drawer.

When the principal entrusts the bank to handle the collection, he/she should submit not only the specified documents but also *the Collection Application* (Generally, it is provided by the remitting bank). The principal and the drawee are the exporter and the importer respectively in the sales contract. Collection application serves as the contract between the principal and the remitting bank, the principal should express his/her real intention and requirement in the collection application, besides the principal should take the sales contract as a reference when he/she fills it in.

In practice, such as the requirement is not filled in accurately, the bank assumes no liability or responsibility for the resulting responsibility. When the principal fills in the collection application, he/she may take the following requirements in *URC522* into consideration:

(1) **Condition of Delivery of the Document**

Article 4 item(B) says: "It is the responsibility of the party preparing the collection instruction to ensure that the terms for the delivery of documents are clearly and unambiguously stated, otherwise banks will not be responsible for any consequences arising therefrom."

(2) **Address of the Payer**

Article 4 item(B) specifies: "If the address is incomplete or incorrect, the collecting bank may, without any liability and responsibility on its part, endeavor to ascertain the proper address." Besides, "the collecting bank will not be liable or responsible for any ensuing delay as a result of an incomplete or incorrect address being provided."

(3) **Time for Presentation**

Article 5 stipulates: "Expressions such as 'first', 'prompt', 'immediate', and the like should not be used in connection with presentation or with reference to any period of time within which documents have to be taken up or for any other action that is to be taken by the drawee. If such terms are used banks will disregard them."

(4) **Delivery Methods of the Document**

It is very important to the parties, especially the principal. Because there is quite a difference on the time to release the documents and the safety, the exporter should definitely define whether it is D/P or D/A, otherwise, the bank will choose D/P in the interest of the clients and will not bear any possible losses. Article 7 (b) stipulates: "If a collection contains a bill of exchange payable at a future date, the collection instruction should state whether the commercial documents are to be released to the drawee against acceptance (D/A) or against payment (D/P). In the absence of such statement, commercial documents will be released only against payment and the collecting bank will not be responsible for any consequences arising out of any delay in the delivery of documents."

### 4.1.2.2 Remitting Bank

The "remitting bank" is the bank which was entrusted by the principal to handle a collection. In China, we also call it the collecting bank. However, even though this bank was entrusted by the principal to collect the payment, it cannot finish the task because it is located in the exporting country. It will send the relevant documents to the collecting bank, which is located in the importing country upon receipt the documents from the principal, so remitting bank that deserves the name.

In practice, the remitting bank should also conduct the collection strictly according to both *the Collection Application* and *URC522*, cannot act overconfidently, otherwise, it will bear the responsibility.

However, the remitting bank bears no responsibility in the following fields:

(1) **Assume No Liability or Responsibility of the Form, Sufficiency, Accuracy, Genuineness, Falsification or Legal Effect of Any Document(s) or Superimposed Thereon**

This is specified in Article 13 in *URC522*. Besides, Article 13 further details: "Nor do they (the banks) assume any liability, condition, packing, delivery, value of existence of the goods represented by any document(s), or for the good faith or acts and/or omission, solvency, performance or standing of the consignors, the carriers, the forwarders, the consignees or the insurers of the goods, or any other person whomsoever."

(2) **Assume No Liability on the Commodities**

Under collection, the bank has no obligation to take care of the commodities. If the principal dispatches the goods to the bank without the permission of the bank, the bank does not assume any liability. As to this, item(a), (b), (c) and (d) of Article 10 in *URC522* has detailed it as follows:

"a. Goods should not be dispatched directly to the address of a bank or consigned to or to the order of a bank without prior agreement on the part of that bank.

Nevertheless, in the event that goods are dispatched directly to the address of a bank or consigned to or to the order of a bank for release to a drawee against payment or acceptance or upon other terms and conditions without prior agreement on the part of that bank, such bank shall have no obligation to take delivery of the goods, which remain at the risk and responsibility of the party dispatching the goods.

b. Banks have no obligation to take any action in respect of the goods to which a documentary collection relates, including storage and insurance of the goods even when specific instructions are given to do so. Banks will only take such action if, when, and to the extent that they agree to do so in each case, notwithstanding the provisions of sub-article 1(c), this rule applies even in the absence of any specific advice to this effect by the collecting bank.

c. Nevertheless, in the case that banks take action for the protection of the goods, whether instructed or not, they assume no liability or responsibility with regard to the fate and/or condition of the goods and/or for any acts and/or omissions on the part of any third parties entrusted with the custody and/or protection of the goods. However, the collecting bank must advise without delay the bank from which the collection instruction was received of any such action taken.

d. Any charges and/or expense incurred by banks in connection with any action taken to protect the goods will be for the account of the party from whom they received the collection."

(3) **Assume No Liability on the Result Arising Out of Delay ETC**

Article 14(a) and (b) stipulates as follows:

"a. Banks assume no liability or responsibility for the consequences arising out of delay and/or loss in transit of any message(s), letter(s) or document(s), or for delay, mutilation or other error(s) arising in transmission of any telecommunication or for error(s) in translation and/or interpretation of technical terms.

b. Banks will not be liable or responsible for any delays resulting from the need to obtain clarification of any instructions received."

**(4) Assume No Liability When Force Majeure Has Happened**

This is shown in Article 15 of the *URC522*:

"Banks assume no liability or responsibility for consequence arising out of the interruption of their business by Acts of God, riots, civil commotions, insurrections, wars, or any other causes beyond their control or by strikes or lockouts."

#### 4.1.2.3 Collecting Bank

It is any bank, other than the remitting bank, involved in processing the collection. In practice, it is a bank entrusted by the remitting bank to present the documents to the drawee and collect payment. Generally speaking, it is the correspondent bank in the importing country.

Generally, the collecting bank is also the presenting bank, who makes a presentation to the drawee. Its obligations are as follows:

**(1) Make Presentation for Payment or Acceptance**

According to *URC522*, in the case of documents payable at sight the presenting bank must make a presentation for payment without delay, while in the case of documents payable at a tenor the presenting bank must first make a presentation for acceptance without delay, and make a presentation for payment at its maturity.

**(2) Collect the Right Currency**

Article 17 of the *URC522* stipulates: "In the case of documents payable in the currency of the country of payment (local currency), the presenting bank must, unless otherwise instructed in the collection instruction, release the documents to the drawee against payment in local currency only if such currency is immediately available for disposal in the manner specified in the collection instruction."

According to Article 18, the presenting bank must release the documents to the drawee against payment in the designed foreign currency in the case of documents payable in a currency of foreign currency.

1) Take the Safety As the First Principle When Releasing the Documents Under Partial Payment.

According to Article 19(b), when partial payments are authorized in the collection instruction, the presenting bank should release the documents to the drawee only after full payment has been received, unless otherwise instructed.

2) Assume the Liability That the Form of Acceptance of Draft Be Complete and Correct Apparently.

#### 4.1.2.4 Drawee

The "drawee" is the one to whom presentation is to be made in accordance with the collection instruction. It is the real payer under collection. Under export collection, the drawee is the importer.

In addition, there is a special party, that is, representative-in-case-of need. *URC522* names it as In-Case-of-Need. Under collection, the exporter will collect after he/she has delivered the goods, which makes him/her meet the difficulty as to how to deal with the goods which have been arrived in or will arrive in the place/port of destination when the payment was dishonored. In practice, the principal will entrust an agent to handle the commodities related (including stocking, clearing the goods for import etc. As to this party, *URC522* also stipulates something on Article 25: "If the principal nominates a representative to act as case-of-need in the event of non-payment and/or non-acceptance the collection instruction should clearly and fully indicate the powers of such case-of-need. In the absence of such indication, banks will not accept any instructions from the case-of-need.").

### 4.1.3 Collection Instruction

Collection Instruction is a kind of document in which the parties concerned (banks) can know how to handle the documents and collect the payment. In China, we divided it into two kinds and name them respectively, we call the instruction to the remitting bank submitted by the principal as collection application while the one to the collecting bank submitted by the remitting bank as collection order.

Article 4 of *URC522* has specified *the Collection Instruction* in detail. It says:

"A i. All documents sent for collection must be accompanied by a collection instruction indicating that the collection is subject to *URC522* and giving complete and precise instructions. Banks are only permitted to act upon the instructions given in such collection instruction, and in accordance with these Rules.

ii. Banks will not examine documents in order to obtain instructions.

iii. Unless otherwise authorized in the collection instruction, banks will disregard any instructions from any party/bank other than the party/bank from whom they received the collections.

B A collection instruction should contain the following items of information, as appropriate.

i. Details of the bank from which the collection was received including full name, postal and SWIFT addresses, telex, telephone, facsimile numbers and reference.

ii. Details of the principal including full name, postal address, and if applicable telex, telephone and facsimile numbers.

iii. Details of the drawee including full name, postal address, or the domicile at which presentation is to be made and if applicable telex, telephone and facsimile numbers.

iv. Details of the presenting bank, if any, including full name, postal address, and if applicable telex, telephone and facsimile numbers.

v. Amount(s) and currencies to be collected.

vi. List of documents enclosed and the numerical count of each document.

vii. a) Terms and conditions upon which payment and/or acceptance is to be obtained.

b) Terms of delivery of documents against:

1) payment and/or acceptance.

2) other terms and conditions.

It is the responsibility of the party preparing the collection instruction to ensure that the terms for the delivery of documents are clearly and unambiguously stated, otherwise banks will not be responsible for any consequences arising therefrom.

viii. Charges to be collected, indicating whether they may be waived or not.

ix. Interest to be collected, if applicable, indicating whether it may be waived or not, including:

a) rate of interest

b) interest period

c) basis of calculation (for example 360 or 365 days in a year) as applicable.

x. Method of payment and form of payment advice.

xi. Instructions in case of non-payment, non-acceptance and/or non-compliance with other instructions."

## 4.2 Characteristics of Collection and *URC522*

Under collection, the bank helps the customers to collect the creditor's rights and discharge the debt by utilizing the relations and the fund transfer channels between him/her and his/her correspondent bank. It depends on the credits of both the principal (exporter) and the payee (the importer) and is a kind of commercial credit.

In detail, according to *URC522*, we can express the commercial credit under collection into three "no obligation" for the banks under collection.

### 4.2.1 Characteristics of Collection

(1) No obligation to Guarantee the Payment

According to the item (b) in Article 1 of *the URC522*: "Banks shall have no obligation to handle either a collection or any collection instruction or subsequent related instructions." Then, Article 2 stipulates that the collection refers to the bank to obtain payment and/or acceptance, or in other terms and conditions. It is easy to draw the conclusion that the banks have no obligation to guarantee payment.

(2) No Obligation to Check the Documents

Under the collection, according to *URC522*, it is sure that "the bank must determine that the documents received appear to be as listed in the collection instruction". However, the "banks will present documents as received without further examination". Besides, according to Article 13: "Banks assume no liability or responsibility of the form, sufficiency, accuracy, genuineness, falsification or legal effect of any document (s), or for the general and/or particular conditions stipulated in the documentary (s) or superimposed thereon."

In addition, Article 13 of *URC522* specifies that the banks do not need to assume any liability, condition, packing, delivery, value of existence of the goods represented by any document (s), or for the good faith or acts and/or omission, solvency, performance or standing of the consignors, the carriers, the forwarders, the consignees or the insurers of the goods, or any other person whomsoever.

(3) No Obligation to Be in Custody of the Goods

We can get the information from the item (a) to (c) in Article 10 *of the URC522*: "a. Goods should not be dispatched directly to the address of a bank or consigned to or to the order of a bank without prior agreement on the part of that bank. Nevertheless, in the event that goods are dispatched directly to the address of a bank or consigned to or to the order of a bank for release to a drawee against payment or acceptance or upon other terms and conditions without prior agreement on the part of that bank, such bank shall have no obligation to take delivery of the goods, which remain at the risk and responsibility of the party dispatching the goods.

b. Banks have no obligation to take any action in respect of the goods to which a documentary collection relates, including storage and insurance of the goods even when specific instructions are given to do so. Banks will only take such action if, when, and to the extent that they agree to do so in each case."

"c. Nevertheless, in the case that banks take action for the protection of the goods, whether instructed or not, they assume no liability or responsibility with regard to the fate and/or condition of the goods and/or for any acts and/or omissions on the part of any third parties entrusted with the custody and/or protection of the goods. However, the collecting bank must advise without delay the bank from which the collection instruction was received of any such action taken."

## 4.2.2 *URC522*

*The ICC Uniform Rules for Collections* were first published by the ICC in 1956. Revised versions were issued in 1967 and 1978. This present revision was adopted by the Council of the ICC in June 1995. It is issued with the title "ICC Uniform Rules for Collections" as ICC Publication No 522. This English language gives the official text of the 1995 Revision.

---

**Cases of Collection Based on *URC522***
**The Case of Releasing Documents not Against Payment in D/P**

**Background:**
Principal: Chinese Firm A
Remitting Bank: Chinese Bank R
Collecting Bank: US Bank C
Presenting Bank: US Bank C
Drawee: US Importer, Firm B

**Circumstances:**
Firm A: Firm A shipped its goods to Firm B in the payment method of D/P at sight, and presented the title documents to Bank R.
Bank R: After completing the internal operating procedures, Bank R forwarded the documents to Bank C in the US with the collection instruction clearly indicating that documents are to be released only against payment.
Bank C: Bank C released the title documents to Firm B without getting payment from Firm B.
Firm B: Firm B took the title of goods immediately from the transport agency. But very soon after that, Firm B was declared by the court to bankrupt.
Firm A: Firm A got the fact and then required Bank R in order to offset its loss.

> **Questions:**
> 1. What was the error of the collecting bank (Bank C) which had led to the loss of Firm A based on *URC522*?
> 2. What might be the final resolution to the problem?
>
> **Answers:**
> 1. Article 7 of *URC522* clearly states that if a collection contains a bill of exchange payable at a future date and the collection instruction indicates that commercial documents are to be released against payment, documents will be released only against such payment and the collecting bank will not be responsible for any consequences arising out of any delay in the delivery of documents. In this very case, Bank C was careless in its handling D/P collection. It released the documents to Firm B not against payment, resulting to the of Firm A.
> 2. The final resolution to the case is that: With the court as a mediator, Firm A and Bank C reached an agreement of mediation. Bank C agreed to make the payment of full value.

## 4.3 Categories and Procedures

### 4.3.1 Categories

According to whether the collection is accompanied by the commercial documents or not, we can divide the collection into two types: Clean Collection and Documentary Collection.

#### 4.3.1.1 Clean Collection

According to the explanation of Article 2 item (c) in the *URC522*, clean collection means a collection of financial documents not accompanied by commercial documents.

*URC522* categorized the documents into financial documents and commercial documents. The financial documents refer to bills of exchange, promissory notes, cheques, or other similar instruments used for obtaining the payment of money; while commercial documents refer to invoice, transport documents, documents of title or other similar documents, or any other documents whatsoever, not being financial documents.

Generally, a clean collection is widely used for the collection of trade and non-trade settlement such as incidental charges, the rest payment, commission, charges for sample etc.

#### 4.3.1.2 Documentary Collection

Documentary collection includes two kinds as follows: the collection of financial documents accompanied by commercial documents and the collection of commercial documents not accompanied by financial documents. Consequently, commercial documents, which are concerned with the shipping documents especially the B/L, is more important than the financial documents. Thus, they should be explained as the commercial documents when we say documents under collection. Generally, a collection of financial documents accompanied by commercial documents is more popular in international trade settlement.

In practice, in terms of condition of releasing the documents, documentary collection can be subdivided into documents against payment(D/P) and documents against acceptance (D/A).

(1) D/P

It refers to that the exporter releases the documents to the importer provided that the importer has made payment. That is to say, the exporter instructs the bank that he/she can only hand over the commercial documents, especially the transport documents to the buyer only when the importer has effected the payment.

According to the time for payment, D/P can be subdivided into two forms: D/P at sight and D/P at a fixed time after sight.

1) Under D/P at sight, the exporter draws sight draft(s) and presents the draft(s) to the importer through the remitting bank accompanied by the commercial documents. The importer can acquire the commercial documents only after he/she has paid immediately on presentation.

2) Under D/P after sight, the exporter draws a time draft which is payable at a future date after he/she has effected the delivery. The collecting bank first presents the draft(s) to the drawee for acceptance, but does not release the documents to the drawee. And when the buyer pays the draft at maturity, the collecting bank releases the documents to the buyer.

The importer can only take delivery of the commodities when he/she has made payment. Under D/P after sight, the commodities sometimes may arrive in the port/place of destination while the importer cannot acquire the shipping document(s) and take delivery of the goods because the time for payment has not expired. In this case, in order to push sales of the goods in time, the importer may consult with the collecting bank to borrow the bills of lading before the maturity of the drafts against the trust receipt (T/R) and make payment on the due dates of drafts.

The so-called T/R is a kind of certificate of guarantee, issued by the importer to the collecting bank, in which the importer guaranteed to the collecting bank that he/she will take delivery of the good, clear the goods for import, stock, buy insurance, sell the goods on behalf of the collecting bank and besides he/she admits that the sales proceeds belong to the collecting bank. The collecting may cancel T/R at any time and get the goods back. Sometimes, the collecting can be entrusted to lend the commercial documents to the importer according to the collection instruction, which is D/P · T/R, which means it is the exporter who finances the importer. If the exporter cannot get the payment, it is the exporter himself/herself to bear the risks.

**Case study 4-1 T/R**

Company A in China sold a batch of sweaters to Company B in Britain, USD 200,000 in value, payment by D/P at sight with Bank C in China as the remitting bank and Bank D in Britain as the collecting bank. Soon after sending the documents, the collecting bank said in its telex that the importer asked to pledge a house for taking delivery of the goods. Bank C informed Company A about this. Company A decided to release the documents to Company B first and then get payment by remittance, as the usual practice of both parties. In spite of Bank C's cautions, Company

A insisted that Bank C notify Bank D to release the documents for nothing. However, while notifying Bank D to release the documents, Bank C did not express explicitly that Company A insisted free release of the documents. Afterwards, Bank C received a message from Bank D that both parties had reached an agreement that the principal and the interest would be paid off at the monthly rate of 0.04% three months later.

Three months later, the conditions of Company B changed greatly so that it was on the brink of bankruptcy. Company A urged Bank C to press for payment. However, Bank D said that it would make payment only when Bank C sent back the draft accepted by Company B. Bank C claimed that it had never received such a draft. Bank D insisted that it would not make payment without seeing the draft.

Company A, who now came to realize the major difference between D/P and remittance, got anxious and called for Bank C's assistance to get the payment. Through its own channels, Bank C learned that because it did not inform Bank D explicitly to release the documents for nothing, Company B had pledged its plant building and obtaining Bank D's guarantee before taking delivery of the goods, therefore, Bank C press Bank D for payment with this fact. In the end, Bank D remitted both the principal and the interest in full.

**Analysis:**

With its poor knowledge about modes of payment in international trade, Company A narrowly escaped a heavy loss.

According to the stipulations of *URC522*, in this case, because Company B had provided a pledge and guarantee for the deal, Bank D had to make payment.

Both importer and exporter should know more about the collection to avoid the mistakes made by Company A.

In addition, the importer may pay before the maturity and acquire the documents.

Article 7 of the *URC522* says: "a. Collection should not contain bills of exchange payable at a future date with instruction that commercial documents are to be delivered against payment. b. If a collection contains a bill of exchange payable at a future date, the collection instruction should state whether the commercial documents are to be released to the drawee against acceptance (D/A) or against payment (D/P). In the absence of such statement commercial documents will be released only against payment and the collecting bank will not be responsible for any consequences arising out of any delay in the delivery of documents. If a collection contains a bill of exchange payable at a future date and the collection instruction indicates that commercial documents are to be released against payment, documents will be released only against such payment and the collecting bank will not be responsible for any consequences arising out of any delay in the delivery of documents."

(2) D/A

Under the D/A, the collecting bank delivers the documents against the drawee's acceptance.

The time draft or usance draft is used. The collecting bank will advise the remitting bank of the date of acceptance and holds the bill until maturity when the collecting bank will present it to the buyer for payment.

### 4.3.2 General Procedure for Collection

#### 4.3.2.1 D/P at Sight

Under the D/P at sight, the collection procedure is shown in Figure 4-1.

1) The Seller and the Buyer both have signed the sales contract, in which both agree to pay by D/P at sight.

2) The Seller makes the goods available, effects the shipment and obtains the shipping documents.

3) The seller fills in *the Collection Application* (See Appendix C),, draws the drafts, presents the commercial document. At the same time, the seller pays the collecting fees and other related expenses (generally shall be borne by the collection side except otherwise specified).

4) Collection bank makes out the collection instruction (also known as collection order) according to the seller's instruction, presents it to the collecting bank with the drafts, commercial documents etc, and requires the collecting bank to collect the payment in accordance with the collection instruction.

5) The collecting bank presents the drafts and the other documents to the importer and asks the buyer to make payment.

6) The importer makes payment immediately.

7) Collecting bank will release all set of documents. It can be called to redeem the documents for the importer.

8) Collecting bank transfers the funds to the remitting bank when he has got the payment.

9) Remitting bank transfers the funds to the principal.

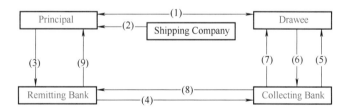

Figure 4-1　General Procedure of D/P at Sight

#### 4.3.2.2 D/P After Sight

Compared with the D/P at sight, the main differences of the D/P after sight are in two fields: one is the exporter draws time draft(s) instead of sight draft; the other is the importer accepts the usance draft(s) first when he/she was presented by the collecting bank and then makes payment on its maturity. Before the importer has made payment, the collecting bank will keep all sets documents on behalf of the remitting bank and present the documents again when it is due. As to the specific procedure of the D/P after sight, they are similar to the D/P at sight, please take Figure 4-1 we will not discuss it in detail.

### 4.3.2.3 D/A

Documents against acceptance means the collecting bank may delivery the documents against the drawee's acceptance instead of the payment under the D/P. The draft under the D/A terms is a time draft. The collecting bank will advise the remitting bank of the date of acceptance and holds the bill until maturity when the collecting bank will present it to the importer for payment.

Under the D/A, the drawee gains possession of the goods before payment is actually affected and can resell them immediately, in which he can raise the necessary funds to pay the bill of exchange. He/she thus obtains a period of credit and is relieved of the need to arrange short-term inventory financing in some other form. In conclusion, the D/A is more favorable to the importer than the D/P.

However, the exporter will bear the risk that the importer would have dishonored on its maturity.

## 4.4 Payment Clause under Collection in the International Sales Contract

The payment clause generally contains the condition of releasing the documents, the importer's obligation to pay or accept, the time for payment etc.

### 4.4.1 Under D/P at sight

For example:

Upon the first presentation, the Buyers shall pay against documentary draft drawn by the Sellers at sight. The shipping documents are to be delivered against payment only.

### 4.4.2 Under D/P After Sight

For example:

The Buyers shall duly accept the documentary draft drawn by the Sellers at... days sight upon the first presentation and make payment on its maturity. The shipping documents are to be delivered against payment.

Or:

The Buyers shall pay against documentary draft drawn by the Sellers at... days after the date of B/L. The shipping documents are to be delivered against payment only.

### 4.4.3 Under D/A

The Buyers shall duly accept the documentary draft drawn by the Sellers at... days sight upon the first presentation and make payment on its maturity. The shipping documents are to be delivered against acceptance.

## 4.4.4 Under the Collection Plus Remittance

Shipment to be made subject to advanced payment or down payment amounting... to be remitted in favour of Sellers by telegraphic transfer with an indication of S/C No... and the remaining part on collection basis, documents will be released against payment at sight.

## Questions:

### Ⅰ. True or False.

1. If a credit stipulates that "Shipment must be effected as soon as possible by the beneficiary", the bank will disregard the expressions such as prompt, immediate, or as soon as possible.
2. When the collecting bank releases the documents to the buyer on the trust receipt, the legal title to the goods remains with the principal.
3. From Bank of America New York's view, a vostro account is a dollar account held for its overseas correspondents.
4. The representative in case of need appointed by the buyer to arrange the warehouse and insurance in the event of non-acceptance and/or non-payment.
5. A payment order, airmail advice or credit advice or please debit advice is an authenticated order in writing addressed by one bank to another instructing the latter to pay a sum certain in money to a specified person or beneficiary named thereon.
6. The only means of authenticating a cable transfer is the authorized signatures.
7. Mail transfer is often used when the client wants to transfer the funds to his/her beneficiary himself/herself.
8. If the remitting bank opens a current account with the paying bank, the reimbursement may be effected by debiting nostro account of the remitting bank.
9. Documents against acceptance offers the greater security to the exporter than documents against payment.

### Ⅱ. Mulitple choice.

1. The presenting bank is responsible for (   ).
   A. the authority of any signatory to sign the acceptance
   B. seeing that the form of the acceptance of a draft appears to be complete and correct
   C. the genuineness of any signature
   D. none of above
2. The (   ) bank must send without delay advice or acceptance to the bank from which the collection instruction was received.
   A. collecting　　　　B. remitting　　　　C. seller's　　　　D. paying bank
3. The presenting bank is responsible for (   ).
   A. the authority of any signatory to sign the acceptance
   B. seeing that the form of the acceptance of a draft appears to be complete and correct
   C. the genuineness of any signature

D. none of above

4. The ( ) bank must send without delay advice or acceptance to the bank from which the collection instruction was received.

   A. collecting　　　　B. remitting　　　　C. seller's　　　　D. paying bank

5. The international uniform customs practice for documentary collection is ( ).

   A. *UCP600*　　　　　　　　　　　B. *ISP98*

   C. *INCOTERMS2000*　　　　　　　D. *URC522*

6. "Documents for collection" means ( ) documents and/or commercial documents.

   A. Insurance　　　　B. financial　　　　C. transport　　　　D. credit

7. "Clean collection" means collection of financial documents not accompanied by ( ).

   A. commercial documents　　B. drafts　　C. bill of lading only　　D. L/C

8. "Documentary collection" does not mean the collection of ( ).

   A. financial documents accompanied by commercial documents

   B. commercial documents not accompanied by financial documents

   C. financial documents not accompanied by commercial documents

   D. A or/and B

9. The principal in collection refers to ( ).

   A. the collecting bank making a presentation to the drawee

   B. the party to whom the presentation is to be made

   C. the party entrusting the handling of a collection to a bank

   D. the party to whom the payment is to be made

10. Banks in the documentary collection will be responsible for ( ).

    A. making further careful examination of the contents of the documents received

    B. any delays resulting from the need to obtain clarification of any instructions

    C. advising the party from whom the collection instruction was received of any documents missing

    D. none of above

Ⅲ. Case study

1. A Chinese company exported a batch of goods by the D/P, and entrusted Chinese Bank A to send the documentary bill to the importing country Bank C for collection by the third country Bank B. It was later learned that Bank C was bankrupt and unable to receive payment. The company requested the return of the relevant documents but received no reply.

   **Question**: Is the collecting bank liable?

2. In February 2012, Chinese Company A and British Company B signed an export contract with the payment terms of D/P 120 Days After Sight. Chinese Bank C sent the documents but didn't receive the payment by August 2012, so Company A asked to instruct British collecting Bank D to do a chargeback. However, despite multiple efforts, the importer, Company B found various excuses to avoid payment and no progress had been made through negotiation between the importer and the exporter. Later, Chinese Bank C repeatedly stressed that the losses of money and goods of the exporter were due to British collecting Bank D's mistake in releasing the documents and

demanded payment of collecting Bank D, but the collecting Bank D refused to reply Chinese Bank C's collection. On October 25, collecting Bank D notified Chinese Bank C that the importer had declared bankruptcy, and a court bankruptcy notice was also attached, so the exporter lost both the money and the goods.

**Question**: Please analyze and comment on this case.

3. A company exported four batches of goods in a certain month, all paid by collection, but in different terms, including D/P at sight, D/P at 30 days after sight, D/P · T/R at 30 days after sight and D/A at 30 days after sight. The collection day of these four businesses was all on July 5, and the mail order (single-way) was 5 days.

   **Question**: What is the date of presentation, acceptance, payment and presentation of the bill of exchange? (Leave aside the reasonable working hours of the bank and the factor of jet lag.)

4. A company of China exported a batch of goods with the settlement method of D/P 90 days. After the bill of exchanges and shipping documents were sent to the foreign collecting bank by the remitting bank, the buyer made the acceptance. But after the goods arrived at the destination, it happened that the market saw a rise in prices, so the payer issued a trust receipt (T/R) to the bank to borrow documents and took delivery of the goods. After the sale of the goods, the importer closed. The collecting bank notified the remitting bank about the foregoing circumstances and informed that the payment was unable to be received.

   **Question**: Should the exporter bear the losses on payment for goods?

5. **Case.**

**Background**:

Principal: Chinese Exporter, Firm A
Remitting Bank: Chinese Bank R
Collecting Bank: New York Bank C
Presenting Bank: New York Bank C
Importer: Firm B

**Circumstances**:

Firm A: On July 11th, 2010, Firm A entrusted Bank R with an export collection business of D/P at sight valued USD200,000.

Bank R: Bank R forwarded the documents with a cover letter to Bank C New York as instructed in the collection order.

Firm B: Five days after Bank R has dispatched the documents, Firm B required Firm A to change the collection of D/P at sight into D/A 60 days after sight in the excuse of having temporary difficulties in immediate payment for the documents.

Firm A: Based on its long-established business relationship with the importer, Firm A agreed to make the change, and requested Bank R to present the order of amendment.

Bank R: Bank R forwarded the instruction of amendment to Bank C as ordered by Firm A.

Bank C: On July 20th, 2010, Bank C released the documents to Firm B after Firm B accepted the draft and then returned the documents to Firm B after Firm B accepted the draft and then returned the document to Bank R with the statement of acceptance.

Firm B: Firm B took the title of goods immediately with the document relieved by Bank C.

Bank R: Bank R has informed Firm A of this acceptance.

Firm A: Firm A asked for payment when the draft had become due. But before this, Firm B had become out of business. Firm A had asked Bank C to pay immediately for the due draft.

Bank C: Bank C refused to make the payment and then made no further responses.

Firm A: The proceeds of the shipment had never been received by Firm A ever since then.

**Questions:**

(1) What are the differences in risks between D/P and D/A?

(2) Was Bank C correct in releasing the document to Firm B?

(3) Was Bank C correct in refusing the payment?

# Chapter 5

# Letter of Credit

**Learning Objectives**

- To understand the definition, characteristics, contents of L/C.
- To grasp the functions of the parties concerned and the general payment procedure.
- To understand the key types of L/C.

Both remittance and collection are based on the commercial credit. They both depend on each other's credit as to whether the exporter can get the payment or the importer get the goods in conformity with the contract. For both sides, there is a big risk in different degrees. To solve the mistrust between the seller and the buyer, the risks, the banks' responsibilities and functions in the international settlement have been continuously strengthened. It is shown that the L/C has been widely used in international trade.

## 5.1 Definition and Contents of L/C

### 5.1.1 Definition

Letter of Credit, also known as Credit, or L/C in short, means any arrangement irrevocable and thereby constitutes a definite undertaking of the issuing bank to honor a complying presentation. Honor means: ①To pay at sight if the credit is available by sight payment; ②To incur a deferred payment undertaking and pay at maturity if the credit is available by deferred payment; ③To accept a bill of exchange ("draft") drawn by the beneficiary and pay at maturity if the credit is available by acceptance (See Appendix D).

### 5.1.2 Contents

In practice, there are no identical L/C in the world, because the contents are related to the complexity of the business. However, the contents can be subdivided into six parts as follows:

#### 5.1.2.1 Information on the L/C Itself

It includes:
1) Form of Credit or Type of Documentary Credit.
2) L/C No. and Date.
3) Amount.

4) Time and Place of Expiry/Validity.

The expiry date is the last day of validity of the credit and the place allowed by the letter of credit(L/C) for the presentation of documents and/or draft(s) for payment, acceptance or negotiation.

In case the validity of an L/C is stated in a period of time, for example, "This credit is valid for one month" or "This credit is available for two months" or "This credit is good for three months", but does not specify the date from which the time is to run, its validity starts from the issuance date of L/C by the issuing bank. The bank normally discourages stating the L/C validity in a period of time.

In case the expiry date and/or the latest negotiation date fall falls on a day on which the bank is closed for reasons not including the acts of God, strikes, riots, civil commotions, lockout, insurrections, wars or any other causes beyond the bank's control, the expiry date and/or the latest negotiation date is extended to the succeeding first day on which the bank is opened. Such extension, however, does not extend the latest date of shipment.

5) Applicant.

6) Beneficiary or "in favor of".

7) Applicant Bank.

8) Available With.../By...

### 5.1.2.2　Description of Goods

It mainly includes the name of commodity, specification, quantity, packing, shipping mark and price terms, etc.

### 5.1.2.3　Shipping

It includes:

1) Shipping on Board/Dispatch/Packing in Charge at/from).

2) Partial Shipment.

3) Transshipment.

4) Transportation to...

5) Latest Date of Shipment. The latest shipment: latest date of shipment or last date for shipment, is the last day of the period of time allowed by the letter of credit (L/C) for shipment, dispatch or taking in charge.

### 5.1.2.4　Draft(s)

It includes the drawer and the drawee as the well as the value and the tenor of the draft. The drawer is always the beneficiary, while the drawee may be the issuing bank or any other bank. This may include a drawn clause, which is used to illustrate the reason for its issuance.

According to *UCP600*, Article 6, "A credit must state whether it is available by sight payment, deferred payment, acceptance or negotiation." Thus, in general terms, there is a clause "Credit available with the Nominated Bank by sight payment I deferred payment I acceptance I negotiation."

### 5.1.2.5　Documents Required

This part lists the documents required, specifies the name, number and specific requirements of the documents respectively. It mainly includes the commercial invoice, bill of lading, insurance documents, etc. In addition, the commodity inspection certificate, certificate of origin, packaging, documents, etc.

### 5.1.2.6 Additional or Additional Instructions

This part shows some special instructions to the beneficiary. Though different C/Ls have different instructions, it mainly contains the following factors:

(1) More of Less Clause

For Example: "Both quantity and amount 10 percent more or less are allowed."

(2) Charges

Under the L/C, besides the issuing bank and the advising bank involved, it may also involve the negotiating bank, the confirming bank, paying bank etc. Customarily, the applicant would pay service charges to the issuing bank, while the charges outside the issuing bank will be on the account of the beneficiary, so the L/C often stipulates: "All banking charges outside the opening bank are for beneficiary's account."

(3) Period for Presentation

(4) Confirmation Instruction

It refers to whether the L/C needs confirmation. In practice, unconfirmed L/C is more popular. In this case, the column shows "without".

(5) Instructions to the Paying/Accepting/Negotiating bank

For example: Discrepant document fee of USD50.00 or equal currency will be deducted from drawing if documents with discrepancies are accepted.

## 5.2 Parties Concerned and Their Rights and Obligations

There are so many parties concerned. Article 2 of *UCP600* has defined the parties as follows:

### 5.2.1 Advising Bank

It is the bank that advises the credit at the request of the issuing bank.

In practice, the advising bank is usually the correspondent bank of the issuing bank in the exporter's country, which verifies the authenticity of the credit and any amendment and forwards them to the beneficiary. Advising bank advises the beneficiary of a letter of credit opened by means of telecommunication and transmitting bank transmits a credit by airmail to the beneficiary. The relationship between the advising bank and the issuing bank is bound by the principal-agent agreement.

1) According to the principal-agent agreement, advising Bank shall advise or transmit the credit correctly to the beneficiary without delay, of course, it may also choose not to advise the credit, and in this case, it must advise all the credit, amendments and advice received, without delay, to the beneficiary.

2) Advising bank shall take reasonable care to check the apparent authenticity of the credit which it advises through checking the test key or signatures of the credit. According to *UCP 600*, if the advising bank cannot confirm such apparent authenticity, it must inform the bank without delay

from which the instructions have been received that it is unable to confirm the authenticity of the credit. On the other hand, if the advising bank elects nonetheless to advise such a credit, it must inform the beneficiary that it is not able to confirm the authenticity of the credit.

3) The obligation of the advising bank is only limited to the accurate transmission of terms and conditions of the letter of credit without engagement on the part of the advising bank, or, undertaking to honor or negotiation.

### 5.2.2 Applicant

Applicant, also called as the opener, it refers to the party at whose request the credit is issued. When the L/C is used for the international trade settlement, the applicant is always the importer, who fills in and signs an L/C application form (See Appendix D) to request his/her bank to issue a credit in favor of the seller. Generally speaking, he/she is subject to the engagement of two sets of contracts: one is the sales contract between him/her and the seller, the other is the application for the L/C between him/her and the issuing bank.

1) According to S/C, the applicant should make an application to the relative bank for issuing an L/C within the reasonable time. This is the most important obligation of the applicant.

2) According to the application for the L/C, the applicant should give the issuing bank reasonable instructions and provide a cash deposit required or offer some collateral.

3) The applicant has the right to examine the documents upon receipt of them from the issuing bank, and also has the right to refuse payment provided that discrepancies are found and to return the documents to the issuing bank.

4) The applicant is liable for timely payment to the issuing bank provided that there is no discrepancy in terms and conditions between the documents and the credit, and the documents are consistent with one another.

### 5.2.3 Beneficiary

It refers to the party in whose favor a credit is issued. In the international trade, the beneficiary is the exporter, who will not only be responsible for the accuracy and correctness of the documents presented to the issuing bank, but also be responsible for that the goods are in conformity with the contract of sale.

In practice, the beneficiary:

1) Should prepare and present documents based on the L/C and ensure that the presentation is "a complying presentation".

2) Have the right to claim payment on the issuing bank or the nominated bank with the complying presentation of the stipulated documents.

3) Have the right to examine the L/C upon receipt of it and decide whether he/she will accept it or not. What he/she should basically examine is to see whether the terms and conditions on the credit comply with those in the sales contract. Once he/she accepts the credit, he/she will be bound by it, and be paid under the credit only against the stipulated documents.

4) Be responsible for the accuracy and authenticity of the documents and the goods conforming to the contract.

In a word, the relationship between the applicant and the beneficiary is bound by the sales contract agreed by them, and the relationship between the applicant and the issuing bank is bound by the application for the L/C, and the relationship between the beneficiary and the issuing bank is bound by the L/C itself. A beneficiary can in no case avail itself of the contractual relationships existing among banks or between the applicant and the issuing bank.

### 5.2.4 Confirming Bank

The confirming bank refers to the bank that adds its confirmation to a credit upon the issuing bank's authorization or request. Confirmation means a definite undertaking of the confirming bank, in addition to that of the issuing bank, to honor or negotiate a complying presentation.

The confirming bank's responsibilities are as follows:

1) The confirming bank is primarily liable for its undertaking under the L/C with almost the same as those of the issuing bank when it adds its confirmation to the credit. Namely, the liability of the confirming bank is the same as that of the issuing bank.

2) The confirming bank must pay at sight, incur a deferred payment undertaking of and pay at maturity, or accept a draft drawn by the beneficiary and then pay at maturity if the credit is available with itself by sight payment, deferred payment or acceptance, or if the credit is available with another nominated bank by sight payment, deferred payment or acceptance or negotiation, which however, fails to do as instructed. If the credit is available by negotiation with the confirming bank, the confirming bank will negotiate without recourse to drawers and/or bona-fide holders of the draft (s) drawn under the credit. The undertaking of the confirming bank is also irrevocable and finally, which means the confirming bank cannot execute the right of recourse after its actual payment based on the documents.

3) The confirming bank undertakes to reimburse another nominated bank that has honored or negotiated a complying presentation and forwarded the documents to the confirming bank. The confirming bank's undertaking to reimburse another nominated bank is independent of the confirming bank's undertaking to the beneficiary.

4) The bank has the right to refuse to add its confirmation to a letter of credit. If a bank as an advising bank is authorized or requested by the issuing bank to confirm a credit but it is not prepared to do so, it must inform the issuing bank of this without delay and may advise the credit to the beneficiary without confirmation.

The issuing bank sometimes does not request the advising bank or some other banks to add their confirmation to the credit or not ask them to add confirmation, but the advising bank, even the other banks, may issue a Guarantee or Letter of Indemnity according to the beneficiary's instructions, which constitutes a "silent confirmation". In this case, the Guarantee or Letter of Indemnity is an independent agreement between the beneficiary and the confirming bank, in this case, the advising bank must undertake to pay or accept the beneficiary's draft drawn and complied with the specified credit. If a bank "confirms" a credit based on "silent confirmation agreement", the bank may not be considered as the "confirming bank" by the issuing bank, and hence acquires no right of claiming reimbursement from the issuing bank.

5) According to *UCP 600*, if a credit is amended by the issuing bank, the confirming bank may extend its confirmation to an amendment and will be irrevocably bound as of the time when it advises the amendment to the beneficiary. If the confirming bank may, however, choose to advise an amendment to the beneficiary but without extending its confirmation and, it must advise this to the issuing bank and the beneficiary respectively without delay.

### 5.2.5 Issuing Bank

The issuing bank, also known as an opening bank, refers to the bank that issues a credit at the request of an applicant or on its own behalf.

The issuing bank is the key party in credit transaction because the triangle contractual arrangements are binding on the issuing bank and the issuing bank may have relations with all other parties concerned.

1) Issuing bank must open an L/C correctly without delay according to the L/C application from the applicant. Besides, the issuing bank has the right to check the L/C application and scrutinize its contents to see whether they generally are consistent with national and international banking and legal requirements and get some collateral in case of need.

2) Issuing bank is primarily liable under the L/C. According to Article 7 of *UCP 600*, an issuing bank is irrevocably bound to honor as of the time it issues the credit provided that the stipulated documents presented complying with the credit and are consistent with one another.

3) The issuing bank must pay at sight, and incur a deferred payment undertaking and pay at maturity, or accept a draft drawn by the beneficiary and pay at maturity if the credit is available with itself by sight payment, deferred payment or acceptance is available with a nominated bank by sight payment, deferred payment or acceptance or negotiation which, however, fails to do as instructed. The undertaking of the issuing bank is irrevocable and finally, which means the issuing bank cannot execute the right of recourse after its actual payment. An issuing bank undertakes to reimburse a nominated bank that has honored or negotiated a complying presentation and then forwarded the documents to the issuing bank. An issuing bank's undertaking to reimburse a nominated bank is independent of the issuing bank's undertaking to honor the beneficiary.

4) The issuing bank has the right to examine the documents and refuse to pay the negotiating bank, the paying bank or the beneficiary if there is any discrepancy with the documents submitted.

### 5.2.6 Nominated Bank

Nominated bank means the bank with which the credit is available or any bank in the case of a credit available with any bank.

### 5.2.7 Presenter

Presenter means a beneficiary, bank or another party that makes a presentation. The presentation means either the delivery of documents under a credit to the issuing bank or nominated bank or the documents so delivered.

## 5.2.8 Negotiating Bank

Negotiation means the purchase by the nominated bank of drafts (drawn on a bank other than the nominated bank) and/or documents under a complying presentation, by advancing or agreeing to advance funds to the beneficiary on or before the banking day on which reimbursement is due to (to be paid the nominated bank).

According to UCP 600, the negotiating bank must examine the documents with reasonable care to determine whether they appear or not on their face, to be in compliance with the terms and conditions of the credit. The only condition for the issuing bank to undertake the payment under the L/C is that the documents which presented to the issuing bank by the beneficiary or his representative should show the terms and conditions of the credit are complied with. Thus, if the negotiating bank wants to claim the reimbursement from the issuing bank after making negotiation to the beneficiary, it must ensure to meet this condition. After the negotiation, the negotiating bank becomes the holder in due course of the draft, and so it normally has the right to recourse against the drawer, namely the beneficiary of the credit, in event of dishonor by the issuing bank.

According to UCP 600, giving for value by the negotiating bank can constitute a negotiation. In a case of a negotiation credit, the bank purchases the drafts and documents under the credit is referred to as the negotiating bank. During its negotiation, the negotiating bank gets a right to charge fees toward the beneficiary.

## 5.2.9 Paying Bank/Accepting Bank

The paying or accepting bank is the bank on which the draft is drawn or the bank who performs payment or acceptance and payment at maturity. The paying bank is always the drawee of draft stipulated in the credit which is available by sight payment or the bank effecting payment under the credit which is available by deferred payment. The accepting bank is the drawee bank of a time bill stipulated in the credit which is available by acceptance. Or, we may say the paying bank or accepting bank is a bank nominated by the issuing bank to make payment or acceptance under the credit. Sometimes, the paying bank or accepting bank is the issuing bank itself.

1) According to UCP 600, a bank nominated by the issuing bank in the credit can be no definite undertaking to pay or accept. That is, as usual, a paying bank or accepting bank is not obliged to follow the instructions of the issuing bank under a credit.

2) According to UCP 600, the paying bank or accepting bank has a right to claim the reimbursement from the issuing bank, confirming bank or reimbursing bank, if any, after it has honored a complying presentation.

3) According to UCP 600, a paying bank or accepting bank must examine. as the nominated bank, all documents under the credit. Once the payment is made by them, it is the final payment without recourse to the drawer and/or the bona-fide holder in event of dishonor by the issuing bank.

According to *UCP 600*, nominated bank means the bank with which the credit is available or any bank in the case of a credit available with any bank. Unless the credit stipulates that it is available only with the issuing bank, all credits must nominate the bank which is authorized to pay, to incur a deferred payment, to accept a draft or to negotiate. In a freely negotiable credit, any bank can be seen as a nominated bank. Furthermore, as shown in the above analysis, unless a nominated bank is the confirming bank, an authorization to honor or negotiate does not impose any obligation on that nominated bank to honor or negotiate.

When a bank effects payment, acceptance or negotiation in accordance with the instruction of the issuing bank, it is entitled to request the issuing bank or the bank nominated by the issuing bank to cover the payment that they have made. Such a paying bank, accepting bank, or negotiating bank, which claims reimbursement from the reimbursing bank, is called the claiming bank.

According to *UCP 600*, if a credit states that reimbursement is to be obtained by the claiming bank on another party (the reimbursing bank), the credit must state if the reimbursement is subject to the *ICC* rules for bank-to-bank reimbursements in effect on the date of issuance of the credit and a claiming bank shall not be required to supply a reimbursing bank with a certificate of compliance with the terms and conditions of the credit. If not reimbursed by the reimbursing bank, the claiming bank is entitled to obtain the reimbursement from the issuing bank. If there is any loss of interest, it should be assumed by the issuing bank. An issuing bank's undertaking to reimburse a claiming bank is independent of the issuing bank's undertaking to the beneficiary.

## 5.2.10 Reimbursing Bank

Reimbursing bank is the one who honors the reimbursement claims of a paying bank or an accepting bank or a negotiating bank (claiming bank) under a particular credit in accordance with the instructions or authorization given by the issuing bank. The purpose of designating a reimbursing bank in a credit is for the convenience of payment or clearing between the issuing bank and the nominated bank. So reimbursing bank is the bank, usually the agent of the issuing bank, with which both the issuing bank and the claiming bank maintain the current accounts.

1) Reimbursing bank can make the reimbursement under the issuing bank's instruction. According to *UCP 600*, if a credit states that reimbursement is to be obtained by a nominated bank claiming on another party, the credit must state whether the reimbursement is subject to the *ICC* rules for bank-to-bank reimbursements. If there is no such statement in a credit, an issuing bank must provide the reimbursing bank with a reimbursement authorization which conforms to the availability stated in the credit.

If reimbursement is not made by a reimbursing bank, the issuing bank is not relieved of any of its obligations to provide reimbursement.

2) Reimbursing bank has no responsibility of checking all documents under the credit. The payment made by the reimbursing bank is just a simple payment for the issuing bank. If the issuing bank refuses to pay after examining the documents presented by the claiming bank the reimbursing bank can ask for the refund from the claiming bank of any reimbursement which has been made

together with interest.

3) Charges to the reimbursing bank should be for the account of the issuing bank. *UCP 600* says if the charges are for the account of another party, the issuing bank should indicate so in the original credit and in the reimbursement instruction and when it is not drawn under the credit, it is the issuing bank to be responsible for the charges. If no reimbursement is made, the reimbursing bank's charges remain the obligation of the issuing bank.

## 5.3　Characteristics of L/C

The L/C is characterized as follows:

### 5.3.1　Issuing Bank Bears the First Responsibility of Payment

According to Article 7 of *UCP 600*, issuing a L/C is a banker's credit, rather than a trader's credit, which is guaranteed by the issuing bank's own credit worthiness. That is, the issuing bank undertakes to effect payment by opening a credit, quite independently of whether the applicant has gone bankrupt or is in default or not, provided that the stipulated documents are presented to the issuing bank or to the nominated bank and comply with the terms and conditions of the credit. Thus, the issuing bank assumes an irrevocable primary rather a secondary liability.

A credit is to be presented to a nominated bank or the issuing bank for sight payment, deferred payment, acceptance or negotiation. The drafts under a letter of credit must be drawn on the issuing bank or any other bank designated by the issuing bank. Or, the drawee of a draft under an L/C must be a bank, the issuing bank or the nominated bank. If a credit is available by sight payment, deferred payment, acceptance or negotiation by a nominated bank, however, if the nominated bank does not pay or incur its deferred payment undertaking or, having incurred its deferred payment undertaking, does not pay at maturity, or does not accept a draft drawn on it or, having accepted a draft drawn on it, does not pay at maturity or, does not negotiate, the issuing bank can't always be exempted from the obligation to honor provided that the documents constitute a complying presentation. In other words, the drawee of a draft under the L/C must be a bank rather the applicant, and if the credit nevertheless calls for drafts drawn on the applicant, banks will treat such drafts as additional documents.

### 5.3.2　The Credit Is an Independent and Autonomic Arrangement/Document

Although a credit is issued on the basis of the contract, according to Article 4 of the *UCP 600*, such credit is a separate transaction from the sale or other contract on which it may be based and banks are in no way concerned with or bound by such contract, even if any reference whatsoever to it is included in the credit.

The L/C is an arrangement between the issuing bank and the beneficiary which should abide by the terms of the credit application and related international practice and customs to regulate the rights and obligations of the all involved parties. As a result, in the credit transactions, the undertaking of a bank to honor, to negotiate or to fulfill any other obligation under the credit is not subject to the engagement or non-engagement by the applicant resulting from its relationships with the issuing bank or the beneficiary. The issuing bank only takes the responsibility for the own credit and only effects payment against documents complied with the terms of credit. The other banks involved in should be fully in accordance with the provisions of the credit itself. Similarly, a beneficiary can in no case avail itself of the contractual relationships existing among banks or between the applicant and the issuing bank.

Article 4 of the *UCP600* stipulates:

"a. A credit by its nature is a separate transaction from the sale or other contract on which it may be based. Banks are in no way concerned with or bound by such contract, even if any reference whatsoever to it is included in the credit. Consequently, the undertaking of a bank to honor, to negotiate or to fulfill any other obligation under the credit is not subject to claims or defenses by the applicant resulting from its relationships with the issuing bank or the beneficiary. A beneficiary can in no case avail itself of the contractual relationships existing between banks or between the applicant and the issuing bank.

b. An issuing bank should discourage any attempt by the applicant to include, as an integral part of the credit, copies of the underlying contract, proforma invoice and the like."

### 5.3.3 Credit Transaction Is the Trade Dealing With Documents Only

Article 5 of *UCP600* specifies: "Banks deal with documents but not with goods, services or performance to which the documents may relate." As long as the documents presented by the beneficiary are complying with the terms and conditions of the credit, the issuing bank or the nominated bank should be honor. "Complying Presentation" means a presentation that is in accordance with the terms and conditions of the credit, the applicable provisions of these rules and international standard banking practice.

## 5.4 General Procedure

Only when the importer and the exporter both have agreed to use the L/C for the payment and signed in the sales contract, can the L/C be used. Generally, there are eight key steps of the operation of the L/C as follows:

### 5.4.1 Application for the Opening of Credit

In practice, the importer(applicant) would apply for the opening/issuing of the credit a little earlier than the time of shipment/delivery according to the sales contract because only when the exporter has got the right credit concerned then will he/she effect shipment. The importer will fill in an application form for the opening of credit in favor of the exporter to his/her relative bank and pay charges to the bank. Generally, the application form includes two basic components: the clauses stipulated in L/C based on the terms and conditions of the sales contract and the statements and promises by the applicant to ensure the responsibilities of both parties.

In practice, the application form(See Appendix E) serves as a contract between the applicant and the issuing bank and it will include statements and promises by the applicant to ensure the responsibilities of both parties and its main contents as follows:

- Full and correct names and addresses of the beneficiary, the issuing bank and the advising bank, if need.
- Kinds of credit, such as irrevocable or revocable, confirmed or unconfirmed.
- L/C amount in figures and words.
- Expiry date and place of the credit.
- Credit to be opened by airmail, cable or telex.
- Credit available by sight payment, deferred payment, acceptance or negotiation.
- Credit transferable or non- transferable.
- Draft needed or not, if needed the name of the drawee, the amount and tenor.
- Details of the shipping documents required, which generally are commercial invoice, insurance policy, B/L, etc.
- Description, quantity, unit price of goods as well as price terms, e. g. CIF, FOB, etc.
- Port of loading and discharge and destination and the latest date of shipment.
- Transshipment allowed or not allowed, partial shipment allowed or not allowed.
- Full name, address and signature of the applicant.
- The applicant admits that the issuing bank has the right to keep a mortgage or lien on the goods and documents under the credit and get the cash deposit or other kinds of collateral relating to the credit, before issuing bank presents the documents and documents of title to goods to him/her for its pay, and he/she has to admit that, if necessary, issuing bank has the right to dispose of these documents to compensate the payment effected under credit. If insufficient, the applicant will be responsible for the difference.
- The applicant admits the issuing bank can accept the "apparently qualified" documents and is not responsible for the correctness, completeness and effectiveness of the documents.
- The applicant guarantees to make the payment including goods, expenses, interest under the credit, and instruct the issuing bank to make foreign payment or acceptance or refuse the documents presented with discrepancies and dishonored after their receipt of full set of documents within three working days.
- The applicant admits that a bank assumes no responsibility for the consequences arising out of delay, loss in transit, mutilation or other errors arising in the transmission of any messages or delivery of letters or documents, according to the stipulations stated in the credit, or when the bank may have chosen itself to transmit or deliver the relative business documents in the absence of such instructions in the credit, unless it is due to direct negligence or dereliction by the issuing bank.

A documentary credit is a conditional undertaking of payment by a bank. The issuing bank undertakes to effect payment by opening a credit, quite independently of whether the applicant is bankrupt or is in default or not, provided that the stipulated documents are presented to the issuing bank or to the nominated bank and complying with the terms and conditions of the credit. In order to guarantee the benefits of the opening bank, generally, the importer must pay collaterals in cash or deposit in the issuing bank.

### 5.4.2 Opening the L/C

#### 5.4.2.1 Checking the Documentary Credit Application

Issuing an L/C is a banker's credit, rather than a trader's credit, which is guaranteed by the issuing bank's own creditworthiness. The issuing bank should draft the credit strictly according to the application form, so he/she will examine it carefully to ensure its accuracy, completeness and consistency. In addition, banks are reluctant to see that the application contains excessive details for the beneficiary to comply with, in which case the possibility of discrepancies will be greatly increased.

In practice, the issuing bank should carefully check the application based on the following points:

- The method the credit is to be opened and whether the documentary credit is transferable or confirmed or not. If the credit is issued in brief cable form, it should be followed by a confirmation.
- The kinds of credit, such as irrevocable or revocable. According to *UCP 600*, a credit is irrevocable even if there is no indication to that effect.
- Expiry date and place of the credit. Expiry period should not be too long or too short so that the beneficiary has enough time to make shipment. In practice, expiry place should be located in the beneficiary's country or advising bank counter effectively.
- The name and address of the beneficiary should be full and correct.
- The name and address of the applicant should be full and correct.
- The quantity and the unit price of the product should be multiplied by the issuing amount. The amount of credit is the maximum amount that the issuing bank undertakes to pay under the credit, and the words "about" or "approximately" used may indicate a 10 more or less tolerance of the drawing amount from the stated amount allowed.
- The credit should be indicated that it is available by sight payment, deferred payment, acceptance or negotiation.
- The detail for shipping, port of loading and discharge and destination and the latest date of shipment and transshipment and partial shipment are allowed or not allowed. China's imports credit transactions generally require that shipping destination port must be in China.
- Description, quantity, unit price of goods should be clear and concise as well as price terms, e.g. CIF, CFR, FOB, etc.
- Bill of lading made out to order, blank usually endorsement in blank.
- Port of loading and discharge and destination and the latest date of shipment.
- Signature of the applicant. The applicant should be in keeping with the client's name and be the same with the name in the column of the applicant, with the detailed address better.
- No contradiction between the terms.

### 5.4.2.2　Opening the Credit

After the issuing bank has agreed to the application form, the issuing bank will open the L/C in accordance with the provisions of the application. The processes of opening a credit are mainly: numbers coding, registering, charging, issuing, file managing, etc. An L/C is usually opened by means of airmail or telecommunication, which depends on how the credit will be forwarded to the advising bank.

#### (1) By airmail

The issuing bank sends the original L/C through an advising bank or the transmitting bank to the beneficiary by airmail. Credit can be airmailed by several ways such as in ordinary, in a register or in express delivery, etc.

For the applicant, it costs least by airmail, but it is the slowest methods for sending the L/C to the beneficiary. When the advising bank received the L/C by airmail, it should check it against the specimen signature. The L/C by airmail is rarely used nowadays as a result of the rapid development of telecommunication technology.

#### (2) By telecommunication

Issuance by telecommunication has taken the forms of issuance by cable or by telex.

For full cable, the full particulars of the L/C are sent to the advising bank by teletransmission and in recent, an authenticated teletransmission will be indicated to be the operative instrument or the operative amendment, and no mail confirmation should be sent. If a mail confirmation should nevertheless be sent, it will have no effect and the advising bank will have no obligation to check such mail confirmation against the operative credit or amendment received by teletransmission.

For a short or brief cable, the credit only contains some of the core contents, such as the applicant, the beneficiary, the amount of the L/C, the expiry date and kinds of documents presented and requirements, etc. A credit issued by short cable is only preliminary advice by teletransmission (such as SWIFT). The teletransmission must states "details to follow" or states that the mail confirmation is to be the operative instrument. The issuing bank has the obligation to forward the mail confirmation to confirm the brief cable informing the advising bank of issuance of the credit without delay.

#### (3) By SWIFT

The full name of SWIFT is Society for Worldwide Interbank Financial Telecommunication who is headquartered in Belgium in 1973. SWIFT's international governance and oversight reinforce the neutral, global character of its cooperative structure. SWIFT's global office network ensures an active presence in all major financial centers.

SWIFT is a global member-owned cooperative and the world's leading provider of secure financial messaging services. SWIFT messaging platform, products and services connect more than 11,000 banking and securities organizations, market infrastructures and corporate customers in more than 200 countries and territories.

SWIFT message standard format, has become an international standard language data exchange between banks. The field of the SWIFT can be subdivided into two kinds: mandatory field and optional field. The former is necessary, while the latter is unnecessary for each credit.

For each field, it includes three parts: the tag (or item code, generally, the tag is described in two digits, and sometimes it is also followed by an English letter); the name of the item and the specific contents.

There are special requirements for the date and number in the SWIFT.

As to the date, it should adopt the form of "YYMMDD". For example, "on December 8, 2017" should be written as "171208". As to the number, SWIFT requires the decimal point should use "," instead of "."; "0,5" instead of "1/2"; 5 percent instead of "5%".

The tags and the field names in the credit and its amendment are shown in Table 5-1 and Table 5-2 respectively.

Table 5-1  Tags and Field Name Used for the Opening of the L/C

| Tag | Field Name |
| --- | --- |
| 27 | Sequence of Total |
| 20 | Documentary Credit Number |
| 40E | Applicable Rule |
| 45B | Description of Goods and/or Service |
| 46B | Documents Required |
| 47B | Additional Conditions |
| 50 | Applicant |
| 59 | Beneficiary |
| 32B | Currency Code, Amount |
| 39A | Percentage Credit Amount |
| 39B | Maximum Credit Amount |
| 39C | Additional Amount Covered |
| 41A | Available with... by... |
| 42C | Drafts at... |
| 42A | Drawee |
| 42M | Mixed Payment Details |
| 42P | Deferred Payment Details |
| 43P | Partial Shipment |
| 43T | Transshipment |
| 44A | Loading on Board/Dispatch/Taking in Charge at/from... |
| 44B | For Transportation to... |
| 44C | Latest Date of Shipment |
| 44D | Shipment Period |
| 45A | Description of Goods and/or Services |
| 46A | Documents Required |
| 47A | Additional Conditions |
| 71B | Charges |
| 48 | Period for Presentation |
| 49 | Confirmation Instruction |

(续)

| Tag | Field Name |
|---|---|
| 53A | Reimbursement Bank |
| 78 | Instructions to the Paying/Accepting/Negotiating Bank |
| 57A | Advising through |
| 72 | Sender to Receiver Information |

Table 5-2　Tags and Field Name Used for the Amendment of the L/C

| Tag | Field Name |
|---|---|
| 20 | Sender's Reference |
| 21 | Receiver's Reference |
| 23 | Issuing Bank's Reference |
| 52a | Issuing Bank |
| 31c | Date of Issue |
| 30 | Date of Amendment |
| 26E | Number of Amendment |
| 59 | Beneficiary(before this amendment) |
| 31E | New Date of Expiry |
| 32B | Increase of Documentary Credit Amount |
| 33B | Decrease of Documentary Credit Amount |
| 34B | New Documentary Credit Amount After |
| 39A | Percentage Credit Amount Tolerance |
| 39B | Maximum Credit Amount |
| 39C | Additional Amount Covered |
| 44A | Loading on Board/Dispatch/Taking in Charge at/from... |
| 44B | For Transportation to... |
| 44C | Latest Date of Shipment |
| 44D | Shipment Period |
| 79 | Narrative |
| 72 | Sender to Receiver Information |

When opening an L/C, the issuing bank should also pay attention to the following relevant provisions of *UCP 600*:

- *The Uniform Customs and Practice for Documentary Credits*, 2007 Revised. *ICC* Publication No. 600 (*UCP 600*) are rules that apply to any documentary credit (credit) when the text of the credit expressly indicates that it is subject to these rules.
- A credit must state the bank with which it is available or whether it is available with any bank. A credit available with a nominated bank is also available with the issuing bank.
- A credit is irrevocable even if there is no indication to that effect.
- A credit must state whether it is available by sight payment, deferred payment, acceptance or negotiation.
- An issuing bank is irrevocably bound to honor as of the time it issues the credit.

- A credit must not be issued available by a draft drawn on the applicant.
- A credit and any amendment may be advised to a beneficiary through an advising bank.
- Except as otherwise provided by Article 38, a credit can neither be amended nor cancelled without the agreement of the issuing bank, the confirming bank, if any, and the beneficiary.
- A requirement for a document to be legalized, visaed, certified or similar will be satisfied by any signature, mark, stamp or label on the document which appears to satisfy that requirement.
- Terms such as "first class" "well-known" "qualified" "independent" "official" "competent" or "local" used to describe the issuer of a document allow any issuer except the beneficiary to issue that document.
- An issuing bank should discourage any attempt by the applicant to include, as an integral part of the credit, copies of the underlying contract, proforma invoice and the like.

## 5.4.3 Notification of Documentary Credit

Generally, the issuing bank has never sent the L/C to the beneficiary directly, but sends the L/C to his/her correspondent bank (notifying or advising bank) and lets the latter notify the L/C to the beneficiary. However, the advising bank will carefully review the credit but before he/she notifies it to the beneficiaries. Quite different from the beneficiary, the advising bank focuses on the review of the negotiation and collection. In operation, more attention should be paid by the advising bank as follows:

(1) **Authenticity of the Authorized Signatures or the Test Key**

Upon receipt of an L/C from abroad, the advising bank should first check the authenticity of the credit by checking its signatures or test key. If the authorized signature (of the letter) or the test key (of the cable) is in compliance with those kept by the advising bank, the advising bank makes a notation on the credit certifying its authenticity. If the signature or the test key is incorrect, the advising bank needs to notify the issuing bank to add the signature or test key again to prove its genuineness. In addition, the advising bank should check the authority of the authorized signatures. If it is not the person who has the authority to sign, the credit is invalid.

(2) **Creditworthiness of the Issuing Bank**

When a bank receives an L/C from a foreign bank, the two banks are usually correspondent banks. In establishing a correspondent banking relationship, a bank usually selects creditworthy banks, so, in practice, if the issuing bank is one of the correspondent banks of the advising bank, the advising bank will accept it as agreed. However, if the credit is from a non-correspondent bank, the advising bank usually only advises the credit to the beneficiary, and in order to avoid risks, will not accept the duty as a negotiating bank, an accepting bank, or a confirming bank, or a paying Bank. To this effect, the advising bank will not investigate the creditworthiness of the issuing bank. If the advising bank intends to negotiate, pay, or confirm the credit, it must investigate the issuing bank's creditworthiness.

(3) **Credit Rating of the Country the Issuing Bank Resides In**

In China, the head offices of different banks are responsible for rating the credit standings of different countries. If the country the issuing bank resides in is below the standard requirements set by its head office, the bank in China will refuse to negotiate, pay or confirm the credit. In this case, the bank only advises the credit to the beneficiary and reminds the beneficiary of the bad credit rating of the country the issuing bank resides in.

If the issuing bank has no correspondent banking relationship with the advising bank, the issuing may require another bank to transmit the credit to the advising bank. Then, the bank, serving as a transmitting bank, will first check the credit's authenticity and then transmit it to the advising bank. The advising bank should examine the credit status of the transmitting bank. If the credit requires the advising bank to negotiate, pay or confirm it, the advising bank must investigate the transmitting bank's creditworthiness. If there is no correspondent banking relationship between the issuing bank and the transmitting bank, what the advising bank should do is only to advise the credit.

If the credit is a transferable credit, and has been transferred by another bank, i. e., the transferring bank, the advising bank should check the credit status of the transferring bank and investigate the creditworthiness of the transferring bank.

## 5.4.4  Checking Credit, Presenting Documents & Applying for Negotiation

Generally, the importer will apply for the issuance of the credit according to the sales contract. However, the credit may contain some clauses which are not in compliance with the sales contract or there are some contractions in the L/C because of this or that reason. Thus, the beneficiary must check the L/C before he/she effects the delivery.

Different from the advising bank, the exporters must review credit carefully from the following aspects:

- The form of the credit. The credit must indicate expressly whether it is revocable or irrevocable. In absence of such indication, the credit is deemed to be irrevocable.
- The date of issue. The date of issue must be clearly indicated. In absence of such a date, the date of the letter or the date of receiving the cable will be regarded as the date of issue. The date of issue is used to calculate other dates, and sometimes used to make sure whether the date of presentation of documents is one after the date of issue. Also, from this date, the beneficiary can know whether the importer opens the credit according to the contractual stipulations.
- "Three Periods" of a credit. The expiry date is the last date allowing the beneficiary to submit the documents to the bank. The beneficiary must present documents to the bank for settlement before or on this date. In the validity column of the L/C, the effective location is often prescribed, that is the expiry place. The expiry place is the place where the beneficiary must present documents to the bank. The place of payment in practice is preferred to be in the place the beneficiary resides in. If the expiry place is in a foreign country, the bank should remind the beneficiary of it and make the beneficiary surrender the documents earlier to assure that the documents will reach the foreign bank within specified time. The date of shipment is the latest date for the beneficiary to ship the goods. The beneficiary must ship the goods before or on the date. The date should contain the year, month and day. A credit usually stipulates a period of presentation of documents. For example,

"Documents to be presented within 15 days after the date of transport documents but within the validity date of this documentary credit." If there is no such a stipulation in the credit, the period of presenting documents, according to *UCP 600*, is within 21 days after the date of shipment and within the validity of the credit.

- Applicant and beneficiary of the credit. The applicant of the credit is the buyer under the sales contract. The beneficiary of the credit is the seller under the sales contract and the credit is opened in favor of him. The credit must indicate clearly the full name and address of the applicant and beneficiary. In the event of missing or error, the advising bank must contact the issuing bank without delay, or notifies the beneficiary of it. Then the beneficiary contacts the applicant to amend the credit.

- No. of L/C. The L/C number is the issuing bank's reference number. When contacting the issuing bank on the L/C transaction, the advising bank must quote the number. It should be clearly indicated in the credit. If the number appears in the credit more than once, one should make sure that they must be consistent with each other. If they are not consistent, the advising bank needs to contact the issuing bank to amend it.

- Currency code and amount. The currency used in the credit must be freely convertible. If the currency is not internationally convertible, the advising bank should remind the beneficiary of it. The currency code must be the ISO currency code. The description of the amount must be in the internationally acceptable form. If the amount is written both in words and figures, the two should be consistent.

- Type of credit. According to *UCP 600*, a credit must be indicated to be available with sight payment, deferred payment, acceptance, or negotiation. When accepting and advising different kinds of credits, the advising bank should perform on different duties. For example, according to *UCP 600*, an advising bank that is not a confirming bank advises the credit and any amendment without any undertaking to honor or negotiate, so if there is not a reimbursing clause, by which the paying bank may claim reimbursement from the issuing bank in a sight payment credit, the advising bank will refuse to be the drawee bank. In this case, the advising bank must notify the issuing bank without delay.

- Drawn clause. This clause authorizes the beneficiary to draw draft(s) under the credit on the issuing bank or another nominated drawee bank for payment, acceptance or negotiation. Under a credit, the drawer of the draft is usually the beneficiary (exporter), and the payee is the negotiating bank or the beneficiary himself/herself, and the drawee may be the paying bank, accepting bank, confirming bank or issuing bank.

- Clause of the goods. The clause of the goods includes the name, quantity, size or specifications of the goods, unit price and price terms, etc. The description of the goods must be complete and precise, but too detailed one will bring trouble to both the beneficiary and the advising bank when dealing with documents. The price terms used in international trade are usually FOB, CIF, CFR, etc. such as "FOB Dalian" or "CIF Liverpool".

- Documents required. A credit usually stipulates a list of documents that the beneficiary must present. The requirements for documents should be consistent. For example, if the clause on bills of lading requires "Freight Prepaid", the price term must be CIF or CFR. If it requires "Freight Collect", the price term is usually FOB.

When the L/C has been accepted by the beneficiary and the time of shipment has come, the beneficiary should deliver the goods according to the sales contract to the shipping company and get the shipping document (in most case, it is the bill of lading), draw the draft(s) and prepare all the other documents required in the L/C. Then, the beneficiary should present the draft(s) and the other documents required in the L/C within the period for presentation but within the expiry date of the L/C for negotiation.

### 5.4.5 Verification of Documents & Negotiation

(1) **Verification of Documents**

Under a credit, the banks which have the responsibility for the examination of the documents are the negotiating bank, the paying bank, the accepting bank, the issuing bank and the confirming bank of the credit. According to *UCP 600*, the standards for examination of documents mainly refer to the following several points:

- A nominated bank acting on its nomination, a confirming bank, if any, and the issuing bank must examine a presentation to determine, on the basis of the documents alone, whether the documents appear on their face to constitute a complying presentation or not.

- A nominated bank acting on its nomination, a confirming bank, if any, and the issuing bank each shall have a maximum of five banking days following the day of presentation to determine if a presentation is complying.

- Data in a document, when read in context with the credit, the document itself and international standard banking practice, need not to be identical, but must not be conflict with the data in that document or any other stipulated document or the credit.

- In documents other than the commercial invoice, the description of the goods, services or performance, if stated, may be in general terms not conflicting with their description in the credit.

- If a credit requires presentation of a document other than a transport document, insurance document or commercial invoice, without stipulating by whom the document is to be issued or its data content, banks will accept the document as presented if its content appears to fulfill the function of the required document.

- A document may be dated prior to the issuance date of the credit, but must not be dated later than its date of presentation.

- A document presented but not required by the credit will be disregarded and if a credit contains a condition without stipulating the document to indicate compliance with the condition. Banks will deem such condition as not stated and will disregard it.

(2) **Negotiation**

After the advising bank has made sure that the documents are complying with the credit, he/she will negotiate the documents.

The general procedure for L/C is shown in Figure 5-1.

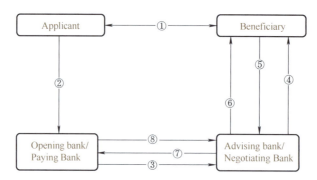

Figure 5-1　General Procedure for L/C

The key work contents for each step are as follows:

① Both the Seller and the Buyer agree to settle the payment by the L/C.
② The Applicant applies to open the L/C.
③ The Opening bank opens the L/C and sent it to the Advising bank.
④ The Advising bank notify the L/C to the Beneficiary.
⑤ The Beneficiary presents the documents required by the L/C and ask for negotiation.
⑥ The Negotiating bank (Generally it is the Advising bank) negotiate the documents.
⑦ The Negotiating bank send the documents to the Paying Bank and ask for reimbursement.
⑧ The Opening bank makes payment when he found the documents presented by the beneficiary and sent by the negotiating bank comply with the L/C.

## 5.4.6　The negotiation bank negotiates the documents according to the terms of the credit

## 5.4.7　The negotiation bank sends the documents to the issuing bank and ask for reimbursement

## 5.4.8　The issuing bank effects the payment when the documents presented by the beneficiary and sent by the negotiation bank comply with the requirements in the L/C

# 5.5　Categories of L/C

## 5.5.1　Reimbursement or Claim Reimbursement between Banks under the Credit

After negotiation or payment is made, the negotiating bank or the paying bank will claim reimbursement from the issuing bank or the reimbursing bank in accordance with the reimbursement terms indicated in the credit and the documents will be sent to the issuing bank.

Upon receipt of the documents, the issuing bank will check them. If the documents have meted the credit requirements, the issuing bank will effect payment in the accordance with the terms of credit. If the documents do not comply with the credit terms, the issuing bank will refuse to pay and at the same time inform the negotiating bank or the paying bank immediately.

In practice the payment between banks depends on the reimbursement terms indicated in the credit and the accounts relationship between the issuing bank and the negotiating bank or the paying bank.

There are so many kinds of credit according to different characteristics.

## 5.5.2 Whether It Is Accompanied with Shipping Documents

### (1) Documentary Credit

A documentary credit refers to a credit under which payment will be made against documents representing title to the goods and thus making the transfer of title possible. It is universally used as a method of payment in the international trade settlement. A credit usually bears the word "documentary" to indicate that it is a documentary credit.

### (2) Clean Credit

A clean credit refers to a credit under which payment will be effected only against a draft without any shipping documents attached thereto or sometimes, against a draft with an invoice alone attached thereto. A clean credit is often used in the international non-trade settlement, such as anticipatory credit standby credit under trade settlement and traveler's credit under the non-trade settlement.

## 5.5.3 Whether Paying Bank can Revoke or not

### (1) Irrevocable L/C

An irrevocable letter of credit cannot be amended or cancelled without the consent of the beneficiary, the confirming bank etc. The payment is guaranteed by the bank if the credit terms and conditions are fully met by the beneficiary. The words "irrevocable documentary credit" or "irrevocable credit" may be indicated in the L/C.

However, in some cases, an irrevocable L/C received by the beneficiary may become invalid without the amendment or cancellation of such L/C, for example, when the trade between the importing and the exporting countries is suspended such as in a trade sanction, or when the issuing bank has gone bankrupt.

Although such a credit gives the maximum flexibility to the applicant, it involves risks to the beneficiary since the documentary credit may be amended or cancelled while the goods are in transit and before the documents may have been presented, before payment has been made.

### (2) Revocable L/C

A revocable letter of credit can be amended or cancelled by the issuing bank at any time without the consent of the beneficiary, often at the request and on the instructions of the applicant. There is no security of payment in a revocable letter of credit (L/C). The words "this credit is subject to cancellation without notice", "revocable documentary credit" or "revocable credit" usually are indicated in the L/C.

Before the 1970s, such a credit was usually used for those businesses between the developing countries, however, it has rarely seen since then in international trade. According to *UCP600*, all credit should be irrevocable nowadays.

According to *UCP 600*, "Irrevocable" means the definite, irrevocable undertaking of the Issuing Bank to pay the seller provided the terms and conditions are met. This credit gives the beneficiary great assurance of payment, whether it will be paid or not depends on the undertaking of the foreign issuing bank, and the precondition for payment is that the stipulated documents are presented and all the stipulations of the credit are complied with, and gives the applicant (the importer) less flexibility as the credit can only be amended or cancelled if all parties thereto agree. More attention is, in an irrevocable credit, the term "Irrevocable" is clearly indicated and a credit is irrevocable even if there is no indication to that effect. Therefore, Article 3 of *UCP 600* stipulates that "A credit is irrevocable even if there is no indication to that effect."

## 5.5.4 Whether There Is a Confirming Bank

(1) Confirmed L/C

Article 2 of *UCP600* says: "Confirmation means a definite undertaking of the confirming bank, in addition to that of the issuing bank, to honor or negotiate a complying presentation." Besides, a confirmed credit should be an irrevocable credit first.

An irrevocable letter of credit (L/C) opened by an issuing bank whose authenticity has been confirmed by the advising bank and where the advising bank has added its confirmation to the credit is known as a confirmed irrevocable letter of credit. The words "we confirm the credit and hereby undertake..." or "we add our confirmation to this credit and hereby undertake..." normally are included in the L/C.

A confirmed irrevocable L/C is assured of payment even if the importer or the issuing bank defaults. The confirmed irrevocable L/C is particularly important from the buyers in a country which is economically or politically unstable.

In a confirmed letter of credit, the exporter or the importer pays an extra charge called the confirmation fee, which may vary from bank to bank within a country. The fee usually is for the exporter's account. The exporter may indicate in the sales contract that the confirmation fee and other charges outside the seller's country are on the buyer's account.

(2) Unconfirmed L/C

An irrevocable letter of credit (L/C) opened by an issuing bank in which the advising bank does not add its confirmation to the credit is known as an unconfirmed irrevocable letter of credit. The promise to pay comes from the issuing bank only, unlike in a confirmed irrevocable L/C where both the issuing bank and the advising bank promise to pay the beneficiary.

In the international trade, the confirming L/C will be used in the following situations, such as the total amount of the credit is too large and may be beyond the solvency of the issuing bank itself; the issuing bank is a small-medium one; there is political and/or economic instability in the importing country; there is a serious shortage of foreign exchange and shall be confirmed by a bank in a third country. In addition, British banks traditionally believed their credit is the most reliable, so they often add confirmation in their own credits, however, such kind of confirmed credit has no essential difference with the irrevocable letter of credit itself.

---

**Case study 5-1 Irrevocable Confirmed L/C**

**Background:**

Type of Credit: Irrevocable Confirmed    Application: UCP600

Issuing Bank: Bank I    Advising Bank: Bank A

Confirming Bank: Bank A    Availability: At sight with the Confirming Bank

**Circumstances:**

Issuing Bank: Bank I issued its irrevocable Documentary Credit in favor of the Beneficiary and advised it through Bank A at a request that Bank A added its confirmation.

Confirming Bank: Bank A advised the Credit to the Beneficiary adding its confirmation.

Beneficiary: The Beneficiary shipped the merchandise and presented the relevant documents with a value of SUD110,000——two days prior to the expiry date of the Credit.

Confirming Bank: Upon receipt of the documents, Bank A examined them and determined that they were not in compliance with the terms of the Credit for the following reasons:

(1) Bill of lading was issued to the order of the shipper and endorsed in blank instead of to the order of the buyer.

(2) The Credit was overdrawn by USD10,000. In view of the fax: that the Credit was about to expire, Bank A telephoned the Beneficiary advising him/her of the discrepancies.

Beneficiary: Upon receipt of the notice of rejection and prior to the expiry date of the Credit, the Beneficiary requested Bank A to telex the Bank I requesting approval to pay despite the discrepant documents.

Confirming Bank: Immediately, upon receipt of such telephonic authorization, Bank A telexed Bank I requesting authority to pay the documents as presented. (After conferring with the applicant, Bank I authorized Bank A to pay the documents as presented.) By the time Bank I had telexed authorization for Bank A to pay the discrepant documents; the political and economic conditions in Bank I's country had deteriorated, Bank A informed the Beneficiary that, although approval had been received to pay the documents as presented, Bank A was not in a position to honor those instructions in as much as the assets of Bank I had been frozen in Bank A's country and did not have any means of obtaining reimbursement from Bank I.

Beneficiary: The Beneficiary immediately contacted his/her lawyers to determine the position he/she should take to protect his/she interest. The lawyers contacted Bank A and informed them that the withholding of the payment was unwarranted and reminded Bank A of that they had confirmed the Credit. As such, under *UCP600*, the confirmer of a Credit could not withdraw their confirmation of the Credit without the Beneficiary's consent.

Confirming Bank: Bank A countered with the statement that their confirmation was valid provided only that the terms and conditions of the Credit were complied with. In view of the fact that the documents presented did not comply with the terms of the Credit, Bank A's confirmation was null and void.

Beneficiary: The lawyers for the Beneficiary responded that Bank A did agree unconditionally to telex Bank I for permission to pay despite the discrepant documents. That course of action was said to constitute consent by Bank A to effect payment upon a positive response from Bank I.

**Questions**:

1. Do you agree with the position taken by Bank A that their confirmation was only valid for the original Credit terms, even though they had agreed to telex Bank I for permission to pay, and that it should not imply their concurrence to pay it although such authority to pay was given by Bank I?
2. What was the position taken by the ICC Banking Commission on a similar case?
3. What course of action should Bank A have taken to protect its interest?

**Answer**:

1. Yes, normally, the position is correct. But in view of the fact that Bank A agreed to request permission to pay discrepant documents, that position had lost its value. It would be a different case if the confirming bank did not agree unconditionally to telex Bank I for permission to pay despite the discrepant documents.
2. A confirming bank is irrevocably bound to honor or negotiate as of the time it adds its confirmation to the credit. Where discrepant documents were submitted by the confirming bank to the issuing bank for approval within the framework of the credit transaction, this action itself was to be regarded in effect as a request for amendment of the credit. During the process of the transaction, the confirming bank remained bound of its obligation to effect payment in the event that the documents were approved by the issuing bank, and were deemed to have agreed to the date of expiry of the credit being automatically extended for a reasonable period so as to allow the issuing bank to have sufficient time to reply.
3. Bank A or the confirming bank should have informed the beneficiary that, as an accommodation, they themselves (the beneficiary) would send the telex requiring the issuing bank to authorize payment despite the noted discrepancies. That action should not infer that the Bank A's confirmation was automatically extended for the period necessary for the issuing bank to review and authorize the payment. Alternatively, the confirming bank could have informed the beneficiary to contact the applicant directly, requesting the applicant to authorize the issuing bank to accept the documents as presented and to instruct Bank A to effect payment, which would also imply that the confirmation was considered to be null and void.

### 5.5.5 Method and Time of Payment

#### 5.5.5.1 Sight Payment L/C

A sight payment credit refers to the credit that provides for payment immediately at the counters of the issuing bank or the confirming bank or the nominated paying bank upon presentation of documents complying with the credit terms.

Under sight payment credit, the beneficiary would receive payment at sight on presentation of his/her draft to the drawee bank or to the issuing bank, once the relevant documents have been verified and found to be complying with the credit.

Generally, there is a clause in the sight payment credit, such as: "This credit is available with Bank A, New York (the issuing bank) or Bank B, Beijing (advising bank) or Bank C, London (another bank) by sight payment against presentation of beneficiary's drafts at sight drawn on Bank A, New York or Bank B, Beijing or Bank C, London, and of the documents detailed herein."

Under a sight credit, if a draft is used, it must be drawn on the party stated in the credit, which could either be the issuing bank or any other nominated paying banks. If no other paying bank is nominated in the credit, the issuing bank is the paying bank, and must directly deliver the drafts drawn on the issuing bank and the stipulated documents to the issuing bank to ask for payment. However, a draft is not necessary in a sight credit to avoid the stamp duty/stamp tax. Payment under a sight credit is sometimes effected only against a receipt of the beneficiary but usually against correct documents without any receipt. For example, a credit can make specified as follows: "This credit is available with us (issuing bank) by sight payment against presentation of the documents detailed herein."

Under a sight credit, the payment of the paying bank is final and without recourse to the beneficiary, so the beneficiary of such a credit normally can obtain the payment immediately after submitting complying documents, thus ensuring his/her immediate use of funds and reducing the risks of the fluctuation of exchange rate and the non-payment by the buyer.

### 5.5.5.2 Deferred Credit

A deferred payment credit refers to the credit that indicates a bank, which is also called the paying bank, to pay on a specified future time after the date of the bill of lading or after the presentation of documents. Deferred credit and acceptance credit mentioned later are usance or time credit, while the difference between these two is that the latter may certainly require drafts and the former may not at all. The reason of no draft required for deferred credit is mainly to avoid the stamp duty. The following provisions will be stipulated in a deferred payment credit: "Available with _____ bank by deferred payment at _____ days after the date of issuance of the transport documents" or "Available at _____ days after the presentation of the documents", etc.

If a credit is available with the issuing bank or the confirming bank, when presenting documents complying with the terms of this credit, the beneficiary will receive, an undertaking in writing of the issuing bank or the confirming bank that the payment will be effected on due date. If a credit is available with another exporter's bank who hasn't added its confirmation to the credit, what the beneficiary may obtain after delivery of the documents is a proof qualified or an authorized in a time of payment in the future, may not be sure of the payment obligation. Therefore, the beneficiary might encounter a lot of risks in this case and his/her general approach is to ask the paying bank or some other reliable banks to add their confirmation to the deferred payment credit.

### 5.5.5.3 Acceptance credit

An acceptance credit refers to the credit that indicates a bank which is called the accepting bank, the issuing bank or another nominated bank, to accept and pay the face value of draft drawn on this bank at maturity. It must be a usance credit and the draft there under the credit must be a time bill drawn on the issuing bank, the advising bank, or any other drawee bank. The clause used in the credit is as follows: "Credit available with _____ bank by acceptance." By accepting the draft under the credit, the accepting bank promises to pay the face value when the draft matures. According to *UCP 600*, in event that the drawee bank other than the issuing bank or the confirming bank does not accept the draft drawn on it or pay at maturity, the issuing bank or the confirming bank engages to accept and pay at maturity the draft drawn by the beneficiary on the issuing bank or the confirming bank, if any. Under an acceptance credit, the beneficiary can only obtain payment from the drawee bank at the maturity date and then if the beneficiary wishes to get paid immediately he/she may discount the accepted draft with a discount house or a commercial bank. Namely, the beneficiary of an acceptance credit may either hold the accepted drafts for security and presents for payment at maturity or discount it with a discounting house to obtain the funds immediately.

Based on whether the discounting charges will be borne by the buyer or the seller, acceptance credits can be subdivided into two types: seller's usance credit and buyer's usance credit. As to the former, discounting charges are for the seller's account, while as to the latter, for the account of the buyer.

(1) **Seller's Usance Credit**

Generally speaking, under an acceptance credit, the beneficiary will receive payment on a specified future time. If he/her discounts the accepted draft in the money market, the acceptance fee and discount charges are for the account of the beneficiary. This is called the seller's usance credit. In this case, clauses in the credit are as follows: "This credit is available with _____ bank by acceptance of draft at 30 days after sight against the documents detailed herein and beneficiary's draft(s) drawn on us." "We hereby engage that drafts drawn in conformity with the terms of this credit will be duly accepted on presentation and duly honored at maturity." Under this situation, the issuing bank is the drawee bank. Or, a seller's usance credit may also mark the clauses as: "This credit available by acceptance of beneficiary's draft at 60 days drawn on advising bank. Acceptance charges and discount fees are for seller's account. At maturity of draft please reimburse yourself from..." Under this situation, the drawee bank is the advising bank, namely the nominated bank.

The seller's usance credit is usually issued if the contract is on time basis. The purpose of an acceptance credit is to give the importer time to make payment. If he/she can resell the goods before payment falls due, he/she can use the proceeds to meet the L/C. In this way, he/she avoids the necessity of borrowing money to finance the transaction. On the other hand, the issuing bank can obtain the documents after acceptance, but it will not release them to the applicant until the applicant redeems the documents at maturity. So, there may be a situation that both documents and goods have arrived but the applicant cannot obtain the documents. Under this situation, the applicant may submit a Trust Receipt(T/R) to the issuing bank to borrow the documents against the issuing bank's approval.

(2) **Buyer's Usance Credit**

A buyer's usance credit is one that the credit is a usance credit but the sales contract on which the credit is issued provides for payment at sight. The draft drawn under a buyer's acceptance credit by the beneficiary is a time draft payable at sight, and the payment is actually from the proceeds of discounting the accepted draft, and the discounting charges are for the buyer's account. Thus, one may find clauses in a buyer's acceptance such as: "The usance drafts are payable on a sight basis, discount charges and acceptance commission are for the buyer's account." "This credit is available by your drafts at 45 days sight at maturity drawn on our New York branch which is payable in Shanghai(our H. O.). Drawn bank's discount charges are for the account of the Applicant." "The usance credit is available by your draft at 90 days sight on Citi bank, N. Y." "Drawee bank's discount and acceptance commission are for the account of the applicant and therefore the beneficiary can receive the face value of the terms drafts as if drawn at sight."

In practice, a buyer's usance credit is also called usance credit payable at sight, and in the credit, we can usually find similar clauses reading as: "The usance drafts are payable on a sight-basis, discount charges and acceptance commission are for the buyer's account." "Drawee bank's discount and acceptance commission are for the account of the applicant and therefore the beneficiary can receive the face value of the term drafts as if drawn at sight."

### 5.5.5.4 Negotiation Credit

A negotiation credit refers to the credit one under which the issuing bank authorizes other nominated bank which is called negotiating bank to negotiate sight or time drafts presented and or documents by the beneficiary.

According to the definition of negotiation of *UCP 600*, We can understand the "negotiation credit" from the following several aspects:

1) The credit must indicate "credit available by negotiation".

2) The credit can be either a sight credit or a time credit, that is, if there is a draft involved, the drafts drawn on the issuing bank or on any other drawee bank under the credit can be payable at sight or in a specific future time.

3) The negotiating bank should have got the authorization from the issuing bank.

4) The negotiating bank should accord to the issuing bank to buy the draft from the beneficiary or to give value for draft and or documents.

5) Only the complying presentation of documents can get advance funds from the negotiating bank.

6) After negotiation, the negotiating bank becomes a holder of the drafts drawn under the credit and normally get a right of recourse against the drawer, namely the beneficiary of the credit, unless the credit has been confirmed by the negotiating bank. Negotiation by the issuing bank or the confirming bank will be without recourse to the beneficiary.

Accordingly, a negotiation credit can be divided into two types: free negotiation credit and restricted negotiation credit.

**Firstly, Free negotiation credit.** In a free negotiation credit, the issuing bank invites or authorizes any bank to negotiate the drafts and the beneficiary may present the drafts and/or documents to and receive money from any bank at his/her choice. Or, any bank can be a nominated negotiating bank, as long as the bank has negotiated the drafts and/or documents, and claim normally the reimbursement from the issuing bank. In this case, the issuing bank usually indicates

"This credit is available with any bank by negotiation" on the credit and expresses its promise to honor drafts properly drawn and negotiated by any bank with clauses such as: "We hereby engage with drawers, endorsers and bona-fide holders of draft(s) drawn under and in compliance with the terms of the credit that such draft(s) will be duly honored on due presentation and delivery of documents as specified."

**Secondly, Restricted negotiation credit.** Under a restricted negotiation credit, the authorization from the issuing bank to negotiate the drafts drawn under the credit and/or documents is restricted to a specific nominated negotiating bank, and the beneficiary can only negotiate the drafts and/or documents with this negotiating bank. The negotiating bank is usually the issuing bank's branch or a correspondent bank. In such credit, there may be clauses such as: "This credit is available with _____ bank (for example, namely the advising bank) by negotiation." "We hereby engage with you that all draft(s) drawn under and in conformity with the terms of this credit will be duly honored on presentation to _____ bank (for example, namely the advising bank)."

However, under an restricted negotiation credit, the beneficiary may choose other banks or financial institutions, rather than a nominated negotiating bank, to negotiate (purchase) his/her drafts at their own risks. In such case, a bank that has negotiated (bought) the beneficiary's drafts is called a non-nominated negotiating bank. This bank just acts a remitting bank or a forwarding bank to forward the documents to the issuing bank on behalf of the beneficiary, and his/her negotiation can't be protected by *UCP 600*. Therefore, only when the documents are to be presented to the issuing bank within the validity of the credit and in compliance with the terms and conditions of the credit, the non-nominated negotiating bank can claim normally reimbursement.

In order to escape the stamp duty levied on any draft in some countries, a credit may indicate that it is a negotiable one although sometimes there is no draft there under.

The above-mentioned classifications of credit are made on the basic characteristics of each letter of credit. The following classification is based on a particular feature that may be for a particular letter of credit.

---

### Case study 5-2 Restrictive Negotiation
**Background:**
The beneficiary drew a draft under an L/C with the payee of Bank of Communications, Nanjing Branch. After Bank of Communications, Nanjing Branch, endorsed the draft, Bank of China, Nanjing Branch sent the documents to and claimed reimbursement from the issuing bank. The issuing bank refused to pay because it believed that Bank of Communications, Nanjing Branch was not a negotiating bank.

**Analysis:**
The refusal is unreasonable. According to *the Law of Commercial Paper*, it is a complete draft. The issuing bank should not refuse the reimbursement claimed by Bank of China as long as the documents presented comply with terms and conditions of the L/C.

### 5.5.5.5 Anticipatory Credit

Anticipatory credit refers to a red clause credit, which is based on the anticipated payment of the credit amount. In other words, it is a credit with a special clause printed in red added there to that authorizes the advising bank or the confirming bank or any other nominated bank to make some or all advances to the beneficiary before presentation of the documents. An anticipatory credit is also called as a packing credit. The special clause, called the red clause or the anticipatory clause, is incorporated into the credit by the issuing bank at the specific request of the applicant. The reason of printing it in red is to draw attention to the unique nature of this credit. This type of credit is used particularly in Australian wool trade.

An anticipatory credit provides funds to assist the beneficiary in paying the cost before shipment such as expenses for labor, materials and package. Essentially, an anticipatory credit is a form of financing provided by the buyer to the seller and is at the specific request of the applicant when the applicant trust exporter fully and would be willing to make a special concession of this nature. According to the anticipatory clause, the beneficiary can advance a part or all amount of the credit from the advising bank or the confirming bank or any other nominated bank. The advising bank or the confirming bank or the other nominated bank will get repayment of the loan plus interest, from the proceeds to be paid to the beneficiary, when the goods are shipped and documents are presented in compliance with the terms of the credit. If the beneficiary fails to ship the goods or present the documents required under the credit, the advising bank or the confirming bank or the other nominated bank will have the right to demand repayment with interest from the issuing bank, which will have a similar right of recourse against the applicant.

The anticipatory clause should usually indicate the following contents:

- The maximum amount or percentage to advance, usually 30 or 40 percent of the amount of the credit.
- The basis to advance such as the receipt or confirmation or guarantee in writing issued by the beneficiary.
- The issuing bank's responsibility for security to the banks who have advance to the beneficiary, as beneficiary fails to ship the goods or present the documents required under the credit.

The anticipatory clause is usually expressed as:"The negotiating bank is authorized to advance 50% of this credit amount to the beneficiary against their undertaking to effect shipment and present compliance documents under this credit within its validity. The relative advance plus interest are to be deducted from the proceeds upon negotiation. In case the beneficiary fails to act according to his undertaking mentioned above, we undertake to refund the negotiating bank for the principal plus interest upon presentation by, the negotiating bank of the mentioned-above undertaking."

Based on the different conditions of advances, anticipatory letters of credit can be divided into the red clause letter of credit and the green clause letter of credit. the green clause letter of credit, its anticipatory clause printed in green printing ink, required the beneficiary to use the bill of exchange and warehouse receipts under the credit as a collateral for getting advance from the negotiating bank prior to export. Stricter anticipatory clauses distinguish the green clause letter of credit from the red clause letter of credit.

## 5.5.6 Whether the Credit can be Transferred

### (1) Transferable Credit

According to Article 38 of *UCP 600*, "Transferable credit means a credit that specifically states it is 'transferable'. A transferable credit may be made available in whole or in part to another beneficiary ('second beneficiary') at the request of the beneficiary ('first beneficiary')." In other words, a transferable credit is normally used in trilateral trade, when the first beneficiary is a middleman who does not supply the merchandise himself, and so wishes to transfer part or all of his rights and obligations to the actual suppliers as second beneficiary (beneficiaries). So transferable credit can have the following characteristics:

Firstly, only credit clearly marked such word as "transferable" is transferable credit. Terms such as "divisible" "fractionable" "assignable" and "transmissible" do not render the credit transferable. If such terms are used, they shall be disregarded.

Secondly, transferred credit means a credit that has been made available by the transferring bank to a second beneficiary. Transferring bank means a nominated bank that transfers the credit, or a bank that is specifically authorized the issuing bank to transfer, and or a bank that transfers the credit to the second beneficiary in case that the credit is available with any bank. An issuing bank may be itself a transferring bank, but other (non-issuing bank) bank that is requested to transfer the credit is not obliged to do so.

Thirdly, a transferred credit can only be transferred once, namely it cannot be transferred at the request of a second beneficiary to any subsequent beneficiary. The rest beneficiary is not considered to be a subsequent beneficiary.

Fourthly, the transferred credit must accurately reflect the terms and conditions of the credit, including confirmation, if any, with the exception of:

- The amount of the credit.
- Any unit price stated therein.
- The expiry dates.
- The period for presentation, or the latest shipment date or given period for shipment.

Any or all of which may be reduced or curtailed.

The percentage for which insurance cover must be effected may be increased to provide the amount of cover stipulated in the credit or these articles. In addition, the name of the first beneficiary may be substituted for that of the applicant in the credit, but if the name of the applicant is specifically required by the credit to appear in any document other than the invoice, such requirement must be reflected in the transferred credit.

Any request for transfer must indicate if and under what conditions amendments may be advised to the second beneficiary. The transferred credit must clearly indicate those conditions.

If a credit is transferred to more than one second beneficiary, rejection of an amendment by one or more second beneficiary does not invalidate the acceptance by any other second beneficiary, with respect to which the transferred credit will be amended accordingly. For any second beneficiary that rejected the amendment, the transferred credit will remain unamended.

In practice, under a transferred credit, the beneficiary can choose to transfer all of his/her rights or part of his rights to one or more second beneficiaries. In these two kinds of circumstances, the beneficiary can also choose to conceal or not conceal the status of actual buyer and supplier. If the beneficiary wants to conceal both parties, he/she may request to transfer the credit with the substitution of documents. Namely, in case of substitution of documents needed, the beneficiary has the right to substitute its own invoice and draft for those of one or more transferees. According to *UCP 600*, the first beneficiary has the right to substitute its own invoice and draft, if any, for those of a second beneficiary for an amount not in excess of that stipulated in the credit, and upon such substitution, the first beneficiary can draw under the credit for the difference, if any, between its invoice and the invoice of a second beneficiary. Additionally, if the first beneficiary is to present its own invoice and draft, if any, but fails to do so on first demand, or if the invoices presented by the first beneficiary create discrepancies that did not exist in the presentation made by the second beneficiary and the first beneficiary fails to correct them on first demand, the transferring bank has the right to present the documents as received from the second beneficiary to the issuing bank, without further responsibility to the first beneficiary.

(2) **Non-transferable L/C**

Non-transferable L/C refers to a credit that cannot be transferred to another party. All those Ls/C which have not mentioned "transferable" are not transferable.

### 5.5.7 Reciprocal L/C

In the operation of a reciprocal L/C, there are two credits under which the applicant of one credit (the original credit) may assume the position of the beneficiary of the second credit (the reciprocal credit), and the issuing bank of the original credit may become the advising bank of the reciprocal credit. The amount of the two credits can be equivalent, or roughly. A special clause specifying that it will be effective only when its beneficiary opens a reciprocal credit through a bank within the specified time limit in favor of the applicant of the first credit must be contained in the reciprocal credit. For example, the first credit is usually stated as: "This is a reciprocal credit against_____ Bank credit No. _____ favoring _____ covering shipment of _____." "This credit is available by draft(s) drawn on us at _____ days after bill of lading date. Payment will be effected by us on maturity of the draft against the above-mentioned documents and our receipt of the credit opener's advice stating that a reciprocal credit in their favor issued by _____ Bank on your account available by sight draft has been received by and found acceptable to them."

A reciprocal credit is mostly used in a barter trade, a trade of processing of incoming materials, incoming drawings and samples, and a compensation trade, there are usually two transactions and credits involved. Two of the reciprocal credit can come into operation at the same time or not. It is apparent that if the two credits become effective separately, the applicant of the first credit is faced with risks. Under a credit operation, banks only deal with documents, i.e., the issuing bank will effect payment so long as the documents presented by the beneficiary on their face comply with the terms and conditions of the credit. In a trade of processing incoming materials, for example, the incoming materials received by the applicant of the first credit might not meet the requirements of the sales contract, if the issuing bank of the first credit has already made duly payment, but the applicant of the first credit will have to assume the loss by himself. Therefore, the two credits under a reciprocal credit operation should simultaneously take effect at best.

### 5.5.8 Back to Back L/C

Back to back L/C refers to a new one that is similar to the original L/C which is opened by the beneficiary (as the applicant) of the original one in favor of the real supplier on the basis of the original L/C.

Because the back to back L/C is opened based on the original L/C, it is also called as the secondary L/C or local L/C.

In practice, when the exporter is not the actual supplier while the importer has opened a kind of non-transferable credit or when the exporter and the importer cannot do business directly.

### 5.5.9 Revolving L/C

This is the so-called revolving L/C according to the credit amount to be used repeatedly, which renews itself after its all or partial amount is drawn. In other words, a revolving L/C is one by which the amount of the credit is renewed or reinstated to the original amount after it has been utilized without specific amendments to the credit. The revolving L/C is mainly applicable to the circumstances under which the importer and exporter may sign a long-term contract, and partial shipment, long-term installment. Using a revolving L/C, the importer can save cost and opening formalities.

The revolving L/C can be renewed or revolved on the basis of time or amount. If renewed on a time basis, it is available for a fixed amount over a given period. For example, such a credit may be stated as "This is a monthly revolving credit which is available for up to the amount of USD 10,000 every month for the first time in May, for the last time in November 2018, and maximum amount payable under this credit USD 60,000." If renewed on an amount basis, the amount of the credit is reinstated whenever it is drawn within the validity period until the total amount of the credit is used up. The wording for such a credit may be as follows: "Amount of the credit GBP 10,000, revolving 6 times to maximum amount GBP 80,000." In practice, the revolving credit revolved on a time basis is quite common.

A revolving L/C, whether on a time basis or an amount basis, can be cumulative or non-cumulative. If it is stated "cumulative", any sum not utilized during the first period carries over and may be utilized during a subsequent period. If it is stated "non-cumulative", any sum not utilized in a period ceases to be available, i.e., it cannot be carried over to a subsequent period.

The specific revolving methods can be formulated in different ways with different words stipulated in the credit:

(1) **Automatic Revolving L/C**

The amount of the credit will be reinstated immediately after its drawings have been made whether it is cumulative or non-cumulative. Such as: "This Credit shall be renewable automatically non-cumulatively twice for a period of one month each for an amount of USD50,000.00 for each period making a total of USD150,000.00."

(2) **Semi-automatic Revolving L/C**

The amount of the credit will be reinstated if no advice to stop renewal is sent from the issuing bank within a specified period as mentioned in the credit. Such as: "The amount shall be renewable cumulatively after each negotiation only upon receipt of Issuing Bank's advice advising that the credit may be renewable."

(3) **Non-automatic Revolving L/C**

The amount of the credit will be reinstated only upon receipt of the issuing bank's notice of renewal as mentioned in the credit. Such as: "Should the Negotiating Bank not be advised of stopping renewed within 7 days, the unused balance of this credit shall be increased to the original amount on the 8th day after each negotiation."

## 5.6 Payment Clause by L/C under Sales Contract

In practice, the L/C can be used solely or used with the other payment methods, such as collection. Thus, in different cases, the contents are different from each other.

### 5.6.1 Payment by L/C Wholly

When payment was made by the L/C wholly, the contents of the payment clause in the sales contract would contain the follows:

(1) **Beneficiary**

Generally, it is the seller who would be the beneficiary.

(2) **Opening Bank**

General rules for "the seller agrees to accept the bank".

(3) **Date of Issuance**

Generally, it would be "at _____ days after the date of the sales contract", "in _____ days before the time of shipment stipulated in the contract" or "_____ days after receiving the seller notice of the stock" etc. The date of issuance and the date of arrival of the L/C are different from each other. In practice, the latter would be better for the exporter.

(4) **Categories**

There are so many kinds of L/C, both parties should make them sure according to the specific transactions.

(5) **Credit Amount**

Generally, it stipulates "according to 100% of the invoice value". When there is "More or

Less" clause in the sales contract, the total amount and the total quantity should also be stipulated correspondingly.

**(6) Date and Place of Expiry**

Example 1: The Buyers shall open through a bank acceptable to the Sellers an irrevocable sight after of credit to reach the Sellers... days before the month of shipment, valid for negotiation in China until the 15th day after the month of shipment.

Example 2: The Buyers shall open through a bank acceptable to the Sellers an irrevocable letter of credit at... days sight to reach the Sellers... days before the month of shipment, valid for negotiation in China until the 15th day after the month of shipment.

## 5.6.2 Partly by L/C and Partly by Collection

The buyers shall open through a bank acceptable to the seller an irrevocable sight letter of credit to reach the sellers... days before the month of shipment, stipulating that 50% of the invoice value available against clean draft at sight while the remaining 50% on documents against payment at sight (or D/P at... days after sight). The full set of the shipping documents of 100% invoice value shall accompany the collection item and shall only be released after full payment of the invoice value. If the Buyers fail to pay full invoice, the shipping documents shall be held by the issuing bank at the Sellers' disposal.

## Questions:

I. True or false.

1. Once shipment of the goods is finished, the seller should present all the documents to the negotiating bank for payment under the terms of the credit.
2. As a documentary credit is opened through banks, therefore, the issuing bank, the advising bank and the negotiating bank, etc. perform the same function.
3. In irrevocable L/C, the seller can receive his payment once he finishes the shipment of contract goods.
4. In the international trade, it is always necessary for the seller to urge the buyer to open the L/C in good time.
5. When the buyer fails to issue the covering L/C within the specified time of the contract, the seller holds the right of declaring the contract avoid.
6. When the L/C stipulates that the quantity of the goods must not be more or less than the prescribed quantity, the seller may still have the right of delivering 5 percent more or less.
7. According to the *UCP600*, a freely negotiable credit must stipulate a place for the presentation of documents for negotiation.
8. Unless otherwise stated in the credit, a transferable credit can be transferred more than once.
9. When the goods do not conform to the sales contract, the bank may stop payment immediately even if the documents are correct and complete.
10. If the Issuing Band appoints the Bank of China as its Advising Bank of the L/C, then the

Issuing Bank may ask the Bank of Asia to advise amendments to the L/C.
11. According to *UCP600*, if documents are in correspondence with L/C's stipulations, discrepancies between the documents themselves are allowed.
12. After the issuance of the letter of credit, the Issuing Bank may refuse payment if the applicant becomes bankrupt.
13. After the negotiating bank negotiates the documents, which are refused by the opening bank later, the negotiating bank may ask the beneficiary for repayment.
14. Banks deal exclusively with documents means they are not in a position to verify whether the goods supplied are actually identical with those specified in the credit.
15. An irrevocable credit cannot be amended, revoked or cancelled.

Ⅱ. Multiple choice.
1. Banks will not accept transport documents indicating a date of shipment (    ) the expiry date stipulated in the credit or amendments.
    A. before         B. prior to         C. later than         D. on
2. Documentary credit means payment against (    ) instead of against (    ).
    A. goods...documents              B. documents...goods
    C. documents...endorsement        D. acceptance...documents
3. The (    ) bank should ensure that the seller's documents are drawn up by complying with the credit terms before such documents are paid for and forwarded to the (    ) bank for final reimbursement.
    A. issuing...negotiating          B. negotiating...issuing
    C. advising...paying              D. paying...advising
4. L/C is (    ).
    A. seller's credit    B. buyer's credit    C. bank credit    D. commercial credit
5. The letter of credit process has been standardized by a set of rules published by the International Chamber of Commerce(ICC). These rules are referred to as *the Uniform Customs and Practice for Documentary Credit* and are currently listed in ICC Publication No. 600. So, it is binding on all parties (    ).
    A. because it is international law
    B. unless expressly modified or excluded by the credit
    C. when the text of the credit expressly indicates that it is subject to these rules
    D. all the above wrong
6. (    ) is the bank that adds its definite undertaking, in addition to that of the issuing bank, to honor or negotiate a complying presentation.
    A. Issuing banks    B. Advising bank    C. Paying bank    D. Confirming bank
7. (    ) is the bank that negotiates or discounts the beneficiary's bill of exchange.
    A. Issuing banks    B. Advising bank    C. Negotiating bank    D. Confirming bank
8. A documentary credit available by sight payment will specifically nominate (    ) which is to pay without recourse (meaning the payment is final), unless payment is made under reserve, the

stipulated sum immediately against presentation to it of the required documents.

 A. Issuing banks    B. Advising bank    C. Negotiating bank    D. Paying bank

9. The Opening Banks of the L/C deal with (　　).

 A. services           B. goods

 C. documents          D. performance to which the documents may relate

10. At the request of the Buyer, L/C is an Conditioned Guaranty of payment Issued by Bank. Here the word "Conditioned" means (　　).

 A. the seller delivers the goods on time    B. the seller makes the shipment on time

 C. the seller prepares the documents on time   D. the doctrine of strict compliance

11. According to Documentary Credit, the (　　), on receipt of a letter of credit, will have to prepare the shipment of the contract goods within the delivery date.

 A. seller      B. buyer      C. customer      D. agent

12. The (　　) bank should ensure that the seller's documents are drawn up in accordance with the credit terms and negotiate them with recourse, then forward to the (　　) bank for final reimbursement.

 A. issuing...negotiating       B. negotiating...issuing

 C. advising...paying        D. paying...advising

## Ⅲ. Case study.

1. There is an export order that both exporter and importer entered into a contract and the exporter had already prepared the goods before the shipment date stipulated in the contract.

 **Questions：**

 (1) If the settlement method is collection, can the exporter load the goods for export immediately? Why?

 (2) If the goods are paid by the L/C, which has not been received from abroad yet, can the exporter load for export immediately? Why?

2. The importer and the exporter had signed a trade contract, in which the commercial specification of the goods specified by the contract was "60g of writing paper". But it was wrongly written to "60g of carbon paper" in the L/C. After the beneficiary loaded the goods, the documents were written to "60g of writing paper" in accordance with the contract.

 **Questions：**

 (1) Is the issuing bank entitled to dishonoring? Why?

 (2) If you are the beneficiary, what can you do in face of such a mistake?

3. If the documents indicate that the goods meet the requirements of the L/C and so do other aspects, that is, the documents are completely in line with the L/C. However, the real cargo condition is not perfect as required in a contract and the issuing bank has already known the truth.

 **Question：**Is the issuing bank entitled to dishonoring? Why?

4. A company exports a batch of goods with a total FOB value of USD 14,500. Now there is a foreign L/C with a value of USD15,000, which does not specify the unit price of goods loaded,

but stipulates that goods should be shipped in one consignment rather than in partial shipment.

**Question**: As for this L/C, will the company be in trouble when performing the contract and calling in loans in the future?

5. The Company MONMEN in Australian imported a batch of goods from a US Company A. MONMEN applied to its domestic Bank I for opening an L/C to Company A and designating the US Company A as the confirming bank of this L/C. Company A shipped the goods as scheduled according to L/C. After that, Company A prepared all the documents and presented for payment to the confirming bank. However, the confirming bank found that the name of the notified party written on the B/L was wrong (MONMEN was wrongly printed as MOMMEN). So, the confirming bank thought the documents were not in confirmation with the L/C and did not pay to Company A. The confirming bank immediately called the issuing bank and required the right to pay to Company A in the presence of the above discrepancies, but the issuing bank persistently refused the authority to pay. Company A thought that the issuing bank was too strict since it refused to pay the loan just because of a misprinted letter, so it sued to a local court and required the confirming bank to make a payment and bear the losses of Company A since it did not pay according to the terms of the L/C.

**Questions**: Which side should the court decide against? Company A or the confirming bank? Why?

6. A chinese company A signed an international sales contract with a US company B to sell a batch of handicrafts. Both parties agreed on the payment terms of the L/C in the contract. Company B opened the L/C according to the contract. According to the L/C, the latest date for shipment was September 30; the B/L was one of the documents that the beneficiary company A should provide to the bank and the expiry date of the L/C was October 15. Company A loaded the goods on September 13 and obtained the B/L. The date of the B/L was September 13. On October 5, company A presented documents to the bank for negotiation, but the bank refused to pay for the reason that the date for presentation of documents had past.

**Questions**: Is it correct for the bank to refuse the payment? What if October 4 is the holiday of the bank?

7. A Chinese foreign trade company exported goods to a company in South Korea by L/C, promising that both quality and quantity would be guaranteed and the cargos would be shipped on time. Subsequently, this company submitted a full set of documents in accordance with the requirements of the letter of credit to the South Korean issuing bank for payment. At that time, the market suffered a fall in price and the issuing bank also found that the name of goods in the invoice that we submitted was the abbreviation, so the bank refused to pay the purchase price. The Chinese company believed that the goods were shipped in accordance with the contract and the Korean company inspected the goods and issued a certificate of inspection, so the Chinese company insisted on the payment.

**Question**: Does the issuing bank have the right to refuse payment and why? What lessons should we learn from this case?

Ⅳ. Practice.

1. Answer the following questions according to the sample L/C:

   (1) How about the requirement on the partial shipment and transshipment?

   (2) Suppose the beneficiary has delivered the goods on Apr. 10, 2009, then when is the last day for the presentation of the documents to the bank?

Irrevocable Documentary Credit

To: Bank of China Shanghai Branch

From: The Hongkong and Shanghai Banking Corporation New York Branch

L/C No. :1678

Applicant: Home Textiles Co. Ltd. 220 Hill Street, New York, USA

Beneficiary: Shanghai Textile IMP and EXP Corporation
    20 Zhong Shan Road, Shanghai P. R. China

Date of Issue: 30 Feb. 2009

Expiry Date and Place: 30 Apr. 2009, Shanghai

Amount: USD 64,500 (Say US Dollars Sixty Four Thousand and Five Hundred Only)

Available by Negotiation with Bank of China

Against Beneficiary's Draft at 30 days sight drawn on us

Shipment From Shanghai To New York

Not Later Than 15 Apr. 2009

Partial shipments allowed

Transshipment not allowed

Documents required: Commercial Invoice in duplicate

Full set clean "on Board" Bills of lading, made out to order marked "freight prepaid" notify applicant.

Insurance Policy/Certificate covering W. A. and War Risk as per CIC 1/1/1981

Covering: 10,000 Meters 100 PCT cotton "print 54/56" at USD 6.45 per meter CIF New York

Shipping Marks: HMCO N. Y. No. 1-100

(Notation: Packed in bales of 100 meter)


2. Please check the L/C according to the related contract

(1) The related contract

SALES CONTRACT

                        S/C NO. : TXT264

                        DATE: SEP. 17, 2007

THE SELLERS: WENZHOU TRADING CO. LTD.

ADDRESS: 12 RENMIN ROAD, WENZHOU CHINA

THE BUYERS: TKAMALA CORPORATION ADDRESS: 6-7, KAWARA MACH OSAKA JAPAN

THE SELLERS AGREE TO SELL AND THE BUYERS AGREE TO BUY THE UNDER MENTIONED GOODS ACCORDING TO THE TERMS AND CONDITIONS AS STIPULATED BELOW

PORT OF SHIPMENT: SHANGHAI PORT
PORT OF DESTINATION: OSAKA PORT
TIME OF SHIPMENT: LASTEST DATE OF SHIPMENT 071020
PARTIAL SHIPMENT: ALLOWED
TRANSSHIPMENT: ALLOWED
INSURANCE: To be covered by the Seller for 110% of total invoice value against covering All Risks and War Risks as per and subject to the relevant ocean marine cargo clauses of the People's Insurance Company of China, dated 1/1/1981.
TERMS OF PAYMENT: L/C AT SIGHT
The Buyer shall establish the covering Letter of credit before sep. 30,2007, failing which the Seller reserves the right to rescind without further notice, or to accept whole or any part of the Sales Confirmation non-fulfilled by the Buyer, or, to lodge a claim for direct losses sustained, if any.
QUALITY/QUANTITY DISCREPANCY: In case of quality discrepancy, claim should be filed by the buyer within 60 days after the arrival of the goods at port of destination, while for quantity discrepancy, claim should be filed by the buyer within 30 days after the arrival of the goods at port of destination. It is understood that the seller shall not be liable for any discrepancy of the goods shipped due to the causes for which the Insurance Company, Shipping Company, other transportation organization/or Post Office are liable.
Force Majeure Clause: In the case of Force Majeure, the seller shall not be responsible for late delivery or non-delivery of the goods but shall notify the buyer by cable.
THE BUYER:                THE SELLER:

(2) The L/C
IRREVOCABLE DOCUMENTARY CREDIT
SEQUENCE OF TOTAL  *27: 1/1
FORM OF DOC. CREDIT  *40A: IRREVOCABLE
DOC. CREDIT NUMBER  *20: XT173
DATE OF ISSUE      31C: 070925
EXPIRY          *31D: DATE 071030 AT NEGOTIATIING BANK'S COUNTY
APPLICANT       *50: TKAMRA CORPORATION
                6-7, KAWARA MACH OSAKA
JAPAN
BENEFICIARY     *59: WENZHOU TRADING CO. LTD. ,
12 RENMIN ROAD, WENZHOU, CHINA
AMOUNT         *32B: CURRENCY USD AMOUNT 32 800.00
AVAILABLE WITH/BY  *41D: OSAKA BANK NEW YORK BRANCH
BY NEGOTIATION
DRAFT AT...     42C: DRAFTS AT 30 DAYS AFTER SIGHT FOR FULL INVOICE COST
DRAWEE         *42D: *FUJI BANK

\* 1013 SAKULA OTOLIKINGZA MACH
\* OSAKA
\* JAPAN
PARTIAL SHIPMENT   43P: NOT ALLOWED
TRANSSHIPMENT      43T: NOT ALLOWED
LOADING IN CHARGE   44A: SHANGHAI PORT
FOR TRANSPORT TO....  44B: OSAKA PORT
LATEST DATE OF SHIP.  44C: 071020
DESCRIPT. OF GOODS 45A: CHINESE GREEN TEA AS PER S/C NO. TXT 264
     CIF OSAKA PORT
DOCUMENTS REQUIRED 46A:
 + SIGNED INVOICE 2 AND 4 COPIES.
 + PACKING LIST 1 AND 4 COPIES.
 + CERTIFICATE OF ORIGINAL GSP CHINA FORM A ISSUED BY THE CHAMBER OF COMMERCE OR OTHER AUTHORITY DULY ENTITLED FOR THIS PURPOSE
 + FULL SET OF NEGOTIABLE INSURANCE POLICY FOR 120PCT OF INVOICE VALUE, COVERING ALL RISKS
 + FULL SET OF ORIGINAL CLEAN ON BOARD MARINE BILL OF LADING MADE OUT OF SHIPPERS AND BLANK ENDORSED, MARKED FREIGHT PREPAID AND NOTIFY APPLICANT
 + QUALITY CERTIFICATE IS TO BE EFFECTED BEFORE SHIPMENT AND IS REQUIRED FROM THE INSPECTING AGENCY DESIGNATED BY THE BUYER FREIGHT PREPAID AND NOTIFY APPLICANT
 CHARGES 71B: ALL BANK CHARGES IN CONNECTION WITH THIS DOCUMENTARY CREDIT EXCEPT ISSUING BANK'S OPENING COMMISSION AND TRANSMISSION COSTS ARE FOR THE BENEFICIARY.
 PRESENTATION PERIOD  48: WITHIN 15 DAYS AFTER THE DATE OF SHIPMENT BUT WITHIN THE VALIDITY OF THE CREDIT.

3. China Camping Shanghai Import and Export Corporation signed a contract with Sport and Camping Co., Ltd. of New York to export 5,000 tents valued at USD10.00/PC FOB Shanghai. Shipping marks are not needed. It was required that all the goods should be shipped before 10 December, 2002. On 25 November, the Company received an irrevocable letter of credit issued by the Bank of New York on 23 November, 2002 with China Camping Shanghai Import and Export Corporation as beneficiary. The issuer was Sport and Camping Co., Ltd. of New York, letter of credit number was A00920, letter of credit amount reached USD50,000.00 (less than 5% decline allowed) and expiry date of the letter of credit is before 23 December, 2002. The company prepared all the goods and shipped goods before 5 December (the latest shipment date stipulated in the letter of credit). The number of shipments has increased by 3% compared with the original plan. The company was prepared to negotiate through the Shanghai Branch of Bank of China. Please make a documentary bill and a commercial bill of exchange in accordance with the above

information.
4. China's exporter X exports certain mechanical product to the United States and applies for a USD2 million credit limit to the export factor. Export factor A contacts the foreign import factor B to obtain a credit of USD1.2 million from the latter. The exporter X signed a USD1.5 million export contract with the U.S. importer Y. After shipping, exporter X applies for financing to export factor A and importer factor B prepays USD1 million. American importer Y refuses to pay, insisting that there is a problem with the quality of the goods (the reason is that the goods are the same type as the previously purchased one that also has the problem). Import factor B exempts bad debt guarantee liability on the grounds of trade disputes. Exporter X believes that Y's refusal should not be accepted. And X further gets to know that the actual reason for Y's refusal is that Y's buyer, a Mexican importer under is bankrupt and the goods are under the bank's control. Thus, Y cannot receive the payment. Therefore, X demands that Y provide quality inspection, yet ignored by Y. Y has not paid yet after the 90-day payment period. X entrusts import factor B to sue Y in the United States, however, Y refuses to cooperate in a negative attitude.

Does importer Y's reason for refusal make sense? Why is the import factor holding a negative attitude? Can it exempt the responsibility of bad debt guarantee?

# Chapter 6

# Bank's Letter of Guarantee

## Learning Objective

- To have a definite understanding of the concept, property, related parties with their rights and liabilities, basic procedures in processing, and main classifications of the bank's letter of guarantee.

## 6.1 An Overview of Bank's Letter of Guarantee

### 6.1.1 The Definition and Property of Bank's Letter of Guarantee

A letter of guarantee, L/G in short, is a written document of credit guaranty given by banks, insurance companies, guarantee companies or individuals (guarantors) to a third party (beneficiary) referring to the request of the applicant, which can ensure that if the applicant fails to fulfill its responsibilities or obligations according to the mutual agreements, the guarantor has to be responsible for the payment or the economic compensation within a certain time and amount limit. Among them, the letter of guarantee given by banks is called a bank's letter of guarantee.

The letter of guarantee can be divided into two parts: letter of accessory guarantee and letter of independent guarantee, based on different situations in the letter of guarantee, including the conditions that beneficiary could obtain payment from the guarantor, the conditions that the guarantor should fulfill his/her responsibilities, or the relations between the letter of guarantee and the basic business contract (such as business contract).

The letter of accessory guarantee is a subsidiary agreement of business contracts, whose legal effects are related to the existence and variations of business contracts. Under the conditions in the letter of accessory guarantee, the bank should bear secondary obligation, which means that when the beneficiary demands compensation, the guarantor should investigate the facts that whether the applicant has fulfilled the basic contracts and confirm that whether the applicant has any non-compliance behaviors, after which the guarantor bank will bear the compensation according to the degree of non-compliance by the guarantor.

The letter of independent guarantee is based on the business contracts, but once set up, it would have independent legal effects which would not be influenced by the existence of business contracts, which can also be called self-sufficiency contract documents. Under the conditions in the letter of independent guarantee, the bank should bear primary obligation, which means that once the beneficiary, under the conditions of letter of independent guarantee, presents a written requirement for compensation and bills according to the letter of guarantee, the guarantor bank has to pay the compensations no matter with the agreement of the applicant or not, and the guarantor bank does not need to investigate the facts that whether the business contracts are fulfilled or not.

The letter of independent guarantee is granted by banks so that it is usually called a bank's letter of guarantee. The guarantor bank bears absolute payment responsibility according to the requirements in the guarantee so that the bank's letter of guarantee is generally demand guarantee.

According to Article 2 of *the Uniform Rules for Demand Guarantees*, ICC Publication No. 758 (*URDG 758* for short) drew up by the International Chamber of Commerce, the demand guarantees are guarantees, bonds and other payment undertakings under which the duty of the guarantor or issuer to make payment arises on "the presentation of a written demand and any other documents specified in the guarantee and is not conditional on actual default by the principal in the underlying transaction".

Accordingly, the guarantor bank of demand guarantees has primary and direct payment responsibility to the beneficiary.

## 6.1.2 The Parties and Their Rights and Liabilities in Bank's Letter of Guarantee

The parties of the bank's letter of guarantee include main parties such as the applicant, the beneficiary, the guarantor bank and so on, and other parties such as advising bank, confirming bank, reissuing bank, counter guarantor and so on. The main responsibilities of these parties and the relationships between them in the bank's letter of guarantee are as follows:

### 6.1.2.1 The Main Parties and Their Rights and Liabilities in Bank's Letter of Guarantee

(1) The Applicant

The applicant, also called the principal, is the person at whose request the bank issues the guarantee.

The main responsibilities of the applicant include to pay the guarantor bank of issuing the guarantee, to bear the obligation of fulfilling the agreement, and to pay compensation to the guarantor bank after its fulfillment of the agreement.

In the process, the identity of the applicant is different according to different business contracts, such as the bidder in the guarantee for a bid bond, the provider of goods and labor in the export performance guarantee, the importer in the import guarantee, and the borrower or debtor in the repayment guarantee.

(2) The Beneficiary

The beneficiary is the person who receives the letter of guarantee and asks for compensation to the guarantor bank according to the items in the letter of guarantee.

The beneficiary wishes to be secured against the risk of the principal's not fulfilling his/her obligations towards the beneficiary in respect of the underlying transaction for which the demand guarantee is given. The beneficiary has his/her responsibility to fulfill the business contract, together with the right to ask the guarantor bank for compensation. Being similar with the principal, the beneficiary is also different from each other in terms with different business contracts and letter of guarantees, such as the tenderer in the guarantee for bid bond, the importer in the export performance guarantee, the owner of project in the performance guarantee and advance payment guarantee of project and so on.

### (3) The Guarantor

The guarantor can be also called the guarantor bank in which the letter of guarantee is issued.

All documents specified and presented under a guarantee, including the demand, shall be examined by the guarantor with reasonable care to ascertain whether or not they appear on their face comply with the terms of the guarantee. Where such documents do not appear so to conform or appear on their face to be inconsistent with one another, they shall be refused.

In practice, after paying back to the beneficiary, the guarantor will have the right to press the applicant for payment. Meanwhile, before issuing the letter of guarantee with the request of the applicant, the guarantor could draw some prerequisite, asking the applicant to provide certain mortgage or counter-guarantee, in order to ensure the security of himself.

Being the same with the documentary L/C, there are three kinds of contract relationships among three main parties mentional-above, basic business contract relationship between the applicant and the beneficiary; contract relationship between the applicant and the guarantor bank, taking the application of issuing a bank's letter of guarantee which is issued by the applicant and accepted by the guarantor bank as the symbol; and contract relationship between the guarantor bank and the beneficiary, with the bank's letter of guarantee as the symbol. In the practical process of operation, in addition to the three main parties above, there is another certain party which is called the advising bank.

### (4) The Advising Bank

The advising bank can be also called the transmitting bank, which would inform or transmit the guarantee to the beneficiary according to the request and application of the guarantor bank. The advising bank is generally the local bank of the beneficiary. There should be a local bank examining the authenticity of the guarantee on behalf of the beneficiary because they could not examine the authenticity of the guarantee they received by themselves. In the process of operation, the advising bank is only responsible to examine the authenticity of the guarantee, including examining the authenticity and accuracy of the seal and the test key of the guarantor bank on behalf of the beneficiary.

#### 6.1.2.2 The Other Parties of the Bank's Letter of Guarantee

In addition to the main parties above, the bank's letter of guarantee will be related to the other following parties:

### (1) The Confirming Bank

The confirming bank, also known as the second guarantor, means adding confirmation to the guarantee according to the requirements of the guarantor. With low publicity, poor credit, and a large amount of guarantee which has exceeded the line of credit of guarantor bank abroad, the bank issuing guarantee would be required by the beneficiary to find other banks who can add confirmation to the guarantee. Once the latter accepts the request and provides confirmation to the relevant guarantees, they can be called the confirming bank.

The confirming bank is entitled to charge a confirmation fee as his/her guarantee of the risks. If it is no use for the confirming bank to fulfill its confirmation responsibilities or the confirming has got compensation after his fulfillment of its confirmation responsibilities, the confirmation fee will be the income of the confirming bank.

(2) **The Reissuing Bank**

In line with the requirements of the guarantor bank, the reissuing bank issues guarantee to the beneficiary with the counter-guarantee of the guarantor bank. The reissuing bank is generally the local bank of the beneficiary.

(3) **The Counter Guarantor**

The counter guarantor would be the person who issues the written letter of counter-guarantee for the applicant to the guarantor bank. And the counter guarantor is generally the applicant's superiors, export credit insurance companies, other banks or non-bank financial institutions and so on.

Anti-guarantor liability is to ensure the applicant to fulfill contractual obligations, and commitment to the guarantor, under the guarantee when the line guarantee payments, guarantee lines can be compensated in full and in a timely manner from the reaction of the guarantor.

The responsibilities of the counter-guarantor are as follows: to ensure that the applicant to fulfill the contractual obligations, and to commit to the guarantor that after guarantor bank's payment according to the guarantee, the guarantor bank could get enough compensation from the counter-guarantor.

## 6.2 The Functions and Contents of Bank's Letter of Guarantee

### 6.2.1 The Functions of Bank's Letter of Guarantee

(1) **To Provide Guarantee**

To provide guarantee means financial compensation should be given to creditors if the primary debtor defaults. In the bank's letter of guarantee, the right to get a payment of beneficiaries depends only on the conditions in the guarantee. The bank will be the primary debtor and will assume all the obligations of the beneficiaries once it agrees to issue the letter of independent guarantee. After paying funds of the guarantee to the beneficiaries, the guarantor bank will have the right of immediate recourse to the primary debtor. Therefore, the guarantor bank would be in a credit risk so that it usually needs compensation to reduce the risk, rather than acting as an insurer.

(2) **To Distribute Risks among Parties**

The distribution of risks among parties can be represented in the bank's letter of guarantee. And the degree and extent of risk distribution depend on the type of the payment terms.

In the demand guarantee, the beneficiary could get payment only with documents which are consistent with the terms of the guarantee superficially. As a trusted financial institution, the guarantor bank usually gives the payment without any delay not only because of its good reputation, but also because of its right of immediate recourse to the primary debtor. However, if the primary debtor believes he/she has fulfilled its contractual obligation correctly, it will be rather difficult for him/her to get the payment back.

**(3) The Redemption Function of the Demand Guarantee**

If the beneficiary believes the primary debtor defaults, he/she will get the payment by submitting documents and bills which are the same with the guarantee superficially without confirmation of the default action of the primary debtor. Another important function of the demand guarantee is that it can make the beneficiaries be enabled to put stress on the debtors with the guarantee in order to make them fulfill the contract in accordance with his/her request.

**(4) To Be a Financing Instrument**

When the primary debtor needs to give advance payment or intermediate payment to the beneficiary, the bank's letter of guarantee can be used as a substitute in order to defer a payment which is equal to giving financial convenience to the primary debtor.

**(5) The Testimony Function**

With the only qualified person, the bank's letter of guarantee can prove the performance capacity of the applicant. Issuing a guarantee means to give an irrevocable commitment of payment so that the banks would not promise to pay without comprehensive investigation of the financial strength and performance capacity of the applicant and satisfactory results. And also, the dealer without the bank's letter of guarantee will not be a trustworthy business partner.

## 6.2.2 Main Contents of Bank's Letter of Guarantee

All instructions for the issue of guarantee and amendments thereto and guarantees and amendments themselves should be clear and precise and should avoid excessive details.

Accordingly, all guarantees should stipulate:

**(1) Primary Parties**

Primary parties include the principal, the beneficiary, and the guarantor.

In practice, if there is any confirming bank, advising bank or reissuing bank, the name and address of them should be listed in the guarantee.

**(2) The Underlying Transaction of the Guarantee**

The underlying contract is the basis of issuing a guarantee. And the relationship with the underlying contract should be explained in the beginning part of the preface of the guarantee, including bid bond, performance guarantee, payment guarantee and so on. Raising an underlying contract which is the basis of issuing a guarantee aims to declare not only the purpose of providing the guarantee and risks prevention, but also with what kind of basic relationship to request the guarantee. The underlying contract should be concise, containing not only names of the applicant and the beneficiary, but also the date when the underlying contract is signed or when the bid document is submitted, and the serial numbers of the contract or bid document, together with other concise description of the object, such as the supply of the goods. The guarantee has pointed out that the underlying contract cannot change the letter of independent guarantee into the letter of accessory guarantee.

### (3) The Maximum Payable Amount and Payable Currency

The payable amount and currency should be stipulated in the guarantee contract definitely (The payable amount could be represented differently from an underlying contract with different currencies). As for the guarantor bank, to clear the specific obligations in the guarantee is of great importance, otherwise, it will suffer the unimaginable risks.

### (4) The Expiry Date and/or Expiry Event of the Guarantee

Firstly, the Effective Date of the Guarantee. The guarantee will be effective once it is issued unless there are other specified terms in it. In advance payment guarantee, performance guarantee, and payment guarantee, once the guarantee goes into effect, the beneficiary can make his/her request to the guarantor bank even if the deadline for the debtor to fulfill contractual obligations according to underlying contract has not yet arrived.

Secondly, the Expiration Date of the Guarantee. The expiration date should be stipulated in the guarantee. No matter there is an expiration term in the bank's letter of guarantee or not, once the guarantee is given back to the guarantor bank or the beneficiary has a written statement to release the responsibilities of the guarantor bank, the guarantee is canceled no matter the guarantee or the amendment is give back to the guarantor bank.

Thirdly, the Extension Term in the Guarantee. In the bid bond or performance guarantee, the beneficiary is often given the right to extend the effective period and the effective period of the guarantee can be extended properly according to the request of the beneficiary.

Fourthly, the Refund Term of the Guarantee. The guarantee should stipulate that the beneficiary should give the letter of guarantee back to the guarantor bank if the guarantee expires. This can not only give the guarantor bank great convenience to do cancellation procedures, but also avoid unnecessary disputes. In practice, it will be difficult to give the letter of guarantee back. If there is such a term in the guarantee, it should be clear that this term does nothing related to the rights of the beneficiary.

E. g. 1: "Upon its expiration, this L/G shall be null and void, and please immediately return it to us for cancellation."

E. g. 2: "If we receive no claim from the beneficiary on or before (date), then this guarantee shall become automatically null and void."

Fifthly, Lack of Expiry Terms. If the expiry date is not specified in the guarantee, the guarantee will be taken into use indefinitely in addition to some exceptional cases.

### (5) The Terms for Demanding Payment

After receiving the written demand for payment or written demand for payment together with other documents stipulated in the guarantee (such as related certification, the judgment report of the court, and the arbitration award), it will be confirmed that whether these documents are the same with the terms in the guarantee superficially which means to pay the payment terms stipulated in the payment guarantee.

Any payment terms in the guarantee shall be in written form, while other files stipulated in the guarantee shall also be in written form.

**(6) Any Provision for Reduction of the Guarantee Amount**

It is also known as the term of diminishing guarantee amount whose function is that when the applicant begins to fulfill the underlying contract, the maximum guarantee amount will be reduced accordingly. And this term is widely used in the advance payment refund guarantee.

In addition, there will be some prerequisite terms which stipulate that the guarantee can be only taken into effect when the prerequisites are fulfilled rather than the issuing date of the guarantee. Therefore, the beneficiary can only request compensation according to the terms in the guarantee when some important prerequisites related to the underlying contract are fulfilled.

## 6.3 The Types of Bank's Letter of Guarantee

The bank's letter of guarantee can be divided into different types in terms of different standards.

### 6.3.1 The Letter of Independent Guarantee and the Letter of Accessory Guarantee

Bank's letter of guarantee can be divided into the letter of independent guarantee and the letter of accessory guarantee according to the liabilities of the guarantor bank. These two categories are described in detail and there is no use to repeat.

### 6.3.2 The Direct Guarantee and Indirect Guarantee

The letter of guarantee can be divided into the direct guarantee and indirect guarantee on the basis of whether the guarantor and the beneficiary are from the same country or region.

The direct guarantee is issued by the bank of the principal directly rather than the bank of the beneficiary's country.

The indirect guarantee is issued by the local bank of the beneficiary. At this time, the principal would make a request to his/her bank (the instructing bank) to give an instruction to the bank of the beneficiary (the guarantor bank) to issue a guarantee. In indirect guarantee, the instructing bank has no contractual relationship with the beneficiary and the beneficiary can request the instructing bank about the payment directly.

### 6.3.3 Letter of Guarantee to Settlement and Letter of Guarantee to Credit

The letter of guarantee can be divided into letter of guarantee to settlement and letter of guarantee to credit according to the basic functions of bank's letter of guarantee.

Letter of guarantee to settlement is a letter of independent guarantee which can be used as a tool for transaction settlement with the guarantor bank taking the primary settlement responsibility. Letter of guarantee to credit is a letter of accessory guarantee or letter of independent guarantee which can be used as a tool for payment guarantee or performance guarantee with the guarantor bank taking the accessory of primary payment or compensation responsibility.

## 6.3.4 Limited Amount Guarantee and Unlimited Amount Guarantee

The letter of guarantee can be divided into limited amount guarantee and unlimited amount guarantee in terms of whether it has a limited amount or not.

Limited amount guarantee means the guarantor is responsible for only a certain amount of the debt (either a cumulative limit or non-cumulative limit), and any debt beyond the limit is not under the responsibility of the guarantor.

Unlimited amount guarantee refers to that the guarantor is responsible for all the debt of the borrower including not only the principal and interest, but also Another debt arises from the loan directly. Another debt here refers to the additional compensation given to the lender from the borrower which comes from the compensation events stipulated in the loan agreements for lenders, such as various taxes, liquidated damages and so on.

## 6.3.5 Revocable Letter of Guarantee and Irrevocable Letter of Guarantee

The letter of guarantee can be divided into the revocable letter of guarantee and the irrevocable letter of guarantee according to the validity of the guarantee.

An revocable letter of guarantee means that the guarantor can do modification and revocation of the original guarantee without the agreements of other parties. An irrevocable letter of guarantee cannot be modified or revoked without agreements of all the related parties.

The guarantees are generally irrevocable. In order to avoid disputes, the beneficiary generally requires the guarantee marked with the words of "irrevocable".

## 6.3.6 Limited Duration Guarantee and Unlimited Duration Guarantee

The guarantee can be divided into limited duration guarantee and unlimited duration guarantee according to the validity.

The limited duration guarantee has stipulated the effective date of the guarantee's responsibility so that the beneficiary should raise payment requirements within a specific period. Otherwise, the guarantor has the right to refuse payment. To stipulate the effective date is very important to the guarantor because the beneficiary will have the unlimited right to ask guarantor for compensation without the stipulation of effective date which may put the guarantor into unpredictable risks.

Unlimited duration guarantee does not stipulate the effective date. The responsibility of the guarantor would not vanish before all the rights of the beneficiary are fulfilled and the beneficiary can ask the guarantor for compensation at any time unless something ruled by the law happens.

## 6.3.7 The Export Guarantee, Import Guarantee, Loan Guarantee and Other Guarantees

The bank's letter of guarantee can be divided into the export guarantee, import guarantee, loan guarantee, and other guarantees according to their different functions.

#### 6.3.7.1 Export Guarantee

Export guarantee refers to various credit guarantees that with the application of international trade exporters, the banks issue these guarantees to the importers in order to give a guarantee of exporters' fulfillment of the bid contracts or certain responsibilities in the trade contract. The export guarantee includes the following five types:

(1) **Tender Guarantee**

The tender guarantor, also called bid bond, is a written guarantee certificate issued by the bank (the guarantor) to the tenderer (the beneficiary), with the application of the bidder (the applicant), in order to guarantee not only the bidder could not cancel the bid or modify the bid conditions by himself/herself before bid opening, but also the bidder should sign the contract, issue performance guarantee or other guarantees required in the bid document, and fulfill the responsibilities committed in the bid document after winning the bid. Otherwise, the guarantor bank has to pay a certain amount of compensation to the tenderer (The amount is generally a percentage of the bidder's total offer.) in order to compensate the losses due to the bidder and to find another bidder. If the bidder loses, the tender guarantee should be returned to the bidder by the tenderer in order to release the guarantee's responsibility of the guarantor.

(2) **The Performance Guarantee**

The performance guarantee is a written undertaking which is issued by the bank to the beneficiary in order to guarantee that the applicant would fulfill the responsibilities in the contract at the request of the applicant. In the effective period of the guarantee, if the applicant defaults contract, the bank (the guarantor) will give a certain amount compensation which is stipulated in the guarantee to the beneficiary at his/her request.

In the process of bidding, the bidders can require the guarantor bank to add terms in the bid bond to describe that if the bidder has won the bid, the guarantee can be transformed to performance guarantee automatically and the amount of guarantee can be adjusted according to specific conditions in order to simplify procedures.

In the contract projects, the performance guarantee is a kind of written credit document which is often issued by the bank to the owners at the request of the contractors in order to guarantee that they could fulfill the contracts. The main responsibilities of the guarantor are to guarantee that the contractors could complete the project on time with good quality and enough quantity. Once the contractor scraps the contract, suspends the project arbitrarily, declares bankruptcy and liquidation and so on, the guarantor has to give all the guaranteed money to the beneficiary as compensation. The guarantee amount of the performance guarantee is often 10% to 25% of the whole project cost.

(3) **The Advanced Payment Guarantee**

The advanced payment guarantee can be also called the down payment guarantee or repayment guarantee, which is issued by the bank (the guarantor) at the request of the goods provided (the applicant) to the goods buyer (the beneficiary). It is also a kind of written credit guarantee. In the advance payment guarantee, if the labor provider could not provide the labors and services according to the contract, the guarantor bank will be responsible to pay the money that is already given by the beneficiary back.

The advanced payment guarantee can be used not only in contract project, but also in the international trade in which it is a written guarantee certificate which is issued by the bank (the guarantor) at the request of the goods provider to the goods importer (the beneficiary). And it has stipulated that if the goods provider cannot provide the labors or goods in terms of the contract, the guarantor bank will be responsible to pay the money that is already paid by the beneficiary back.

### (4) The Quality Guarantee or Repair/Maintenance Guarantee

The difference between the quality guarantee and the repair guarantee is that the quality guarantee is often used in the import and export business while the repair guarantee is more often used in the international labor and service contract projects. However, in the export of complete sets of projects, aircraft, ships and other large projects, the repair guarantee is also used.

In the export and import business, the buyer often requires the seller to provide the bank's letter of quality guarantee in order to ensure the received goods are qualified. If the goods delivered by the seller could not reach the quality standard in the contract, the seller has to change goods or give compensation to the buyer. Otherwise, the guarantor bank is responsible for the compensation. In the international labor and service contract projects, the owners of the projects would require the contractors to provide the bank's letter of repair guarantee in order to ensure the quality of the projects. If the quality of the projects is not inconsistent with the contracts, the contractors have the responsibility to repair or to give the compensation. Otherwise, the guarantor bank has to give the compensation to the owner of the project.

### (5) The Retention Money Guarantee

In the export and import of large-scale machinery equipment in the international trade and the international contract projects, when the importers or project owners pay for the goods or projects, they often leave certain amount of retention money which can be given to the exporters and contractors according to the conditions of the projects after the successful testing, accepting and using imported equipment or a period after the completion of the projects. However, with a large projects and large amount of capital, it will bring much inconvenience to the exporters and contractors. In order to get retention money back in advance, the exporters and contractors usually give applications to domestic banks to issue retention money guarantee, with the importers and project owners as the beneficiary. If the seller could not provide qualified goods or complete qualified project according to the contract, the exporters and contractors would give the retention money back to the importers or the project owners. Otherwise, the bank is responsible for the compensation. The amount of the guarantee is often 5% of the total price in the contract, and the effective date is different because of different subject matters which are determined by the contracting parties.

### 6.3.7.2 Import Guarantee

The import guarantee, at the request of the importers in the international trade, is issued to the exporters in order to ensure that if the exporter has fulfilled the trade contract, the importer will make payment according to the contract or fulfill the obligations in various credit guarantees and payment guarantees. The import guarantees can be divided into the following three types:

(1) **The Payment Guarantee and Deferred Payment Guarantee**

This is a written guarantee document which is issued by the bank at the request of the importers in order to ensure that the importers would fulfill part of or all the payment obligations after the exporters have provided the related goods and technical materials. Otherwise, after receiving the compensation claim notification from the exporters, the guarantor bank has to pay all the funds instead of the exporters. In the deferred payment guarantee, with the importer's fulfillment of the contract, the responsibility and the amount of payment would decrease correspondingly.

(2) **The Shipping Guarantee**

The shipping guarantee can be also called the letter of guarantee for production of bill of a lading (L/G for Production of B/L). In credit business, when the goods reach the port of destination before the shipping documents, importers would like to take delivery of the goods, declare goods at the customs and sell them timely before getting the bill of lading in order to avoid deterioration or backlog of the goods. The shipping companies will require the importer to provide a guarantee with the sign of the bank in order to avoid losses. The guarantee claims that importers are responsible for the losses of shipping companies because of the advanced delivery and they should give the documents back after they get the B/L of the goods.

When requiring these kinds of guarantees to the banks, the importers need to make guarantees to the credit issuing bank that whether the document is conforming to the provisions of the letter of credit or not, they make payment on time. The banks should also pay attention to this when signing such bill of lading and mark out "Guaranteed Delivery" on the L/C, together with charge of the importers.

(3) **The Leasing Guarantee**

The main reason for the leasing guarantee which is generally a written guarantee document issued by the bank, is to ensure the repayment of the rental fee. If the lessee does not fulfill or not completely fulfill the responsibility of paying the rental fee when it expires, the guarantor bank should be responsible for paying the rental fee.

In general, the guarantee will take effect since the issuing day. In practice, when issuing the leasing guarantee, the guarantor and the applicant should try their best to make the leasing guarantee come into effect after the arriving and successful checking of the objects, or after the delivery of the objects of the lesser and providing the bills which can prove the delivery of the objects. The specific time depends on specific circumstances, which comes from the negotiation of both the applicant and the beneficiary. The expiry date of the guarantee is the day when the last payment of the rental fee is finished, but it will be better to determine a definite expiration date. It should be stipulated clearly in the leasing guarantee that the guarantee is responsibility of the guarantor in the leasing guarantee will decrease with each part of the payment is made. In addition, it can be also noted in the guarantee that the lessee or the guarantor has the right to take all the taxes and other expenses of the lesser at the location of the lessee off from the lease payment.

### 6.3.7.3 Counter Trade Guarantee

The counter trade can be called as the import-inspiring trade, which mainly includes compensation trade and outward processing trade and it is the common trade which is commonly used in developing countries in the early stages of the economic development. In the counter trade, the two parties export and import from and to each other. To use the bank's letter of guarantee rationally can be the better safeguard of the interests of the parties and the transactions. These kinds of guarantees include the following several types:

**(1) The Guarantee under Compensation Trade**

In compensation trade, from the provision of equipment and technology to the completion of the compensation trade will take such a long time so that the party who provides the equipment and technology often requires guarantee about introducing equipment and technical direction in order to avoid the interest losses.

**(2) The Guarantee for Processing of Imported Material**

The guarantee for processing of imported material is a kind of written guarantee document which is issued by the banks at the request of importers in order to guarantee that after receiving the raw materials and components which are inconsistent with the contract from the exporters, the importers can use them to process and assemble, and then deliver the end product to the exporters and a certain third party according to the basic contract. If the importers could not fulfill the contract or pay the raw materials, components and additional interest in cash, the guarantor bank will make the payment instead. The amount of the guarantee for processing of imported material is usually the price of raw materials and components.

### 6.3.7.4 Loan Guarantee

The loan guarantee refers to various credit guarantees that are provided by the debtor to the creditor, in which a bank guarantees that the debtor would fulfill his/her responsibilities of repayment, otherwise, the guarantor bank is responsible for a certain amount of compensation to the creditor, among different forms of international loan relationships.

**(1) The Bank Guarantee for Loan**

Before making loans, the lender usually does a thorough investigation of the creditworthiness, ability to repay, and other aspects of the borrower. In addition, the lender often requires the borrower to provide a bank's letter of guarantee which can be a guarantee of repayment in order to ensure the loan can be repaid. This kind of bank's letter of guarantee is the bank guarantee for a loan. It is a written guarantee document issued by the guarantor bank to the lender at the borrower's request, which can ensure that the borrower can repay the loan with interests according to the provisions in the loan agreement. If the borrower defaults, the guarantor must repay all the money that should be repaid by the borrower to the lender.

**(2) The Overdrawn/Overdraft Guarantee**

Overdraft is a kind of lending that the bank allows depositors to draw checks and be given payment beyond their bank balance within the agreed period. The customers have to pay for the interests of the overdraft payment and be responsible to repay at any time. Overdraft which needs customers to provide collateral is called overdraft secured while overdraft without any collateral is called fiduciary overdraft. The overdraft guarantee is the written guarantee document which is used by outward contracted engineering construction companies or other overseas institutions. When they are doing business or construction abroad, they can make applications to local banks of overdraft accounts in order to guarantee that the applicant can make up the overdraft repayment, together with interests and fees of the bank on time according to the overdraft contract. The amount of overdraft guarantee is usually the overdraft limit which is stipulated in the overdraft contract by the principal and a local bank.

#### 6.3.7.5　Other Special Guarantees

**(1) The Guarantee for the Customs Duties**

This kind of guarantee is applied in the international contracted project, exhibitions, fairs and so on, and the amount of the guarantee is often the tariff regulated by the customs. In the international contracted project, the construction sector of one country is doing construction in another country. When they transport the construction machinery to the target country, the customs in target country will impose a tariff which will be returned to the contractor when they transport the machinery back to their own country. If the contractor does not transport the machinery back country, the machinery will be imposed the imported goods so that the tariff will not be returned. In this case, the contractor often makes request to local banks to issue a guarantee for custom duties to guarantee that the contractor would transport the machinery back to the country after finishing the construction project to the customs of the target country in order to accelerate cash flow and avoid the troubles of capital tying up and tariff returning. Otherwise, the guarantor bank will pay the tariff.

In the international exhibitions and fairs, one country would encounter the same situation when they ship the exhibitions to another country. Exhibitions holders and fairs holders would provide the same bank's letter of guarantee in order to avoid the troubles of capital tying up and tariff returning. The content of the guarantee is the same as above.

**(2) The Guarantee for Maritime Accident**

With the guarantee for maritime accident, in the processing of transportation of the goods with ships and other means of transport, the ships owner or the transportation company would pay the compensation to the goods owner or the party with losses when there is an accident happening, including the shortage of goods, damage of goods, and losses caused by the ships owner or the transportation company, or other accidents at sea including collision with damages of seaport facilities and other ships, disputes of ship contracts, maritime accidents, marine pollution, and detaining because of violation of laws such as being suspected of being involved in the smuggling. Otherwise, the guarantor bank would pay the compensation. The reason why the ships owner and the transportation company apply for guarantees is that when these accidents happen, the authorities would detain the ships in order to do an investigation, obtaining of evidence and then the final court judgment for a period of time which will take a long time. And the transportation company could take the guarantee as a kind of bail to be in exchange for the release of the detained ships in order to avoid economic losses which are caused by the detaining of the ships for a long time.

# Chapter 6  Bank's Letter of Guarantee

## Questions:

### Ⅰ. Multiple choice.

1. To issue a letter of guarantee represents a certain legal obligation and the division of responsibility between (    ).
   A. the accountee and guarantee bank
   B. accountee and the advising bank
   C. accountee and beneficiary
   D. the guarantee bank and the transmitting bank

2. The letter of guarantee that seller or the contractor (the accountee) entrusts the bank to issue to the buyer or the proprietor (beneficiary) to guarantee the refund the payment that equals to the amount of advance payment, or the amount of advance payment corresponding to the part of the contract which has not been fulfilled when failing to fulfill the contract, is called (    ).
   A. Maintenance Guarantee
   B. Performance Guarantee
   C. Retention Money Guarantee
   D. Advance Payment guarantee

3. The beneficiary of the shipping guarantee is (    ).
   A. Bank
   B. Exporter
   C. Shipping company
   D. Importer

4. Which of the following is not the common feature shared by a bank letter of guarantee and the documentary letter of credit? (    )
   A. Both are commitments made by the bank.
   B. Both have similar forms.
   C. Both are documentation businesses.
   D. The auditing responsibility of the documents of a bank in both cases is only on the surface.

5. In (    ), the guarantor's reimbursement obligations are subordinate to or dependent on the accountee's obligations under the transaction contract. Whether the accountee breaches the contract or not should be based on the provisions of the basic contract and the actual performance, which often results in the dilemma that the bank is involved in trade disputes between buyers and sellers.
   A. Letter of Accessory Guarantee
   B. Letter of Independence Guarantee
   C. Payment Guarantee
   D. Overdraft Guarantee

6. The recipient of the security interests under the guarantee, that is, the party entitled to claim the fund according to the provisions of the guarantee by submitting a document or statement to the guarantee bank, is the (    ) of a letter of guarantee.
   A. Accountee
   B. Guarantee Bank
   C. Beneficiary
   D. Counter-guarantee Bank

7. The accountee of tender guarantee letter is (    ).

A. Government of the tendering country

B. Tenderee

C. Bidder

D. Successful bidder

8. Which of the following does not belong to the import guarantee? (    ).

    A. Payment Guarantee

    B. Lease Guarantee

    C. Shipping Guarantee

    D. Quality Guarantee

## II. True or false.

1. Issuing a guarantee means that the guarantee bank has assumed a certain liability. Therefore, in regard of its own interests, the guarantee bank will often make a detailed investigation on the accountee's basic credit and financial status, collateral and counter-guarantee measures, feasibility and effectiveness of the project, the content of the application for a guarantee or the entrusted guarantee agreement before issuing the guarantee.

2. Reissuing the guarantee is one of the most basic methods to issue a guarantee.

3. In a letter of independence guarantee, the guarantor undertakes the primary liability of payment, that is, the guarantor's payment liability is independent of the accountee's obligations under the transaction contract.

4. The amendment to the guarantee must be unanimously approved by the parties concerned. Any amendment made to the terms of the guarantee by a single party is considered invalid.

5. Any bank guarantee has confirming bank as a basic party.

6. When issuing bank guarantee for the accountee, banks will ask accountee to provide counter-guarantee in order to control possible risks on their own.

7. Amendment to bank guarantee must be unanimously approved by the parties concerned. The beneficiary applies to the guarantee bank with a written application after the approval is achieved.

8. Bank guarantee has a wider range of usage than the ordinary documentary L/C. It can be used to guarantee the fulfillment of different responsibilities and obligations of any party in the economic activities.

9. The guarantee bank assumes the guarantee is responsibility only within the guarantee period. Therefore, the beneficiary must make a claim to the guarantee bank within the prescribed time limit, otherwise, the guarantee bank may not pay or refuse to fulfill the obligation of compensation.

10. After paying the beneficiary, the guarantee bank has the right to claim against the accountee or the counter-guarantor. If the accountee cannot immediately repay the amount paid by the guarantee bank, the guarantee bank is entitled to dispose of the margin or the collateral. If the compensation is still insufficient after the disposal, the guarantee bank shall bear the loss at its own discretion (it still has the right to claim the uncompensated part).

# Chapter 7

# International Factoring

**Learning Objectives**

- To master content, nature and business processes of the international factoring.
- To understand the main parties and their responsibilities by means of the international factoring.

## 7.1 Concept and Characteristics of International Factoring

### 7.1.1 Definition

International Factoring, also known as the acquisition of accounts receivable, refers to that exporters sell goods in the form of commercial credit and then receive all or part of loan by selling invoices, bills of exchange, bills of lading and other relevant documents to factoring organizations or specialized financial companies immediately after the shipment, so as to obtain financial services. It is a form of short-term credit for the foreign trade.

After the World War II, with the development of international trade, factoring business developed rapidly. It was demonstrated in three aspects. Firstly, the number of organizations engaged in factoring business of expanding scale has been increasing, as well as the number of related organizations. There appeared Factor Chain International (FCI) internationally, which facilitates the information exchange among acquisition of accounts receivable companies of all countries and advances the development of international factoring business. Secondly, more and more countries have begun to start the factoring business. Besides Britain, which was the first country to open this business, other developed countries have also opened the factoring business. For example, the first Japanese factoring agency was approved to the establishment by the Ministry of Finance in 1972. Since then, some developing countries have been conducting factoring business in succession. Thirdly, the factoring business involves extensive trade areas. The traditional factoring business arises from the textile trade operated by means of consignment. At present, the factoring business provides service not only for the textile, food and general merchandise trade areas, but also for electronic products, furniture, machinery products and other trade areas.

### 7.1.2 Characteristics

(1) **Credit Risk Borne by Factoring Agencies**

The exporter sells the document to the factoring agency, which means that the factoring agent will not be able to exercise the right of recourse against the exporter once the importer refuses to pay the money or fails to pay on time, and the risk will be borne by the exporter himself/herself. In order to reduce the risk, the exporter who wants to allocate funds in the form of factoring shall consult with the importer on the basis of investigation results of importer's credit and suggestion on possible trade amount. It is generally requested that the trade amount should be within the recommended amount. In addition, the factoring agencies generally have a special department to conduct a comprehensive, detailed and accurate investigation of the credit information of importers. Therefore, the transactions carried out on this basis can avoid the risk of not receiving payment.

(2) **Extensive Service Factoring Business**

Factoring business provides not only convenient ways of allocating funds for exporters, but also a series of services for exporters, including the credit investigation, the collection of accounts and the commission for accounting process.

(3) **Advanced Payment**

After selling documents, exporters will immediately receive cash and finish allocating fund. This is called a typical factoring business. Of course, if exporters boast abundant fund, they can ask the factoring agency for a loan even after the expiration of the bill. The rate of service charge, depending on deadline and exchange rate risk, generally accounts for 1.75% to 2% of the total accounts receivable. Factoring service charge includes the following:

1) Proposals for importers concerning credit limit and period, which are the results of a careful investigation of the factoring agencies.

2) The credit risk assessment work.

3) The costs of keeping records of the trade negotiations between importers and exporters, and of accounting treatment.

---

**Case study 7-1  Opening up the International Market with the Help of Factoring Services**

**Detail:**

China Taiwan Merida Industrial Co., Ltd. is one of the world's famous bicycle manufacturers. Established in 1972, the company has exported its products to Asian and European countries. Mature technology of bicycle resulting in a fierce completion. Most companies had no choice but to meet the customers' demand for credit. The company's first concern caused by credit sales was customers' bad debts. The company ever used credit insurance to lift bad debts. However, in the event of bad debts, the company still has to bear at least 20% of the loan loss, and the procedures for this are not easier than those for a letter of credit. Later, the company contacted Chailease Finance Company attached to FCI and began to understand and use factoring services. The customer credit information and a full set of account management services provided by factoring services save a lot of manpower for the company. Most importantly, the cost of factoring is much lower than that of the credit insurance. The manager of the company said that if in this way, they could calmly face the competition and assuredly develop new customers.

**Analysis:**

To adopt credit sales, exporters must first consider transference problem of the buyer's credit risk. Like the exporter in this case, for many years, many exporters have chosen export credit insurance to solve this problem. However, compared with factoring, credit insurance has many disadvantages. First of all, export credit insurance generally requires exporters to ensare all sales (that is, all payments should be insured), but exporters can ensure part of goods selectively on the basis of risk in factoring business. Second, the export credit insurance costs are higher, and the highest premiums can reach to 4% of the total amount of exports in the international community, which are much higher than the factoring service commission. Again, with regard to the credit insurance, the credit risk of the importer is generally shared by the insurance company and the exporter. The insurance company generally only covers and compensates 70% to 90% of the bad debts in the credit line, and the claim procedure is cumbersome and time-consuming. The pay period is from 120 to 150 days after the loan expires. In the factoring business, the factoring company bears all the bad debts within the credit limit, and the claim procedure is simple and convenient. The factoring company's maximum pay period will not exceed 90 days. Most importantly, by using the factoring services, exporters can not only successfully transfer the credit risk of the buyers, but also obtain other services including financing, account management, and account collection, which are not provided by the credit insurance. The company's manager said that these services are essential to exporters, and are beneficial to the development of exporters' business.

**Enlightenment:**

At present, the international cargo market has generally become the buyer's market, especially those goods whose production technology are relatively mature and stable. Due to the relatively mature production process, fixed production cost and other reasons, the traditional means of export competition, such as improving quality or reducing the price, produce little effect. As a result, many exporters have chosen to provide importers with better payment conditions to fuel their competitiveness. In other relatively equivalent circumstances, the exporter who can provide more favorable payment terms, such as credit settlement convenience, will be able to seize the export opportunities. Even the world's leading companies, in this case, are also faced with such competition pressure and choice of competitive means. The factoring service is the best choice to solve concern of exporters' credit sales and enhance the export competitiveness, so great importance should be attached to it.

## 7.2 Types of International Factoring

According to different classification criteria, the factoring business can be divided into different types.

## 7.2.1 Whether Factoring Agents Shall Immediately Pay to the Exporter

According to whether the bank or professional agents that undertake factoring business should immediately pay to the exporter or not (payment will be after the documents of accounts receivable is purchased), factoring can be divided into maturity factoring and advance factoring.

(1) **Maturity Factoring**

Maturity factoring means when the exporter sells the relevant documents to factoring agent, the factoring agent shall pay the cash immediately to the exporter, and confirm and agree to pay the amount in the invoice to the exporter when the invoice expires with the right of non-recourse.

(2) **Advance Factoring**

Advance factoring means that factoring agent shall pay the amount in the invoice to the exporter when the exporter sells relevant documents to factoring agent. Because advance factoring is more common, it is called Standard Factoring.

## 7.2.2 Whether the Factoring Agent Is Disclosed to Exporters

According to whether the factoring agent is disclosed to exporters, the factoring can be divided into disclosed factoring and undisclosed factoring.

(1) **Disclosed Factoring**

Disclosed factoring means when the exporter sells the documents to the factoring agent, the factoring agent collects money from the importer while the exporter informs the importer of the payment to the factoring agent.

(2) **Undisclosed Factoring**

Undisclosed factoring is also known as concealed factoring. In this way, the exporter is reluctant to let the importer know that he/she needs factoring due to lack of floating capital. Therefore, after the document is sold to the factoring agent, exporter still collects money from the importer himself/herself and then transfers to the factoring agent.

## 7.2.3 Whether Factoring Agent Shall Bear the Risk of Bad Debts and Buyout Accounts Receivable

According to this creterion, factoring can be divided into recourse factoring and non-recourse factoring.

(1) **Recourse Factoring**

In this way, the factoring agent acquires effective the invoice from the exporter, finishes advance payment at a pre-negotiated rate, and gets all money back from the importer. If the importer pays total par value of payment within due date, factoring agent will deduct advance payment and interests and the relevant expenses, and give the balance to the exporter; if the importer delays paying the price of goods due to credit reasons or fails to pay because of disputes and bankruptcy, which causes that factoring agent is unable to recall loan timely, the factoring agent has the right to require exporters to repurchase invoices to repay advance payment and interests, so it is called recourse factoring.

### (2) Non-recourse Factoring

In this mode, the factoring agent assumes all risks and has no right to require the supplier to repurchase the invoice and return the prepayment. Non-recourse factoring is dominant in international factoring. The factoring agent conducts credit investigation based on the list of importers provided by exporters and certifies the corresponding credit line of each importer for exporters. With regard to exporters' credit within the credit line, the factoring agent has no recourse right to the acquisition of account receivable.

## 7.2.4 Mode of Operation

According to operating modes, factoring can be divided into the single-factor system and two-factor system. In the international factoring business, the factoring agent can be divided into export factoring agent and import factoring agent. As the name suggests, the factoring agent located in the exporting country/region is called export factoring agent, and the factoring firm located at the importing country/region is called the import factoring agent.

### (1) Single-factor System

Single-factor system means that only export factoring agent or import factoring agent is involved in a factoring business, that is to say, a factoring agent undertakes factoring business between exporters and importers at the same time.

### (2) Two-factor System

The two-factor system means the factoring business involves both the factoring agents from the importers and exporters. At present, the international factoring business employs this mode more. In this way, exporters and export factoring agents sign a factoring agreement to transfer their accounts receivable abroad to the export factoring agents, and the export factoring agents and the import factoring agents sign an agency agreement to transfers the relevant accounts receivable to import factoring agents. The import factoring agent is entrusted to contact the importer directly and collect payment and at the same time, the import factoring agent provides service including full protection against bad debts, debt collection and sales approval.

To exporters, importers and factoring agencies, goods of the two-factor system have certain advantages, details of which are as follows:

For exporters, two-factor system has the following advantages:

1) It can provide importers with more competitive payment conditions, such as: O/A, D/A, and is conducive to expand the market and increase sales.

2) It can obtain bank financing in advance, speed up its capital turnover, change the accounts receivable into cash income, and optimize the financial statements, which help to improve the enterprise's credit rating and financing capacity.

3) It can improve the quality of accounts receivable because factoring agent assumes credit risk of importer within approved credit line in this mode.

4) It can ease the relevant burden on the enterprise and reduce management costs, because the credit investigation, accounting management and account collection are responsible for by the factoring

agents.

5) It can save cumbersome procedures of letter of credit transactions, which helps to improve the business efficiency.

For importers, the two-factor system has the following advantages:

1) It can get preferential payment terms, reduce financial pressure, speed up the flow of funds and expand the turnover.

2) It can simplify the import procedures, and provide convenient conditions for the purchase. Under the two-factor system, the importer can obtain the credit amount only by the company's reputation and good financial performance while no additional guarantee is required.

3) It can save the cost and time of opening the letter of credit and handling the complicated documents.

For banks (factoring agencies), the two-factor system can generate interest income and higher intermediary business income because the factoring charges are generally higher than the conventional financing service such as letters of credit; the two-factor system also helps to increase international business settlement.

---

**Case study 7-2  Importer and Factoring Services**

**Detail:**

British Tex UK, which operates daily textiles, imports goods mainly from China, Turkey, Portugal, Spain and Egypt. A few years ago, when the company imported goods from China for the first time, payment could be paid by L/C. The initial use of this payment was beneficial for both parties, but as the volume of the imports has grown, they have increasingly recognized that this way was cumbersome and inflexible, which required sufficient mortgage provided by the issuing bank. In order to maintain the business growth, the company began to seek for credit payment at least 60 days. Although this company has established a good relationship with our exporters, considering the high risk of foreign exchange, our suppliers did not agree with this method. Later, the company turned to Alex Lawrie, a domestic factoring agent, to seek for a solution. British import factoring agent approved certain amount of credit for this company, and informed our exporters through the Bank of China. Through the factoring mechanism, importers received preferential payment terms for credit sales, and exporters have received 100% risk protection and trade finance accounting for 80% of the invoice amount. At present, Tex UK has extended its factoring business to five Chinese suppliers and Turkey's exporters.

**Analysis:**

As Mr. Jeremy Smith, director of Tex UK, said, the company was actively seeking factoring services because the factoring business could provide importers with good payment terms of non-guarantee deferred payment and relieved Chinese concern about payment collection, made the credit payment possible, thus helping expand its import volume from China. Exporters will add the factoring costs to the import price, but for importers, the import cost has been determined when the delivery price is settled and the transaction contract is signed, so importers will no longer need to pay the letter of credit charges and other additional costs.

> **Enlightenment**:
> The above case tells us that although the factoring service is provided for the exporters, in fact, it is also very beneficial to the importers, which is a win-win settlement. Thus, in the transaction, importers should also take the initiative in using factoring settlement, and then strive for favorable credit sale to them.

### 7.2.5 Different Payment Object for Debtor

According to this criterion, factoring can be divided into direct factoring and indirect factoring. The former refers to that the debtor directly pays to factoring agent under the factoring contract, while the latter means that the debtor pays to the supplier or the exporter under the factoring contract.

### 7.2.6 Operation Mode of Factoring Business

According to this criterion, factoring can be divided into bulk factoring and one-by-one factoring.

Under the bulk factoring, the factoring agent provides the supplier with factoring service for all sales or a series of sales activities, that is, the factoring agent grants a maximum credit limit to the importer, within which the importer can reuse the amount without application until the factoring agent revokes this approval.

Under the one-by-one factoring, the supplier shall inquire the factoring agent about every business and ask for factoring ways that provide factoring service for customers.

### 7.2.7 The Number of Factoring Contracts Involved in Sales Activities

According to this criterion, factoring can be divided into single factoring and back-to-back factoring. Single factoring means that only one factoring contract is involved in the general factoring way. The back-to-back factoring involves two factoring contracts, one of which considers factoring risk based on another factoring contract. The back-to-back factoring is produced when the importer is a middle-man.

## 7.3 Procedure of Factoring Business

If the exporter wants to sell goods by means of credit sales and collect sales payment in time by means of factoring, that is, the exporter must sign the contract concerning factoring business with the factoring agent and clarify the responsibilities and rights of exporters and factoring agents before signing the trade contract with the importer so the exporter can obtain the financial intermediation from the factoring institution. The agreement may specify a period of validity (generally one year) or not specify a period of validity but the validity period within which some inappropriate content can be modified.

After the agreement is signed, the factoring business is generally carried out through the following procedures:

1) The exporter reports the name of the importer who wishes to trade with the exporter and the relevant transaction information to the national factoring institution and entrusts the factoring agency to investigate the credit status of the importer.

2) After arranging the relevant documents, the Factoring institution of the exporting country informs the importer factoring institution and entrusts it to understand the relevant situation of the importer.

3) The factoring institution of the importing party carries out investigation according to the requirements of the exporter factoring institution and informs the exporter's factoring institution of the detailed investigation result and the suggestion on the amount of credit that can be provided to the importer.

4) The exporter factoring institution verifies the proposal above and ensures credibility and correctness, and then informs the exporter of the results.

5) According to the above survey results, the exporter makes it clear that payment is made through factoring business in the negotiation and transaction with the importer and writes it into the trade contract.

6) After loading and shipping the goods as requested, the exporter will prepare the documents according to the stipulations listed on the contract and the agreements signed with factoring agency and submit them to the exporter factoring institution. The exporter factoring institution deducts interest and relevant costs, and then the payment is paid to the exporter immediately or on the date agreed by both parties.

7) The exporter factoring agency sends the relevant documents to the importer factoring institution and entrusts the agent to collect the money from the importer.

8) The importer factoring agency receives payment from the importer and pays the money to the exporting factoring agency.

# Questions:

### Ⅰ. True or false( T for true and F for false).

1. International factoring, also known as the international insurance agency, refers to the legal relationship formed in the process that factoring agents obtain export claim through transferring and provides comprehensive financial services for exporters.
2. The international factoring business can bring many benefits to exporters and importers such as an increased turnover, risk protection, cost saving, simplified procedures and higher profits and improved credit.
3. The adoption of international factoring will not reduce the risk of foreign exchange.
4. The factoring agent has the right to claw back all payment paid to exporters.
5. International Factoring is suitable for payments such as O/A, D/A and D/P.
6. Maturity factoring can provide trade finance for exporters, because trade finance is one of the functions of factoring services.

7. Factoring serves as a multi-functional and comprehensive financial service, but its core content is providing the trade financing through the acquisition of claims.
8. On the whole, the international factoring can be approximately regarded as an international settlement between the international settlement (credit and collection) based on commercial credit and the settlement (letter of credit) based on bank credit.

II. Multiple choice (including single answer and multiple answers).

1. The financial management services provided by factoring agents include (    ).
   A. credit analysis and credit evaluation on the importer
   B. collection services of accounts receivable
   C. financing of recognized accounts receivable
   D. undertaking accounting work of accounts receivable

2. The parties related to the international factoring business include (    ).
   A. exporter                      B. importer
   C. export factoring agent        D. import factoring agent

3. In the international factoring service, the focus of factoring agents' credit evaluation is (    ).
   A. exporter
   B. importer
   C. the legal system of the importing country
   D. the quality of each account receivable

4. In the approved credit limit, the maximum premium of debt for exporters provided by factoring agents is (    ).
   A. 70%          B. 80%          C. 90%          D. 100%

5. In the factoring business, the credit risk is borne by (    ).
   A. exporter     B. importer     C. factoring agent     D. insurers

6. In the following items, (    ) is/are not function(s) of the factoring business.
   A. collection of accounts          B. verification of credit line
   C. risk guarantee                  D. sales account management
   E. trade financing                 F. opening guarantee letter

7. Based on the fact that whether the sales loan is paid directly to the factoring agent or whether the debtor is informed of the transference of the claim, the factoring business can be divided into (    ).
   A. maturity factoring              B. advance factoring
   C. disclosed factoring             D. undisclosed factoring

8. Based on the factor that whether financing is provided for the exporter, the factoring business is divided into (    ).
   A. maturity factoring              B. standard factoring
   C. disclosed factoring             D. undisclosed factoring

9. In accordance with *the Code of International Factoring Customs*, when providing services, the import factoring agent is considered to be (    ).

A. responsible for the supplier (exporter)
B. responsible for the export factoring agent
C. responsible for the importer
D. determining the object to be responsible for according to the provisions in the agreement

10. Exporters who want to use international factoring services must have the conditions such as (    ).
    A. the exporter must undertake a legitimate business
    B. the exporter has certain experience and qualifications
    C. the debtor must be the exporter's old customer
    D. the exporter's business must have a large scale
    E. trade goods are non-capital goods
    F. distribution of exporters' customers is relatively scattered

# Chapter 8

# Standby Letter of Credit

## Learning Objectives

- To master content, nature and business processes of the standby L/C.
- To understand the main parties and their responsibilities by means of standby L/C.

## 8.1 The Connotation and Type of Standby Letter of Credit

### 8.1.1 The Connotation of Standby L/C

Standby L/C, also known as the guarantee L/C, refers to the kind of credit that does not pay the price of goods but aims at loan financing or guaranteeing debt repayment (See Appendix F).

The standby L/C is a financial instrument developed in the United States that aims to circulate funds and guarantee the debt. The standby L/C originated in the United States. At the beginning of the 19th century, the relevant laws of the United States restricted banks to handle the guarantee business. As a response, some commercial banks provided guarantee service in the disguised form of the commercial L/C, that is, the standby L/C. Since then, the scope of application of the standby L/C has gradually expanded. It has rapidly evolved into an international financial instrument. Thus, the standby L/C is a kind of payment commitment with the nature of bank guarantee.

In the standby L/C, the issuing bank ensures that when the accountee fails to fulfill its obligations, the beneficiary can be paid by the issuing bank when it provides the declaration or document that proves the accountee's failure of fulfilling its obligation and draws a draft to the issuing bank. The standby L/C is only applicable to part of the terms of the *Uniform Customs and Practice for Documentary Credits (UCP 600)*.

### 8.1.2 The Nature of the Standby L/C

The standby L/C has the following natures:

**(1) Irrevocable**

Once the standby L/C is issued, the issuer shall not modify or revoke its obligations under the standby L/C unless there is another provision in the standby L/C or with the consent of both parties.

**(2) Independent**

Once the standby L/C is issued, it exists independently as a self-contained document. Under the standby L/C, the obligation of the issuer is entirely dependent on whether the terms of the standby L/C and the documents presented by the beneficiary meet the provisions of these articles on the surface and do not depend on the follows: ① The issuer's right and ability to obtain reimbursement from the accountee. ② The beneficiary's right to obtain payment from the accountee. ③ A reference to any reimbursement agreement or underlying transaction in the standby L/C. ④ Weather the issuer has understood the performance or breach of any reimbursement agreement or underlying transaction.

(3) Documentary

The standby L/C also has a documentary requirement. And the performance of the issuer's repayment obligation depends on whether the document submitted by the beneficiary meets the requirements of the standby L/C or not. The documentary nature of standby L/C is no different from the commercial L/C. However, the latter is mainly used for international trade settlement. Its documents are mainly drafts and shipping documents. And standby L/C is more commonly used for international business guarantees. It usually only requires beneficiaries to submit non-shipping documents that include drafts and declaration of accountee's default.

(4) Enforceable

Once the standby L/C is issued, it is binding whether the accountee is authorized or not, whether the issuer is paid or not, or whether the beneficiary receives the standby L/C or takes certain action because of reliance on the standby L/C or modify it or not. It is enforceable to issuing banks.

The mentioned-above four legal aspects of standby L/C complement each other and create the excellent qualities of this financial product. "Irrevocable" fixes the issuer's obligations and thus more effectively protects the interests of the beneficiaries. "Independence" inherits the nature of independence of the L/C and independent guaranty, endowing it established legal attributes. "Documentary" limits the issuer's obligations to the basis of "voucher" principle and is beneficial to the implementation of "independence". And "enforceable" is the strict implementation of the obligations of the issuer. Its integration with "irrevocable" fully reflects the liability and seriousness of the issuer's obligations, helping to prevent the interference of non-normal factors. Based on these key legal nature, the standby L/C combines the advantages of commercial L/C and independent guaranty, reflecting its unique functional advantages in practice.

## 8.1.3 The Difference between the Standby L/C and the General Commercial L/C

1) The general commercial L/C is used only when the beneficiary presents the relevant documents that prove they have fulfilled the basic trading obligations, then the issuing bank will pay the sum of money under the L/C. While the standby L/C is used when the beneficiary presents the documents that prove the debtor has not fulfilled the basis trading obligations, then the issuing bank will pay the sum of money under the L/C.

2) The issuing bank of general commercial L/C is willing to pay the beneficiary's drafts and documents in accordance with the provisions of the L/C, as this indicates that the basic transaction relationship between the buyer and the seller is normal. The issuing bank of the standby L/C does not want to pay the beneficiary's drafts and documents in accordance with the provisions of the L/C,

as this indicates that problems arise in the transaction between the exporter and the importer.

3) The accountee of the general commercial L/C is always the importer of goods and the exporter is the beneficiary. The accountee and beneficiary of the standby L/C can be either the importer or the exporter.

## 8.1.4 The Difference Between the Standby L/C and the Bank Guarantee

There are similarities between the bank guarantee and the standby L/C:

1) Both are of reserve nature.

2) Both require the claiming of reimbursement when submitting documents.

The difference are as follows: first of all, the bank guarantee and the standby L/C are subject to different international practices. The international practice of the guarantee is *The Uniform Rules for Demand Guarantees ICC Publication No. 758* (*URDG758*). The international practice of the standby L/C is, as aforementioned, *International Standby Practice 1998* (*ISP98*). Secondly, *URDG 758* provides that the rights of the beneficiaries under the letter of guarantee are not transferable. While in *ISP98* there are relevant provisions that provide the means of transferring the right of withdrawal of the beneficiary, which means the standby L/C is allowed to be transferred. Thirdly, the guarantee has counter-guarantee as a guarantee. While there is no such item in the standby mode. Fourthly, the guarantee has primary liability and secondary liability. However, the standby L/C only has primary liability.

> **Case study 8-1 Dispute About the Standby L/C**
>
> Bank A in State S received a standby L/C issued by Bank B from State W that nominated Bank A as the beneficiary and requested a credit of USD 1 million for Client D. Due to the lack of Bank B's seal, Bank A went to a branch of Bank B for verification. Although the two sides contended with each other during the process of verification, in the L/C endorsed with words that said "Seal match, Bank B", inscribed with the signature of two staff of Bank B's branch. Then, Bank A verified the signature of the two staff according to the seal of Bank B's Sydney branch in their hands and it was fully consistent. In this regard, Consumer D withdrew USD 1 million from Bank A. Later, Bank A contacted Bank B for minor modification of the L/C. However, Bank B denied that they had issued such an L/C, and would not assume any responsibility to that L/C. Thus, Bank A's request of withdrawing USD 1 million according to the L/C was refused by Bank B. Bank B claimed that the L/C was forged, and certain contents of the L/C was sufficient to alert Bank A. Bank A refuted that the seal was matched, indicating the L/C was authentic. Therefore, Bank B should be responsible for the L/C.
>
> According to the court, the plaintiff Bank A's proof submitted was in accordance with the practice of local banks. Its proof was how they had handled the verification of the seal during the process of inward remittance. Therefore, it was an effective way to confirm the authenticity of the L/C. And if the authenticity could be confirmed through the verification of seal in banks with proxy, then the verification of seal through the branch bank of issuing bank would be capable of

confirming the authenticity of the L/C. The defendant claimed that the contents of the L/C should make Bank A alert thus the defendant was unrestricted. The court held that the defendant was unrestricted only when the plaintiff was totally aware of the authenticity of the perjury. For the plaintiff, it was reasonable for them to take the defendant's L/C as an authentic one because they did not know it was forged.

The court ruled that the defendant was fully responsible for the L/C.

**Analysis:**

The L/C, in this case, is a standby L/C. Standby L/C, also known as commercial paper L/C or secured L/C, is a special form of clean L/C. The standby L/C refers to a service that the issuing bank issues to the beneficiary to ensure that the accountee will fulfill the contract. And when the accountee fails to fulfill its obligations, the issuing bank will make a written guarantee commitment of a certain amount of payment with the submission of the beneficiary's documents.

The focus of the dispute, in this case, is the authenticity of the standby L/C and the question concerning the assignment of responsibility and right between the "issuing bank" and the beneficiary with the forged credit. In the case, Bank B claimed that the L/C was forged and suggested that if the issuing bank had a proxy relationship with the verification bank, the verified seal could be a suitable method for confirming the authenticity of the credit. However, Bank B had no proxy relationship with its branch. Therefore, Bank A's verification of seal in its branch could not prove that the standby L/C was authentic. As a matter of fact, Bank A was acting in accordance with the practice of local banks when they used the verification of the seal during the process of inward remittance as a proof. Therefore, it was an effective way to confirm the authenticity of the L/C. And if the authenticity can be confirmed through the verification of a seal in banks with proxy, then the verification of seal through the branch bank of issuing bank will be capable of confirming the authenticity of the L/C. Because the branch does not have an independent legal personality, the responsibility for its legal action directly goes to its head office. Bank B also claimed that the contents of the L/C should make Bank A alert. Thus, it was unrestricted. In such business, the issuing bank must be responsible for any of their own negligence. The issuing bank's L/C is a payment commitment. If the beneficiary trusts such a commitment, then the law does not allow the issuing bank to overthrow its previous commitment. The beneficiary is not obliged to explore the real intention of the issuing bank outside the scope of reasonable integrity. These are based on the principle of fairness. If the beneficiary knows that the issuing bank is wrong and takes advantage of it, the situation will be different. However, Bank A was not aware that the L/C was forged. And it verified the forged one according to the local bank practice, in line with the principle of prudence. Therefore, Bank A bank had reason to rely on the commitment of the issuing bank.

In addition, the trial of the case applies to *UCP400* and other relevant laws. If the *UCP500* and *UCP600* are applicable, the court's judgment may be different, because the article 2 of paragraph 2 of *UCP500* that was introduced on 1 January 1994 provides that, for the purposes of this customary provision, one bank that has set up different branches in different countries are considered to be another bank. The *UCP600* which was amended on July 1, 2007, retains this article (*UCP600* Article 3). Therefore, the branches of the same bank may, on an organizational and managerial basis, be the same as their head office, but in the business related to the L/C it should be regarded as a separate bank. In this case, the Bank A verified the seal in Bank B's branch, which would not be able to prove that the L/C was issued by the Bank B because Bank B and its Sydney branch in such business were considered as separate banks, and there was no evidence that there existed a proxy relationship between them. Therefore, Bank B had no relationship with the L/C in the legal sense. It is reasonable that Bank B would not take the responsibility for payment. It is necessary to clarify this provision of *UCP600*. From the bank's perspective, it should not be burdened with the L/C from other relevant banks. From the perspective of the beneficiary, the legal relationship should be clarified and it should not be bewildered.

**Enlightenment**:

1. The standby L/C is the written guarantee commitment made by the issuing bank to the beneficiary. Therefore, for the beneficiary, it should carefully verify the issuing bank's signature. The confirmation of the authenticity of the standby L/C is essential, directly affecting whether the beneficiary's rights and interests can be guaranteed or not.

2. For the issuing bank of the standby L/C, once the L/C is issued, it should abide by the commitments when the beneficiary puts forward the requirement of reasonable payment or compensation, maintaining its own credibility.

3. Both the issuing bank of the L/C and its beneficiary should be familiar with the business practices and laws that applied internationally. They should also make corresponding business adjustments to avoid a passive situation that is caused by the ignorance of the latest practices and the law applicable.

## 8.2 Types of Standby Letters of Credit

The different roles that the standby L/C play in the basic transaction can be divided into the following eight categories:

### 8.2.1 Performance Standby L/C

It supports the performance of an obligation other than payment of the money, including compensation for the loss caused by the accountee's breach of contract in the basic transaction.

### 8.2.2 Advance Payment Standby L/C

It is used to guarantee the accountee's obligations and liabilities to the beneficiary's prepayment. This standby L/C is normally used to pay for 10% to 25% of the project advance payment paid by the landlord to the contractor in the international engineering contracting project, and for the prepayment paid by the importer to the exporter in the import and export trade.

### 8.2.3 Counter Standby L/C

It is also known as separate standby L/C, which supports another standby L/C issued or other commitment made by the beneficiary of counter standby.

### 8.2.4 Financial Standby L/C

It supports the payment obligations, including any documents that prove the obligations of repayment of borrowings. At present, the standby L/C used by foreign-funded enterprises to mortgage RMB loans is a financial standby L/C.

### 8.2.5 Tender Bond Standby L/C

It is used to guarantee the contractual obligations and responsibilities of the accountee after the successful implementation of the bid. If the bidders fail to fulfill the contract, the issuer must perform its compensation obligation to the accountee in accordance with the provisions of the standby L/C. The amount of the tender bond standby L/C is generally 1% to 5% of the insured price (the specific proportion depends on the provisions of the tender documents).

### 8.2.6 Direct Payment Standby L/C

It is used to guarantee the due payment, especially the principal and interest should be paid when there is no default of the contract. It has broken the traditional guarantee nature of the standby L/C that is not used but to standby. It is used to guarantee the obligation to pay the principal and interest due to the issuance of the bonds or the establishment of the debt contract of the issuing bank.

### 8.2.7 Insurance Standby L/C

It supports the accountee's insurance or reinsurance obligations.

### 8.2.8 Commercial Standby L/C

It means the guarantee of the accountee's payment obligations to the goods or services when the payment cannot be fulfilled in other ways.

At present, China's foreign-invested enterprises are increasingly becoming an important force for the export. There are three types of foreign-funded enterprises, including Chinese-foreign joint ventures, Chinese-foreign co-operative enterprises and solely foreign-owned enterprises. And their export volume accounts for about 60% of that of China. With the gradual improvement of the domestic investment environment, the procurement and investment of foreign-invested enterprises in the domestic market increase year by year, forming a huge demand for RMB funds. The domestic banks are cautious about the financing of foreign-invested enterprises, because the operating centers of most foreign-invested are located overseas, making it difficult for banks to accurately assess the financial situation of enterprises. And the collaterals of enterprises such as plants and machinery equipment are not of high values and weak in transforming into cash, therefore it is hard for banks to provide large financing. The standby L/C is increasingly becoming an important financing instrument for foreign-invested enterprises, considering its great flexibility and simple operability.

### Case study 8-2  Fraud on Import of Standby L/C

At the beginning of the year, Company D (the accountee) submitted a contract, an application form and a standby L/C form to Bank B (issuing bank) and kept a 100% margin, requiring the issuance of a standby L/C worth USD500,000 for imported cars. The beneficiary (the seller) was the Company T from Hong Kong. When auditing the relevant information, the bank handler found on the contract where the seller section was Company T. And there existed the signatures of both the buyers and the sellers. The terms of the contract also provided that "Company T ensures that, upon receiving the standby L/C issued by the issuing bank, Company T will start delivery immediately. The buyer will complete the payment in a year without any interest". However, there existed questions in the code format of the standby L/C:

(1) In the format (allegedly the standard format of Bank C), the accountee and the beneficiary were Company T and Bank P from Hong Kong instead of Company D and Company T.

(2) The liability clause served as a guarantee by a bank to ensure that Company T would return the loans to Bank P, rather than guarantee the Company D's payment.

So, Bank B reminded Company D to be cautious about this. And it provided a standby L/C as a special payment guarantee to the Company D as a reference. Company D faxed this format to Company T for confirmation. However, Company T refused to accept, and falsely alleged that: "This format cannot be applied in Hong Kong." And it insisted that the format must be applied according to the original example and must be issued to Bank P, otherwise, the goods would be sold to others. Seeing the increase in car market prices, Company D was afraid of losing the opportunity of making money and repeatedly asked for the issuance of the L/C from the issuing bank. In view of this, the issuing bank sought to investigate the beneficiary's credit quality and the ability to repay loans through a Hong Kong advisory institution. It learned that Company T had the criminal record of taking advantage of the standby L/C to defraud the supplier's goods and the deposit of the buyer. The issuing bank immediately notified the accountee and then called Bank C for investigation. The reply from Bank C denied the issuance of the standby L/C in the format above. The fraud was exposed at last. Therefore, the companies avoided economic losses.

**Analysis:**

Claiming to provide goods in short supply, the defrauder cheats or uses shoddy goods to force the accountee to apply for irrepealable standby L/C from the buyer's bank in order to defraud the goods of the actual supplier or the deposit of importers financing of the bank.

This kind of fraud often has the following characteristics: firstly, the fraud uses providing goods in short supply as a bait to lure buyers into applying for a separate L/C to the bank. Secondly, the standby L/C is based on the contract signed between the buyers and sellers and the payment period is one year in the long term. Thirdly, the fraud requires the buyer to instruct the bank to issue the L/C according to the so-called "standard format" provided and designates a certain bank as the beneficiary. Fourthly, the standby L/C is of a large amount of money which is used for a large amount of fraud. Fifthly, the fraud's targets range from domestic importing enterprises, the actual foreign suppliers and banks.

**Enlightenment:**

Since the buyers and sellers are located in different countries in the international trade, normally they lack sufficient understanding of each other's credit. In this case, domestic enterprises should pay special attention to the following aspects:

1. Before signing the contract, they should know each other's operation style, financial situation and credibility in different ways as much as possible. Even a tiny problem deserves enough concern.

2. In face of some concessional terms along with improper payment, offered by other companies, domestic companies should work closely with banks. With domestic banks' specialty and network advantages, they should know the real intentions of other companies and timely expose the conspiracy to avoid any losses.

For domestic banks, they should be very cautious when issuing standby L/C. In the premise of ensuring their own security (in this case, the accountee provided 100% margin), they should actively guard for customers to find out questions and doubts detection of problems timely to draw the attention of customers.

## 8.3 The Operating Principle of Standby Letters of Credit

Since the standby L/C originated from the family of L/C, the business process of the standby L/C basically conforms to the operating principles of L/C.

Firstly, the accountee (the debtor of the basic transaction contract) applies for the issuance of the standby L/C to the issuer (bank or non-bank financial institution).

Secondly, the issuer should strictly examine the accountee's credit capability, financial status, the feasibility of the project. If the issuer agrees to issue the standby L/C, he/she shall inform the beneficiary (creditors of the underlying trading contract) of the standby L/C through the notifying bank.

Thirdly, if the issuer fulfills the obligation of payment due to the agreement of the basic trading contract, the accountee does not need to fulfill the obligation of payment for the issuance of standby L/C. It shall be discharged from the guarantee obligation when reaching the expiry date of the validity of the credit. If the accountee fails to perform the credit, the standby L/C will bring its function of payment guarantee into play. In the latter case, the beneficiary may submit the bill of exchange, the proof of accountee's breach of contract and the compensation document in accordance with the provisions of the standby L/C to ask for compensation.

Fourthly, the issuer should verify and confirm that the relevant compensation documents are in line with the stipulation of the standby L/C. After that, the issuer must pay the beneficiary unconditionally to fulfill its guarantee obligations.

Finally, after fulfilling the payment, the issuer should claim the reimbursement of advance payment to the accountee. And the accountee is responsible for compensation.

## 8.4 International Practice of Standby L/C

There are currently two types of practice applicable to the standby L/C. One is International Standby Practice and the other is *UCP600*. In this section, the first one will be introduced because we have learned the *UCP600 before*.

### 8.4.1 Background

*Uniform Customs and Practice for Documentary Credits* is mainly the rule established for business L/C. Therefore, many features of standby L/C cannot be fully embodied in these rules. For example, there is no detailed requirement of issues related to the long term of the standby L/C, its automatic extension, the demand on transfer, and the request of making a commitment from one beneficiary for another. Thus, it results in the uncertainty of explanation of standby L/C, easily leading to disputes.

In response to the above background, on April 6, 1998, *International Standby Practice* was drafted through the joint effort of the United States International Financial Services Association, Institute of International Banking Law and Practice and the International Chamber of Commerce Bank Technology and Practice Committee. In December, 1998, International Chamber of Commerce announced the *International Standby Practice*. It came into force on January 1, 1999, and was designated as ICC Publication No. 590 to be promoted around the world. It has filled the gaps in the standard of international standard of standby L/C.

### 8.4.2 Main Contents

Based on the *United Nations Convention on Independent Guarantees and Stand-by Letters of Credit* and referring to *Uniform Customs and Practice for Documentary Credits* (*UCP500*) and *The Uniform Rules for Demand Guarantees* (*URDG758*), *International Standby Practice* (*ISP98*) was established in accordance with the characteristics of the standby L/C. It determined the definition of those commonly used standby L/C, such as performance standby L/C, advance payment standby L/C, tender bond standby L/C, counter standby L/C, financial standby L/C, insurance standby L/C, commercial standby L/C and direct payment of standby L/C.

International Standby Practice included the preamble and text which were divided into ten sections with a total of 89 clauses. The ten sections were General Provisions (The scope, application, definition and explanation, general rules and terms of the provisions), Obligations, Notice, Examination, Transfer, Assignment, and Transfer by Operation of Law (Transfer of Drawing Rights,

Acknowledgment of Assignment of Proceeds, Transfer by Operation of Law), Revocation, Reimbursement Obligations, Timing and Syndication/Participation.

# Questions:

## I. True or false.

1. The standby L/C is formally similar to a documentary L/C and is similar in nature to a bank guarantee.
2. Standby L/C can be involved in any area that needs bank guarantees. It has been used widly than the documentary L/C.
3. Standby letters of credit, the same as bank guarantee, is divided into subordinate one and independent one.
4. Standby L/C is mainly used for the process of settlement in foreign trade as a payment method of commodity trading. Documentary L/C can be involved in any area that needs bank guarantees. It has a wider range of usage than standby L/C.
5. The legal parties of standby L/C and bank guarantees generally include the accountee, the issuing bank or the guarantee bank (the two are in the same position) and the beneficiary.
6. The contents of the standby L/C are similar to that of the documentary L/C. And it requires the beneficiary to submit the shipping documents, commercial invoice, insurance document, commodity inspection list, etc. that meet the requirements of the L/C as the basis for the claim.

## II. Multiple choice.

1. The basic client of the standby L/C does not include the (    ).
   A. issuing bank    B. guarantee bank    C. beneficiary    D. accountee
2. Which of the following is not the common feature shared by the standby L/C and documentary L/C? (    )
   A. Both have similar forms.
   B. Both are bank credit.
   C. Both are paid by vouchers or documents in accordance with the L/C's requirements.
   D. The issuing bank has the primary liability of making payment in both cases.
3. A set of independent international rules of standby L/C on a worldwide basis is (    ).
   A. UCP 600    B. URC522    C. ISP98    D. URDG758
4. Which of the following statement about the standby L/C is incorrect? (    )
   A. The purpose of issuing standby L/C is to ask the issuing bank to take the primary liability of making payment to the beneficiary.
   B. If the accountee fails to fulfill the relevant obligations as stipulated in the contract, the bank is responsible for compensating the beneficiary for economic losses.
   C. If the accountee fulfills the relevant obligations as stipulated in the contract, the beneficiary needs not submit the declaration of default to the issuing bank.
   D. Standby L/C is a kind of document that is often ready just in use.
5. Which of the following does not belong to the basic content of the standby L/C? (    ).

A. The number and issuing date of the standby L/C

B. The validity of the standby L/C

C. The documents, certificates and reminders that the beneficiary needs to provide when claiming compensation

D. A brief description of the name quantity, price and packaging of the goods

**III. Case study.**

It is rare for China's institutes or companies to issue the standby L/C to foreign countries, however, in 1993, there was an abortive L/C fraud worth USD 10 billion which caused a stir nationwide. In this fraud case, the standby L/C was issued by Agricultural Bank of China, Hengshui Brach worth USD 10 billion.

In March 1993, two Chinese-American Mei Zhifang (Mei in short hereafter) and Li Zhaoming (Li in short here after) came to Agricultural Bank of China, Hengshui Brach. They submitted written and words to the former vice presidents Zhao Jinrong (Zhao in short hereafter) and Xu Zhiguo (Xu in short hereafter). Mei and Li lied to Zhao and Xu that the "Asian Union Cooperation" they ran in the US had many strong partners and could introduce "foreign investment" to Hengshui. In this condition that Hengshui Central Branch of Agricultural Bank of China must issue the standby L/C to "Asian Union Cooperation" for investment. They also lied that these standby Ls/C were only used to prove the Overview of relevant funds into China, and Hengshui Agricultural Bank of China "do not repay, do not pay interest and do not bear any economic and legal responsibility" to the introduced funds.

Both Zhao and Xu did no study on the economic capabilities of the "Asian Union Cooperation" advocated by Mei and Li, nor did they try to understand the feasibility of capital absorption via consultation. They did not report the details of the transaction and the ways to collect the premium or securities to their leaders for approval, either. They signed the agreement for capital absorption that totaled at USD 10 billion on April 2, 1993. On April 5, Zhao Jinrong overstepped his authority to sign his name on the 200 standby Ls/C that totaled USD 10 billion according to the sample Mei and Li provided when they two did not provide any margin or pledge. These standby Ls/C were of one-year duration, irrevocable, and transferable. The deputy chief of foreign exchange business section in Agricultural Bank of China Hengshui Branch, Liu Shudong also signed on the standby L/C and stamped the official seal of Hengshui Central Branch of Agricultural Bank of China on them.

With the assistance of Interpol and the police from related countries, on October 18, 1994, with more than six months passing by, 200 standby letters of credit with the total amount of USD 10 billion issued by the deceived Agricultural Bank of China Hengshui Branch were all clawed back. Try to analyze the above cases and put forward measures to prevent fraud on standby letters of credit.

# Chapter 9

# Documents for International Settlement

**Learning Objectives**

- To understand the significance, basic requirements and general rules of making documents for international settlement.
- To grasp the essentials of making various documents and be familiar with the production of main documents in international settlement.
- To learn basic procedures of electronic documentation and accurately make a full set of documents under any form of settlement.

## 9.1 General Overview on Documents for International Settlement

### 9.1.1 The Definition and Function of Documents for International Trade Settlement

Documents for International Settlement refer to various documents and certificates used in the international trade settlement. *Uniform Customs and Practice for Documentary Credits* (2005 Revised Edition) of ICC (International Chamber of Commerce) stipulates that "In the L/C business, they are documents that are dealt with instead of goods, service, and/or other action that may by concerned". This shows the significance of documents in the documentary credit business; moreover, through the practice of international trade, documents play an extremely important role and that is mainly reflected in the following aspects:

(1) Documents are Important Bases for Contract Performance

In the domestic trade of a country, contract performance is usually achieved by the exchange of goods and currency. While in international trade, limited by time and space, mostly it's very difficult to directly exchange but to take a document as the medium of it. This is the main cause that people claim FOB, CFR and CIF as symbolic delivery.

Besides, documents plays the most essential role in the performance of the export contract. If anything is wrong with the preparation of the goods, issuance of the L/C, commodity inspection, chartering and booking shipping space, insurance, customs declaration, shipping, etc., which cannot be found and corrected in time, it finally will be exposed in the documents and some can be sometimes corrected. So, documents play the role of guarding and monitoring during the contract performance.

(2) Documents are Important Tools to Collect Payment

When the collection of export trade applies the form of collection, L/C or international factoring, the main basis of payment is a document. Even if remittance is applied, a document is also the basis for payment (i. e. pay in cash when you get a document). With the development of the international trade, documentation of international goods makes the convection principle of the convection between the documents and the goods become a general rule in the international trade.

(3) **Documents are Bases for Party Concerned in Dealing with Dispute**

The insurance policy serves as a proof of compensation, if the goods are found damaged when the buyer takes delivery of them and claim to the insuring company. If concerned with the calculation of amount of compensation, the invoice would be the basis. Thus, export documents can be seen as documents concerning foreign law.

Furthermore, export documents are of political significance. For example, customs invoices or consular invoices may be used by the customs of the importing countries to check whether the goods belong to dumping. The GSP certificate of origin provides the basis for the implementation of the general preference system and customs duty exemption from the importing countries. Therefore, export documents are documents that reflect a country's policies and guidelines.

## 9.1.2 Types of Documents for International Trade Settlement

There are many types and division creteria for the international trade settlement documents. According to the characteristics of documents, they can be divided into financial bills, commercial bills and official bills.

(1) **Financial Bills**

Financial bills refer to bills of exchange, promissory notes, cheques etc. , and other documents that represent certain monetary claims, such as bonds, coupons and bank certificates of deposit.

(2) **Commercial Bills**

Commercial bills are used as certificates of the seller's performance and certificates of the goods. Here the goods contain two meanings. First, it means that the buyer holds a bill and then understands the goods conditions by it, that is "Seeing bills is Seeing the goods". Second is that in commercial bills, there are bills of lading which can be used to take delivery of the goods. Once the buyer holds the bill, he/she keeps the real right proof, which means he gets the goods. In the L/C, commercial bills are the main basis for determining whether an exporter can safely obtain the foreign exchange proceeds. The quality of commercial bills must be guaranteed and be strictly in line with the terms and conditions stipulated in the L/C.

(3) **Official Bills**

There are two ways to understand "Official" in business. One is to interpret "Official" as "official" or "governmental", which means that "Official Bills" must be issued by the government authorities, such as documents issued by the Ministry of Commerce and the Commodity Inspection Bureau. Another, the "Official" is interpreted as "formal" and "normal". In addition to the state organizations, some documents issued by non-governmental organizations such as Chambers of Commerce and Trade Unions are also "Offbeat Bills".

## 9.2 Basic Requirements of Making Documents for International Settlement

Although different international settlements require documents with different types and numbers, the principle of "Accurate, Complete, Timely, Concise, Clean" shall be followed:

### 9.2.1 Accurate

The correctness of documents is the fundamental principle, the premise and the starting point of the work of the export document. The correctness of documents mainly displays in two aspects:

**(1) Documents Shall Be in Accordance with the International Practice and the Regulation on Both Importing and Exporting Countries**

**(2) Documents with the Payment of L/C Shall Ensure "Three Consistence"**

Firstly, the documents shall be consistent with the L/C. It is the requirement of payment of the L/C itself to the documents. If any inconsistency occurs, banks may dishonor the payment.

Secondly, the documents shall be consistent with themselves. In a same business, the corresponding items on different documents shall be in conformity with each other, rather than contradict themselves. Not only the contents of each clause, but also the spelling of each letter shall be exactly the same.

Thirdly, the documents shall be consistent with the goods. In other words, the contents described in the documents shall be consistent with the actual goods, which actually requires the seller to fulfill the trade contracts strictly.

In the "Three Consistency", "documents shall be consistent with the L/C" is the premise of the others, it plays the most important role. From the perspective of receiving remittance safely, the documents shall be made and prepared in accordance with the regulation of the L/C, otherwise, they will be easily refused by the issuing bank.

### 9.2.2 Complete

"Complete" generally includes the following three meanings:

**(1) The Types of Documents Shall Be Complete**

Each documentary credit stipulates various documents, such as invoice, bills of lading, insurance policy and commodity inspection certificate. Documents will be incomplete if any is omitted.

**(2) The Content of Documents Shall Be Complete**

Due to the different roles and functions, the contents of the document are different. For example, bills of lading shall include the name of consignor, consignee and notifier, port of shipment, the name of vessels, numbers of packages, weight, the name of products and other items. Documents will be incomplete if any is omitted. When the L/C fails to stipulate one item, which is the necessary one in the document, it shall not be omitted, or it will be perceived as incomplete. For example, in the bills of lading we mentioned above, although there is no regulation on the L/C

# Chapter 9 Documents for International Settlement

that numbers of packages shall be listed (goods in bulk are excluded), as for the document, without specified numbers of packages, the contents of documents is incomplete.

### (3) Copies of Documents Shall Be Complete

Generally, the L/C stipulates numbers of copies of documents when submitted to the bank, and they shall be submitted in accordance with the number. The followings are the two ways of representations of copies of documents stipulated in the L/C:

| | |
|---|---|
| In Duplicate | In 2 folds |
| In Triplicate | In 3 folds |
| In Quadruplicate | In 4 folds |
| In Quintuplicate | In 5 folds |
| In Sextuplicate | In 6 folds |
| In Septuplicate | In 7 folds |
| In Octuplicate | In 8 folds |
| In Nonuplicate | In 9 folds |
| In Decuplicate | In 10 folds |

In addition, even if the L/C does not provide specific numbers of copies, unless otherwise specified in the L/C, the document is incomplete. For example, when the bill of lading shows that it issues three originals, it is incomplete if only one or two copies are provided.

In order to ensure the completeness of the documents, you'd better read the L/C before making documents and mark the important provisions so as not to leave anything out. Then fill out the examination sheet in accordance with the L/C.

## 9.2.3 Timely

The work of making documents is time-sensitive, and each kind of document has an appropriate issuing date. Issuing documents in time include two interpretations. On the one hand, the date of issuing documents shall be reasonable and feasible, in other words, the date cannot exceed the expiration date stipulated in the L/C or the reasonable date formed by trade practice. For example, in the condition of CIF, the issuing date of insurance policy shall be earlier or no later than the date of bills of lading, and the issuing date of bills of lading shall not be earlier and later than the shipping date stipulated in the L/C. On the other hand, when it comes to the negotiation of documents, the date of negotiation to the bank shall not exceed the expiry date of delivering documents stipulated by the L/C, or if the delivering date is not stipulated, the document shall be delivered within 21 days after the shipping document issued. Of course, under the condition permitted by the L/C, the beneficiary may also deliver documents and conduct a negotiation in advance.

In order to ensure the principle "timely", people who make documents shall clear about the priorities. Documents with a large amount of money and about to expire shall be first made out. If necessary, produce documents first and the date, name of vessels and other items can be made up later.

## 9.2.4　Concise

The content of documents shall be in accordance with the provisions of the L/C and the international practices. "Concise" requires that the design of documents shall be standardized and normal. The arrangement of the content shall be clear and in order, and key projects shall be prominent and eye-catching. Altered documents shall be minimized or even are not approved. The amendment of documents shall have a limit, at the same time, many amendments in one document are not allowed. Documents shall be made out again if too many errors appear. The altered part must have the seal of proofreader. Some items such as the payer and the amount of money must not be altered. Once go wrong, the documents must be made out again.

Besides, in order to fulfill the five requirements mentioned-above, people who make documents and clerks shall cooperate with each other and exchange information, which can avoid various errors because of inconsistent ideas. Re-check regulation shall be established. The documents shall be re-checked by others because it is not easy to find errors by themselves. Besides, one should make close contact with banks in case of an error occurs.

Making documents for the international settlement shall be concise. *UCP 600* prescribes that "In order to prevent confusion and misunderstandings, banks shall discourage the following intentions: 'adding too many details in the L/C or any other amendment.'" It is for avoiding complication, because of the more complicated the documents, the larger the probability of the errors.

## 9.2.5　Clean

The content of clean documents shall be clear and easy to recognize, and the surface shall be clean and good-looking.

# 9.3　Commercial Documents: the Making of Invoice

There are many categories of commercial bills, which include invoices, transport documents, insurance documents, packing lists, weight lists etc. This section describes the invoice and its making.

In the international trade, an invoice includes various categories, such as commercial invoice, proforma invoice, banker's invoice, combined invoice, manufacturer's invoice, customs invoice, consular invoice, etc. The latter two are official bills and will be introduced in the next section.

The most common one is the commercial invoice (See Appendix G), which is often known as an invoice. It is the core of the whole set of documents, and the basis for exporters to make other documents. In this section, we will focus on all items of commercial invoice and the detailed elaboration of its making method. And then we will briefly introduce the basic knowledge of other invoices.

## 9.3.1　The Basic Contents and Making Method of Commercial Invoice

Invoice is a list that includes the goods' name, quantity, price etc. It performs as the main document with which both buyers and sellers can transfer the goods and do the payment. In addition, it is a proof of customs declaration.

The invoice format is different in export trade. The formats of the commercial invoice are different from China's foreign trade enterprises, but the main items and the basic contents are consistent.

(1) Heading

**1) Invoice Name**

Either invoice or commercial invoice should be in accordance with the L/C or the contract requirements, and marked in a prominent position.

**2) Invoice No. and Date**

The invoice No., which represents the number of a full set of documents, is an important item that cannot be omitted. And the No. of the bill of exchange must be in line with the invoice No.

**3) Letter of Credit and Contract No.**

The L/C number is usually filled in the invoice under the L/C payment. If there is no contract number in an L/C, it may not be filled. If it is specified, fill it out according to the original sentence, such as "As Per Contract No..." or "Other terms as per contract No...". The invoice in the collection form is filled with contract number.

**4) Consignee**

Unless the L/C has specified stipulations, the invoice is opened by the L/C and the applicant is the consignee's name.

The consignee name of the invoice under collection shall be filled out by the buyer's name as stipulated in the contract.

**5) Means of Transportation and Routes of Transportation**

Strictly in line with the L/C and the B/L, this column includes the port of loading, port of destination and means of transportation. If the L/C stipulates original port for "Any Chinese Port", some Chinese ports must be marked. If only "Chinese", any inland city or port in China is OK. Land transportation shows "Per Rail" and ocean shipping shows "Per Vessel".

(2) Body

**1) Shipping Marks**

Shipping marks, according to the stipulation of ISO (International Organization for Standardization), are made up of four parts: the buyer's abbreviation or code name, reference number, the name of destination port and the number of packages. Their functions are to facilitate the loading and unloading, transportation and storage of the goods. The stipulation concerned in the L/C should be strictly made word by word according to the requirements of the L/C. And each character's order, layout and newline of shipping marks should absolutely conform to the wording of the L/C. Otherwise, it can be taken as nonconformity between documents and terms of the L/C.

If there is no stipulation of shipping marks in the L/C, fill it out in accordance with the contract or let the exporter select it by himself/herself.

**2) Description**

The description of the goods in the invoice contains the name, specifications, package and quantity. Among them, name and specifications in principle should be in line with the L/C. If some letters of the name of a commodity in the L/C are wrong, it is better to correct the L/C, or copy word by word as last option. And quantity and package should be in line with actual shipment as well as the requirements of the L/C. Some letters of credit contain more or less clause, and a certain amount of quantity elasticity is allowed at this moment.

### 3) Unit Price, Total Value and Payment Terms

Unit price should be marked out according to the L/C stipulation. If not specified, it may not be made but prepared by contract, and then the total number and total amount must be consistent with the L/C.

Payment Terms are one of the most important items of the invoice and cannot be omitted. They involve the responsibility and risk of both buyers and sellers.

Some certificate price, including commission or discount, should be dealt with according to the L/C stipulation. It should be followed if a commission must be deducted in the invoice. In some countries, the L/C stipulates that under CIF price term, freight, insurance and FOB price should be listed on the invoice. And the sum of FOB value, freight and insurance should be equal to the CIF price. The invoice value shall not exceed the maximum amount that stipulated in the L/C.

### 4) Other Contents

If there is a special clause in the L/C, the invoice must be filled with an item or a statement, and it should be recorded in the invoice by rules and not be omitted. For example, fill production unit, license number and another reference number, or claim the validity and authenticity of the invoice as well as place of origin of goods. Pay attention to the correctness and coherence of the typing statement sentence, and "E. & O. E." (Errors & Omissions Excepted) printed at the end of the invoice should be deleted.

### (3) Complimentary Close

The main form of complimentary close is the exporter's company stamp and signature. All the stamps must be consistent the beneficiary stipulation in the L/C and shall be the same as that in the other documents. At present, many companies print the company name and official's signature at the bottom right corner of the invoice. But it is noticeable that if the L/C asks for a signature, you must add it to the leading official.

## 9.3.2 Proforma Invoice

Proforma invoice is an informal invoice opened by the seller at the buyer's request. It is an important basis for the buyer to apply for the foreign exchange or import license.

Proforma invoice is an informal document that is legally binding on both the seller and the buyer. It has no uniform format, except the name of proforma invoice, which declares that: "This invoice is supplied to enable you to apply for the necessary Import License. Actual orders shall be subject to our final confirmation." And other contents shall be consistent with the commercial invoice.

## 9.3.3 Banker's Invoice

When the goods' name, specification and packaging methods stipulated in the L/C are much more abbreviated than these in the contract provisions, the exporter may put every item aforementioned on the invoice list according to the contract of sales signed by both parties. And then it is delivered to a bank for negotiation, the bank often refuses to pay because the documents are inconsistent with the L/C. The bank is unwilling to take the responsibility beyond the L/C terms, because the negotiating bank and the issuing bank usually check documents with reference to the L/C terms only. At this time, the exporter can only send the detailed invoice to the importer and issue a brief invoice as required by the L/C in order to meet the requirements of the bank. This is what we call a banker's invoice.

### 9.3.4 Manufacturer's Invoice

Manufacturer's invoice is the invoice that issued by the factory that produces export commodities in its domestic currency and used to prove the manufacturer's price of export commodities. It is also for the importer's customs valuation, tax accounting: The importing country/region will use it to determine whether the exporter is dumpingnot.

In addition, as exports to China Hong Kong and China Macao, the manufacturer often combines commercial invoice with a certificate of premises and weight list so as to form a combined invoice.

## 9.4 Business Documents: Transport Documents

Transport documents, which are issued by a carrier or his/her agent to a shipper, performs as a proof that the goods have been loaded aboard or the departure of goods is under the carrier's control. They serve as documents related to the liabilities and ownership of the parties to a contract for the carriage of goods. Besides, they play an important role in taking delivery, handling claims and doing exchange settlement or the bank's negotiation.

The transport documents may take different forms in terms of transport mode, such as ocean shipping documents, railway documents, air way bill, parcel post receipt and multimodal transport documents. Among all, the ocean shipping documents are the most important.

### 9.4.1 Ocean Shipping Documents

#### 9.4.1.1 Bill of Lading

(1) Definition

Bill of lading (B/L for short) is a document issued by a carrier or his/her agent to the shipper to make sure that the goods have been loaded onto a specified vessel, or are ready to be loaded onto a specified ship for a designated port. In addition, it also performs as a document or proof to be presented when the consignee takes delivery at the port of destination (See Appendix H).

In the early days, there were no specific sectors for trade and transport. All the cargos were shipped by the trader themselves. In the 16th century, however, fueled by the development of the international trade and marine technology, transport separated itself from the international trade and became an independent sector, which gave rise to the appearance of the B/L. At that time, the only function of the B/L was to serve as a receipt from the carrier to the shipper. A B/L did not become a document of title until 18th century and then developed into negotiable securities that could be transferable or mortgaged by endorsement. The wide use of the B/L increasingly improves the terms on it.

(2) **Roles and Purposes of B/L**

1) **Receipt of the Goods**

A B/L signed and issued by a carrier or his/her agent to a shipper can be used as a proof by the fact that carrier has received the goods, which are the same as the contents listed on it. Though it is a receipt of cargos, it does not guarantee that the goods have already been loaded onto a vessel. Usually, the shipper sends the goods to a specified warehouse or place designated by the carrier. Then the carrier can issue a received-for-shipment B/L at the shipper's requirements and later convert it to an on-board B/L once the goods have been loaded.

2) **Evidence of the Contract of Carriage**

The B/L itself is not a contract of carriage. During the transit process, when the shipping company or its agent issues a shipping order and agrees to accept the shipper's cargos, then both parties enter into a contract of carriage. The contract of chartering a vessel belongs to transport contract. A B/L is issued after that. Despite this, a B/L shares the same conditions and terms as normal transport contract, which serves as explanatory terms for the settlement of disputes.

3) **Documents of Title**

A B/L represents the goods written on it. The holder of a B/L is entitled to received the goods from the carrier and the carrier must hand over the goods to the consignee according to the contents of B/L. In this case, the B/L performs as document of title for the goods. It can be negotiated via legitimate procedure. Negotiation of the B/L is equal to that of ownership. Though as a negotiable security, the B/L is different from the normal bills.

Besides, the B/L could also perform as freight evidence and apply for a mortgage from a bank.

(3) **Related Parties**

When a B/L performs as a contract of carriage, then there are two main parties involved. One is the carrier and the other is the shipper. However, from the perspective of contents, there are more parties, like consignee and notify party. If a B/L is negotiated, there will be assignee and the owner involved.

1) **Carrier**

The carrier, which enters into a contract with the consignor, is responsible for the shipment of goods, as well as the damage and loss in transit. It is not the real carrier, nor the owner or charter.

2) **Consignor/Shipper**

A consignor is a shipper sending a shipment to be delivered. Besides he is entitled to designate a consignee. Sometimes according to the L/C rules, if the buyer performs as a shipper, then the consignor is an applicant for the opening of the L/C.

3) **Consignee**

A party related to a sales contract, which is entitled to take delivery at the port of destination by presenting a B/L to the carrier, is usually a buyer. How to fill the document depends on specific circumstance.

**4) Notify Party**

Notify party refers to someone informed by a carrier to take delivery of the goods at the port of destination, who may be irrelevant to the title of goods.

In addition, a notify party can be the assignee or the owner.

(4) **Contents Indicated on a B/L**

Generally, contents indicated on a B/L include both the front clauses and back clauses.

**1) Front Clauses on a B/L**

① Clauses offered and written by a consignor include consignor, consignee, notify party, itemized contents, shipping marks, the number of packages, gross weight, measurement etc. If filling in incorrectly, the shipper must be consequently responsible for the missing, loss, and cost caused by it.

② Clauses offered by carrier include two parts: printed clauses and written clauses.

**Printed clauses are as follows:**

Fine appearance clause: The goods which are in good condition have been loaded onto the above-mentioned vessel and would be shipped to and discharged at a designated port of destination where the vessel can park there safely.

Unknown content clause: The carrier fails to check the descriptions of goods offered by the shipper, such as weight, measurement, shipping marks, number of packages, quality, and value.

Agreement and acceptance clause: Consignor, consignee, and the owner of the B/L agree to and accept the regulations, disclaimers, and conditions printed and written both on the front of and back of a B/L.

**2) Back Clauses of a B/L**

Clauses printed on the back of a B/L specify the rights, responsibilities and liability exemptions between the carrier and the shipper. It serves as a legal basis when handling the disputes.

(5) **Types of B/L**

B/L may take various forms, which could be classified as follows:

**1) Being Classified by Whether the Goods are Loaded or not:**

① On Board B/L or Shipped B/L. After loading all the cargos onto a vessel, the carrier will issue a shipped-on-board B/L which indicates when and where the cargos have been loaded. An on-board B/L is widely adopted in the international trade, for it is more secure for the consignor to receive the cargos on time.

② Received for Shipment B/L. A received for shipment B/L denotes that merchandise has been received, but indicates no specific date or the name of ship. Whether the goods have been loaded or shipped is not guaranteed. Even the goods are paid by documentary letter of credit, the banks will not accept it. Most of the time, when the goods have been loaded onto a vessel, the shipper exchanges the received for shipment B/L for an on-board B/L. Or the carrier adds "have been loaded vessel..." and date on it and stamps. However, a received B/L is acceptable in container transport.

**2) Being Classified by Whether the Carrier Makes a Statement (Clause) or not:**

A B/L denotes that merchandise is in good condition upon being loaded, and with no statement (clause) like damaged packages added by the carrier. When presenting for negotiation, the exporter must provide a clean B/L. Meanwhile, the importer must present a clean B/L when transferring B/L.

An unclean B/L will have a statement (clause) about the appearance or other bad conditions of goods, such as obscure marks, loose packages, foul or broken packages. A bank will never allow for such foul B/L. Under this circumstance, the shipper must repair or change the commodities, or show a letter of indemnity to the carrier, then the shipping party will issue a clean B/L.

**3) Being Classified by Transport Mode:**

Direct B/L denotes that the cargos are shipped directly to the port of destination by one vessel, with no transshipment halfway.

Transshipment B/L denotes that the cargos, after being loaded onto a vessel, are transshipped halfway instead of being taken to the destination directly. Normally a transshipment B/L indicates descriptions like "Port of transshipment: ×××".

Through B/L involves two or more modes of transport, normally including ocean transport. It is issued by the initial carrier who may continue to be responsible for the rest of the transport.

Both transshipment B/L and through B/L cover the whole journey. The carrier or his/her agent requires on the B/L that he/she is liable under a contract of carriage only for his/her own phase of the journey, regardless of other phases after the goods have been discharged.

With the rapid development of container transport, there appeals a containerized door-to-door shipment that involves two or more modes of transport. Under this circumstance, the bill issued by a carrier or his/her agent is called combined transport B/L, which is now, for example, adopted by COSCO (China Ocean Shipping Group) in China.

**4) Being Classified by Format:**

① Short form B/L is also known as blank black B/L, which is one where the terms and conditions are not printed on the reverse. Short form B/L could be further divided into charter party B/L and liner B/L.

• A charter party B/L bears a sentence like "All terms and conditions as per charter party dated …". Suck kind B/L is governed by the charter party, which itself is not an independent document. Therefore, banks generally refuse to accept such B/L unless there are specifications under the L/C.

• A liner B/L is adopted for the sake of simplification of the B/L. On a liner B/L, we can find "The receipt, storage, carriage and freight of goods listed on this bill are subject to all the terms and exceptional terms appearing on the front and reverse of this long form B/L of our company, either printed, written, stamped and printed. This long form B/L is kept in our company, branch and agents for your reference at any time." According to the conventions of international banking services, a bank could pay with this B/L.

② A long form B/L has terms and conditions of responsibilities and liabilities of the carrier and the shipper printed on its reverse.

**5) Being Classified by Different Consignees:**

A straight B/L indicates the specified name of a person or a company as the consignee. A straight B/L is generally accepted to be one that makes the goods deliverable to a named consignee, which avoids probable risks brought about during the negotiation process and makes sure that the goods are always under the control of the shipper. In this way, however, the consignee may transfer the B/L through property transferability. So the banks probably refuse to accept a straight B/L when negotiating payment.

Blank B/L (also known as open B/L or bearer B/L) denotes that there is no specific consignee, but words like "To Bearer" on it. Anyone who holds the B/L can pick up the goods from the port of destination. A bearer bill can be negotiated by the physical delivery, the potential risk of which results in the rare use of it in international trade.

Order B/L denotes that there are only words like "To Order" or "To Order of" filled in the blank of the consignee. The object of "To Order of" could be the order from the shipper or from the importer's bank. Order B/L could be transferred to a third party by endorsement without permission of the person who issues the original B/L.

Endorsement takes two forms: blank endorsement and special endorsement. The former denotes that only an endorser(shipper) signs his/her name on the reverse without an endorsee's (assignee's) name. The latter denotes that in addition to an endorser's signature, the endorsee should also sign his or her name on the bills. If the assignee of a special B/L needs to transfer it, another endorsement should be added. Generally, we describe an order B/L with a blank endorsement as "blank order and endorsement B/L", which is widely used in the international trade.

**6) Being Classified by the Effects:**

An original B/L has a signature signed by the carrier, captain or his/her agent. An exporter must present an original one to the bank when negotiating payment and an importer must do the same thing when taking delivery of the commodities. There are two or more original bills of lading in a service and when one of them comes into force, the rest automatically voids.

A copy B/L has no signature by the carrier, captain or his agent. It only serves as a reference for the business. Different from the original one, there are words like "Copy" or "Not Negotiable" on the copy one.

**7) Stale B/L**

A stale B/L denotes that the consignee receives the goods after the vessel has arrived at the port of destination, which is often happening in near-sea shipping cases. At present, if a payment is done by the L/C, a stale B/L that is delivered later than the last date specified on the L/C, or 21 days after a B/L is issued if there is no specific regulation, will affect related parties' benefits. Therefore, according to ICC *Uniform Customs and Practice for Documentary* (revised in 2007), a stale B/L is rejected by banks.

**8) Advanced B/L**

When the loading of goods is completed later than the loading date specified in a contract or the loading date and last date specified on L/C, a carrier would issue a B/L in advance the shipment. An advanced B/L is often adopted when a vessel arrives later than expected or a shipper fails to offer the goods on time. If it is the shipper who should bear the responsibilities, he/she needs to present a letter of indemnity. A carrier, however, still needs to take the blame like issuing a fake B/L.

### 9) Anti-dated B/L

When the real loading date is later than the one specified on the L/C or in a contract, a carrier changes the date to be in line with the regulations at a shipper's requirement. A carrier shall bear similar risks happening in an advanced B/L, so he/she seldom adopts it.

### 10) On Deck B/L

An on-deck B/L is issued by a carrier to prove that the goods are loaded on deck. According to Hague Rules, a carrier bears no responsibilities for the damages or missing of goods on deck during the journey or on the open sea. Therefore, a shipper should buy insurance covering on deck risks in case of any losses in the future.

In addition to the above-mentioned bills, there are combined B/L, separate B/L, switch B/L, house B/L etc., which would not be reiterated here.

## (6) How to Complete a B/L

### 1) Shipper

If the payment is done by the L/C, unless there are other stipulations, generally the shipper is the first beneficiary. If it is a negotiable L/C, the shipper could be the assignee (second beneficiary).

If the payment is done by collection, the consigner could be the shipper.

### 2) Consignee

If the payment is done by the L/C, this blank must be filled in according to the L/C stipulations. Because it has a direct influence on whether a B/L is negotiable, as well as on the ownership of the goods. Normally, we adopt an order B/L where the consignee blank should be filled with "To Order" "To Order of XXX Co." "To Order of XXX Bank" or "To Order of Shipper".

If the payment is done by collection, the consignee is a blank order.

### 3) Notify Party

If the payment is done by the L/C, this blank must be filled in according to the L/C stipulations.

A notify party is the agent of a consignee. When the goods arrive, a notify party should ask the consignee to make preparations for taking delivery. Therefore, the address of a notify party must be offered for a carrier or his agent. If an L/C does not specify a detailed address, to keep in line with the shipping documents, this part on an original B/L could be left blank.

### 4) Ocean Vessel Voy. No.

This part is about the name and No. of a vessel involved.

### 5) Port of Loading

This part is about the name of the actual port of loading, which should be in line with the stipulations in the L/C.

### 6) Port of Discharge

If the goods are directly delivered to the port of destination, with no transshipment, then filling the final destination in. If the goods are transshipped at a port halfway, then the transshipment port. For example, the cargos transshipped at Hong Kong China, then filling "Hong Kong China (W/T)" in, which means "With Transshipment at Hong Kong China".

### 7) Final Destination

This part must be filled according to the L/C stipulations. If the ports share the same name, then the country name must be added.

### 8) Freight Payable at

If the trade term is FOB, then filling in the port of destination. If the trade term is CFR or CIF, then the port of loading. Normally, this part could be left blank.

### 9) Number and Kind of Packages

The number and kind of packages should keep the same with the real situation. The number of packages should be printed in capital letters. If there are two or more packages, like iron drums and cartons, the number of different packages should be listed separately, and then a total number below the descriptions. For example:

200 Cartons

<u>300 Iron Drums</u>

500 Packages

When shipping the bulk cargos, filling in "In Bulk" is OK and the "Total Number of Packages" could be left blank.

### 10) Shipping Marks

This part should be filled in according to the contents of the L/C and must keep the same with the shipping marks on the other documents.

### 11) Description of Goods

A simple description is enough, no need to list in detail.

### 12) Gross Weight and Measurement

Unless there are specific stipulations on the L/C, there is no need to fill in the net weight. Only gross weight is enough, whose unit is kilogram and could be rounded to one digit. The unit of measurement is the cubic meter, rounded to three decimal places.

### 13) Freight

If the payment is done by the L/C, the fees of B/L delivery depend on the payment terms of a contract or the L/C stipulations. In a FOB contract, "Freight to Collect" "Freight Payable at Destination" or "Freight to be Paid at Destination" should be mentioned. In a contract of CFR or CIF, "Freight Prepaid" or "Freight Paid" should be mentioned, but no statements like "Freight Pre-payable" or "Freight to be paid".

### 14) Place and Date of Issue

The place where a B/L is issued should be the same as the port of lading. According to the international conventions, the date of issue is when the goods are loaded. Therefore, the date of issue must not be later than the date of loading.

### 15) Number of Original B/L

If the payment is done by the L/C, the number of original B/L must be in confirmity with the number specified on the L/C. For example, statement like "Full set 3/3 original clean on-board ocean B/L" means three original bills of lading are required. Some letters of credit have no explicit requirements about the number, but requirement like "... available by Beneficiary's drafts at sight drawn on us and accompanied by the following documents in duplicate" which denotes that all the shipping documents must have one original and two copies.

**16) Signed for the Carrier**

The signature must be done by the shipping company or its agent.

### 9.4.1.2 Sea Waybill

Like ocean B/L, a sea waybill is a document issued by a carrier or his/her agent to the shipper to make sure that the goods have been loaded onto a specified ship, or are ready to be loaded onto a specified ship for a designated port. A sea waybill serves as a receipt of cargos, as well as an evidence of the contract of carriage. The difference is that a sea waybill could not perform as a document of title, but a guarantee for the shipment of goods. When the carrier breaks the contract, such as delivery of wrong cargos, the shipper could ask for compensation by means of sea waybill. Though the ownership of goods is not negotiable, the rights and liabilities of a shipper to a carrier could be transferred to the consignee on a sea waybill.

The shipping company only issues one original sea waybill, sometimes two or more if required by a shipper. A week before the arrival of the ship, the shipping company would send an arrival advice to the consignee, who may sign the order and exchange it for a B/L. The consignee must present this B/L when taking delivery from the shipping company.

At present, a sea waybill is used more than before and has been accepted by banks.

1) The sea waybill shall be subject to any International Convention or National Law, which is compulsorily applicable thereto.

2) The sea waybill is not rejected by a bank.

3) Both parties to a contract and the port of destination are clear.

4) The consignee agrees with the use of sea waybill.

5) There is no need to negotiate the document of title.

After meeting the above-mentioned requirements, we encourage the use of sea waybill when facing the following conditions:

1) When shipping the goods by vessels (Both parties to a contract and the port of destination are clear).

2) When shipping the goods by high-speed vessels, like container ships.

3) When the journey is not long during a through shipment.

4) When a contract is done between two intimate parties or between a parent company and its subsidiary.

5) When a bank which issues the L/C is willing to be a consignee of the sea waybill.

### 9.4.2 Railway Transport Documents

Railway transport takes two forms: One is International through Railway Transport and the other is Railway Transport of Goods for Hong Kong China, each of which has its own documents. The former adopts an International Railway though Waybill, a contract of carriage between the railway line and the shipper. It stipulates the rights, liabilities and responsibilities of delivery for the railway line, shipper and consignee. Besides, it has legal effect on these three parties. In express transport, on both the front and back of the bill, there is a red line (1cm) on both top and bottom margin to show the difference with slow transport. Fill in the bill by the language of a forwarding country and add Russian (or German) translation under each line. For goods transported within China and North Korea or Vietnam, there is no translation. While within other countries, the text is translated into Russian. On a rail waybill, the part with the bold line below is completed by railway line; other parts are completed by the shipper. Rail waybills are issued in one set of different-color pages.

(1) **Original Railway Bill**

When the goods arrive at the station of destination, both original railway bill and arrival notice would be handed into the shipper, who could pick up the goods by presenting the original one.

(2) **Train Journal**

It serves as a proof related to the cargo handover, responsibilities, transport expenses, cargo volume and incomes. A train journal arrives at the station along with the goods.

(3) **Copy Railway Bill**

After the establishment of a contract of carriage, the copy will be given to the shipper, which does not have a legal effect as the original one, but may serve as a proof of the receipt of goods by a railway line. Besides, according to the regulations between China and North Korea, Vietnam, Mongolia, Russia and Eastern European countries, when a shipper asks for money from a consignee via two countries' banks, he/she must present a copy with a date stamp. When a shipper or a consignee ask for compensation from the railway or the change of route, he/she must also present a copy.

(4) **Delivery Order**

A delivery order arrives at the station along with the goods, which is signed by a consignee when taking delivery.

(5) **Arrival Notice**

An arrival notice arrives at the station together with the goods. Then both arrival notice and original railway bill are presented to the consignee.

Apart from that, additional train journals must be prepared for cross-border roads.

A Cargo receipt is adopted in railway transport of goods for Hong Kong China. It serves as a document of carriage between a carrier and a shipper that responsible for the whole journey to Hong Kong China, which is issued by forwarders (international companies of different places) to industrial and trading companies. Besides, it must be presented when a shipper negotiates payment with a bank and it is a proof for the consignee who is located in Hong Kong China to take delivery from the station.

A set of cargo receipt has four pages: one original, two copies and one copy for reference. The number could be changed according to the real situation. The contents are similar to those of ocean bill of lading. It should be noted that the contents should be written in Chinese or both Chinese and English, where the Chinese must be simplified characters by State Council. The consignee should be a Hong Kong bank, while the "Notify Party" should be the real consignee in Hong Kong China.

### 9.4.3 Airway Bill

An airway bill (AWB) is a receipt issued by an international airline for goods and an evidence of the contract of carriage, but it is not a document of title to the goods. Hence, the air waybill is non-negotiable. Each set of airway bill has three originals and at least six copies. These three originals are printed in different colors. The first original, blue in color, performs as a cargo receipt, which is issued by a carrier or his/her agent for a shipper. The second original, green in color, performs as an evidence of the interior accounting. The third original, pink in color, is delivered with the goods and given to a consignee as an evidence of cargo receipt when arriving at the station. One copy, yellow in color, performs as a delivery receipt and a consignee shall sign his/her name on when taking delivery and keep it for the check. The rest copies are in white color and are separately sent to the agent, the port of destination and first, second and third carrier. The number of copies could be increased if in short. On the right side of each airway bill, there is a number. The first three digits are the Airline Prefix, China's civil aviation, for example, is 999. The rest eight digits are the serial number of the Airway Bill.

There are two kinds of airway bills: One is Master Airway Bill (MAWB), issued by an airline, and the other is House Airway Bill (HAWB), issued by a freight forwarder. A freight forwarder offers a consolidation service and will issue its own airway bill or bill of lading. An airline only issues one set of airway bill. Both airway bills share similar contents and have similar legal effects. But in a HAWB, a freight forwarder bears all the responsibilities of cargo transport.

### 9.4.4 Parcel Post Receipt

Parcel post receipt is the main document in parcel post transport, which is issued by a post office when they receive the parcel. A consignee could present it when picking up the parcel. If a parcel is damaged or missing, the receipt could also perform as a proof for compensation, but not a document of title.

### 9.4.5 Multimodal Transport Documents

Multimodal transport documents (MTD) are used under the transportation of goods which are performed with at least two different means of transport. They are issued by a multimodal transport operator (MTO) to prove that he has taken over the goods. An MTD is responsible for the whole process of the carriage. To keep pace with the development of unitized transport and containerized transport, more and more multimodal transport documents are adopted in the international delivery services.

## 9.5 Commercial Documents: Insurance Documents

### 9.5.1 The Definition and Function of Insurance Documents

The insurance document is the insurance contract between the insurance company and the applicant, which specifies the rights and obligations of both parties. It is also the insurance certificate for the insurer issued by the insurance company. When the insured goods suffer from the loss of insurance liability, the insurance bill is the main basis for the insurer to claim against the insurance company. It is also the basis for the insurance company to settle the claim. At the same time, the insurance bill is a major part of a full set of shipping documents.

The insurance policy of general property insurance is not an adjunct to the insurance subject and cannot be transferred with the passing of title of insurance subject. However, the international cargo transportation insurance policy has its specialty. According to the international practice of insurance, endorsed by the insured, cargo transportation insurance policy can be transferred with cargo ownership instead of asking for the permission of the insurer or informing the insurer. This is because the international cargo transportation is not controlled or managed by the insured but finished by the third party. The insured fails to exert his influence on the goods shipped in transit, that is to say, the risk that may happen in transit is the same even the insured are different. There are stipulations aforementioned in many countries' insurance law, PICC (The People's Insurance Company(Group) of China Limited), for example, also handles insurance business according to the international practice.

#### 9.5.1.1 Party to an Insurance Policy

The person who collects the premium is responsible for the loss in accordance with a marine insurance contract, also known as the insurer.

#### 9.5.1.2 The Assured or The Insured

Known as applicant or proposer, the insured is the person who enters into an insurance contract with the insurer and pays the premium. In the event of loss of insurance subject, the insured has the right to claim against the insurer and accept all or part of the compensation of the insurable interest. According to the usual practice, the insured shall be eligible for the indemnity only if he meets two conditions as follows:

(1) **The Insured Shall Have an Insurable Interest in the Insurance Subject**

The insurable interest refers to the insured's certain legitimate economic interest of the insurance subject. In marine insurance, such economic interest embodies the insured's ownership and security interest of the insurance subject or the bearing of economic risk and responsibility. The insured shall benefit from the safe or anticipated arrival of insurance subject as well as be damaged or be liable for the loss of the subject.

(2) **The Insured Shall Have Good Faith**

It means that the insured shall honestly introduce the goods, means of transportation and routes of transportation, which is the principle of "utmost good faith" in the insurance business.

#### 9.5.1.3 Insurance Agent

Authorized by the insurer, the insurance agent instead of the insurer solicits insurance business to issue the cover note or insurance policy within the prescribed scope of authorization. And the insurance agent is a middleman who inspects and adjusts the loss. The insurance company signs a contract with the insurance agent in terms of many businesses that cannot be completed. The agency fee is paid by the insurance company, and the rights and obligations of agency acts are directly undertaken by the insurance company.

#### 9.5.1.4 Insurer Broker

It is the middleman between the insurer and the insured, who especially represents the insured to sign a contract with the insurance company and collect commissions from the company.

At present, in the foreign trade of most countries in the world, the importer and exporter do not directly contact the insurer for insurance but entrust the insurance broker to do the business. The marine insurance needs special knowledge because of its professional and complicated procedures. The insurer broker specializes in the insurance business and is trusted by importers or exporters. Legally, the insurance broker has a special position, who is an agent on behalf of the insured to apply for insurance with preferential terms and low premiums. But the due commission is deducted by insurance personnel from the premiums. When the insurer broker accepts the insurance business, he/she issues a cover note and ensures the insurer, thus the cover note is not an insurance contract but an agreement of insurance agency.

### 9.5.2 Types of Insurance Policy

#### 9.5.2.1 Being Classified by Forms of Insurance Policy

(1) **Insurance Policy**

An insurance policy (See Appendix I) is a formal insurance contract. The insurance policy is used to cover the loss of a certain cargo within a specified voyage, and is legally binding on the insurer and the insured. It's divided into two parts: front clauses and back clauses. The main contents of front clauses include: the name and address of the insured; the name of the insured goods, amount and marks; the amount of insurance; means of loading and transporting, shipment date, the port of loading and port of destination; conditions; name and address of the insurance agent; claim payable at; date and place of making an insurance policy as well as signature of the insurer, etc. On the back, the rights and obligations of the insurer and the insured are stipulated in detail. In a contract with CIF and CIP, the buyer usually requires an insurance policy.

(2) **Insurance Certificate**

The insurance certificate does not record detailed terms of the rights and obligations of the insurer and the insured. Other items in it are the same as insurance policy and have an equal legal effect, but if the buyer requires an insurance policy, insurance certificate cannot replace it.

(3) **Combined Certificate**

The combined certificate is a combination of the invoice and insurance policy. It is a more simplified insurance document than an insurance policy, but it has the same legal effect as an insurance policy. The insurance company fills the types, amount and number of insurance in the applicant's invoice. And other items shall be the same as the invoice stated. It is mainly used for the export between some Chinese businessmen and these businessmen who are located in Hong Kong China, Macao China, Singapore and Malaysia.

## Chapter 9 Documents for International Settlement

### (4) Cover Note

It is an informal and temporary insurance policy, which is pre-issued by the insurer in the event that the insured does not know the name of the vessel and the shipment date. The applicant immediately informs the insurer of the ship name and sailing date, and then exchanges formal insurance policy or adds it on the cover note by endorsement. In general, banks do not accept a cover note issued by a broker.

### (5) Endorsement

If the insured wants to add or change the contents of an insurance policy after its issuing, he may submit a written application to the insurance company. After asking permission, the document that has marked change and supplement of contents issued by the insurance company, is called an endorsement. Endorsement and the original insurance policy constitute a new insurance contract, which is legally binding on the applicant and the insurer.

## 9.5.2.2 Being Classified by Forms of Insurance

### (1) Floating Policy

The floating policy only ensures conditions of insurance but is uncertain of goods. The floating policy only displays a list of categories of goods, conditions, grades of carrying vessels and navigation area, total amount insured, and etc. After the shipment of goods, the insured declares the name of the vessel and goods to the insurer until the value of insurance policy runs out. And the floating policy provides a way to withdraw an insurance policy. The policy remains valid as long as it has not been withdrawn and the total amount insured has the balance.

In order to prevent many concentrated risks, the insurer adds to the list "Per Ship Clause" and "Place Limit Clause", etc.

### (2) Open Policy

Actually, the open policy is the open contract, which is an insurance policy that ensures all the goods shipped within a certain period of time. The open policy specifies the insured goods' coverage, conditions, premium rate, utmost insurance amount, methods of premium payment, etc. In order to facilitate the trade companies and increase business, the insurance company can book the insurance business of transportation of import and export goods. Once the goods under open insurance are shipped, they will be automatically insured according to conditions stated in the open policy. The insured needs not handle insurance of each shipment. But after the insured is informed of shipment of each cargo, the insurer shall be informed of the name of goods, number, insurance amount, types and name of means of transportation, terminal place of the voyage, sailing date, etc. in writing (or in the form of shipment notice).

The open policy facilitates the companies that often import and export. It can prevent the losses caused by missing the insurance and eliminate the procedures of the individual insurance.

### (3) Blanket Policy

Blanket policy, also known as closed policy, is the insurer's total slip of subject matter insurance within the agreed period of insurance.

## 9.5.3 The Making of Insurance Policy

The insurance policy is made by the insurance company according to the insurance application, commercial invoice, transport document and the L/C that offered by the insured.

Generally, the name and address of the insurance company as well as both Chinese and English name of the insurance policy are printed, we only analyze the columns that need to be filled out.

**(1) Policy No.**

Policy No. generally consists of three parts: district number, year and a serial number of the insurance company.

**(2) Invoice No.**

This column is filled out according to No. of the commercial invoice.

**(3) Insured**

The insured is filled out after "At the request of" in the insurance policy, which customarily has three methods as follows:

1) If the L/C stipulates or requires "Endorsed in Blank", the beneficiary's name shall be filled out and detailed address can be omitted, and meanwhile the export company shall endorse in an insurance policy.

2) If the L/C stipulates the endorsement to... bank, i.e. "Endorsed to the order of... Bank", the beneficiary's name still shall be filled in and sentences like "To order of... Bank" or "Claim if any pay to order of... Bank" shall be filled out in the insurance policy. And there shall be the beneficiary's signature.

3) If the L/C designates... Company or... Bank or someone as the insured, the column remains unchanged and the exporter does not endorse.

**(4) Marks & Nos**

This column shall be consistent with invoice and the B/L. It can be filled as "As Per Invoice No...." if the L/C has no special provisions.

**(5) Description of Goods**

These two columns shall be consistent with the related invoice.

**(6) Amount Insured**

The L/C generally stipulates that the amount insured shall be filled out according to 110% of the CIF invoice value. And this column must be in accordance with Total Amount Insured.

**(7) Premium & Rate**

These two columns are generally known by the inside of the insurance company and "As Arranged" is printed on the insurance policy, so they may not be filled. But you should fill them out if it is stipulated by the certificate.

**(8) Per Conveyance S.S.**

This column shall be filled out the name of vessel and voyage if there is a direct vessel in the ocean carriage. The name of the vessel of the first and second voyage shall be filled out and they shall be connected with "With Transshipment" in case of transshipment en route. It shall be filled in accordingly if there are other means of transportation, such as "By Train, Wagon No. . ." "By Airplane" and etc.

(9) SLG. On ABT

Fill it out according to the date of transport document.

(10) From. . . to. . .

It shall be filled according to the transport document. And it must be filled out if there is transshipment en route, i. e. "From Shanghai to London W/T Hong Kong China"; if the port of destination on the B/L is New York but Chicago is stipulated in the L/C, it shall be filled out as "From Shanghai to New York and thence to Chicago".

(11) Conditions

The conditions of the insurance policy under the L/C shall be handled according to the stipulations of the L/C.

Conditions are the most important parts of an insurance policy, so particular attention must be paid to the correctness and preciseness of conditions.

If the L/C stipulates "Covering All Risks and the Risk of War", the insurance policy may be filled as "Covering All Risks as per Ocean Marine Cargo Clauses and Ocean Marine Cargo War Risks Clauses".

(12) The Company's Agent

The detailed address of the company's agent shall be filled in the blank. The consignee may immediately contact the agent if any insurance accident of insured goods happens.

(13) Claim Payable at. . .

If there are no specific stipulations in L/C, port of destination shall be filled in this column.

(14) Place and Date of Issue

The issue date of insurance policy shall be earlier than or the same as transport document but definitely no later than that. Place of issue shall be the one where the beneficiary locates and usually it is already printed in the insurance policy.

(15) Authorized Signature

The insurance policy takes effect an the insurance company's signature and usually the signature is printed on the policy.

The insurance document must be carefully made and it's better not to alter so as to keep its tidiness. Any mistakes, omissions and modifications shall be filled with proofreading.

## 9.6 Other Commercial Documents

### 9.6.1 Packing List and Weight List

#### 9.6.1.1 Packing List

A packing list is also referred to as a packaging list or a packing slip. It specifies the goods packaging and detailed information of each packaging unit, such as the specification, pattern and color and design of each item, so packing list is also referred to as Specification of Contents (See

Appendix J). In international trade practice, the document of general machine parts, clothing, textiles, handicrafts and non-quantitative packaging of goods requires to be issued; in particular, packaging conditions of the non-quantitative packaging of goods shall be listed one by one. Import customs inspection, survey or inspection and goods check by importers shall be based on a packing list.

At present, the packing list format in those international trade companies is different in China, but its main format and items are similar. The contents are as follows:

(1) **Name**

Customarily, it is a template with the words "Packing List" printed on top by the export companies. In some cases, the importer would ask for a Packing List along with a Weight Note. If combined form documents are acceptable, the exporter could also present one like these. Under this circumstance, the shipper should add words "and Weight Note" after "Packing List", better with a confirmation stamp.

(2) **Invoice Number**

Generally, it shall fill out the invoice number.

(3) **Date of Issue**

It should be the same as the date of issue of invoice, no later than the date on B/L, and the expiry date of L/C.

(4) **Number of L/C and Contract**

If there are no specific requirements on L/C, this field could be left blank.

(5) **Name of Buyer**

It is the name of the applicant. It shall omit the full address or fill out "To Whom It May Concern".

(6) **Shipping Marks**

Contents in this section shall stay the same with those of invoice and the B/L.

(7) **Description of Goods and Quantity**

Name of goods can be called by a joint name. If there are no special requirements on the L/C, it shall give a brief description of the goods packaging and fill out the number of packages in both words and numbers. If the L/C requires a detailed packing list, then specific descriptions concerning the cargo loading shall be provided, as well as the details of each package. Sometimes if the L/C requires to state the origin or to make a statement on the packing list, the shipper shall follow these accordingly.

(8) **Weight**

It includes both the gross weight and net weight of the goods. If the L/C requires to list the gross weight or tare of a single item, the shipper shall follow the requirements accordingly.

(9) **Size or Measurement**

This file shall be filled out based on the real measurement, which must be in line with the L/C stipulations.

### 9.6.1.2 Weight Memo, Weight Note or Weight List

It is a document used in the international trade to describe the weight of each packaging unit

(See Appendix K). If both parties enter into a contract based on the shipping weight, the shipper must present a weight list to the consignee during loading, who may use it for checking when taking delivery. Weight list is more suitable to commodity trade where the weight of the goods is the key element, such as foods etc. and the contents emphasize the record and the proof of detailed weight of the goods.

A weight list could be issued by the exporters, commodity inspection agencies, surveyors, weight surveyors and so on. If the weight list is issued by commodity inspection agency, it is referred to as Weight Certificate. At the time of delivery at the port of loading, if the exporter provides weight list or other documents which are in line with the provisions of the contract, the delivery is completed. In case of short shipment of goods arrived at the port of destination, the importer must submit a certificate of weight in order to make a claim against the exporter, shipping company or insurance company.

A weight list generally includes the invoice number, date, the name of goods, shipping marks, gross weight, net weight, tare and the total number of packages.

The weight list is also a subsidiary document of the invoice as a packing list. When issued, its contents should be consistent with the related items of invoice, B/L, etc. Date of issue shall be the same as that of invoice but no earlier than the invoice date.

## 9.6.2 Shipping Company's Certificate

It is a document issued by a shipping company to an importer, who would present it when the government wants to know about the carriage conditions.

Common Shipping Company's Certificate:

### 9.6.2.1 Certificate of Vessel's Nationality

It refers to a certificate issued by the shipping company stating the nationality of the carrying vessel. If there are specific requirements for the nationality of the carrying vessel, certificate of vessel's nationality must be in line with the L/C stipulations.

### 9.6.2.2 Certificate of the Vessel's Age

It refers to a certificate issued by the shipping company stating the age of the carrying vessel. Generally, vessels with the age of more than 15 years are overage vessels. The age of the carrying vessel is often stipulated by importers in the L/C. For example, the L/C stipulates that "Shipment to be effected by regular liner under 15 years of age otherwise the overage premium, if any to be paid by the beneficiary". If the carrying vessel's age is required in the L/C, exporters shall require the shipping company to issue the certificate of vessel's age, even if it is not clearly demanded in the L/C. The document is used by exporters to prove they have acted upon what is required in the L/C.

### 9.6.2.3 Certificate of Classification

It refers to a certificate issued by shipping company stating that the carrying vessel meets certain classification criteria. Common ship classification terms in the L/C is: "A certificate from an international classification society, stating that all ship cargo gears are in good working order and condition is required" and "Goods to be shipped by vessels covered by Institute Classification Clause". In case of such similar terms, the exporter shall provide the certificate of classification issued by the shipping company.

### 9.6.2.4 Black List Certificate

It refers to a certificate issued by the shipping company stating that the carrying vessel is not included in the blacklist. The blacklist made by Arab countries lists the vessel names, which have dealings with Israel. If the vessel is on the blacklist, Arab countries shall not allow any transport business with the country. Therefore, an import business in Arab countries or in the L/C, the blacklist certificate requires to be issued by the shipping company.

### 9.6.2.5 Route Certificate

It is a certificate presented by the captain or the ship's agent stating the ports, ports of call, routes and nationality of the vessel during the voyage. The contents of the route certificate, under the L/C, are entirely based on the requirements of the L/C. If there is a difference between the contents and the L/C, the document is discrepant.

The most common content of the route certificate is as follows:

To whom it may concern:

This is to certify that S. S. "..." flying the flag of the People's Republic of China. will not call at any Israeli ports during this present voyage, according to the schedule, and so far as we know that she is not blacklisted by the Arabian countries.

The shipping company or the ship is often required to issue such certificates in the Red Sea and the Persian Gulf region. Certainly, the format and content are not fixed.

### 9.6.2.6 Certificate of Transshipment Notice

It is a document proving that the captain, the agent or the shipper transship the goods halfway, with which the forwarder could inform the consignee of related stuff. If the L/C stipulates that the certificate must be issued, the second carrying vessel's name must be advised to the consignee when certifying transshipment.

In case transshipment is allowed, port of transshipment and the second carrying vessel's name should be advised to the consignee and beneficiary's certificate to accompany the documents.

### 9.6.2.7 Captain's Receipt

Captain's receipt is issued by the captain to certify that the exporter has entrusted the document to the captain to deliver. In practice, to prevent the document arriving later than goods or for other reasons, the importer often requires the exporter to deliver a certain document or one set of originals or copies to the captain of the carrying vessel when shipping and the captain deliver it to the consignee. The certificate of receipt issued by the captain after he/she receives the document from the exporter is Captain's Receipt. It indicates the type and number of documents received and states that the document will be delivered to the designated person upon arrival at the port of destination.

Under the L/C, a captain's receipt is issued in accordance with the terms of the L/C. For example, the term of the L/C is like this: "Original certificate of Quality, Weight and Analysis should be handed to the Captain of the carrying vessel, and a captain's receipt to accompany the document." The exporter must submit a receipt from the captain of the carrying vessel who has received Original Certificate of Quality, Weight and Analysis, and a captain's receipt to accompany other documents to the bank for negotiation.

The main content of a captain's receipt can be made by the exporter himself/herself and then handed to the captain to review, sign and return.

## 9.6.3 Beneficiary's Statement

Beneficiary's Statement is, by means of payment of the L/C, to certify that the exporter has fulfilled some obligation or handled some work in accordance with requirements of the L/C. In practice, the common statements are about the quality of goods, packaging, sent shipping notice, sent samples and non-negotiable documents. The beneficiary shall make a statement with a formal signature in accordance with the L/C stipulations.

Generally, the beneficiary is required to certify that the goods are not of Israeli origin in the L/C from countries in the Red Sea and the Persian Gulf. This beneficiary's statement is sometimes required only to be proved in the invoice. The beneficiary's statement can be as follows:

This is to certify that the goods are not of Israeli origin and that on materials of Israeli origin have been used in their manufacture.

Wooden packing is not allowed in some countries, such as Iraq. The requirement of Australia, New Zealand, South Africa and other countries for the packing of imported goods is: Wood should be fumigated or heat-treated in case of use of wooden case (including wooden used in pallet or export wooden) in packing. Otherwise, the goods will be burned at the arrival of the port of destination and the loss shall be borne by the shipper. Statement of wooden packing or statement like this is often required in the L/C from these countries.

The common terms of wooden packing in the L/C are:

(1) Do not use plant stuff in packing to avoid plant disease.

(2) No wooden containers or wooden packing have been used in the packing of goods covered by this invoice.

For term 1, the beneficiary's statement can be as follows:

We declare that we have not used plant stuff in packing to avoid plant disease.

For term 2, the beneficiary's statement in the invoice can be as follows:

We state that no wooden containers or wooden packing have been used in the packing of goods.

Some L/C require that the exporter should send one set of non-negotiable documents to the applicant (importer) after loading. Apart from that, the exporter should also present a receipt from the courier to the importer. For example, the document must be submitted in the L/C is:

Beneficiary's certificate of airmailing one set of non-negotiable documents to the applicant after the shipment.

Under the terms of the L/C, the beneficiary's statement can be as follows:

We certify that we have airmailed one set of non-negotiable documents to the applicant.

## 9.7 Official Documents

The official document is one of the most important types of documents in the international settlement business. In the international business, the common official documents include customs invoice, consular invoice, commodity inspection certificate and certificate of origin, etc.

### 9.7.1 Customs Invoice

Customs invoice is a kind of invoice with a fixed format made by the customs in some countries and shall be filled out by foreign exporters. It has three different names: Customs Invoice, CCVO-Combined Certificate of Value and Origin and Certificate Invoice in accordance with... customs regulations.

This invoice is required by the importer mainly as a basis for the evaluation of tax clearance and the imposition of differential treatment customs duties and anti-dumping duties and could also be used for compiling statistics. The invoice should be handed to the customs by the importer at customs entry.

pay attention to the notes as follows in filling out customs invoice:

1) Each country (or region) has its own customs invoice of its own format which is changeable, and these customs invoices with different formats should not be mixed up.

2) The contents shared by commercial invoice and customs invoice should be in line with each other.

3) The section "Domestic Market Price in the Exporting Country" is an important basis for the customs of the exporting country to decide whether to impose the anti-dumping duties or not. Therefore, it should be handled carefully according to the relative regulations when filling in.

4) If the transaction price is the CIF, CFR, freight and insurance should be listed separately and the sum of the three should be equal to the value of CIF.

5) Both the signatory and certifier shall act in their personal capacity and cannot be the same one. The signature shall be valid by hand.

### 9.7.2 Consular Invoice

Consular invoice is a document with a fixed format made by the consulate of the importing country. It shall be signed by the consulate of the importing country in the exporting country after the seller fills it in. But sometimes it can be replaced by the commercial invoice which is a counterpart of customs invoice. Some certain consular charges when the consular invoice is issued by consulates of different countries. At present, if the foreign L/C requires the consular invoice from our side, generally we will not accept it except the companies located in Beijing.

### 9.7.3 Commodity Inspection Certificate

#### 9.7.3.1 Function of Commodity Inspection Certificate

In the import and export trade, Commodity Inspection Certificate is issued by the inspection agency set by a country/region or by an independent authentication institution which is registered by the government and serves as the third party. It certifies the quality, specifications, health, safety, quarantine, packaging, quantity, weight, damage, shipping conditions and shipping technology of the import or export goods. Generally speaking, the import or export commodity inspection is an integral part in the process of the goods transfer.

Commodity Inspection Certificate serves as a proof and is related to economic responsibility and rights and interests of the parties concerned. It serves:

1) As a basis to inspect whether the quality, weight, quantity, packaging and sanitary conditions of goods delivered by the seller conform to the regulations of the contract.

2) As a certificate for the buyer who may raise a question about the cargo's quality, quantity, weight and package, reject the receipt of goods or ask for compensation.

3) As one of the documents for the seller to negotiate with the bank.

4) As a valid document presented in customs clearance of exporting and importing countries.

5) As a proof which demonstrates the actual conditions of goods in shipment and discharge and transport as well as freight settlement and defined attribution of responsibility.

### 9.7.3.2 Types of Commodity Inspection Certificate

The certificates of inspection and authentication issued by China Commodity Inspection Bureau are as follows:

**(1) Inspection Certificate of Quality**

It certifies the quality, specifications or grade of import (export) goods.

**(2) Inspection Certificate of Weight**

It certifies the weight of import (export) goods.

**(3) Inspection Certificate of Quantity**

It certifies the quantity, length, area and so on of import (export) goods.

**(4) Veterinary Inspection Certificate**

It certifies that the export animal products and animals have been inspected by veterinary before export and meet quarantine requirements.

**(5) Sanitary Inspection Certificate/Inspection Certificate of Health**

It certifies that the export food and animal product are not infected by diseases, can be consumed and conform to the sanitary standards.

**(6) Disinfection Inspection Certificate**

It certifies that the export animal products have been disinfected.

**(7) Inspection Certificate of Origin**

It also referred to as Certificate of Origin, certifies the origin of the exported products. For those countries which offer GSP treatment to our country, the GSP shall be issued by the Commodity Inspection Bureau of China.

**(8) Inspection Certificate on Damaged Cargo**

It certifies the damage of import goods, assessment of the degree of damage and ascertainment of causes of damage.

(9) Inspection Certificate of Value

It certifies the actual value of import (export) goods.

(10) Certificate of Measurement and/or Weight

It certifies the weight or measurement of goods.

In addition, there are also inspection certificates of hold, certificate of storage, certificate of stowage, certificate of temperature measurement, certificate of tank/hold, certificate of load damage, certificate of the container, certificate of raw silk classification and conditioned weight, certificate of fumigation, certificate of radioactivity, etc.

## 9.7.4 Certificate of Origin

A Certificate of Origin is a document certifying the origin or place of the manufacture of goods (See Appendix L). In the import and export trade, the Certificate of Origin is provided by the exporter at the request of the importer, which is mainly to provide the customs in the importing country with the origin of the goods, so as to coordinate the implementation of the corresponding trade policies and measures.

At present, certificate of origin submitted by the export company in China under the L/C includes General Certificate of Origin and Generalized System of Preference Certificate of Origin.

### 9.7.4.1 General Certificate of Origin (Certificate of Origin of China)

*Rules of the People's Republic of China on the Origin of Export Goods and Implementing Measures* (came into effect from May 1, 1992) promulgated by the State Council of the People's Republic of China stipulates that export goods that meet the certain criteria shall apply for General Certificate of Origin. General Certificate of Origin is a document to certify that the export goods are made or produced in the People's Republic of China and an important basis in the customs clearance, settlement of exchange and trade statistics dealt with by the parties concerned. It stipulates that the State Administration for commodity inspection and its branches in various localities, the China Council for the Promotion of International Trade (referred to as CCPIT) and its branches and other organizations authorized by the State Department in charge of foreign economic relations and trade are responsible for signing and issuing certificates of origin. The person who issues the certificate, in reality, shall depend on the specific requirements of the L/C. However, if the letter requires the certificate from our official agency, it shall be applied to the State Administration for Commodity Inspection. However, no matter who issues it, the format is the same. Only the issuer is different.

The general certificate of origin has a total of twelve sections (The section Name and Certificate No. in the top right corner are not included and they have been printed, see Appendix L). The key points are as follows:

(1) The Full Name and Address of the Exporter

If there are no specific stipulations on the L/C, generally the full name, address and country of the beneficiary shall be filled out and shall not be left blank. The address shall be filled out in detail and be in line with the L/C.

(2) The Full Name and Address of the Consignee

This section shall be filled out accordingly if there are specific stipulations on the L/C. If not, generally the notify party of the B/L provided by the L/C shall be filled out. Customarily it shall be added in this section "To Whom It May Concern".

(3) **Transport Mode and Route**

Generally, the port of loading, port of discharge and means of transport shall be filled in. In the case of transshipment, the place of transshipment shall be marked and be in line with that of B/L. For example, "Shipment from Shanghai, China to London Per Vessel".

(4) **Port of Destination**

The final port of destination shall be filled out.

(5) **For Certifying Authority Use Only**

The agency applying for certificate of origin shall leave this column blank. The certifying authority adds the content if the content is needed, such as the missing of the certificate, reissue, and declaration of revocation of Certificate No. ×××  and so on.

(6) **Shipping Marks**

It shall be filled out in accordance with the L/C stipulations and be in line with that of the invoice and the B/L.

(7) **Description of Goods, Number and Kind of Packages**

The filling method of this section shall be basically consistent with that of the B/L and shall be in line with the the L/C stipulations. The full name of goods shall be required. The section shall be used when the foreign the L/C requires to add the L/C No. or a statement.

(8) **H. S. Code**

H. S., short for Harmonized Commodity Description and Coding System, serves as a method to classify a variety of goods developed by the Customs Cooperation Council. The H. S. code consists of 4 digits. The first two digits refer to the H. S. Chapter. The last two digits refer to the H. S. heading in each Chapter. This section shall be filled out correctly.

(9) **Quantity or Weight of Goods**

Units of measurement shall be filled out in this section, usually in the unit of weight. Gross weight and net weight shall be specified and generally the gross weight. For example, "Gross Weight 18,650kg".

(10) **Number and Date of Invoice**

It shall be filled out in accordance with commercial invoice. In order to avoid misunderstanding, the date shall be abbreviated in English. For example, "May 8th, 1994".

When Section 6, 7, 8, 9 and 10 is completed, the sign "******" shall be added in the end.

(11) **Declaration by the Exporter, Signature and Seal**

The content of the printed Declaration by the Exporter is that "The undersigned hereby declares that the above details of goods and statements are correct and that all the goods are produced and manufactured in China, which is completely in line with the rules of the People's Republic of China on the Origin of Export Goods."

The signatory of the applicant institution shall possess the legal personality and have registered at the certifying authority. The applicant institution shall stamp in this section, and the signature of the signatory shall be legible. The signature shall not overlap with the seal on the certificate.

Place and date of the declaration shall be filled out, for example, "Nanjing, China Feb. 15, 1994". Please note that the date of the declaration shall be no earlier than the date of the invoice and no later than the date of the B/L.

(12) **Certification of Certifying Authority, Signature and Stamp**

The content is that "It is hereby certified that the declaration by the exporter is correct."

The certificate shall be signed by the authorized signatory and stamped after examining it by the certifying authority. Place and date shall be marked. Note that the date of issue in this section should not be earlier than both the date of invoice (Section 10) and the date of declaration (Section 11) and that they can be the same day at the earliest.

Generally, the Certificate of Origin, stipulated by the Ministry of Commerce, shall be printed in English with one original and three copies of each certificate. In addition, copies of the certificate are specifically printed to meet the requirements in some L/C for providing more copies.

The General Certificate of Origin shall not be altered in the process of filling in. Be careful that if the certificate signed and issued has to be changed, a change of procedures shall be applied to the Certifying Authority for a request for a new certificate.

Since the new rules on the origin of goods have been promulgated since May 1, 1992, the Certificate of Origin issued by the exporting company and the manufacturer is no longer in use unless otherwise stipulated in the L/C.

### 9.7.4.2 Generalized System of Preference Certificate of Origin

Generalized System of Preference Certificate of Origin is referred to as GSP Certificate of Origin. GSP is a preferential system that the developed countries generally provide unilateral tariff reduction and exemption for manufactured goods and semi-manufactured goods from the developing countries. Its principle is universal, non-reciprocal and non-discriminatory. At present, about 20 countries have provided this preferential treatment for our country. If our export goods are entitled to GSP treatment, generally the Certificate of Origin shall be handed to the preference-giving country.

There are many kinds of GSP Certificate of Origin, but the most common one is GSP. The method of filling out this certificate will be introduced as follows:

The contents and filling method of Section 1, 2 and 3 of the certificate shall be the same as those of the General Certificate of Origin. The contents and filling method of Section 1, 2 and 3 of the certificate shall be referred to those of the General Certificate of Origin.

Section 4, Official Use

This section "Exporter" shall be left blank, which is similar to Section 5 of the General Certificate of Origin.

Section 5, Item Number

Under the same consignee and carriage conditions, if there are different varieties of a batch of goods, the number "1" "2"...... shall be marked separately in terms of variety and invoice number. If the type of goods is single, "1" shall be filled out in this section or this section shall be left blank.

The contents and filling method of Section 6 and 7 of the certificate shall be the same as those of the General Certificate of Origin. The contents and filling method of Section 6 and 7 shall be referred to those of the General Certificate of Origin.

Section 8, Origin Criteria

This section is the core item in customs verification. Generally, it shall be filled out as follows:

"P" shall be filled out, which indicates that the goods are fully indigenous and have no imported ingredients.

"W" shall be filled out, which indicates that the goods contain imported ingredients but meet the criteria of the place of origin.

"F" shall be filled out, which indicates that the goods are exported to Canada and they contain imported ingredients (below 40% of goods factory price). If the goods are exported to Norway, Switzerland, Sweden, Finland, Austria, the Europe Union and Japan, it shall fill "w" out and mark beneath with the H. S. Code.

The contents and filling method of Section 9 and 10 of the certificate shall be the same as those of the General Certificate of Origin.

Section 11, the Certificate of Certifying Authority, Place, Date, the Signature of Authorized Signatory and Stamp of Commodity Inspection Agency

Form A has one original and two copies. The authorized signatory shall only sign the original certificate after verification. The date of issue shall not be earlier than the date of invoice (Section 10) and the date of declaration (Section 12), but no later than the date of the B/L.

Section 12, Declaration by the Exporter

"CHINA" on the line of origin is generally printed on the certificate. The exporting country shall be filled out correctly. If there are specific stipulations on the L/C, it shall fill it out accordingly. Otherwise, it shall refer to the nationality in Section 3.

The applicant shall also hand in a GSP Certificate of Origin application and a copy of invoice when applying to Commodity Inspection Bureau for the bill.

## Questions:

### True or false.

1. The promissory note is a commitment to pay without acceptance. The drawer is always the main debtor. Usance bills need to be accepted by the payer. The drawer is the main debtor before the acceptance. Once accepted, the acceptor becomes the main debtor and the drawer downgrades to the accessory debtor.
2. Shipping marks are written in the "marks and nos." column. They should be in accordance with ones that fill in the same column on the invoice or bill of lading, or fill in "As Per Invoice No. . . . ". If there is no mark, then fill in "N/M".
3. Endorsement in blank is also known as an anonymous endorsement. The endorser of endorsement in blank only needs to sign on the back of the bill so that the bill can be transferred without

recoding the name of the endorsee. Endorsement in blank can freely circulate with no need to endorse to transfer.
4. The issuing date of various documents should be consistent with the logic and the international practices. The usual date of the insurance policy is the latest issuing date of the negotiable document.
5. Commercial documents include commercial invoices, bills of lading, insurance policy, consular invoices, customs invoices, certificate of origin, packing list, quality certificate, weight list, the certificate for the dispatch of documents, certificate of the sample, shipping advice, the age of vessel advice.
6. Enterprises in the audit of the letter of credit to conduct a comprehensive review of the main audit alone are consistent with the documents are consistent, the single goods are consistent and the documents and the contract are consistent.
7. The integrity of a document refers to the integrity of a complete set of documents.
8. The main basis for the compilation and examination of international trade documents is the contract of sale, letter of credit, the original materials of the relevant commodities, relevant international practices, relevant domestic regulatory requirements and the requirements of relevant foreign clients.
9. When examining, banks use *UCP600* as the examination basis if there are no special provisions in the letter of credit.
10. "Consistency of documents and letters" holds an important position because "consistency of documents" is based on the premise of it. The payment will be refused even when documents are consistent without such a premise. As for "consistency of goods and documents", it mainly refers to the contents of the documents should be consistent with the actual delivery of goods, that is, consistent with the contract. "Consistency of goods and documents" should also meet the premise and conditions of "consistency of documents and letters".

# Chapter 10

# International Settlement Risks & Management

**Learning Objectives**

- To learn about the international settlement risks and the related management methods.

## 10.1 An Overview of International Settlement Risk

### 10.1.1 Risks and Risk Factors

The import and export activities, the profit acquisition, and the survival and development of the enterprises are running on under the conditions of overcoming the impacts of various risks and effective management of them.

As early as 1901, Dr. Wright from the United States defined the risk as "Risk is the objective embodiment of the uncertainty of the affairs which people are unwilling to happen." for the first time in his thesis named *The Economic Theory of Risks and Insurance*. In 1921, Economist Knight differentiated the risks and the uncertainty in the book named *Risk, Uncertainty and Profit*. Then in 1964, William and Hans published *Risk Management and Insurance*, in which they put the subjective factors of risk analysts into the conception of risk and they claimed that risk is a kind of objective state which is existed to anyone while uncertainty is the subjective judgment of the principal. In 1983, a Japanese scholar Takeiisao defined the risk as "Risk, which exists in the specific environment among specific period naturally, is the changes which can lead to the economic loss." And the famous Chinese scholar Zhao Shuming concluded and defined risk as "Risk is a kind of uncertainty, which exists objectively in a specific environment and in a specific period, leads to the emergence of expenses, loss and damage and can be clarified and controlled." in his masterpiece, *International Business: Risk Management*.

### 10.1.2 The Characteristics of Risk

Although there are different kinds of definitions of risk, the three basic characteristics of risk are the same in general. They are as follows:

Objectivity: Risk exists everywhere which is independent of the will of the human beings. People need to control and eliminate risks through various means in order to avoid or reduce losses.

Relativity: Risk may or may not lead to losses, or even profit. Meanwhile, with respect to the different subject or environment, the content of risk and its degree are changing.

Controllability: Risk can be reduced to some extent or the uncertainty of risk can be controlled as the increasing of people's ability to identify and defend risk. Through detailed investigation and demonstration, strategy to defend or avoid risk can be made which can resist the occurrence of risk or reduce the losses together with the risk.

## 10.1.3 The Elements of Risk

A risk is usually composed of three elements, including risk factors, risk accidents and risk losses.

### (1) Risk Factors

Risk factors are factors which can lead to or increase the frequency and extent of a kind of loss. This is not only the condition but also the cause of the production of operational risk in enterprises. According to different forms, risk factors can be divided into two different aspects including factors about the matter and factors about the people, with different representation forms respectively.

### (2) Risk Accidents

Risk accidents, caused by the comprehensive effects of risk factors, are the reasons which can lead to risk losses, or the mediums which can lead to risk loss.

### (3) Risk Losses

Risk losses are the unintentional, unplanned, and unintended reducing of profit or increasing of losses caused by risk accidents. It shows two different forms: direct losses and indirect losses.

## 10.1.4 International Settlement Risk

The so-called international settlement risk refers to the uncertainty of the principals involved due to the influence of various factors in the process of the international settlement.

There are so many kinds of international settlement risks from different criteria as follows:

### (1) In Terms of the Reasons

It can be divided into natural risk and artificial risk. Artificial risk, also known as subjective risk, refers to the risks caused by people's behaviors, as well as various political and economic activities.

### (2) In Terms of Whether the Risk can be Managed or Not

According to whether the international settlement risk can be predicted or controlled, it can be divided into the manageable risk and the unmanageable risk. The former refers to predictable and controllable risk while the latter refers to unpredictable and uncontrollable risk. Whether the risk can be managed or not depends on the collection of related information and the level of risk management ability. Moreover, with the enrichment of information collected and the increasing level of management skills, some unmanageable risk may be transferred into manageable risk.

### (3) In Terms of the Representation Forms

In terms of the representation forms, it can be divided into bill risk, settlement risk, and fraud risk. And the analysis of this chapter is based on this points of view.

## 10.2 Bill Risks and Prevention

As the important payment document in the international settlement, bills are widely used throughout the world. The risk in the process of using bills is generally existed due to the variety of bills and properties, together with the lack of identification ability because most domestic residents are rarely exposed to foreign bills.

### 10.2.1 The Definition and Types of Bill Risk

(1) **Definition of Bill Risk**

Bill risk refers to the risk for principals of profit loss because of the existence of uncertain factors in the process of issuing and circulating a bill.

(2) **Categories of Bill Risk**

Bill risk refers to the risk of damage to the parties concerned due to the existence of uncertain factors in the issuance and/or circulation of bills or notes.

The causes of bill risk include economic factors and non-economic factors.

According to different presentation forms, bill risk can be divided into acceptance risk, discount risk, transfer risk, re-discount risk, repurchase risk and collection risk etc.

In terms of different forms, bill risks include short-term, long-term, hidden and obvious ones. Especially, with the rapid development of bill business, there are new characteristics of bill risks. Above all, the first feature is "high" which means the risk of bill business is gradually increasing. Then the second feature is "novel" or "new" which refers to that bill business is no longer a simple acceptance and discount business, and new varieties and new operation ways in bill business have come into being. The third feature is "miscellaneous" which is because that the presentation forms, causes, and types of dispute of bill risk are complex and various. The fourth one is "big". Bill risk are related to all aspects of economic and financial activities so that the amount of bill risk has a significant increase. The final one is "difficult" which refers to that the prevention and control of bill risk are difficult and professional.

### 10.2.2 Prevention of Bill Risks

The bills mainly used in the international trade settlement are the bill of exchange, promissory note and check. Among them, the payment methods, including collection, the L/C, international factoring and so on, are often related to the use of bill of exchange (Remittance by banker's demand draft would make use of bank draft under which circumstance the risk of bill of exchange for the seller is very low on the basis of bank's credit.). And for these payment methods, the exporter issues the bill of exchange to the importer (in the collection or international factoring) or bank (in the L/C) respectively in order to request the payment at sight or at a fixed time after sight while the issue of bill of exchange is often after the shipment of goods. The buyer could safeguard his interest through a number of ways if the seller fails to complete the delivery according to the contract or if there is another adverse circumstance happening. However, the seller's risk is higher when the buyer issues a promissory note or a check as the payment method. Considering this, we will discuss the ways to prevent the risks of accepting a promissory note, especially a check, from the seller's point of view.

The seller needs to pay attention to the following tips in order to prevent bill risk.

(1) To Choose a Customer with Good Credit Standing

Before closing the deal, it is necessary to investigate the credit status of the customer through various methods and choose a customer with good credit standing to make a deal. The seller should pay special attention to those customers with unknown credit standing or those who are from less developed areas or countries with a tight foreign exchange or volatile situation.

(2) To Sign a Foreign Trade Contract Conscientiously

Both buyers and sellers should sign a sales contract on the basis of equality and mutual benefit.

(3) To Review the Bills Carefully

All the bills submitted by the customers need to be reviewed by the entrusted bank in advance in order to ensure the security of exchange collection.

(4) To Send Goods Off before the Other Party Getting the Payment from the Bank in Order to Avoid Loss of Both Payment and Goods

(5) To Accumulate Experience in Order to Strengthen the Prevention of Counterfeit Notes and Bills

Even the check by the paying bank with the world's best credit standing cannot ensure the payment all the time. Recently, some foreign unscrupulous businessmen use counterfeit bills and remittance receipt for fraud in the domestic market and the number of cases has an upward trend which cannot be taken lightly.

## 10.3 Collection's Risk and Management

With the rapid development of the international trade, the international settlement methods have experienced a number of evolution with the changes in the international trade methods and technical means. However, no matter in which stage, there is more or less different kinds of risks which would affect the interests of the parties concerned. As there are mainly three kinds of international settlement methods, namely remittance, collection and the L/C, this book would focus on the overview of the risk management for these three settlement methods.

The international trade settlement mainly involves three parties of principals, including exporters, importers, and banks. Different payment methods may need different banks. For example, the collection will involve at least two banks, remitting bank and collecting bank, while the L/C will involve the issuing bank and the negotiating bank generally. This section focuses on the risk management under these two commonly used international settlement methods, collection and the L/C.

### 10.3.1 Risk Factors for the Collection

Collection involves four parties concerned, namely exporters (principal), importers (payer),

# Chapter 10 International Settlement Risks & Management

remitting bank and collecting bank. Different parties are faced with different kinds of risks so that the risk factors are different respectively (see Table 10-1).

Table 10-1 Risk Factors of Principals in the Method of Collection

|  | External Environment | Within Enterprises |
|---|---|---|
| Risk of Exporters | 1. Rejection to make payment by the importer (such as poor credit standing of importers, bankruptcy and insolvency, adverse changes of the market for the buyers, changes of trade policies in importing country, failure in the application for foreign exchange and so on)<br>2. Losses of goods in transit (under FOB, CFR and other contract terms in which buyers are responsible for the risk in transit) or goods without insurance so that buyers would not make redemption or delay the redemption in order to avoid occupation of funds<br>3. A special understanding of the terms in importing countries<br>4. The collusion between collecting bank and importers (for example, under the method of forward D/P, the collecting bank allows the buyer to make the receipt for a loan with T/R.) | 1. Unknown to the credit standing of importers<br>2. Incorrect bills<br>3. Improper choice of collecting methods<br>4. Improper choice of remitting bank<br>5. Improper choice of terms of price<br>6. Failure to fulfill the obligation of delivery according to the contract<br>7. Unknown to the trade laws, regulations, customary rules, and policies of the other country |
| Risk of Importers | 1. Fraud of Exporters, such as using a forged bill of lading to get the payment of goods<br>2. Failure to perform delivery obligation according to quality and quantity requirements in the contract<br>3. Sales of goods that are not owned and owned by a third party or using a "cloned" bill of lading to sell the same assignment of goods to multiple buyers | 1. Lack of a deep understanding of the credit standing and operation style of the exporters<br>2. Incorrect auditing of the bills (such as lack of judgment ability of the authenticity of the bill of lading which will lead to receiving a fake bill of lading.) |
| Risk of Remitting Bank | 1. Poor credit standing of exporters (providing trade financing to the exporters with poor credit standing, such as bill purchased or discounting bills of exchange)<br>2. Improper choice of collecting bank with poor credit standing | Failure to handle the business in terms of collection instruction |
| Risk of Collecting Bank | 1. Rejection to make payment on maturity after taking delivery of goods with T/R from the importers<br>2. Be responsible for the risk that the importers refuse to make payment in forward and on demand D/P business. | Failure to handle the business in terms of collection instruction |

(Source of materials: Self-arrangement and induction.)

## 10.3.2 Management Measures

### 10.3.2.1 Exporter's Risk Management Strategy

(1) Pre-control Measures

Exporters are proactive in avoiding risk before choosing a method of collection and the available methods includes:

Above all, to improve the quality of business personnel, establish comprehensive rules and ordinances, follow the URC exactly and operate as authorized.

Secondly, to make transactions only with those importers with good credit standing and integrity of the operating style. In the collection business, exporters should establish a credit file for the main customers so that the credit level of these customers can be evaluated and the credit risk of buyers can be controlled before closing the deal. As for the new customers, exporters should collect information about them through various means in advance, such as through the Bank of China or other commercial banks handling collection business, China Export and Credit Insurance Corporation, and other institutions, or they can authorize credit investigation agencies (such as Dun & Bradstreet Company) to do investigations in order to avoid unnecessary losses. The exporters should be more thoughtful for those businesses which have exceeded the importer's operation ability so as to avoid loss.

Thirdly, to sign a trade contract correctly. To specify the terms of the contract in detail can avoid the losses of both the commodities and the payment which is caused by the rejection of payment of importers or the commodities have been accused because of retention in the destination port.

Fourthly, to master the credit line. It is not appropriate to use the collection for those transactions with a large amount.

Fifthly, to study the laws, regulations on both the foreign trade and foreign exchange in the importing countries or regions, and to use the method of collection as less as possible with the businessmen in the countries with more stringent regulations on trade and foreign exchange.

Sixthly, to choose payment in advance, the L/C, international factoring and other methods to collect payment.

Seventhly, to cover export credit insurance in order to shift the risk of export earnings. The export credit insurance, taking the financial funds as the background and aiming to encourage and expand exports by a government, is a policy-type risk guarantee system which is provided by specific insurance agencies to exporters in order to ensure their safety of export earnings. It is not done for financial gain, so it is not the same as the general commercial insurance. After ansuting this kind of insurance, the risk of collecting the foreign exchange in collection business faced by the exporters will be transferred safely and effectively to the export credit insurance institutions, who will be responsible for the risk of collecting the foreign exchange. As for exporters, the export credit insurance is an effective risk-transferring system which can prevent the risk.

(2) **Course-control Measures**

Once forced to choose the collection, the exporters would be more passive. However, there are still many good measures to manage the risks, such as:

Above all, to choose a scientific type of shipping. Try to avoid railway transportation and air transportation. Because when these transport methods are used, the importers would take delivery of the goods just after receiving the notice of the arrival of the goods given by the relevant transport department after the arriving of the goods at the destination in which circumstances, the buyers would find excuses to refuse payment or lower prices which will put the exporters in a passive situation.

Then, to choose the price terms reasonably. For example, it would be better for the exporters to use CIF, CIP and other price terms in which buyers are responsible for the insurance. Because the exporter may claim compensation to the insurance company with the insurance policy to protect their own interest when the importers have refused to pay for goods after have gotten the news that the goods have been damaged or lost. If the price term in which the importers are responsible for the insurance has been chosen, the exporter should cover "seller's interest insurance" additionally (a kind of independent risk of the marine cargo insurance business in which the insurer shall bear the liability when the buyer has refused to take delivery of the commodities.)

Next, to take control of the export documents and bills in good order. Exporters can control the exported commodities mainly by the negotiable bill of lading. Generally, the bill of lading is the certification to the title of the real goods. To own the B/L means that the party who holds it can have the right to the goods shipped. However, whether the bill of lading is the certification to the title of the goods depends on the order of the B/L. If the column of the "Consignee" in the B/L was marked with "To Order" or "To Order of the Shipper", the exporters can transfer the right of the goods through the endorsement on the bill of lading. By the way, the exporter may require the remitting bank and/or collecting bank to transfer the B/L to the importer only when he has made payment so as to reduce the related risk.

Fourthly, the two priority principles should be followed strictly when choosing the methods of collection. For example, the exporter should prefer D/P over D/A; while prefer the D/P at sight over the D/P after sight. Besides, the exporter should pay attention to that some countries have their own explanation on D/P after sight. For example, some countries in South America and the Middle East put the D/P after and the D/A on the equal footing. While the *URC522* specifies clearly that the local laws should be chosen when the provisions are contrary to the provisions of a national, state or local law and/or regulation which cannot be departed from.

Fifthly, to choose collecting bank carefully which can speed up the collection of foreign exchange. According to the *URC522*, it is stated that the principal should choose the collecting bank voluntarily and the principal can also ask the remitting bank to choose instead. Generally speaking, the principal often chooses the bank of deposit of the importers as the collecting bank without enough understanding of its credit standing so that the speed of collecting exchange will be reduced and the risk of collecting exchange will be increased if the choice is not proper. Therefore, it is recommended that the principal entrust the remitting bank to choose the collecting bank because the remitting bank often handles the international settlement business, has overseas branches, or has firsthand data and information of the credit standing, business conditions, and quality of service of the foreign banks. Under no circumstance should the principal accept the bank which is designated by importers as the collecting bank in order to prevent the collusion of the two parties, such as taking the delivery of the goods with the receipt for a loan through the T/R.

Sixthly, to choose the combined method of payment, such as the combination of collection and remittance, the combination of collection and the L/C etc.. When the later was chosen, it is recommended to choose the combination of documentary collection and clean L/C which can ensure that the documents are not out of control.

(3) Post-control Measures

Once the risk occurs, the exporters would be limited to a very passive situation. However, there are still some measures that can reduce the loss as long as the exporters have done the following steps:

Firstly, to identify the problems and deal with them immediately, such as strengthening the monitoring of collection time in order to get a timely collection of the payment because a long delay may mean trouble, and entrusting representative in case-of-need to deal with the goods at the destination port in time. Meanwhile, it is essential to choose our country's local company as the representative in case-of-need.

Secondly, to resort laws for legal preservation.

Thirdly, to claim compensation in time. For example, if the exporter has insured the export credit insurance in advance, the exporter could claim compensation to the relevant insurance company with the related insurance policy.

### 10.3.2.2 Importer's Risk Management Strategy

(1) Pre-control Measures

Firstly, do not choose collection methods which is the easiest method. But the characteristic of the seller's monopoly of some products in the international market makes the buyers could not avoid the choice of collection methods sometimes.

Secondly, choose exporters with good credit standing to make transactions.

Thirdly, choose reasonable price terms. For example, to choose the FOB and other price terms that the buyers are responsible for the transportation as far as possible can help the buyer to avoid the occurrence of the collusion of the sellers and the ship owners.

(2) Course-control Measures

When the importer has been forced to choose the collection, he can use the following methods to hedge or control the risks:

Firstly, to choose a specific collection method scientifically

As for the choice of collection methods, importers should obey the following two prior principals, that is to prefer D/A over D/P and prefer D/P after sight over D/P at sight.

Secondly, to investigate the documents and bills carefully

In order to prevent that the exporters cheat the importers for the payment with fraud bills or defective goods, the importers should require the exporters to provide certificate of quality of the goods which is issued by the assigner or the assigned institutions in the export places required by the importers, or by the impartial inspection agency in the export places, or by the international inspection agency with recognized authority throughout the world, such as the SGS inspection agency in Swiss. In addition, in accordance with the provisions of *URC522*, the relevant bank is not responsible for the investigation of the documents and bills under the method of collection which requires the importers to take the responsibility. The importers must make redemption or acceptance after the requirements of "two consistencies" (which means the consistency between bills and trade contract and the consistence among the bills) are fulfilled. The bill of lading with the function of real right should be paid attention to in the investigation of bills and documents.

Thirdly, to track detail status of the commodities in transit in time

The importer may check the registration of the carrying vessel, dead-weight tonnage, navigability, port of departure, date of shipment and other information of the ships, timely master the operation status of the ship in the B/L and identify fraud behaviors timely through the shipping information channels such as Lloyd Maritime Information and Service Limited Company, Dynamic References of Lloyd Shipping etc.

(3) Post-control Measures

Once the importers have redeemed the documents but only to find the exporters fail to fulfill the delivery of goods according to the contract, the importers can only claim against the sellers according to the sales contract and relevant laws and regulations. If the exporter has used fraudulent documents and bills to cheat, sometimes the importer will get compensation through legal channels. However, in most cases, the importer can only take the responsibility themselves and learn from the losses.

#### 10.3.2.3 Remitting Bank's Risk Management Strategy

There are two principles of the risk management measures for the remitting bank:

Firstly, follow the rules of the *Uniform Rules for Collection* to the letter. The remitting bank has only a limited obligation under the collection business. The remitting bank can eliminate the risk of business if he can just play it safe according to the *URC522*, namely to investigate the documents and bills submitted by the exporters superficially, remit the documents to the collecting bank in consistent with the content in the collection order and then instruct the collecting bank correctly.

Secondly, not to provide trade financing to the exporters with poor credit standing.

#### 10.3.2.4 Collecting Bank's Risk Management

It is easy for the collecting bank to avoid and control the risks as long as he can follow the following three principles.

Above all, follow the rules of the *Uniform Rules for Collection* strictly.

Then, to strengthen the credit investigation of the importers. When financing the importers, the collecting bank is also faced with the problem that whether the credit standing of the importers is good or not. Even with the trust receipt submitted by the importers, the collecting bank cannot give financing to the importers with poor credit standing or without enough investigation, and cannot accept their requirements to modify the original conditions of the long-term document against payment. Only in this way can the collecting bank avoid the risk that the importers refuse to pay after financing.

And next, be cautious to deal with the emerging financing business of "D/P after sight while paying at sight". For such business, the collecting bank should review the credit standing of the importers carefully so as to be passive.

## 10.4 Risk Management Strategy under L/C

The L/C should be used on the basis of the credit standing of the bank, but the parties concerned involved in the L/C may face much more complicated risk which are difficult to avoid because when dealing with business, the exporters, banks, importers and other relevant parties in the L/C take the provisions of L/C as the basis and the documents and bills submitted by the exporters as the center which will lead to the separation of documents and the goods that are shipped.

## 10.4.1 Risk Factors for L/C

The risk factors in L/C are listed in Table 10-2.

Table 10-2  Risk Factors of Different Principals in L/C

|  | External Environment | Within Enterprises |
|---|---|---|
| Risk of the Beneficiaries | 1. The importers may not issue the L/C according to the contract<br>2. The period of the validity which is given by the L/C to the bank, the date of shipment of the goods, and the presentation date of the exporters are relatively short<br>3. The consignee of the bill of lading stipulated by the L/C is the applicant which will make the exporters lose the control of goods<br>4. 1/3 or 2/3 of the original bill of lading is sent to the applicant, stipulated by the L/C, which will do harm to the control of goods by the exporters<br>5. The period and place of validity are both in the local place of issuing bank<br>6. The exporters are responsible for the charges of the bank in the L/C which will increase the cost of exporters<br>7. L/C with soft clauses<br>8. The issuing bank refuses to pay as a result of bankruptcy<br>9. Documents do not match the L/C or the documents do not match with each other | 1. Inadequate information on the credit standing of importers<br>2. Misunderstanding of the L/C<br>3. Incorrect operation of issuing and presenting the L/C<br>4. Lack of experience to identify the fraud of the L/C |
| Risk of the Applicants | 1. The exporters may use forged documents to cheat issuing bank or other designated bank to get payment<br>2. The exporters may submit goods which do not match the requirements of the contract with the use of characteristics of business with the L/C<br>3. The exporters may delay the delivery of goods or abscond with the money after getting the payment in advance under the anticipatory L/C<br>4. The delay of issuing the L/C after importing goods or equipment will make the importers suffer loss | 1. To choose the exporters with poor credit standing<br>2. Lack of enough confirmation on the submitted documents and bills |
| Risk of the Issuing Bank | 1. The applicant refuses to make redemption or payment of full amount of the L/C<br>2. Incorrect documents submitted by the beneficiary<br>3. The exporters may refuse to deliver goods or delay the delivery under the anticipatory L/C<br>4. The importers refuse to pay for the goods under the fraud forward L/C | 1. The investigation of the credit standing of the applicant is not strict enough<br>2. The investigation of the documents and bills under the provisions of the L/C is not strict enough |

Chapter 10　International Settlement Risks & Management

（续）

| | External Environment | Within Enterprises |
|---|---|---|
| Risk of Negotiating Bank | 1. The beneficiary may have no payment ability when the credit standing is poor or the recourse happens<br>2. The issuing bank refuses to pay<br>3. Documents do not match the L/C or the documents do not match with each other | 1. Inexperienced business personnel<br>2. Inadequate investigation of the credit standing of beneficiaries |
| Risk of Advising Bank | L/C fraud, such as the forged L/C imprinted by the exporters, or by the collision with exporters and the banks | Advising the beneficiary about the L/C but the fact that whether the L/C is authentic or not is omitted when the Test No. or signature is uncertain |
| Risk of Confirming Bank | 1. Poor credit standing of the issuing bank<br>2. Political risk exists in the importing country<br>3. Incorrect documents and bills submitted by the beneficiary | Inadequate investigation of the confirming qualification |

## 10.4.2　Risk Management under the L/C

### 10.4.2.1　Risk Prevention of the Beneficiaries

Under the L/C, when receiving the L/C with various provisions which are issued by the bank at the request of the importers, together with the payment guarantee, the exporters should do as follows:

Firstly, to master the real status of the credit standing of the issuing bank, including the external payment status of the issuing bank itself, the domestic situation of exchange control, economic strength and so on. Otherwise, the exporters are faced with the risk of not being able to get the payment even though the bills submitted by the exporters after shipment of the goods meet the request that the documents are consistent with the L/C and the documents are consistent with other documents and bills. If the status of the issuing bank is unclear, the exporters can request the importers to instruct the issuing bank to invite the bank in the place of export to issue a confirmation of the L/C so that when the exporters get the confirmed L/C, they have a payment protection from a second bank in addition to the issuing bank. Therefore, the risk of exporters will be reduced.

Secondly, the exporters should review various provisions in the L/C after receiving. The provisions in the L/C are conditions for the exporters to get payment. The exporters have the right to request the issuing bank to modify the L/C through the importers until they are satisfied with it if there are some provisions which are difficult to fulfill or which will do harm to the interest of exporters. In this way, the exchange earnings of the exporters can be protected.

Thirdly, exporters should pick up the methods to control the goods through the use of documents. In general, the bill of lading is the certification of real right and the cheque payable should be blank which is favorable for the exporters so that exporters could transfer the bills to the commissioned bank through endorsement in order to control the goods effectively.

Fourthly, exporters should ensure export credit insurance in the insurance institutions of host country because even though the L/C is on the basis of the bank's credit, it does not mean that there is no risk for the exporters. Before shipping the goods, exporters could ensure export credit insurance in the insurance institutions in the exporting country which can transfer or reduce the risk of earnings in order to safeguard the process of the earning.

Fifthly, if the issuing bank refuses to pay, the measures that can be taken are as follows:

- To Study the Reasons of Refusal and Discuss Countermeasure with the Corresponding Bank

After receiving the notice of refusal from the bank, the exporters should study carefully that whether the refusal reasons are sufficient or not, and whether there is something wrong with the documents and bills which will lead to the variance between documents and the L/C or among the documents. If these are not the reason or there are only small inconsistencies which cannot lead to refusal general, other reasons should be taken into consideration. The other common reason is that the issuing bank may use some insignificant defects to refuse the payment intentionally because the poor credit standing or financial situation of the buyer and the issuing bank fear that the buyer cannot pay the redemption. If this happens, the relevant provisions (which must follow No. 600 publication, *Uniform Customs and Practice for Documentary Credits*) in the laws, regulations and conventions should be paid attention to and the initial discussion with professionals in the corresponding bank is of great importance. If the refusal reason is inadequate and strained, exporters can claim for justice in accordance with the uniform rules through the corresponding bank.

- To Negotiate with the Buyers or Their Agents

The transaction with the L/C is a kind of document transaction which means that only when the documents submitted by the seller comply with the provisions in the L/C, will the issuing bank make payment. The seller could not force the issuing bank to make payment even there is a little defect in the documents in which case the seller needs to negotiate with the buyer or the agent, for example, to make negotiation about the relevant provisions in the contract, to sell with a lower price or to commission the other party to sell, and so on.

- The Handling of the Freight Documents and the Preservation of the Goods

Before the reimbursement of exporting goods is made, the seller is responsible for the discharge of the goods and documents so that the seller should put emphasis on both the handling of the freight documents and the preservation of the goods. The freight documents are preserved by the commissioned issuing bank generally. If the negotiation with the buyer has worked, the seller will instruct the issuing bank through the corresponding bank to deliver the documents to the importers to take delivery the goods. If the goods have been shipped to the port of discharge, the seller will still be responsible for the risk in order that if the case of refusal of the payment cannot be solved, local agent or a trusted third party will be commissioned to deliver the goods on behalf of the corresponding bank and then to preserve the goods or to ensure an insurance to protect goods. If there is no suitable person to the commission, the issuing bank can be commissioned to handle the preservation procedures through the corresponding bank, for example, to deposit the goods within bonded warehouses and to of the goods with the storage period which can avoid being forced to sell.

- To Resell or Return the Goods

## Chapter 10    International Settlement Risks & Management

To resell the goods to another buyer or to ask a local company with a good credit standing to change the L/C into D/P or D/A are desirable measures if the negotiation with the buyer does not work. If not, the goods should be resold to other regions or be returned to host country, in which circumstances, whether the loading costs, freight, insurance premiums and other additional costs are worthwhile, should be taken into consideration.

- Mediation and Arbitration

If the sellers want to claim compensation after being refused for payment, they need to negotiate with the buyers directly and propose mediation or arbitration. Mediation refers to that a mediator designated by both the seller and the buyer draws up a mediation solution which will be regarded as the standard for solving the dispute. However, if the principals of one of the two parties, or two parties do not agree with the mediation solution, the mediation is invalid. Arbitration refers to that the seller and the buyer designate an arbitration institution according to a prior agreement based on the business contract or an afterwards agreement and the arbitrator will make a fair and reasonable judgment in order to solve the dispute according to the materials submitted by the two parties. The arbitration has the constraining force which is valid to the two parties.

Sixthly, the available measures of the bankruptcy of the issuing bank.

The main function of the L/C is to use the credit standing of the issuing bank to replace the commercial credit of the buyer in order to ensure the payment of the goods. If the issuing bank declares bankruptcy, there will be a great impact on the principal of the L/C under which circumstance the legal rights and obligations of the relevant principals are different in accordance with the different beginning stages of the bankruptcy in the procedure of transaction of the L/C:

A. Bankruptcy Before Issuing the L/C

If the bankruptcy happens before issuing the L/C, the buyer can discharge the contract with the bank while the seller also has the right to request the buyer to choose another bank to issue another new L/C.

B. Bankruptcy After Issuing the L/C

If the L/C is issued but it is not used by the beneficiary, it will not be used any more generally so that even though this offer is still valid legally and the beneficiary could submit the documents to the bank, the right to claim payment is only ordinary bankruptcy creditors.

C. Bankruptcy After the Acceptance of the Bill of Exchange

The principals have different rights and obligations under this circumstance: in forward acceptance credit, after receiving documents and the acceptance of the bill of exchange, if the issuing bank declares bankruptcy before the bill of exchange expires, the negotiating bank could claim a recourse to the seller after finishing the procedures of refusal certifications. After giving compensation to the negotiating bank, the seller can claim a recourse to the buyer, and can also claim the right of liquidator to the issuing bank with the acceptance bill of exchange; if the seller, negotiating bank, confirming bank and other parties with documents or acceptance bill of exchange, claim a liquidation to the liquidator of the issuing bank, they will be located only in the position of general creditor without any priority; if the issuing bank has delivered the documents to the buyer according to the trust receipt after acceptance and before payment, the buyer can also participate in the payment of bill of exchange of the seller as well in order to get the bill of exchange which can offset the debt in the trust receipt without loss.

D. Bankruptcy After the Payment of the L/C

After the issuing bank has paid for part of or all the payment of the documents in the L/C, if the buyer has paid the security deposit in advance, the security deposit can be offset when paying redemption to the liquidator which means the offset right of creditor's rights and debts. If the amount of security deposit is larger than the amount of redemption, the difference can be only recovered by the method of apportionment after bankruptcy.

After the bankruptcy of the issuing bank, the confirming bank cannot refuse payment or negotiation of the beneficiary of the L/C, while the designated negotiating bank can refuse negotiation. After the payment, the confirming bank can neither claim recourse to the beneficiary because of the bankruptcy of the issuing bank, nor request the buyer to make redemption without consideration about the liquidator of the issuing bank.

### 10.4.2.2 The Risk Prevention of Importers

The importers involved in the L/C can take the following measures to prevent the risk they are faced with:

A. To Strengthen the Investigation of Credit Standing of the Exporters

In the international trade business, not only the exporters need to get information about the importers, but also the importers need to get information about the exporters. Only in this way can both parties take precautions. Specifically, the exporters should get known about the operation conditions, business strength, business scale, whether there are poor shipping record and other detailed information of the exporters.

B. To List the Detailed Information of Goods in the L/C

As the buyers in the business of the L/C, the importers are concerned about the goods shipped by the exporters. However, one of the characteristics of the business about L/C is the separation of documents and actual goods so that the importers need to add some additional provisions into the L/C in order to restrain the shipment of goods by the exporters. The commonly used methods are as follows:

① Exporters are required to submit relevant inspection certifications of the commodities, including inspection certification of quality, quantity, weight and so on. In this way, the importers can take control of the goods shipped by the exporters in order to avoid that the exporters do not ship goods, ship the fake goods, ship goods with less amount, and so on.

② The shipment status of the exporting goods should be stipulated, such as the date of shipment, the port of shipment, the place of discharge, whether partial shipment is allowed or not, whether transshipment is allowed or not, and so on, in order to avoid that the exporters do not ship the goods on time or the importers cannot get the shipped goods on time.

③ The date that the exporters should present the documents to the bank after shipping the goods should be stipulated. The stipulation of this date is equally important for importers. If the exporters delay the presentation of the documents after shipping the goods, in addition to a lot of unnecessary expenses, the importers will not get the goods on time which will also have an impact on the cash flow of the importers.

In general, the date when the exporters need to submit documents to the bank is stipulated in the L/C specifically which is usually 7 days, 14 days, 15 days or so after the date of shipment. If there is no such stipulation in the L/C, the date is usually within 21 days after the date of shipment according to the *UCP600*. And 21 days is such a long period for the importers.

C. In the L/C, it should be stipulated that after receiving the L/C issued by the bank of the other party, the L/C issued by the bank in the host country can be taken into effect. Only with this provision added to the L/C, can the importers of materials and equipment avoid the loss that the goods produced by themselves cannot be exported, which is caused by the exporters who refuse to issue the L/C after exporting the goods or who do not issue the L/C immediately in the term of trade called "Custom Manufacturing with Imported Materials".

D. In the anticipatory L/C, the importers should require the issuing bank to add the provision that "prepayment in this L/C should be paid in batches with the preparation and shipment conditions of the exporting goods". In addition, if possible, the importers should send someone to monitor the processes of goods preparation and delivery, only through which can the importers avoid to be faced with the risk that the exporters refuse to ship goods or abscond with money after receiving the prepayment from the bank.

### 10.4.2.3 Risk Prevention of the Issuing Bank

The main risk prevention measures for the issuing bank in the business of the L/C are as follows:

A. Examine the credit standing of the importers carefully. As for importers with different credit standings, the issuing bank could issue the L/C to the exporters only with the credit standing, low percentage security deposit of issuing the L/C or high percentage security deposit delivered by the importers so that the issuing can reduce the loss if the importers with poor credit standing refuse to make redemption. Meanwhile, the issuing bank can make the consignee of the bill of lading stipulated in the L/C as "To the Order of the Issuing Bank" so that the issuing bank can take delivery of the goods and resell them with the documents they have when the importers refuse to pay the redemption in order to offset or reduce the loss.

B. For the financing under the anticipatory L/C, the issuing bank can demand the bank in the exporting country to deliver the financing in batches according to the schedule of goods preparation and delivery of the exporters in order to reduce the risk that the loss of both payment and goods because of one-time prepayment.

### 10.4.2.4 Risk Prevention of Advising Bank

When providing advising services, the advising bank should examine the authenticity of the L/C in strict accordance with the provisions of *UCP600*. If the authenticity of the L/C is unclear, the advising bank should inform the relevant principals in order to avoid the loss caused by their own reasons or the application of forged L/C.

### 10.4.2.5 Risk Prevention of the Negotiating Bank

When providing negotiation to the beneficiaries, the negotiating bank should strengthen business training of their personnel to improve their professional level so that they can examine the documents submitted by the exporters strictly in order to avoid the refusal payment caused by contraction that they believe the documents are consistent with the L/C while the issuing bank disagrees. Next, the credit standing of the issuing bank should be examined carefully in order to avoid the situation that the issuing bank refuse to fulfill the obligations of liquidation after the alternative payment has been made because of the poor credit standing of the issuing bank. Thirdly, to strengthen the understanding of the credit standing of the exporters involved in the L/C or to ask the exporters to provide guarantees or collateral can reduce the possibility of suffering further loss. Fourthly, it is necessary to refuse negotiation in order to avoid risk when getting known about that the issuing bank is suffering great domestic political risk.

### 10.4.2.6 Risk Prevention of the Confirming Bank

When providing confirming services to a specific bank, it is necessary to check the credit standing of the issuing bank and the degree of political risk in the host country in order to avoid suffering loss caused by the refusal of payment by issuing bank after the payment by the confirming bank. The confirming bank can refuse the confirming invitation of the issuing bank if the risk they are faced with is greater. In addition, if the issuing bank requires a specific bank to provide the confirming services, it means that the issuing bank has opened an account there with a certain amount of funds. Without this relationship, the designated bank should deal with the business cautiously.

## Questions:

### Ⅰ. True or false.

1. The payee of the draft is written as "Pay to John Store or order", indicating that the draft is a draft with demonstrative order and can be endorsed for transfer.
2. D/P at... days after sight refers to the reminder that collecting bank should make immediately after receiving the documents. It should remind the importer of draft and documents. If the documents are correct, the importer should accept the draft immediately and pay the collecting bank on the due date for payment. And the collecting bank will present the document after the fare is collected. As shown in the definition of D/P after sight, the presentation of the documents from collecting bank is based on the payment of importer when the D/P after sight uses the collection.
3. The settlement using the letter of credit in international trade belongs to the category of bank credit. The issuing bank makes payment commitment to their own credit and assumes primary liability for payment. However, drafts in the form of the letter of credit are usually issued by the seller of import and export trade, thus they belong to the category of the commercial draft.
4. In practice, there are occasions when an exporter directs banks to provide financial facilities to importers. The exporter authorizes the remitting bank to notify the collecting bank and notifies the importer in the collection application that the importer can issue a debit memorandum to the collecting bank on the basis of its own trust receipt after accepting the draft to dispose goods prior

## Chapter 10　International Settlement Risks & Management

to payment and pay on the due date. Then the collecting bank can release documents directly with the trust receipt of the importer after the latter has accepted the drafts, without requiring the importer to provide security or collateral. This is often referred to as D/P & T/R. If the buyer takes delivery by the T/R, yet fails to pay, the exporter alone should take the responsibility.

5. Export credit insurance is the general method adopted by all governments to resist export risks.

II. Case Analysis.

1. One Chinese company exported goods to a foreign Company A. Company A issued an irrevocable sight negotiation L/C on time and this L/C is advised and confirmed by the Bank B which is a foreign bank that is located in China. After the goods were shipped, the Chinese company sent a full set of qualified documents to Bank B and negotiated the payment. It had received the payment then. However, when Bank B claimed reimbursement to the issuing bank, it knew that the issuing bank had declared bankrupt due to poor management. As a result, Bank B requested that the Chinese company should refund the negotiated payment and advised the company to entrust it to claim payment directly from Company A. In this regard, what do you think the Chinese company should do and why?

2. One Chinese company exported a number of native products to Japan. The contract worth 3 million Japanese yen, using D/P six months after sight. After the signing of the contract, statistics released by the Japanese government showed that Japanese fiscal deficit in the previous quarter rose sharply, leading to the significant increase in the balance of payments deficit and inflation. In order to reduce the foreign exchange risk, how should the Chinese company settle and why?

3. Company A in China exports a batch of goods to the Company B in South Korea with the payment method of D/P at 90 days after sight. After the shipment of goods, the bill of exchange and shipping documents were sent to a collecting bank in South Korea through the remitting bank in exporting place and Company B has accepted the bill of exchange. After the arrival of goods at the port of destination, Company B presents a trust receipt(T/R) to the local collecting bank in order to get the shipment documents and to deliver the goods to resell the goods because of the anxiety of getting goods. When the bill of exchange expires, Company B has no payment ability due to poor management and operation. The collecting bank informs the remitting bank and advises the Company A to claim payment directly from Company B because the payer of the bill of exchange refuses to make payment. At this time, there are 30 days left before the bill of exchange expires. Please analyze the possibility of recovering payment by Company A when the bill of exchange expires and put forward advice to deal with the case. Please make comments.

4. Company A from China and Company B from Indonesia had signed an export contract with the amount of 20 thousand dollars on March 11, 2003, and the Company B requested the payment in the form of D/P at sight. After the shipment of goods, Company B required the domestic exporter to mark the consignor and consignee as Company B on the bill of lading and to send the copy of bill of lading to Company B. After arrival of goods at the port of destination, Company B did not make payment for redemption with the reasons such as temporary lack of money for goods and so

on, and then required the exporter not only to change the method of payment into the D/A, but also to allow the Company B to take delivery of goods in advance, otherwise Company B would reject the goods. As the consignee of the bill of lading was marked as Company B, the domestic exporter could not resell the goods to other customers and could only meet the requirements. Then, the Company B would handle with the procedures of taking delivery of the goods with the copy of the bill of lading to the shipping company, according to the guarantee and copy of the business license, because goods were on Company B's own grounds. After the delivery and resale of goods, Company B would not make payment to the bank on schedule and could not be contacted, so that the Company A would suffer the loses of both goods and money. Please analyze the case.

5. In June, 2009, an export company in Zhejiang Province and an importer from Indian had signed an exporting contract of cashmere yarn series with the total amount of 60 thousand us dollars in which it was stipulated that the trade conditions are CFR NEW DELHI BY AIR, and the payment method was the 100% irrevocable L/C at sight. The date of shipment was in August of 2009, from Shanghai to New Delhi. After signing the contract, the importer had issued the L/C through a commercial bank in India, and the advising bank and the negotiating bank were both a domestic bank, and the price term in the L/C was "CNF NEW DELHI" which the exporter did not pay attention to. After receiving the L/C, the exporter shipped the goods and prepared various bills and documents according to the requirements in L/C after which they handled with the negotiating procedures. However, the negotiating bank received the refusal notification from the issuing bank soon after sending the relevant documents to it and the reasons for refusal was the documents are not consistent with L/C, which referred to that the price term "CFR NEW DELHI" was not the same as the "CNF NEW DELHI" in the L/C. After knowing this, the exporter contacted the importer immediately to request the importer to pay for redemption, and sent a telex to the issuing bank through the domestic negotiating bank to clarify the refusal reason was not proper so that the counter party should perform the payment obligation in time according to the provisions of *UCP600*. Both the importer and the issuing bank ignored the measure taken by the exporter. In this case, the exporter contacted the carrier of goods at once and the agency in New Delhi informed the exporter that the goods have been taken away. In such a passive situation, the exporter had to agree with the 20% reduction of the price in order to solve the problem. Please analyze the case and analyze the specific prevention measures of the L/C risk in the mode of air transportation.

6. An import and export Company X in City A of China and a trade Company Y in Australia have signed a trade contract, in which Company Y will export a batch of hard-to-get supplies to Company X and the place of delivery is stipulated in the contract as City A. Company X applies to the Bank Z to issue a documentary L/C in which the negotiating bank is not specified. Subsequently, the date of shipment has come, and Company X suspects that the Company Y has cheating behaviors so that it requires the bank to refuse to negotiate with the negotiating bank. Company Y finds a guarantee company which has promised that the goods are loaded and shipped

to the port of destination. Afterward, the applicant informs the issuing bank to authorize the negotiating bank to negotiate. The negotiating bank is an international Bank U. After receiving the authorization, Bank U gives payment to Company Y of the beneficiary the next day according to the requirements in *UCP600*. And then, the buyer, Company X does not receive the goods from Company Y so that it applies preservation order to the court in A to require the court to frozen the payment issued by Bank Z under the provisions of the L/C, because of fraud of the beneficiary (However in fact, the issuing bank agrees the negotiating bank to negotiate, and the negotiating bank has given the relevant funds to the beneficiary). If you are a judge, how would you make court decisions of the above case?

# 第1章

# 国际结算概述

## 1.1 国际结算的含义与特征

### 1.1.1 国际结算的含义与类型

作为一种经济行为,结算是由于商品交易、服务贸易和资金移动与调拨等原因而产生的货币收支及清算债权、债务的行为。而国际结算则是指营业地在不同国家/地区的当事人之间因政治、经济、文化、外交、军事等方面的交往或联系而产生的以货币表示的债权、债务关系的清偿或资金转移行为。作为一项重要的国际经济活动,国际结算是保障与促进国际各项活动与交往正常进行的必要手段。

根据国际债权、债务关系发生的原因,可将国际结算分为国际贸易结算和国际非贸易结算两大类。国际贸易结算是指基于货物进出口而引起的国际货币收支和国际债权债务的结算,又称为有形贸易结算。它是国际结算的基础和主要内容。国际非贸易结算是指货物进出口以外的其他各种因国际政治、经济及文化交往活动引起的结算,也在一定程度上反映了一个国家/地区对外开放的广度和深度。

### 1.1.2 国际结算与国内结算的区别

国际结算与国内结算的区别主要有以下几点:

**1. 货币的活动范围不同**

在国内结算中,其货币活动不越出国界;而国际结算则是跨国界进行的。

**2. 使用的货币不同**

在国内结算时,收付双方一般使用同一种货币;而国际结算则往往使用不同的货币,经常需要进行货币兑换,因而不可避免地会遇到汇率风险,特别是交易风险。

**3. 遵循的法律不同**

在国内结算中出现问题后,有关当事方一般遵循同一法律。但在国际结算中,若发生纠纷,则很难简单地用所涉及的两国/地区中任何一国/地区的法规解决,而须根据国际惯例或根据事先由双方当事人共同议订的某一法律或惯例进行裁决。

此外,国际结算与国内结算在支付工具、外汇管制及其所引起的业务处理等方面也有不同。

### 1.1.3 国际结算的内容

国际结算主要研究国际债权债务清偿所使用的信用工具(结算工具)、结算方式和结算单据。同时，结算资金的划拨以及国际结算风险也是国际结算研究的内容。

**1. 结算工具**

当代国际结算主要采用非现金结算，为表明资金的转移收付关系，主要借助票据进行。票据是国际贸易结算使用的主要工具，有汇票、本票和支票三种基本类型。为使票据能有效地发挥其应有的职能，各国都通过法律对票据的形式、内容及相关行为进行规范，并明确票据的性质和特点。本书将在第2章中对上述三种票据进行详细分析。

**2. 结算方式**

国际结算方式即国际货币收付的途径、手段及渠道，它主要解决资金（外汇）如何从进口地转移到出口地的问题，这是国际结算中最主要的内容。国内外常见的国际结算方式主要包括汇款、托收、信用证、银行保函、备用信用证、国际保理服务和包买票据业务等七种方式。在很长一段时期内，信用证曾被广泛使用，但其业务程序相对于其他支付方式更为复杂。

**3. 结算单据**

商品单据化和单据商品化是当代国际贸易运作模式的发展趋势。为使资金转移和货物交接顺利结合，保障当事人的合法权益，以利于国际贸易顺利进行，各种相关单据即成为国际结算业务的一项重要内容。

国际结算单据主要包括商业发票、运输单据、金融单据及保险单等。其中，运输单据中的海运提单和多式联运提单代表了货物所有权，是最重要的单据。除以上单据外，有时还会涉及一些附属单据。

**4. 结算资金的划拨**

当代国际结算通过有关银行间的资金划拨实现。为安全、迅速、高效地办理好相关业务手续，建立好银行间的联行、代理行和账户行等关系，并根据实际业务需要，从密集的银行业务网络中选出最便捷的途径和手续，结算资金的划拨也成为国际结算的内容之一。

**5. 国际结算风险**

虽受金融危机等多方面因素的影响，近年来国际贸易发展速度呈下降趋势，但规模仍在不断扩大。同时，国际贸易竞争受多方面因素影响也变得日趋激烈，这促使国际结算方式处于不断变化和发展之中。特别地，随着全球性买方市场的形成，对买方有利的托收和汇付等结算方式越来越受到青睐。国际贸易结算方式的发展变化，不仅未使贸易争端及贸易风险减少和降低，反而使其日趋加剧。国际贸易相关各方（出口方、进口方及银行）如何针对不同结算方式的特性、优劣势，有效地防范相应结算方式项下的业务风险，正成为国际结算领域研究的重要课题。

### 1.1.4 国际结算制度

国际结算主要以银行为媒介，随着国际结算业务量的飞速增长，为保证国际结算的正常进行，逐渐形成了进行国际结算时所须遵循的原则或行为规范，以服务于世界各国/地区银行的国际结算业务。这种国际进行结算时所遵循的原则或行为规范，通常称为国际结算制度。

根据使用的结算货币是否可自由兑换，可将国际结算制度分为以下三种形式：

**1. 自由的多边国际结算制度**

以使用国际可自由兑换货币为特点，且凡使用国际可自由兑换货币的国家相互间的债权、债务均可互相抵冲。

**2. 管制的双边国际结算制度**

以使用不可自由兑换的货币为特点，一般做法是：在外汇管制条件下，由两国政府通过签订支付协定，双方分别在对方设立清算账户，采用集中冲销彼此之间债权、债务的方法来进行国际结算。

**3. 区域性经济集团内部的多边国际结算制度**

欧盟及过去"经互会"各成员之间的国际结算即属此。

## 1.2　国际结算的演进

国际结算随着社会经济制度变革、生产力发展、国际贸易发展、货币制度及信用制度的发展而产生和发展。迄今为止，大致经历了现金结算、非现金结算及电子结算三种模式。

### 1.2.1　现金结算

随着西方主要国家进入资本主义时期，国际贸易开始产生，并因此促进了国际结算的产生与发展。但在国际贸易的早期阶段，国际结算业务通常采用现金或使用黄金、白银等贵金属进行结算。因为远途运送金银风险大、费用高、占压资金时间长，且计数之外还需鉴别金银真伪，当贸易量大时清点和支付金银也很不方便，故随着贸易规模的扩大及交易日趋频繁，贵金属及现金作为结算工具已不能适应国际贸易大规模发展形势的需要，从而为非现金结算提供了发展的空间。

### 1.2.2　非现金结算

11世纪，地中海沿岸的商品贸易渐具规模，商人开始用字据来代替现金。14～15世纪，意大利一些重要城市商业发展较快，出现了银行，并开始通过银行使用汇票办理国际结算。18世纪，单据化的概念被普遍接受，单据结算的优越性也不断显现，这使得国际结算逐步从现金结算发展到非现金结算。19世纪末20世纪初，凭单据付款的结算方式已基本完善，国际结算出现了融资与结算相结合的特点，其标志表现为银行信用逐渐加入国际结算，银行成为国际结算的中枢。银行通过买卖各种不同货币、不同金额及不同期限的票据，将两国进出口商之间的结算变为两国银行之间的结算。结算后出现的余额由债权国银行以存款的形式存入债务国银行，而不必通过运送现金解决，单据也从一般的货物收据演变为可转让的凭证。

### 1.2.3　电子结算

第二次世界大战以后，随着国际贸易规模、贸易方式、运输方式及商品结构的巨变，世界各国/地区的银行结算业务量迅猛增长，对国际结算的速度与服务质量提出了更高更新的要求。同时，随着电子技术的迅速发展，发达国家的银行把现代通信技术和电子计算机结合起来，构成了"银行电子国际结算系统"，大大提高了国际结算效率。目前，具有代表性的

"银行电子国际结算系统"主要有四个,分别为:

**1. 纽约银行同业电子结算系统**

纽约银行同业电子结算系统又称交换银行相互收付系统(Clearing House Interbank Payment System,CHIPS),是一个为大额交易活动设立的美国私人清算所。该系统于1970年夏天由设在纽约的100多家美国和外国银行分支机构共同成立,由纽约清算协会所拥有并经营,现有140多家成员银行,其中2/3为外国成员银行,分布于43个国家。纽约清算协会是一个自发组织的协会,通过使用装置在每家会员银行与该系统主机相连的终端来办理银行收付业务,其实质是一个国际美元收付网络。凡通过上述系统清算的业务,如发生纠纷时,将依据纽约的法律解决。

**2. 伦敦银行同业自动支付系统**

伦敦银行同业自动支付系统(Clearing House Automated Payment System,CHAPS)是1984年2月在伦敦建立的一家英国清算系统,提供当天的英镑资金转移。该系统具有以下特点:高度自动计算机化的信息传递部分取代了依靠票据交换的传递,使以伦敦城以外的交换银行为付款人的部分交易也可实现当天结算;继续维护英国银行双重清算体制(Two Ties Clearing System)。所有商业银行,先通过往来的清算银行进行清算(为初级清算),再由国家清算银行之间进行集中清算(为终极清算)。因此,所有商业银行须在清算银行开立账户,在初级清算中轧算差额;清算银行在英格兰银行开立账户,在终极清算时轧算差额。

**3. 环球银行金融电讯系统**

环球银行金融电讯系统(Society for Worldwide Inter-Bank Financial Telecommunication,SWIFT)是在首席执行官Carl Reuterskiold领导下于1973年在布鲁塞尔成立的,得到了来自15个国家的239家银行的支持。SWIFT成立后,开始建立用于金融交易、共享数据处理系统和全球通信网络的共同标准,并于1975年建立基本操作程序、责任规则等,于1977年发送第一条消息。

SWIFT是一套能为世界各地金融机构以安全、标准、可靠的方式发送与接收金融交易信息的网络。SWIFT以高度安全的方式传输金融信息,也向那些使用SWIFT网络的金融机构出售软件及服务,但不持有其会员账户,且不进行任何清算或结算。目前,国际银行间的大多数信息使用SWIFT网络进行传递。截至2010年9月,SWIFT联系着在世界209个国家/地区的9000多家金融机构,平均每天交换1500万条以上的信息。

**4. 美国联邦资金转账系统**

美国联邦资金转账系统又称全美境内美元支付系统(Federal Reserves Wire Transfer System,FEDWIRE),成立于1913年,将全美划分为12个联邦储备区、25个分行和11个专门的支付处理中心,将美国联储总部、所有的联储银行、美国财政部及其他联邦政府机构连接在一起,提供实时全额结算服务,主要用于金融机构间的隔夜拆借、行间清算及企业间大额交易结算,美国政府与国际组织的记账债券转移业务等。此外,美国的个人和非金融机构可通过金融机构间接使用FEDWIRE。

FEDWIRE系统有专用的实现资金转移的电码通信网络,其权威性、安全性较高,每天运行18个小时,每笔大额的资金转账从发起、处理到完成,全部自动化。1960年,FEDWIRE建立了簿记证券系统,其主要目的在于降低证券交易成本,提高交割与结算效率及安全系数。

### 1.2.4 国际结算的特征

（1）用于国际结算的货币为国际可自由兑换货币。
（2）按国际惯例进行。
（3）实行"推定交货"原理。
（4）商业银行成为结算和融资的中心。

## 1.3 国际结算中的往来银行

### 1.3.1 银行信用与国际结算

在国际结算业务中，银行是不可或缺的主体。银行办理国际结算具有以下优点：

**1. 便利**

银行网络和国际代理行网络的普遍建立，使国际结算不受时间和地点的限制，能够满足世界各地客户的需求。

**2. 安全**

银行资金雄厚，银行信用优于商业信用，使国际结算更加安全可靠。

**3. 经济**

银行集中了大量的债权债务关系，可最大限度地加以抵销，有助于缩短结算路径，节约时间、费用及利息的支出，使国际结算更为经济。

**4. 规范**

通过有关国际惯例的颁布和实施，银行办理国际结算有统一的规章可循，使之更加合理化和规范化，有助于减少和避免国际贸易纠纷。

**5. 快捷**

随着高新技术，特别是计算机技术和通信技术在银行业务中的应用，人工处理纸张与票据的国际结算逐渐转向电子化作业与管理，使得国际结算不断朝着安全可靠、经济合理、方便迅速的方向发展。

### 1.3.2 银行在国际结算中的作用

银行在国际结算中居于中心枢纽地位。国际银行业务通过世界各地商业银行间的合作进行。离开了商业银行间的合作，国际结算就无法正常进行。具体到国际贸易结算，银行的作用主要有以下几个方面：

**1. 国际汇兑**

国际汇兑（International Exchange）是指银行应汇款人或债务人要求，将一种货币兑换成另一种货币，并委托收款人所在地银行向收款人或债权人支付一定金额，以结清国际债权债务关系的金融活动，属于银行的一项中间业务。

**2. 提供信用保证**

国际贸易结算的风险主要在于买卖双方不能一手交货，一手收款。进出口商均不愿先将货款、货物或代表货物所有权的单据交给对方，这就需要一个双方均信得过的第三方来充当中间人和保证人，对此，银行显然是最好的选择。在信用证、银行保函等结算方式下，通过银行的信用保证，国际贸易才得以顺利地进行。

**3. 融通资金**

取得银行的资金融通是进出口商从事国际贸易的一个重要条件。任何一个企业，其自有资金总是有限的，如要经营对外贸易，通常须借助于银行的资金融通。除一般贷款外，银行还可在办理具体贸易结算过程中，以进出口押汇方式向客户提供融资、向进口商提供信用证开证额度、向出口商提供票据贴现等，从而推进国际贸易的开展。

**4. 减少外汇风险**

进出口贸易线长面广，从签约到履约（即卖方交货、收款，买方收货、付款）通常需要2~3个月，甚至更长时间，这就给货款收付双方带来外汇风险。银行可通过远期外汇交易、货币期货交易和货币期权交易等手段，为进出口商降低甚至消除外汇风险。例如，我国银行目前开展的远期结售汇业务，就是一种为企业提供的避免外汇风险的工具。

## 1.3.3 国际结算中的往来银行

在国际结算业务中，收付行为一般习惯通过银行间的清算来进行。因此，办理国际结算的基本条件是须有一个国际性银行网络。

银行间往来包括中央银行往来、同业银行往来、联行往来和代理行往来。一般而言，尽管经营外汇业务的商业银行在海外都设有分支机构，但不可能在发生债权债务的所有国家/地区均建立分支机构，于是就需要与其他国家/地区的银行密切合作，进而形成一个高效率的资金转移网络。在境外的往来银行主要包括以下类型：

**1. 境外分行**

境外分行是办理国际金融业务的商业银行获得东道国批准后，在东道国境外设立的营业性分支机构。境外分行与总行属于同一法人，其资产负债及相关费用、收益均并入总行的会计报表，并由总行承担连带法律责任，且有权使用总行的一切资源。

**2. 子银行**

子银行简称海外子行，是由总行按东道国法律在东道国注册的、具有独立法人地位的银行。这类银行的大部分或全部股权归总行所有。根据子银行注册资金的来源不同，可将其分为全资子银行和控股子银行两类。

**3. 海外附属行**

海外附属行是一家在东道国注册的银行，总行在该行持有一部分股权，但尚未达到控股程度。附属行的其他股东可以是当地机构，也可以是其他海外银行。海外附属行有时是专门成立的，有时则由国内总行购买当地银行的部分股权形成的。在法律上，海外附属行是受东道国管理的当地金融机构，东道国允许其从事正常的银行业务，故而允许它们为其国外股东的客户提供银行服务。

**4. 国外办事处**

一家银行在某国设立办事处的主要目的是方便总行的客户在该国及其邻国进行生意往来。办事处的主要功能在于为总行的客户提供信息和咨询服务。国外办事处不是营业性机构，不许接受存款，不能贷款，亦不能提供汇票、信用证等国际贸易支付服务。对于国际贸易结算业务而言，国外办事处的缺点在于不能开展普通的银行业务。尽管它也能通过地方代理银行提供贸易支付便利，但过程可能缓慢且麻烦，难以满足商家的需求。

### 5. 联营银行

联营银行又称为合资银行。这是一国银行在东道国与东道国共同出资组建的银行，也可能有多个外国投资者参与，但外国投资者的出资都未达到控股程度，主要由东道国银行控股。正因如此，东道国对这一类银行业务范围的限制要比前四类少。

### 6. 代理行

代理行是指与其他国家银行签订协议，接受对方委托，代理所委托的各项结算业务的银行。一家银行办理的国际结算业务可能遍及全球各地，但从其本身经营管理的核算角度考虑，加之受到东道国监管的限制，最多也只能在国外的金融中心和部分中心城市设立分支机构和子银行、联营银行。

### 7. 账户行

账户行也称为账户代理行。为满足业务中资金划拨的需要，办理国际结算业务的银行对账户行的选择比代理行严格。因此，应从众多的代理行中选择发展历史长、国际信誉高、业务能力强、经营效率高、服务质量良好、互委业务量大、资金实力强、账户条件比较优惠、所在国的货币是世界上广泛使用的清算货币的银行开立现汇账户。这些被选择开立账户的银行就称为账户行。

目前，中国银行是国内办理国际结算历史最悠久、国际结算业务量最大、代理行关系最多的一家外汇指定银行。中国银行建立了遍及世界五大洲160多个国家/地区的5000多家代理行的网络，有选择地与一些代理行相互建立账户关系，并与全球200多家大银行保持着经常性的资金往来关系，根据需要相互进行资金融通。中国银行这个覆盖全球的代理行网络，大大便利了中国与其他国家/地区的贸易和非贸易结算，也促进了中国银行本身国际结算业务的不断发展。

# 第2章

# 国际结算票据

## 2.1 票据概述

票据是出票人自己承诺或委托付款人在指定日期无条件支付一定款项的一种凭证,是国际结算中最主要的工具。

### 2.1.1 票据的特性

**1. 设权性**

票据的设权性即票据与其代表的权利不可分,是指持票人的票据权利随票据的设立而产生,离开了票据,就不能证明其票据权利。

**2. 要式性**

要式性是指票据的做成须具备法定的形式,票据上所记载的必要项目必须严格遵守规定且记载完全。如果不具有法定的形式,就不能产生票据效力。

各国法律对票据上必须具备的形式要件和内容均做了详细规定。例如,我国票据法明确规定,汇票必须记载下列事项:表明"汇票"的字样;无条件支付的委托;确定的金额;付款人名称;收款人名称;出票日期;出票人签章。各类票据的当事人须严格遵守这些规定,不得随意更改,否则票据就是不合格的和无效的,因而就得不到法律的保护。英国票据法则规定,支票是可以流通的,但倘若无收款人的名字或未填写金额,该支票即不可流通。票据在流通中,各当事人的权利和义务关系,全凭票据上的文义确定,若票据记载事项的方式不统一,或某些重要事项记载不明,则当事人的权利义务就难以确定,就会使票据的可接受性降低。

**3. 流通性**

可流通转让是票据的基本特性。票据的受让人获得票据的全部法律权利,受让人取得票据后,有权用自己的名义起诉票据上所有的当事人。善意而支付过对价的受让人的权利不因前手对票据的权利有缺陷而受到影响。

票据受让人拥有的权利是有条件的,具体条件包括:

(1) 转让须是付过对价的。
(2) 受让人须是善意地取得票据的。
(3) 票面完整而合格(参见要式性)。
(4) 票据处于可交付的状态。

**4. 无因性**

无因性又称条件支付性,即票据须无条件支付。票据是否有效,不受出票或转让原因影响,即出票或背书的原因无须在票面记载,只要符合法定要式,在票据到期时,付款人就须无条件支付。票据受让人无须调查出票和转让原因,只要票据记载合格,就能取得票据文义载明的权利。

**5. 金钱性**

票据的金钱性是指票据所表示的权利,是一种以金钱为给付标的物的债权,因而票据债务人只能支付款项,而不能用物品支付。

**6. 提示性**

票据的提示性是指持票人要求付款时,须在法定期限内向付款人出示票据,以显示占有这张票据,才能要求付款。否则,付款人不予理会。例如,我国票据法规定,即期汇票自出票日起一个月内向付款人提示付款。

**7. 返还性**

票据的返还性是指票据的持票人领到支付的票款时,应将票据交还付款人;如不交还,债务人可不付款。票据由于具有返还性,不能无限期地流通,在到期日付款后就结束流通。这说明票据在模仿货币的功能上仍有局限,一经付款就不能继续流通。

**8. 可追索性**

票据的可追索性是指票据的付款人或承兑人如果对合格票据拒绝承兑,或拒绝付款,则正当持票人为维护其票据权利,有权通过法定程序向所有票据债务人追索,要求得到票据权利。

### 2.1.2 票据功能

**1. 结算功能**

国际结算的基本方法是非现金结算,在这一方式下,要结清国际债权、债务就须使用一定的支付工具。票据是一种能起到货币支付功能和结算功能的支付工具。

**2. 信用功能**

票据并非商品,不含有社会劳动,自身没有价值,它是建立在信用基础上的书面支付凭证。如果交易时,买卖双方约定交货后一个月付款,买方可向卖方开立一个月期付款的本票,即买方一个月期付款的信用以本票代替。

**3. 流通功能**

票据经过交付或背书转让给他人并能连续多次转让。背书人对票据的付款负有担保责任,故背书次数越多,对票据付款的负责人也就越多,票据的身价也就越高。背书转让使得票据在市场上广泛流通,成为一种流通工具,既节约了现金使用,又拓宽了流通手段。

### 2.1.3 票据法

票据在国际结算及社会经济生活中发挥着十分重要的作用,因此各国政府都极为重视,相继对票据流通规则进行立法,即票据法。票据发源于欧洲,最早在法国立法,随后德国、英国也都相继进行了票据立法。由于各国票据法的立法时间有先后,各国的经济水平、商业习惯及法制思想存在差异,因此形成了多个法系,主要有英美法系和大陆法系两大法系。

**1. 英美法系**

英美法系的票据法以英国的国内法《英国票据法》为蓝本。英国于 1882 年颁布施行票据法，美国及大部分英联邦成员国，如加拿大、印度等，都以此为参照制定本国的票据法。美国在 1952 年制定《统一商法法典》，其中第三章商业证券，即是关于票据的法律规定，也就是美国的票据法，它在英美法系国家的票据法中也具一定的代表性和影响力。美国和其他英联邦国家的票据法虽在具体法律条文上与英国票据法有所不同，但总体说来，英美法系国家的票据法基本上是统一的。

**2. 大陆法系**

大陆法系又称日内瓦法系，以国际公约《日内瓦统一法》为依据。以法国、德国等欧洲大陆为主的 20 多个国家参加了 1930 年在日内瓦召开的国际票据法统一会议，签订了《日内瓦统一汇票、本票法公约》，1931 年又签订了《日内瓦统一支票法公约》。两个公约合称为《日内瓦统一法》。《日内瓦统一法》是有关票据方面的国际私法的重要渊源，参加签字的大陆法系的国家在制定或修改本国的票据法时都要依循这一国际公约。大陆法系国家的票据法又以法国和德国的票据法最有代表性。另有一些非大陆法系国家的票据法也参照《日内瓦统一法》制定本国的票据法（如我国的票据法）。在实际内容上，大陆法系国家的票据法基本趋于统一。

## 2.2 汇票

### 2.2.1 含义

根据英国票据法第三条："汇票是一种书面的无条件支付的命令，由一人开给另一人，并由签发命令的人签名，要求受票人见票或定期或在某一可预定之日期，将一定金额之款项付与规定之人或其指定人或来人。"

按照《日内瓦统一汇票、本票法公约》的规定，汇票字样可用 Bill of Exchange、Exchange、Draft 等表示。

### 2.2.2 汇票要式

汇票的要式即根据票据法规定在汇票上必须记载的项目，也就是说，汇票必须具备形式要件才能产生法律效力。

我国票据法第 22 条规定："汇票必须记载下列事项：①表明'汇票'的字样；②无条件支付的委托；③确定的金额；④付款人名称；⑤收款人名称；⑥出票日期；⑦出票人签章。汇票上未记载前款规定事项之一的，无效。"第 23 条还规定："汇票上记载付款日期、付款地、出票地等事项的，应当清楚、明确。"

### 2.2.3 汇票当事人及其权利、义务与责任

汇票有三个必要的当事人：出票人（即签发汇票的人）、收款人及受票人或付款人。当事人同时也是汇票进入流通领域前的基本当事人。除此之外，汇票有时还会涉及背书人、被背书人及保证人等其他当事人。

根据参与汇票活动时间的不同，各当事人可分为基本当事人与非基本当事人两种。

**1. 基本当事人**

基本当事人是指基于最初的汇票行为而明确的当事人,包括出票人、收款人和(受托)付款人,其名称或商号均记载于汇票的正面。

(1) **出票人**。出票人是指开出汇票的企业或银行。中国票据法第 20 条的规定:"出票是指出票人签发票据并将其交付给收款人的票据行为。"既然出票是一种票据行为,行为人的资格就须符合法律的规定,因此具有行为能力是签发票据的必要条件,无行为能力者的出票行为由其法定代理人或监护人代理。

(2) **收款人**。收款人是指汇票上记载收取票据款项者。

(3) **受票人**。汇票的受票人同时也是汇票的付款人,是履行汇票付款的责任者。

(4) **承兑人**。承兑人即承担到期付款责任的责任者,通常情况下,承兑人即受票人。

**2. 汇票的非基本当事人**

国际结算业务中,汇票的非基本当事人主要包括两个:

(1) **被背书人**。被背书人是指受让票据后取得票据权利者,在票据签发时与票据无关,通过被背书受让成为汇票权利人。背书受让包括背书转让、背书质押、背书贴现三种方式。被背书人可作为背书人再次转让汇票,转让后便丧失权利人的地位,并且成为新的连带债务人,在汇票得到付款之前须准备承受持票人的追索。

(2) **保证人**。保证人是指为保证收款人或者持票人能够得到付款而承担担保付款的连带责任者。在签发票据时做保证人是为出票人做担保,在承兑时做保证人是为承兑人做担保(这两种保证都是为主债务人所做的保证),在背书环节做保证人是为背书人做担保。保证人在票据上不记载被保证人时视为对主债务人做保证。因为保证人是在出票后加盟的,所以是票据的非基本当事人。

### 2.2.4 汇票的类型

汇票可按不同的标准进行分类,通常有以下几种分类标准:

**1. 按出票人划分**

(1) **商业汇票**。这是由工商企业或个人签发的汇票,其付款人可以是工商企业或个人,也可以是银行。在国际贸易结算中,出口商按合同规定装运货物后向进口商开立的汇票即是一种商业汇票。在国际贸易中,商业汇票最为常用。

(2) **银行汇票**。银行汇票即由银行签发的汇票,其付款人是银行,通常用于汇款业务。

**2. 按汇票抬头(即收款人)划分**

(1) **限制式抬头汇票**。这种汇票又称记名汇票,它只能由汇票上指定的收款人收款,不能背书转让。

(2) **指示式抬头汇票**。这种汇票在业务中最常用,可通过背书转让。

(3) **来人抬头汇票**。这种汇票无须背书即可转让。

**3. 按付款时间划分**

(1) **即期汇票**。它是指在持票人提示时,付款人须立即付款的汇票。

(2) **远期汇票**。它是指在一定期限内付款的汇票。

**4. 按承兑人划分**

(1) **商业承兑汇票**。这是以工商企业或个人为付款人并由工商企业或个人进行承兑的远期汇票。商业承兑汇票建立在商业信用的基础上，如果承兑人因破产或其他原因无力支付款项，持票人在到期日将无法得到汇票款项。

**（2）银行承兑汇票。** 它是由工商企业或个人开立的以银行为付款人并经银行承兑的远期汇票。银行承兑汇票建立在银行信用基础上，汇票经银行承兑后，持票人通常能按期得到票款。

**5. 按提示要求付款时有无货运单据划分**

**（1）跟单汇票。** 这种汇票又称信用汇票、押汇汇票，是指随附货运单据（通常为提单）的汇票。此种汇票多用于国际贸易结算中的信用证托收项下。商业汇票多为跟单汇票。

**（2）光票。** 这是由出票人开立的不附带任何货运单据的汇票。

**6. 按票面使用的货币划分**

按此标准可分为本币汇票及外币汇票两类。

**7. 按出票地与付款地是否在同一地划分**

按这一标准可分为国内汇票（即出票地与付款地均在同一国家/地区的汇票）和国外汇票（即出票地与付款地不在同一国家/地区的汇票）。

以上仅是汇票的部分分类。汇票按其特征分类，并不意味着一张汇票只具备一种特征，而是可同时具备多种特征。

## 2.2.5　汇票行为

汇票行为是指围绕汇票所发生的、以确立一定权利和义务关系为目的的行为，一般包括出票、提示、承兑、付款等。如需转让还需背书。此外还有退票、追索等。

**（1）出票。** 它包括两个动作：一是出票人制作汇票并签字，二是将汇票交给收款人。汇票的交付可以是实际的交付或推定的交付，即可以是汇票这一实物的转手，也可以是清晰表示有交付意向的某种行为。出票后，出票人成了汇票的主债务人，对汇票债务负有担保承兑或担保付款两方面责任，如汇票不能获得承兑或付款，出票人须自己清偿债务。

**（2）提示。** 这是指持票人将汇票提交付款人要求承兑或付款的行为，分为付款提示和承兑提示。

**（3）承兑。** 承兑是指远期汇票的付款人明确表示同意按出票人的指示于票据到期日付款给持票人的行为，包括两个动作：①写成"承兑"字样并签名，两张一套的，付款人只承兑一张。②交付。付款人将承兑后的汇票交给持票人（可实际交付也可推定交付，即付款人通知持票人某日已做承兑）。

**（4）付款。** 付款是指在即期汇票或经承兑的远期汇票到期时，持票人提示汇票，由付款人或承兑人履行付款。汇票一经付款，汇票上的一切债权债务即告终止。付款人一般还要求持票人出一张收款收据或在汇票背面签字作为收款证明并收回汇票，在汇票上注明"付讫"字样，汇票即注销了。如部分付款，只要持票人接受仍可保留票据，持票人可对未付金额进行追索。此时，付款人须在汇票上注明已付金额，同时要求持票人出具收据。

**（5）背书。** 背书是指持票人在汇票背面签名并把汇票交付被背书人的行为。它包括两个动作：①写成背书；②交付。

**（6）退票**（拒付）。持票人提示汇票要求付款人承兑或付款时遭拒绝，称为退票或拒付。此外，付款人虽未表示不承兑或不付款，但在规定期限内未做承兑或付款，付款人避而不见或付款人已倒闭破产或死亡导致付款无法实现等也属拒付。

**（7）追索**。这是指汇票遭到拒付时，持票人对其前手（背书人、出票人）行使要求偿还汇票金额和费用的权利。持票人可向自己的前手进行追索，也可向任一背书人或出票人行使追索。根据票据法，只要在票据上签过字，就须对票据债务负责。但在实务中，一般持票人大多向主债务人追索，在提示承兑遭拒付时，向出票人追索，已承兑票据提示付款时被拒付，也是向出票人追索。这时尽管承兑人是主债务人，但其拒付时，只能找第一从债务人——出票人进行追索。

## 2.3 本票与支票

### 2.3.1 本票

**1. 含义**

本票也称期票。《英国票据法》第83条将本票定义为："本票为一项书面的无条件付款承诺，由一人开给另一人，并由出票人签名，保证凭票或在规定日期，或在某一可预定之日期，将一定金额之货币付与规定之人或其指定人或来人。"

**2. 本票的关系人**

**（1）出票人**。出票人即签发本票的人，因承诺付款（Make a Promise），故本票出票人习称为"Maker"。

**（2）收款人**（受款人）。即本票的抬头人。

**3. 本票的内容**

根据《日内瓦统一汇票、本票公约》的规定，本票应具备以下内容：①写明"本票"字样；②无条件支付承诺；③收款人；④出票人签字；⑤出票日期和地点（未载明地点时，出票人名字旁的地点视为出票地点）；⑥付款期限（未载明时视为即期）；⑦一定金额；⑧付款地点（未载明时，出票地视为付款地点）。

**4. 本票的种类**

本票的划分方法多种多样。根据签发人的不同，可分为商业本票（又称"一般本票"）和银行本票。根据付款时间的不同，可分为即期本票和远期本票。根据有无收款人之记载，可分为记名本票和不记名本票。根据其金额记载方式的不同，可分为定额本票和不定额本票。根据支付方式的不同，可分为现金本票和转账本票。其中，一般本票（Promissory Note）的出票人为企业或个人，票据可以是即期本票，也可是远期本票。银行本票（Casher's Order）的出票人是银行，只能是即期本票。

### 2.3.2 支票

**1. 含义**

支票是银行存款户对银行签发的授权银行在见票时支付一定金额给某人或其指定人即持票人的一张无条件书面命令。《英国票据法》把支票作为汇票的一种，认为支票是以行为付款人的即期付款的汇票。支票的格式不是由出票人自己设计的，通常是由支票存款户的开户银行提供设计、印刷的。

**2. 支票与汇票的区别**

1）支票为支付工具；汇票除具有支付工具性质外，还具有借贷工具的职能。

2）支票均为即期；汇票可分为即期和远期两种。

3）支票的付款人仅限于银行；而汇票则可是银行、企业或个人。

4）支票无须承兑；汇票除即期汇票外，一般均须承兑。

**3. 支票的内容**

1）写明"支票"字样。

2）无条件支付一定金额的命令。

3）付款人名称。

4）付款地点（未载明时，以付款人所在地为付款地点）。

5）出票日期、地点（未载明地点时，出票人姓名旁地点视为出票地点）。

6）出票人签字。

**4. 支票种类**

支票主要有以下几种：

（1）**记名支票**。这种支票在收款人一栏注明收款人姓名，取款时须经收款人签名。

（2）**不记名支票**。这种支票的收款人可以是任意持票人，银行对持票人获得支票是否合法不负责任。

（3）**划线支票**。这种支票是指支票正面印有两条横向平行线的支票，划线支票不得由持票人提取现款，只能由银行收款。划线支票可起到防止遗失后被人冒领，保障收款人利益的作用。

（4）**保付支票**。这种支票是由付款银行加注"保付"字样的支票。付款银行保付后即须付款。支票经保付后，信用提高，有利于流通。

# 第3章

# 汇　　款

## 3.1　汇款的含义与当事人

### 3.1.1　汇款的含义

汇款又称汇付，是指银行接受客户的委托，通过其自身所建立的通汇网络，使用合适的支付凭证将款项汇交收款人的一种结算方式，属于商业信用。汇付主要是利用银行间的资金划拨渠道，将银行之外的一方当事人的资金输送给另一方当事人，以完成收、付款方之间债权、债务的清偿。它所使用的凭证是支付授权书（Payment Order，P. O.）。由于支付授权书的传递方向与资金流向相同，因此，汇付属于顺汇性质，又称汇付法。在汇付方式下，原始付款人与最后收款人均非银行。在国际贸易结算中，汇款方式最简便，只是利用国际银行间相互划拨款项的便利，不涉及银行信用，买卖双方能否履行合同，取决于彼此间的信用，故纯属商业信用。

### 3.1.2　汇款业务的当事人

汇款业务主要涉及四个基本当事人，他们分别为：
(1) **付款人**。付款人即请求银行将资金汇给收款人的那个当事人，也称为汇款人。
(2) **收款人**。收款人称受款人，即收取款项的人。采用汇付支付货款时，出口商为收款人。
(3) **汇出行**。汇出行即受付款人委托汇出款项的银行。
(4) **汇入行**。汇入行又称解付行，它受汇出行委托将款项解付给收款人。业务中，在受理汇款业务前，汇出行与汇入行之间已经订立有委托代理合同。

## 3.2　汇款类型

汇款主要包括电汇、信汇和票汇。

### 3.2.1　电汇

这是汇款人将一定金额的汇款及汇款手续费付给当地一家银行，要求该银行用电传或电报通知其国外受款人所在地的分支行或代理行将汇款付给收款人。

### 3.2.2　信汇

这是汇款人（即债务人，货款支付时，该当事人为进口商）将汇款及手续费交付给汇款人所在地的一家银行，委托该银行通过信件方式转托受款人所在地的银行，将货款付给出口人。

### 3.2.3 票汇

在该方式下，汇款人向其当地银行购买银行即期汇票，并直接寄给收款人，收款人收到该汇票即可凭此向指定的付款银行取款。

## 3.3 汇款的偿付与退汇

### 3.3.1 汇款的偿付

汇款的偿付即汇款头寸的调拨，是指汇出行因汇入行代其解付汇款而予以偿还款项的行为，俗称"拨头寸"。

### 3.3.2 汇款的退汇

汇款的退汇指在汇款解付之前，由汇款人或收款人要求撤销该笔汇款的行为。退汇可以由收款人提出，也可以由汇款人提出。

**1. 电汇和信汇的退汇**

当选择电汇或信汇时，若收款人提出退汇，汇入行可用电报、电话或航邮通知汇出行将汇款收回，退给汇款人即可。若汇款人提出退汇，汇出行在接受汇款人的退汇要求后，应立即用电报、电传或航邮通知汇入行停止解付，撤销汇款。若汇款已解付，汇款人则不能要求退回，只能直接与收款人交涉退回。

**2. 票汇的退汇**

当选择票汇时，作为汇款人在将汇票交付汇出行后，一般不能止付，但如遇到汇票遗失、被窃等原因时，可办理挂失止付、退付手续。汇款人要向汇出行出具保证书，保证汇出行因票汇退汇而可能遭受的损失，由汇款人承担，并保证如以后发现汇票时把原票缴回汇出行。

**3. 退汇的手续**

（1）汇出行退汇手续：①汇款人提出申请，详细说明退汇的缘由，必要时提供保证；②汇出行审查；③向汇入行发出要求退回头寸的通知；④收到汇入行同意退汇的通知和头寸后，即注销，同时将汇款按汇率折算成本币汇款入账。

（2）汇入行退汇手续：①核对退汇通知的印鉴，看汇款是否已付；②若汇款已付，将收款人签署的汇款收条寄回，表示汇款已经解付；③若未付，则退回头寸，寄回汇款委托书或汇票。

### 3.3.3 汇款的支付条款

在汇付方式下，支付条款的内容主要包括汇付的时间、具体的汇付方式和金额等。例如"买方应不迟于10月10日将100%的货款用信汇预付交至卖方"。

## 3.4 汇款的使用

汇款既可用于贸易结算,又可用于非贸易结算。鉴于汇款方式建立在商业信用基础上,可靠性差,故很少用于贸易结算,而更多地用于贸易从属费用结算或非贸易结算。

根据货款的交付和货物运送时间的关系,可将汇款分为预付货款和货到付款两种。

### 3.4.1 预付货款

预付货款是进口商将货款的一部分或全部支付给出口商,出口商收到货款后再发货的汇款方式。

### 3.4.2 货到付款

货到付款是出口商先发货,待进口商收到货物后,或在一定时间内将货款汇交出口商的一种汇款结算方式。这种方式实际上是赊销或延期付款。

# 第4章

# 托 收

## 4.1 托收的概念与托收指示

### 4.1.1 托收的概念

关于托收，国际商会制定了相关国际惯例——《托收统一规则》，目前生效的是该规则1995 年的修订本，即国际商会第 522 号出版物，英文名为 The Uniform Rules for Collections（1995 Revision, ICC Publication No. 522），简称 URC522。URC522 第 2 条（a）款将托收定义为：托收是指银行依据所收到的指示处理相关单据，以便于 I. 取得付款和/或承兑；或 II. 凭以付款或承兑交单；或 III. 按照其他条款和条件交单。

结合进出口贸易实践，可将进出口贸易中使用的托收定义为：出口商（债权人）在发运货物后，开具汇票委托出口地银行通过其在进口地的代理行或往来银行向进口商（债务人）收取货款的一种结算方式。

### 4.1.2 托收指示

托收指示是指托收业务中授权相关当事人处理单据的完全和准确的条款。业务中，相关当事人申请办理托收时均须提交托收指示。在我国外贸实践中，将委托人对寄单行发出的托收指示称为托收申请书，而将寄单行对代收行发出的托收指示称之为托收委托书。

## 4.2 托收的当事人及其责任与义务

### 4.2.1 当事人

URC522 第 3 条将托收的当事人分为两类：一类是托收关系人，另一类是受票人。有时还会需要代理（Representative in case of need）。代理又称预备付款人，是委托人指定的在托收遭到拒付时代为处理货物，如存仓、转售、运回或改变交单条件的人。

**1. 托收关系人**

根据 URC522 的规定，托收关系人主要有四个：委托人、寄单行（托收行）、代收行和提示行。

**(1) 委托人。** 委托人即委托银行办理托收业务的有关人。在国际贸易实务中，出口商委托银行向国外进口商（债务人）收款时，经常须开具汇票，故也可称其为出票人（Drawer）。

（2）寄单行。寄单行即受委托人委托办理托收的银行。在我国外贸业务中，习惯称其为托收行，但鉴于其在托收业务中，虽受委托人委托办理托收，但其主要工作是在收到委托人交来的单据并同意办理托收后，将相关单据寄送给下述的代收行，故称寄单行。在出口托收时，寄单行通常为出口商所在地的银行。业务中，寄单行须严格按托收指示及 URC522 的规定办理，而不能擅自行事，否则将承担由此引起的责任。

（3）代收行。代收行是指除寄单行以外的任何参与处理托收业务的银行。它是接受托收行委托、向付款人收款的银行，通常是托收行在付款人所在地的联行或代理行。根据 URC522 的规定，代收行必须按托收指示行事。

（4）提示行。提示行即向付款人做出提示的银行，通常提示行由代收行担任。

**2. 受票人**

URC522 第 3 条（b）款规定：付款人为根据托收指示向其提示单据的人。实务中，常将其称之为付款人；出口托收业务中，受票人为进口商。

此外，在实际业务中，托收有时还会有一个特殊的当事人，即需要时的代理人。

### 4.2.2 托收的性质

托收时银行利用其联行或代理行的关系和资金划拨渠道，使两头均是客户间的债权、债务得以清偿，依托委托人与付款人之间的信用以完成偿债关系。因此，托收属于一种典型的商业信用。

托收之所以属于商业信用，还可结合 URC522 将商业信用的特点概括来理解：在托收业务下，银行"三不负责"。"三不负责"是指：

（1）**不负责保证付款的责任**。对此，URC522 第 2 条关于托收的定义即已明确："托收是指银行依据所收到的指示处理下述（2）款所限定的单据，以便于：取得付款和/或承兑；或凭以付款或承兑交单；或按照其他条款和条件交单"，即银行不承担保证付款的责任。

（2）**不负责审核单据**。在托收方式下，有关银行除对照托收指示书审核相关单据与托收指示书是否相符外，对任何单据的格式、完整性、准确性、真实性或其法律效力，或对在单据中载明或在其上附加的一般性和/或特殊性的条款等均不承担责任或对其负责。

（3）**不负责保管托收项下的货物**。对此，URC522 第 10 条（a）、（b）、（c）款分别进行了规定：（a）未经银行事先同意，货物不得以银行的地址直接发送给该银行，或者以该行作为收货人或者以该行为抬头人。然而，如果未经银行事先同意而将货物以银行的地址直接发送给了该银行，或以该行做了收货人或抬头人，并请该行凭付款或承兑或凭其他条款将货物交付给付款人，该行将没有提取货物的义务，其风险和责任仍由发货方承担。（b）银行对与跟单托收有关的货物即使接到特别批示也没有义务采取任何行动包括对货物的仓储和保险，银行只有在个案中如果同意这样做时才会采取该类行动。（c）然而，无论银行是否收到指示，它们为保护货物而采取措施时，银行对有关货物的结局和/或状况和/或对受托保管和/或保护的任何第三方的行为和/或疏漏概不承担责任。但是，代收行必须毫不延误地将其所采取的措施通知对其发出托收指示的银行。

## 4.3 托收的种类与一般支付程序

### 4.3.1 托收的种类

根据托收时是否向银行提交货运单据，可将托收分为光票托收和跟单托收两种。

**1. 光票托收**

根据 URC522 第 2 条（C）款的解释，光票托收是指随附有金融单据而不附有商业单据项下的托收。URC522 将单据分为金融单据和商业单据两类：金融单据是指汇票、本票、支票或其他类似的可用于取得款项支付的凭证；商业单据是指发票、运输单据、所有权文件或其他类似的文件，或者不属于金融单据的任何其他单据。

**2. 跟单托收**

跟单托收有两种情形：一种是附有商业单据的金融单据的托收，另一种是不附有金融单据的商业单据项下的托收。由此可见，在金融单据及商业单据两者中，商业单据因为涉及运输单据特别是海运提单这一具有物权凭证的单据，尤为重要，故在一定意义上将跟单托收中的"单"理解为商业单据。在国际贸易中所用的托收多为前者，即托收时，同时附有商业单据及金融单据。根据业务中按代收行向受票人提交商业单据的条件，可将跟单托收进一步细分为付款交单和承兑交单两类。

**（1）付款交单**。付款交单是指出口商的交单以进口商的付款为条件，即出口商将汇票连同商业单据交给银行托收时，指示银行只有在进口商付清货款时，才能交出商业单据，特别是运输单据。按支付时间的不同，付款交单又分为即期付款交单和远期付款交单。

**（2）承兑交单**。承兑交单是指出口商的交单是以进口商的承兑为条件，也即出口商在装运货物后开具远期汇票，连同商业单据，通过银行向进口商提示，进口商承兑汇票后，代收行便将商业单据交至进口商，待汇票到期，进口商支付货款。承兑交单方式只适用于远期汇票的托收。

### 4.3.2 托收的一般支付程序

**1. 即期 D/P**

在即期 D/P（付款交单，Documents against Payment，简称 D/P）下，款项顺利时，其支付程序为：

1）在贸易合同中，买卖双方约定以即期 D/P 方式支付货款。

2）出口商按合同规定发货后取得运输单据。

3）填写托收指示（我国习称托收申请书），开具即期汇票，并连同发票等商业单据一并送交寄单行，委托托收行代收货款。同时，向托收行支付代收手续费和其他有关费用（除托收委托书特别注明外，一般应由发出托收的一方负担）。

4）托收行根据出口商的指示缮制托收指示（我国习称托收委托书），将其同汇票、商业单据等一并寄交代收行，要求代收行按照托收指示代收货款。

5）代收行收到汇票及单据后，应及时向进口商做付款提示。

6）进口商应立即付清货款，代收行同时向进口商交出全套单据，对进口商而言，可称之为"付款赎单"。

7）代收行收到货款后，便将货款拨付给托收行。

8）托收行收到代收行拨交货款后即转交出口商。

**2. 远期 D/P**

与即期 D/P 相比，远期 D/P 的主要不同在于：当代收行向进口商提示时，进口商先承兑远期汇票，其后代收行代为保管全套单据，待付款期限到时，再次向进口商提示已被进口商承兑的远期汇票，进口商立即付款赎单。其他业务流程则与即期付款交单相同。

**3. D/A**

D/A（承兑交单，Document against Acceptance，简称 D/A）的一般支付程序为：

1）在贸易合同中，买卖双方约定以 D/A 方式支付货款。

2）出口商发运货物后，取得货运单据。

3）填写托收指示（我国习称托收申请书），开具远期汇票，并连同发票等商业单据一并送交寄单行，委托托收行代收货款。同时，向托收行支付代收手续费及和其他有关费用（除托收委托书特别注明外，一般应由发出托收的一方负担）。

4）托收行根据出口商的指示缮制托收指示（我国习称托收委托书），将其同汇票、商业单据等一并寄交代收行，要求代收行按照托收指示代收货款。

5）代收行收到汇票及单据后，应及时向进口商作承兑提示。

6）代收行做出提示后，进口商应立即承兑远期汇票，并交还代收行保管。

7）进口商到期后，付款赎单并及时向进口商交出全套单据，对进口商而言，可称之为"到期付款赎单"。

8）代收行收到货款后，即将货款拨付给托收行。

9）托收行收到代收行拨交货款后即转交出口商。

## 4.4 托收支付条款

在托收方式下，支付条款的内容主要包括交单条件、买方的付款或承兑责任以及付款期限等。举例说明。

### 4.4.1 即期 D/P 条款

例：买方应凭卖方开具的即期跟单汇票于第一次见票时立即付款，付款后交单。（Upon first presentation, the Buyers shall pay against documentary draft drawn by the Sellers at sight. The shipping documents are to be delivered against payment only.）

### 4.4.2 远期 D/P 条款

例1：买方对卖方开具的见票后××天付款的跟单汇票，于第一次提示时应予承兑，并应于汇票到期日即予付款，付款后交单。（The Buyers shall duly accept the documentary draft drawn by the Sellers at... days sight upon first presentation and make payment on its maturity. The shipping documents are to be delivered against payment.）

例2：买方应凭卖方开具的跟单汇票，于汇票出票日后××天付款，付款后交单。（The

Buyers shall pay against documentary draft drawn by the Sellers at... days after date of B/L. The shipping documents are to be delivered against payment only.）

### 4.4.3　D/A 条款

例：买方对卖方开具的见票后××天付款的跟单汇票，于第一次提示时应即承兑，并应于汇票到期日即予付款，承兑后交单。（The Buyers shall duly accept the documentary draft drawn by the Sellers at... days sight upon first presentation and make payment on its maturity. The shipping documents are to be delivered against acceptance.）

在实际业务中，对一些老客户合同中的托收条款，有时可订得较简单。如将即期付款交单简写为"D/P 即期"（D/P at sight or D/P sight）；把远期付款交单简略成"D/P 见票后××天"（D/P at... days sight or D/P at... days after sight），或简写为"D/P××天"（D/P... days）；把承兑交单简略为"D/A 见票后××天"（D/A at... days sight or D/A at... days after sight）。但对新客户或某些按当地习惯对 D/P、D/A 有特殊理解者，如有的把 D/P 解释成"付款交货"（Delivery against payment），把 D/A 解释成"承兑交货"（Delivery against acceptance），则除了应在交易磋商时就向对方明确说明各种托付方式的具体含义和做法外，在合同中也应做出详细规定，列明托收方式的全文，以免造成不必要的争议和损失。

### 4.4.4　托收与汇付相结合的条款

例：凭电汇汇给卖方总金额××%的预付货款（或定金），汇款时列明合同号×××，其余部分货款以托收方式即期付款，付款后交单。（Shipment to be made subject to advanced payment or down payment amounting... to be remitted in favour of Sellers by telegraphic transfer with indication of S/C No... and the remaining part on collection basis, documents will be released against payment at sight.）

# 第5章

# 信  用  证

汇款、托收方式属于商业信用，出口商能否收到货款或进口商能否收到符合合同的货物，均依赖于相互间的信用，对双方而言，均不同程度地存在较大风险。为解决买卖双方互不信任、风险较大的问题，促进国际贸易的进一步发展，银行在国际结算中的责任、作用不断加强。这体现为信用证结算方式在国际贸易中的广泛运用。

## 5.1 信用证的定义与基本内容

随着信用证（Letter of Credit，L/C）被越来越广泛地使用，迫切需要加强对信用证业务的管理。为此，国际商会在1930年制定了有关信用证的国际惯例，即《跟单信用证统一惯例》（The Uniform Customs and Practice for Documentary Credits，UCP），于1933年正式公布，并建议各国银行采用。其后分别于1951年、1974年、1983年、1993年及2007年相继对其进行了修订，其中1993年修订本及2007年修订本分别为国际商会第500号及第600号出版物，分别简称UCP500及UCP600，当前生效版本为UCP600。

### 5.1.1 信用证定义

UCP600第2条将信用证定义为：信用证是指一项不可撤销的安排，无论其名称或描述如何，该项安排构成开证行对相符交单予以兑付的确定承诺。兑付是指：a. 如果信用证为即期付款信用证，则即期付款；b. 如果信用证为延期付款信用证，则承诺延期付款并在承诺到期日付款；c. 如果信用证为承兑信用证，则承兑受益人开出汇票并在汇票到期日付款。

### 5.1.2 信用证的内容

实践中虽没有两份完全相同的信用证，内容依业务的复杂程度不同而各异，但其包括的主要项目是相同的，主要包括：

**(1)** 关于信用证本身的说明。此部分主要包括：①信用证形式；②信用证号码和开证日期；③信用证金额；④有效期限；⑤到期日期和地点；⑥开证申请人；⑦受益人；⑧开证行；⑨支付方式。

**(2)** 关于货物的说明。此部分主要包括商品名称、规格、数量、包装、唛头及价格条件等。

**(3)** 关于运输的说明。此部分主要包括：①装运港或启运地；②分批装运事项；③转运事项；④目的地（港）及最迟装运期等。

**(4)** 关于汇票的说明。此部分主要包括汇票金额、汇票期限及受票人。

(5) **关于单据的说明**。一般列明需要的单据，分别说明单据的名称、份数和具体要求。此部分主要包括商业发票、提单、保险单据等，其他的还有商检证、产地证、包装单据等。

(6) **其他说明**。此部分是开证行在信用证业务下对受益人的一些特殊指示。

## 5.2 信用证的当事人及其权利与责任

信用证的当事人众多，UCP600 在其第 2 条"定义"部分对相关当事人进行了界定，下面按界定顺序分别介绍。

### 5.2.1 通知行

通知行是指应开证行的要求通知信用证的银行。

### 5.2.2 申请人

申请人又称开证申请人，即要求开立信用证的一方。进出口业务中的开证申请人通常为进口商。进口商填写开证申请书并签字，请求银行开出以国外出口商或卖方为受益人的信用证。进口商有义务在适当或合理的时间内，按照销售合同条款申请开出信用证。在开证行付款后，开证人在单据正确时须付款给银行，但若单据有问题，可拒绝付款。如开证行错误地拒绝对受益人付款，开证人可向银行要求赔偿因此造成的损失。如货物是劣质品或与销售合同不符，开证申请人只能根据具体情况，向出口商、保险公司或承运人索赔。

### 5.2.3 受益人

受益人是指接受信用证并享受其利益的一方。在进出口业务中，受益人是出口商或卖方。受益人不仅须对提交开证行的单据的正确性与真实性负责，还须对货物与销售合同相符负责。

### 5.2.4 保兑行

保兑行是指根据开证行的授权或要求对信用证加具保兑的银行。保兑是指保兑行在开证行承诺之外做出的承付或议付相符交单的确定承诺。业务中，保兑行与开证行处于相同地位，在开证行无法履行付款时，保兑行履行验单付款之责。在已经议付或代付之后，开证行倒闭或无理拒付，保兑行无权向受益人追索。

### 5.2.5 开证行

开证行是指应申请人要求或者代表自己开出信用证的银行。业务中，在受益人所提交的有关单据与信用证条款相符时，开证行承诺向受益人即期付款、承兑或议付受益人所开汇票和/或单据。如开证申请人在开证行付款后不付款，开证行有权出售货物，并向开证申请人索款；如销售所得款项不足以支付受益人的款项，开证行对受益人仍承担第一付款人责任，而不管开证申请人是否违约。

### 5.2.6 指定银行

指定银行是指信用证可在其处兑付的银行，如信用证可在任一银行兑付，则任何银行均为指定银行。

### 5.2.7 提示人

提示人是指实施交单行为的受益人、银行或其他人。提示（Presentation）是指向开证行或指定银行提交信用证项下单据的行为，或指按此方式提交单据的行为。

### 5.2.8 议付银行

议付银行即愿意买入或贴现受益人交来的跟单汇票的银行，可以为通知行或受益人指定的当地往来银行，由信用证的条款规定。

## 5.3 信用证的特点

信用证支付方式具有以下特点：

**1. 开证行承担第一性付款人责任**

信用证是一种银行信用，它由开证行以自己的信用做出付款保证，即只要受益人提交的单据与信用证要求相符时，开证行必须无条件地向受益人或其指定人付款、承兑或议付，而不考虑开证申请人是否破产或违约。

**2. 信用证独立于销售合约**

信用证的基础是买卖双方签订的贸易合同，但信用证一经开出即成为独立于贸易合同以外的一项契约，不再受贸易合同的约束。对此，UCP600第4条"信用证与合同"的（a）款对二者之间的关系进行了明确规定。

**3. 信用证是一种单据买卖**

在信用证业务下，各方当事人仅处理单据，而非与单据有关的货物、服务和/或其他行为。对此，UCP600第5条规定：银行处理的是单据，而不是单据所涉及的货物、服务或其他行为。特别是对开证行而言，须对相符提示予以兑付。所谓"相符提示"是指与信用证中的条款及条件、本惯例中所适用的规定及国际标准银行实务相一致的提示。

## 5.4 信用证的业务流程

### 5.4.1 信用证行为

采用信用证方式结算要经过多道环节，或称之为信用证行为。主要包括：

**1. 开立信用证**

进口商银行根据开证申请书的内容向出口商（受益人）开出信用证。开证行可以根据申请人的要求采用信开、电开或SWIFT方式。其中，SWIFT方式目前使用得更为广泛。

**2. 通知或转递信用证**

通知行收到开证行开来的信用证后，核对无误后，即将信用证通知或转递给受益人（出口商）。

**3. 议付**

议付行收到受益人交来的符合信用证规定的单据后，进行议付。

**4. 索偿**

### 5.4.2 信用证支付的一般程序

一般情况下，信用证的支付程序需要经过八步，具体为：

1) 进出口商在贸易合同中约定，双方的货款支付选择信用证支付方式。

2) 进口商向其所在地银行提交开证申请书，开证申请书应以合同为依据进行填写，并向开证行交纳押金或提供其他保证，请银行（开证行）开证。

3) 开证行根据申请内容，并在获得押金或进口商提交的其他保证后，开出以出口商为受益人的信用证，并寄交出口商所在地的分行或代理行（统称通知银行）。

4) 通知行审核无误后，将信用证交与出口商。

5) 出口商对照合同审核信用证，在其与合同相符后，按信用证规定装运货物，并备齐信用证规定的各项货运单据，开出汇票，并在信用证有效期内，将信用证规定的全套单据交其所在地银行进行议付。按惯例，议付行通常就是信用证的通知行。

6) 议付行收单后，按信用证条款审核无误后，按照汇票金额扣除利息，将货款垫付给出口商。

7) 议付行将汇票和货运单据寄给开证行（或其指定的付款行）索偿。

8) 开证行（或其指定的付款行）核对单据无误后，付款给议付行。

## 5.5 信用证的种类

### 5.5.1 按是否附有货运单据分类

**1. 跟单信用证**

跟单信用证普遍用于国际贸易货款的支付。它是凭跟单汇票或仅凭规定的单据付款的信用证。

**2. 光票信用证**

光票信用证是不附任何货运单据只凭汇票（有时附有发票）付款的信用证，如预支信用证、备用信用证及非贸易结算中使用的旅行信用证等。

### 5.5.2 按开证行的付款责任分类

**1. 不可撤销信用证**

不可撤销信用证是指信用证一经开出，未经受益人、保兑行等有关当事人同意，开证行不能片面修改和撤销的信用证。只要受益人提供了符合信用证规定的单据，开证行必须履行付款责任。

**2. 可撤销信用证**

可撤销信用证是指开证行在信用证开出后不必征得受益人或有关当事人的同意，有权随时修改或撤销的信用证。

### 5.5.3 按是否有开证行以外的银行对信用证加以保兑分类

**1. 保兑信用证**

根据 UCP600 第 2 条规定：保兑是指保兑行在开证行之外对于相符提示做出兑付或议付的确定承诺。故保兑信用证是指由保兑行对与信用证条款规定相符的单据履行付款义务的信用证。需注意的是，保兑信用证只适用于不可撤销信用证。

**2. 不保兑信用证**

在开证行开出的不可撤销信用证中，通知银行未增加其保兑责任的信用证被称为不保兑信用证。此时，保证付款的承诺仅仅来自开证行，这与保兑信用证中开证行与通知行同时承诺对受益人付款是不同的。

**3. 自由议付信用证**

在自由议付信用证下，开证行授权对受益人进行支付并不局限于一个特定的银行，任何银行均可成为被指定银行，只要其愿意支付、承兑汇票，承诺延期付款，或对信用证进行议付。此时，"本信用证并不局限于某一银行议付"或"这份信用证可在任何银行议付"或类似的语言会显示在信用证上。

**4. 限制议付信用证**

在限制议付信用证项下，开证行仅限定由特定的指定银行对受益人进行付款。

### 5.5.4 按照付款时间分类

**1. 即期信用证**

即期信用证是指开证行或付款行收到与信用证条款相符的跟单汇票和/或单据后，立即履行付款义务的信用证。在即期信用证中，有时还加列"电报偿付条款"，加列此种条款的信用证，议付行在议付单据后当天即可用电报要求付款行偿付，付款行应以电汇偿付。但如规定开证行或付款行于收到汇票和/或单据与信用证条款核符后才以电汇方式汇付的，则是单据到达后电汇付款的信用证。

**2. 远期信用证**

远期信用证是指开证行或付款行收到符合信用证条款的单据时不立即付款，而是根据规定的付款期限到期才付款的信用证。远期信用证可分为以下几种：

（1）承兑信用证。承兑信用证是开证行或付款行在收到符合信用证条款的汇票和单据后，先办承兑手续，待汇票到期时才履行付款的信用证，分为银行承兑信用证和商业承兑信用证。

（2）延期付款信用证。延期付款信用证又称迟期付款信用证，是指开证行在信用证中规定货物装船后若干天付款，或开证行收单后若干天付款的信用证。此种信用证大多用于大型机器、成套设备的交易。因其远期付款期限较长，达一年或数年不等，往往利用出口国银行中长期信贷来代替短期的贴现作为融资手段，故延期付款信用证一般不要求出口商开立远期汇票。

## 5.5.5 按信用证受益人权利是否可转让分类

**1. 可转让信用证**

信用证原则上是一种非让渡性（不可转让）证券。UCP600 第 38 条规定，只有开证银行在信用证上确切注明"可转让"字样者，信用证受益人才能将信用证权益依法转让给他人。

一般而言，信用证如需转让，应由原受益人提供信用证正本及信用证转让申请书向转让银行办理转让。

**2. 不可转让信用证**

不可转让信用证是指受益人不能将信用证的权利转让给他人的信用证。凡信用证未注明"可转让"者，就是不可转让信用证。

## 5.5.6 预支信用证

预支信用证是指开证行授权议付行在出口商装货交单前预付全部或部分货款的信用证。由于预支款是供受益人收购及包装货物所用，故该种信用证也称为打包放款信用证。它与远期信用证正好相反，进口商付款在先，出口商交货交单在后。

## 5.5.7 对开信用证

对开信用证是指两张信用证的开证申请人互以对方为受益人开立的信用证。对开信用证的性质是，第一张信用证的受益人（出口商）和开证申请人（进口商）同时又是第二张信用证（也称回头证）的开证申请人和受益人。第一张信用证的开证行往往是回头证的通知行，两证的金额大体相等。对开信用证上一般加列表示对开证的条款，两证可以同时互开，也可以分别先后开立。信用证的生效办法在信用证中规定，一般有两种办法：①两张信用证同时生效，第一张信用证开出后暂不生效，等对方开来第二张回头信用证经受益人认可后，通知对方银行，两证同时生效；②两张信用证分别生效，这种办法对于先开证一方来说，须承担对方不开证的风险，因此，运用时需谨慎。对开信用证可用于两批不同商品的易货或换货、补偿贸易、来料加工等业务。

## 5.5.8 对背信用证

对背信用证又称转开信用证，是指受益人要求原证通知行或其他银行以原证为基础，以该行为开证行，以该受益人为开证申请人，以实际供货人为受益人开出的与原证内容相似的新信用证。因为对背信用证是以原证为基础开立的，故也称从属信用证。如果是开给当地供货人的，也称为当地信用证。

## 5.5.9 循环信用证

它是指当受益人全部或部分使用信用证金额后，其使用信用证金额的权利能够重新恢复到原证金额再度被使用，周而复始直到该证规定的次数或总金额用完为止。循环信用证可用于买方在一段时间内购买的各种货物（通常在一年或几个月内）。循环信用证可以分为按时间循环的信用证和按金额循环的信用证两种。

## 5.5.10 按付款方式分类

**1. 付款信用证**

付款信用证是指定某一银行付款的信用证，付款信用证中没有明显的"Payment Credit"字样，但可从其条款内容加以识别：①证内一般不规定需要汇票；②证内明确规定"当卖方提交规定的单据时，即行付款"；③证内列有开证行"保证履行付款责任"的条款。前述的即期信用证和延期付款信用证就属于付款信用证。

**2. 承兑信用证**

承兑信用证是指定某一银行承兑受益人提示的远期汇票的信用证。它的条款内容的特点是：①证内明确规定"当卖方提交远期跟单汇票时，即予承兑"；②证内列有开证行"保证履行承兑和承担到期付款责任"的条款。前述的银行承兑信用证和商业承兑信用证属于承兑信用证的范围。

**3. 议付信用证**

议付信用证是开证行允许受益人向某一指定银行或任何银行交单议付的信用证。在议付信用证下，只要受益人提交的单据符合信用证规定，议付行在扣除利息和手续费后，将票款付给受益人。议付和付款的主要区别在于议付银行（保兑行议付时除外）如因单据不符而不能向开证行收取货款时，可向受益人追索；而付款行在付出货款后，无权向受益人追索。议付信用证可分为公开议付信用证和限制议付信用证。

## 5.6 信用证支付条款

实践中，信用证支付方式可单独使用，但有时也与托收方式结合使用。因此，在不同情形下，支付条款的内容也有所差异。

### 5.6.1 全部使用信用证支付

当货款仅凭信用证收付时，国际货物买卖合同中支付条款的内容一般包括：

（1）**受益人**。一般规定为"以卖方为受益人"。

（2）**开证银行**。一般规定为"卖方同意接受的银行"。

（3）**开证日期**。一般规定为"在合同订立后××天内开证""在合同规定的装运期前……天开到""接到卖方备货通知书后××天内开证"等。开证日期和开到日期的含义不同，在出口合同中，争取规定开到日期对我方较为有利。

（4）**信用证种类**。信用证种类繁多，交易双方应根据具体交易来定。

（5）**信用证金额**。一般规定为"按发票金额100%"。如合同中规定"溢短装"条款时，对总金额和总数量也应规定可有相应的增减幅度。

（6）**信用证有效期和到期地点**。一般规定为"议付有效期至装运期后第15天"。以便装运后有充分的时间制作单证。到期地点一般应定明出口方所在地。

### 5.6.2 部分信用证和部分托收

信用证一般单独使用，但也可与其他支付方式结合使用，如信用证与托收相结合。此时，应注意有关单据须全部随附于托收项下，尤其是在出口业务中，必须待全部货款收妥后，银行方可将单据交给买方。对此，不仅在买卖合同中，而且要求在对方开立的信用证中都应做出具体规定。

# 第6章

# 银 行 保 函

## 6.1 银行保函概述

### 6.1.1 银行保函的含义与性质

保函又称保证书,是指银行、保险公司、担保公司或个人(即担保人)应申请人的请求,向第三方(即受益人)开立的一种书面信用担保凭证,保证在申请人未能按双方协议履行其责任或义务时,由担保人代其履行一定金额、一定期限范围内的某种支付责任或经济赔偿责任。其中,由银行签发的担保书就称为银行保函。根据《见索即付保函统一规则》(国际商会758号出版物)(The Uniform Rules for Demand Guarantees ICC Publication No. 758,URDG 758):无论其如何命名或描述,是指根据提交的相符索赔进行付款的任何签署的承诺。

### 6.1.2 银行保函的当事人及其权责

银行保函除了申请人、受益人、担保人及通知行等主要当事人外,还可能有通知行、保兑行、转开行和反担保人等。银行保函业务的这些当事人的主要责任及其相互关系如下。

**1. 银行保函的主要当事人及其权责**

(1) **申请人。申请人又称委托人**,即向银行提出申请,要求银行开立保函的一方。其主要责任包括:向担保行交纳保函开立费用及履约义务,并在担保行履行担保责任后向担保行补偿其所支付的费用。

(2) **受益人**。URDG758规定受益人是指接受保函并享有其利益的一方。受益人的责任是履行其有关商务的合同义务,在此基础上,他获得向担保行要求偿付的权利。与委托人相似,受益人视原商务合同及保函的不同而不同。具体而言,投标保函项下受益人通常为招标人;出口履约保函项下为进口商;在承包工程的履约保函和预付款保函项下通常为工程的业主等。

(3) **担保人**。担保人也称担保行,即开立保函的银行。

(4) **通知行**。通知行也称转递行,即应担保行的要求和委托,将保函通知或转递给受益人的银行。通知行通常是受益人所在地银行。由于受益人自身不可能核验所收到的银行保函的真实性,故须有其当地的银行代为核验所收保函的真实性。业务中,通知行仅负责核验保函表面的真实性,如代受益人核对担保行的印鉴、密押是否真实、正确等。

**2. 银行保函的其他当事人**

除上述三个主要当事人外,银行保函有时还会涉及以下几个当事人:

**（1）保兑行**。也称第二担保人，即根据担保人要求在保函上加具保兑的银行。开立保函的银行由于国外知名度不高、信誉较差或担保金额较大，超过担保行的授信额度等情形时，受益人往往会要求担保行另找其他银行为其开立的保函加具保兑，一旦后者接受请求，对相关保函进行保兑，则成为保兑行。保兑行有权向担保行收取保兑费，作为自己的风险保证。

**（2）转开行**。转开行即根据担保行要求，接受担保行的委托向受益人开出保函的银行。转开行通常为受益人所在地银行。

**（3）反担保人**。反担保人即为申请人向担保行开出书面反担保函的人。反担保人通常为申请人的上级主管单位、出口信贷保险公司、其他银行或非银行金融机构等。反担保人的责任是：保证申请人履行合同义务，同时向担保人承诺，当担保行在保函项下付款后，担保行可以从反担保人处及时得到足额的补偿。

## 6.2 银行保函的作用与内容

### 6.2.1 银行保函的作用

**1. 提供担保**

提供担保即在主债务人违约时给予债权人以资金上的补偿。在银行保函下，受益人获得支付的权利仅依赖于保函中规定的条件。银行一旦同意开立独立性保函，即成为主债务人，并承担对受益人的一切义务。担保行向受益人支付了保函的款项，即取得对主债务人的立即追索权。故担保行处于一种信贷风险中，它通常要求以补偿来降低这种风险，而不是作为一个保险人行事。

**2. 在当事人之间分配风险**

银行保函代表了当事人之间风险的分配。风险分配程度或范围取决于付款条件的类型。在见索即付保函下，受益人仅需提供表面与保函要求一致的单据即可得到付款，而担保行作为值得信赖的金融机构，既因其信誉良好，也因为它有对主债务人的立即追索权，通常均会毫不延迟地付款。但如主债务人认为他自己已正确履行了合同义务，那么他想重新取回已支付的款项就相当困难了。

**3. 见索即付保函的清偿功能**

受益人认为主债务人违约时，通过提交与保函要求表面一致的单据即可得到支付，而无须首先证实主债务人的违约。见索即付保函另一个非常重要的作用是能使受益人通过实现担保对债务人施加压力，使主债务人按照他的要求完成合同。

**4. 提供融资便利**

在主债务人需要向受益人支付预付款或进行中间付款时，银行保函可作为替代品，起到暂缓付款的作用，从而等于向主债务人提供了融资的便利。

**5. 见证作用**

银行保函可以证明委托人的履约能力，从一开始就把不具备资格的人排除在外。因为提供保函就意味着不可撤销的付款承诺，所以，在对债务人（委托人）的资金实力和履约能力进行全面审查并得到满意的结果前，银行是不会轻易做付款承诺的，而不能得到银行为其开立保函的交易商也不会是一个值得依赖的贸易伙伴。

## 6.2.2 银行保函的主要内容

URDG758 第 3 条规定:"开立保函及其修改的所有指示以及保函和修改本身都必须清楚、准确,且应当避免过多的细节。"

据此要求,所有的保函都应当规定:

**1. 主要当事人**

主要当事人具体包括申请人、受益人及担保人。实践中,若有通知行、保兑行或转开行,还应列明通知行、保兑行或转开行的名称和地址。

**2. 要求出具保函的基础交易**

即保函开立的依据——基础合同。保函应在开头或序言中说明与基础合同的关系,如投标保函、履约保函、付款保函等。在保函中提出开立保函依据的基础合同,其目的在于说明提供保函的目的及防范的风险,同时也意味着根据何种基础关系对担保提出要求。关于基础合同的文字一般须简明扼要,除申请人、受益人名称外,还包括基础合同签订或标书提交的日期、合同或标书的编号,有时还包括对标的的简短陈述,如货物供应等。保函指出基础合同并不会把独立性保函变成从属性保函。

**3. 可支付的最高金额和支付的币种**

担保合同中须明确规定一个确定的金额和货币种类(担保的金额可以用与基础合同不同的币种表示)。对担保行而言,明确保函项下的特定债务十分重要,否则将遭受难以承担的风险。

**4. 保函的到期日和/或到期事由**

(1)保函生效日期。除非保函另有规定,否则保函自开立之日起生效。在预付金保函、履约保函及付款保函中,这意味着保函一旦生效,即使根据基础合同债务人履行合同义务的期限尚未到来,受益人也可以对担保行提出要求。

(2)保函失效日期。保函应规定保函失效日期。不论银行保函中是否规定失效条款,当保函退还给担保行或受益人书面声明解除担保行的责任时,则不管是否已将保函及其修改书还给担保行,都认为该保函已被取消。

(3)保函延期条款。投标保函与履约保函往往赋予受益人将保函有效期延长的权利,即经受益人要求,保函有效期可适当延长。

(4)退还保函条款。保函中应规定,保函到期后,受益人应将保函退回担保行。这样做既便于担保行办理注销手续,也避免发生不必要的纠纷。但在实践中,退还保函的条款有时难以奏效。如果在保函中有这样的条款,也应明确规定该条款与受益人的权利无关。

(5)失效期条款的欠缺。若保函中未规定失效期,除例外情况,将意味着保函是无限期的。

**5. 要求付款的条件**

担保行在收到书面索赔书保函中规定的其他文件(如有关证明书、法院判决书或仲裁裁决书)后,确认这些文件表面上与保函条款一致时,即支付保函中规定的款项。保函项下的任何付款条款均应是书面规定,保函规定的其他文件也应是书面的。

**6. 减少担保金额的任何规定**

该条款也称担保金额递减条款。其作用在于随着申请人逐步履行基础合同，担保的最大数额相应减少。在预付金退还保函中，该条款被普遍使用。

## 6.3 银行保函的类型

按照不同的标准，银行保函可划分为不同的种类。

### 6.3.1 独立性保函与从属性保函

根据担保行承担的责任，可分为独立性保函与从属性保函。这两类保函上述已详述，不再重复。

### 6.3.2 直接保函与间接保函

根据担保行与受益人是否在同一个国家/地区，可分为直接保函与间接保函：直接保函是由委托人的银行直接开立的，而不是由受益人本国银行开立的；间接保函是由受益人本国/地银行开立的，此时，委托人要求他的银行（指示行）向受益人所在地银行（担保行）发出开立保函的指示。在间接保函中，指示行与受益人间无任何合同关系，受益人不能直接要求指示行付款。

### 6.3.3 结算保函与信用保函

根据银行保函的基本功能，可划分为结算保函与信用保函：结算保函是指担保行承担第一性付款责任的用作交易结算工具的独立性保函；信用保函是指担保行承担从属性或第一性支付/赔偿责任的用作支付担保/履约担保工具的备用性的从属性保函或独立性保函。

### 6.3.4 限额保函与非限额保函

根据保函有无限额，可划分为限额保函与非限额保函：限额保函是指担保人只对一定数额（既可以是累积限额，也可以是非累积限额）的债务承担保证责任，超过此限额的任何债务都不属于担保的责任范围；非限额保函是指担保人对借款人的债务（本金和利息）和直接产生于贷款债务的其他债务都承担保证责任。这里的其他债务是指借款人对贷款人的额外补偿或赔偿，它产生于贷款协议中规定要求借款人进行补偿的事件，如各种税收或违约赔偿金等。

### 6.3.5 可撤销保函与不可撤销保函

根据保函的有效性，可划分为可撤销保函及不可撤销保函：通常情况下的保函都应是不可撤销保函。但为避免纠纷，受益人一般都要求保函注明"不可撤销"字样。

### 6.3.6 期限保函与无期限保函

根据保函的有效期，可划分为期限保函与无期限保函：期限保函是指在保函中规定担保责任的有效期，受益人须在规定期限内提出付款要求，否则，担保人可拒绝付款（规定保函期限对担保人而言十分重要,因为,若保函无此项规定,受益人就会无期限地享有对担保人的索偿权,使担保人总是处于不可预测的风险中);无期限保函是指保函中不规定保函有效期,除非依据法律规定的某些事件发生,否则,担保人的责任须在受益人的全部债权被满足后才能消灭,而受益人可随时向担保人提出索偿要求。

### 6.3.7 出口保函、进口保函、对销贸易类保函、借贷保函与其他特别保函

根据银行保函的用途,可划分为出口保函、进口保函、对销贸易类保函、借贷保函及其他特别保函。

**1. 出口保函**

出口保函是指银行应国际贸易出口商申请,向进口商开立的用以担保前者履行投标合同或贸易合同某项义务的各种信用保函。出口保函主要有以下几种:

(1) 投标保函。投标保函是银行(担保人)应投标人(申请人)的请求而出具给招标人(受益人)的书面担保凭证,保证投标人在开标前不撤销投标或片面修改投标条件,中标后签订合约并及时开出履约保函或投标保函中要求的任何保函以及忠实履行投标时承诺的各项义务。否则,担保行负责向招标人赔付一定金额的款项(该金额通常为投标人报价总额的一定比例),以补偿招标人由于投标人违约而给其造成的损失以及重新选择中标人所支付的费用。如果投标人未中标,招标人则应退回投标人的投标保函,以解除担保人的担保责任。

(2) 履约保函。履约保函是银行应申请人请求,向受益人开立的保证申请人履行合同中某项义务的书面保证文件。在保函有效期内,如发生申请人违约情况,银行(担保人)将根据受益人的要求向受益人赔偿保函规定的金额。在招投标业务中,投标人为了简化手续,也可要求担保行在投标保函中加列条款说明,若该投标人中标,则保函自动转化为履约保函,担保金额根据具体情况,可做相应调整。在承包工程项下,履约保函一般为银行根据承包人的要求向业主出具的保证承包人履行承包合同的一种书面信用文件。担保人的主要责任是保证承包人按期、按质、按量地完成所承包的工程。一旦承包人中途毁约,或任意中止工程施工,或者宣布破产、倒闭等,担保人就得向受益人支付担保的全部金额作为赔偿。此类履约保函的担保金额一般为承包工程价款的 10%~25%。

(3) 预付款保函。预付款保函又称定金保函或还款保函,是指银行(担保人)应劳务提供方(申请人)的请求,开给劳务的购买者(受益人)的书面担保凭证。预付款保函除用于工程承包外,还用于国际贸易,是指银行(担保人)应货物提供方(申请人)的请求,开给货物进口人(受益人)的书面担保凭证。其中规定,如货物提供方未能按有关合同提供劳务或交付货物,担保行将负责偿还受益人已付或预付给申请人的金额。

(4) 质量保函与维修保函。这两种保函的区别在于:质量保函主要用于进出口业务中,而维修保函主要运用在国际劳务承包工程中。但在成套项目出口或飞机、轮船等大型项目的出口中有时也使用维修保函。

(5) 留置金保函。在国际贸易的大型机械设备进出口及国际承包工程业务中,进口商或工程业主在支付货款或工程款时,总要留置一定比例的款项,待进口设备调试、验收并投入正常生产或等工程完工一定时期后,再视情况将这部分款项支付给出口商或工程承包方。但由于项目均较大,占压资金也较多,从而给出口商或承包商带来诸多不便。为能提前收回

这部分留置款项，出口商或承包商通常向本国银行申请开立以进口商或工程业主为受益人的留置金保函，保证如果卖方提供的货物或承包工程达不到合同规定的质量标准，出口商或承包商将把这部分提前收回的留置款项退给进口商或工程业主，否则，银行负责赔偿。此类保函的金额一般为合同总价的5%左右，有效期视合同标的物的不同，由合同双方确定。

**2. 进口保函**

进口保函是指应国际贸易进口商的申请向出口商开立的用以担保当后者履行了贸易合同义务时，前者必定偿付合同价款或履行对应义务的各种信用保函或结算保函。进口保函主要有以下三种：

(1) **付款保函/延期付款保函**。这是开立付款保函/延期付款保函的银行应进口商的要求向出口商出具的一份书面保证文件，保证在出口商交运有关货物或有关技术资料后，进口商一定履行部分或全部付款义务。否则，就由担保行在收到出口商的索偿通知后，偿付出口商应付未付的全部款项。

(2) **提货保函**。提货保函又称承运货物收据保证书。在信用证业务中，有时货物早于货运单据到达目的港，为避免货物压仓或变质等，进口商有时希望在获得提单之前便从船公司提货，办理报关并及时销售。船公司为防止因此而遭受损失，便要求进口商提供一份经银行加签的保证书，保证承担因先行提取货物而可能给船公司造成的损失，并保证在收到所提货物的单据后立即交还提单等。

(3) **租赁保函**。租赁业务担保的主要原因是偿还租赁费的担保，一般是银行出具书面保证函。当承租人到期未履行或未完全履行其应承担的支付租赁费的责任时，担保行保证履行此项支付租赁费的责任。

**3. 对销贸易类保函**

对销贸易，又被称为以进带出贸易，主要是补偿贸易和对外加工贸易，是发展中国家在经济发展初期阶段普遍采用的贸易方式。对销贸易双方互有进出口，合理地使用银行保函可以更好地保障当事人的合同权益和交易的顺利进行。这类保函主要有以下几种：

(1) **补偿贸易保函**。在补偿贸易下，由于从提供设备、技术到补偿贸易完成通常需要相当长的一段时间，提供设备和技术的一方为保证其权益不受损害，常常要求引进设备和技术的另一方向其提供担保。

(2) **来料加工保函**。来料加工保函是银行应进口商要求开立的书面担保文件，保证进口商在收到出口商与合同规定相符的原料或元件后，以该原料或元件加工装配，并按基础合同规定将成品交付出口商或其指定的第三方。如进口商未履约又不能以现汇偿付来料或来件价款及附加的利息，则担保行将负责偿付。来料加工保函的金额通常为来料或来件价款。

**4. 借贷保函**

借贷保函是指在各种形式的国际借贷关系中，债务方依约向债权方提供的由（另外）一家银行担保债务方将依约履行其还贷义务，否则担保行承担给予债权方保函规定金额内赔偿的各种信用保函。具体又可分为借款保函和透支保函。

在借款保函下，贷款人在放款前，除对借款人资信情况及偿还能力等方面做深入调查了解外，为确保贷款能按期归还，贷款人往往要求借款人提供一份银行保函作为还款的保证。

透支是银行允许往来存款户在约定期间内超过其存款余额签发支票并给以兑付的一种放

款形式。客户对透支放款须支付利息，并有随时偿还的义务。透支需要提供抵押品的，称为抵押透支；无抵押品的，称为信用透支。透支保函是为对外承包工程公司或其他驻外机构在外国施工或开展业务，向当地银行申请开立透支账户而由本国银行出具的书面保证文件，用以保证申请人按透支合同的规定按时补足透支款项并支付利息和有关银行费用。透支担保的金额通常为委托人与当地（外国）银行签订的透支合同中所规定的透支限额。

**5. 其他特别保函**

（1）**关税保函**。此类保函适用于国际承包工程或国际展览、展销等活动，保函金额通常为各国海关规定的关税金额。在国际承包工程中，一国施工部门在另一国施工，将施工机械运往工程所在国时，该国的海关要对施工机械征收一笔关税，待工程完工、机械运回国时，海关再将这笔关税退还给承包商。若这些机械不运回本国，则把施工机械视为进口货物，不再退还关税。在这种情况下，承包商为了加速资金周转，避免资金占压和退税的麻烦，常要求其本国银行向工程所在国的海关出具关税保函，保证承包商工程完工之后，一定将施工机械运回本国，否则，担保行将支付这笔税金。

在国际展览或展销活动中，一国将展品运往他国，也会遇到同样的情况。展览/展销方为避免占压资金及退税的麻烦，也会提供同样的银行保函，保函内容同上。

（2）**海事保函**。海事保函是指载运船只或其他运输工具在运输途中，由于船方或运输公司的责任而造成货物短缺、残损以及使货主受损，或因海上事故如撞损海港码头设施、其他船只、船舶合同纠纷、海难事故、海洋污染或涉嫌走私等触犯他国法律而被扣留时，船方或运输公司将按照法院判决赔偿货主或受损方所受的损失。否则，担保行将支付这笔赔偿金。船方或运输公司之所以申请保函，是因为发生上述事故后，有关部门都要先扣留船只，然后，经过一段时间的调查、取证、及至最后的法院判决，有时会拖很久。船公司为了避免长久被扣留船只，影响自己的经济效益，就需要以保函作为保释金，换取法院或港务局放行被扣的船只。

## 6.4 银行保函的业务操作程序和业务处理

### 6.4.1 银行保函的申请

在合同或项目协议中，如申请人与受益人没有规定一个特定的银行提供保函，则一般由申请人向其往来银行申请开立银行保函。申请人须向银行提交书面申请，即《开立保函申请书》。

### 6.4.2 银行保函的审查

由于保函业务涉及面广、风险性大，担保行收到申请人递交的《开立保函申请书》和有关文件资料后，要从申请人的资信情况及项目的可行性等方面对担保内容进行审查。然后，再根据审查结果和风险程度来决定是否接受申请人提交的申请。银行保函的审查工作主要有以下几方面：审查申请人资格及资信情况；审查受益人资信情况；审查交易合同或项目；审查保函的主要内容及审查反担保。

### 6.4.3 开立银行保函

在申请人的条件符合银行规定,其《开立保函申请书》、反担保措施落实情况、受益人和有关文件资料被银行审查通过后,银行应与申请人、反担保人签订各项法律文件,以明确双方的权利和义务,并在此基础上对外开具保函。

### 6.4.4 银行保函项下的业务处理

银行保函项下的业务处理主要包括银行保函的修改与撤销、转开与保兑、收取担保费用、处理索偿与赔付等诸多事宜。

**1. 银行保函的修改与撤销**

**(1) 银行保函的修改。**通常,一笔保函业务从担保人正式出具保函到保函最终失效,要经过一段较长的时间,短则几个月,长则几年甚至更长时间。在保函有效期内,当事人会由于各方面的原因而涉及保函条款的修改,如交易或工程项目的延期、交易货物或工程项目所需的机器设备价格的变动、金融市场变动、政策调整、新法规出台、国际政治关系剧变等,均可能会使保函条款做相应的变动。现代的银行保函大都属于无条件的、不可撤销的保函,为防止责任和风险的加大,修改保函必须经有关当事人各方一致同意后方可进行。

当申请人向原出具保函的担保行提出修改保函的要求时,必须向银行提出书面请求及修改保函的编号、金额、开立日期和有权签字人签字和公章,以及一切因修改保函而引起的责任条款,并随附受益人要求或同意修改的书面材料以供担保人参考。

**(2) 银行保函的撤销。**保函到期后应及时办理撤销手续。当担保收到受益人退回的保函时,应将存档原卷调出核对,同时在正本和原卷上用红字注明撤销。如是电开保函,应由受益人来电证明原保函已失效后,才可办理撤销手续。对那些到期或已失效而尚未收回的保函,应及时向受益人索回,并在查明原因后,在原卷上用红字注明撤销。

保函到期如不办理撤销,担保行仍然承担着被索偿的风险,而且担保行也将继续向申请人收取担保费用。担保费用一般是一年计收一次,即使保函在本年内只有几天时间,担保行也会按整年计收担保费用。

**2. 银行保函的转开与保兑**

银行保函的转开与保兑通常是基于外国法律或外国政府的规定以及受益人或银行的要求而进行的,属于正常情况。在我国,银行对保函的转开与保兑一般持谨慎态度。

**3. 银行保函的担保费用**

担保行提供各种类型的保函,应按规定的收费标准按期向申请人收取担保费。

**4. 银行保函的索偿与赔付**

保函开出后,可能因为各种因素的影响,如申请人未能按规定履行合同、借款人不向贷款人偿还其贷款、承包商未按期或按规定的质量标准建设项目等,造成受益人在保函规定的有效期内向担保行或转开行或保兑行索偿。只要受益人在保函规定的有效期内提交了与保函的规定表面上相符的证明文件(包括证明文件之间的一致),担保行即可认定所规定的支付或赔偿条件已经具备,索赔有效,银行即应付款而不必过问索赔理由是否属实、合同是否实际执行以及这些单据和书面文件是否真实等。这是因为:根据 URDG758 的规定,担保行(或转开行或保兑行)作为商业交易的中介,提供的是银行信用,既无义务、也无必要、更无可能对合同实际执行情况进行调查和判定受益人的索赔是否合理；而且担保行在办理保函业务时，处理的只是保函所规定的应由受益人提供的证明文件，并不过问其真伪，对证明文件在邮递过程中的遗失、延误以及受益人与申请人之间是否发生纠纷等概不负责。

受益人的索赔有效时，担保行应按保函规定的担保金额及时进行支付或赔偿受益人的损失，不能借各种理由来推迟偿付，否则，不仅会使担保行信誉受损，而且还会承担由于拖延而导致的各项费用或利息。担保行向受益人赔付时，要注意使用责任递减条款，减轻自身承担的责任或减少对外支付的款项。同时，担保行在对外赔付前，应要求受益人或由受益人通过其往来银行进行确认，在受益人收到赔付款项后，担保行在保函项下的责任自动解除，保函自动失效。受益人有义务将失效的保函退还担保行，担保行收到失效的保函后办理注销手续，并凭反担保函向申请人或反担保人索偿。

# 第7章

# 国 际 保 理

## 7.1 国际保理的概念与特点

### 7.1.1 概念

国际保理,又称承购应收账款业务,是指出口商以商业信用形式出售商品,货物装运后立即将发票、汇票、提单等有关单据,卖断给承购应收账款组织或专门的财务公司,收进全部或一部分货款,从而取得资金融通的业务。它属于对外贸易短期信用的一种形式。

### 7.1.2 保理业务的特点

**1. 保理机构承担信贷风险**

出口商将单据卖断给保理机构,意味着一旦进口商拒付货款或无法按期付款,保理机构将无法向出口商行使追索权,风险将全部由其自行承担。因此,保理机构为减少风险,欲以保理方式融通资金的出口商须根据其对进口商的资信调查结果和可能的贸易金额建议,与进口商进行磋商,贸易金额一般须在保理机构的建议金额之内。另外,保理机构一般都有专门的部门,有条件对进口商资信情况进行全面、细致、准确的调查。因此,以此为基础所进行的交易,可避免货款收不到的风险。

**2. 保理业务内容广泛**

保理业务不仅为出口商提供了资金融通的便利,还向出口商提供资信调查、托收、催收账款甚至代办会计处理等一揽子服务。

**3. 预支货款**

典型的保理业务,出口商在出卖单据后,立即收到现款,得到资金融通。当然,如果出口商资金雄厚,也可在票据到期后向保理机构索要货款。视期限、汇价风险大小而定,手续费的费率一般为应收账款总额的 1.75%~2%。保理手续费主要包括以下费用:向进口商提供赊销额度建议的费用;信贷风险评估费及会计与记账处理费。

## 7.2 国际保理的类型

依据不同的分类标准,可将保理业务分为不同的类型。

### 7.2.1 根据保理商是否须立即向出口商付款分类

根据承办保理业务的银行或专业保理商购入应收账款的单据后,是否须立即向出口商付款,可将分为到期保理和预付保理两类:到期保理是指出口商将有关单据出售给保理商后,保理商无须立即向出口商支付现款,而是确认并同意在票据到期时无追索权地向出口商支付票据金额;预付保理则是指出口商将有关单据出售给保理商后,保理商立即支付票款。业务中,由于预付保理较为常见,故其被称为标准保理。

### 7.2.2 根据是否将保理商向进口商公开分类

根据此标准,分为公开保理和幕后保理两种:公开保理是指当出口商将单据出售给保理商后,由保理商出面向进口商收款,同时出口商也通知进口商将货款付给保理商;幕后保理,又称隐蔽型保理,在此方式下,出口商不愿让进口商得知其缺乏流动资金而需保理,故在将单据出售给保理商后,仍由自己向进口商收款,然后再转交给保理商。

### 7.2.3 根据保理商是否承担坏账风险、买断应收账款分类

根据此标准,可将其分为有追索权保理和无追索权保理两类。

**1. 有追索权保理**

在此方式下,保理商向出口商收购有效发票,按预先协商的比率支付预付款,其后凭发票向进口商追偿货款。若进口商到期支付全部票面金额货款,保理商扣除预付款本息及相关费用,将余额交给出口商;若进口商因信用原因延期支付货款,或因争议、破产而无力支付货款,从而导致保理商无法按时追回货款时,保理商有权要求出口商回购发票,偿还已获预付款本息及相关费用,故称之为有追索权保理。

**2. 无追索权保理**

在此方式下,保理商承担一切风险,并无权要求供应商回购发票、返还预付款。无追索权保理在国际保理中占主导地位。保理商根据出口商提供的进口商名单进行资信调查,并为出口商核定出针对每个进口商的相应的信用额度。出口商在信用额度内的赊销,保理商对应收账款的收购没有追索权。

### 7.2.4 根据运作模式分类

根据运作模式不同可分为单保理和双保理:单保理是指一项保理业务中只涉及出口或进口一方的保理商,即同一保理商在出口商、进口商间进行保付代理业务;双保理是指在一项保理业务中同时涉及进、出口双方的保理商。目前,国际保理多采用双保理方式。

### 7.2.5 根据债务人付款对象分类

根据此标准,可分为直接保理和间接保理两种:前者是指根据保理合同,债务人直接向保理商付款;而后者则是根据保理合同,债务人应向供应商/出口商付款。

### 7.2.6 根据保理业务操作方式分类

据此标准可分为批量保理和逐笔保理两类:在批量保理下,保理商向供应商提供关于全部销售或某一系列销售活动的保理服务,即保理商批给进口商一个最高信用额度,在此额度范围内,进口商可循环使用额度,不必每次申请,直到保理商撤销此批准;而在逐笔保理下,供应商须逐笔向保理商询价,并要求提供保理服务的保理方式。

### 7.2.7 根据销售活动中涉及的保理合同的数量分类

根据此标准，可将其分为单一保理和背对背保理：单一保理是指只有一个保理合同的普通保理方式；而背对背保理则涉及两个保理合同，其中一个保理合同是根据另一个保理合同来考虑保理风险的保理方式。背对背保理是在进口商是中间商的情况下产生的。

## 7.3 保理业务的程序

出口商若以赊销方式出售商品，而欲将销售货款以保理方式及时收回，即出口商要想从保理机构取得资金融通，须在与进口商签订贸易合同之前，先与保理机构签订从事保理业务的协议，明确出口商与保理机构的责任和权利。协议可以规定有效期（一般为一年），也可以不规定有效期，只规定对部分不适宜内容进行修改的期限。

协议签订后，保理业务一般经过以下程序进行：

1）出口商将欲与之进行贸易的进口商的名称及有关交易情况报告给本国保理机构，委托保理机构对进口商的资信状况进行调研。

2）出口方保理机构将有关资料整理后通知进口方保理机构，委托其了解进口商有关情况。

3）进口方保理机构按出口方保理机构的要求进行调查，并将调查结果及可以向进口商提供赊销金额的具体建议通知出口方保理机构。

4）出口方保理机构在对以上建议审核，认为可信、无误后，将调查结果告知出口商。

5）出口商根据以上调查结果，在与进口商的交易磋商中，言明以保理业务进行支付，并将此写入贸易合同中。

6）出口商根据合同装运后，将按贸易合同及与保理机构签订的协议要求制作的单据提交给出口方的保理机构，出口方的保理机构在扣除利息及有关费用后，将货款立即或在双方商定的日期支付给出口商。

7）出口商的保理机构将有关单据寄交进口方的保理机构，委托其向进口商催收货款。

8）进口方的保理机构收到进口商支付的货款后，向出口方的保理机构划付款项。

# 第8章

# 备用信用证

## 8.1 备用信用证的内涵与类型

### 8.1.1 备用信用证的内涵

备用信用证又称担保信用证,是指不以清偿商品交易的价款为目的,而以贷款融资或担保债务偿还为目的所开立的信用证。

在备用信用证中,开证行保证在开证申请人未能履行其应履行的义务时,受益人只要凭备用信用证的规定向开证行开具汇票,并随附开证申请人未履行义务的声明或证明文件即可得到开证行偿付。备用信用证只适用《跟单信用证统一惯例》(UCP600)的部分条款。

### 8.1.2 备用信用证的性质

备用信用证具有如下性质:

(1) **不可撤销性**。备用信用证一经开立,除非在备用信用证中另有规定,或经对方当事人同意,开证人不得修改或撤销其在该备用信用证下之义务。

(2) **独立性**。备用信用证一经开立,即作为一种自足文件而独立存在。在备用信用证下,开证人的义务完全取决于备用信用证条款和受益人提交的单据是否表面上符合这些条款的规定,而不取决于:①开证人从申请人那里获得偿付的权利和能力;②受益人从申请人那里获得付款的权利;③备用信用证中对任何偿付协议或基础交易的援引;④开证人对任何偿付协议或基础交易的履约或违约是否了解。

(3) **跟单性**。备用信用证也有单据要求,且开证人付款义务的履行与否取决于受益人提交的单据是否符合备用信用证的要求。备用信用证的跟单性质和商业信用证并无二致,但后者主要用于国际贸易货款结算,其项下的单据以汇票和货运单据为主;另外,备用信用证更普遍地用于国际商务担保,通常只要求受益人提交汇票以及声明申请人违约的证明文件等非货运单据。

(4) **强制性**。备用信用证一经开立,即具有约束力,无论申请人是否授权开立,开证人是否收取了费用,或受益人是否收到或因信赖备用信用证或修改而采取了行动,它对开证行都是有强制性的。

备用信用证的上述四个法律性质相辅相成,共同造就了这一金融产品的优异特质:"不可撤销性"锁定了开证人的责任义务,进而更有效地保障了受益人的权益;"独立性"传承了信用证和独立性"独立"品格,赋予了其既定的法律属性;"单据性"将开证人的义务限定于"凭单"原则的基准之上,有益于"独立性"的实施;而"强制性"则是对开证人义务履行的严格规范，它与"不可撤销性"的融合充分体现了开证人责任义务的约束性和严肃性，有助于杜绝非正常因素的干扰。基于这些关键的法律性质，备用信用证融合了商业信用证和独立性担保之特长，在实践中体现出独特的功能优势。

### 8.1.3 备用信用证与一般商业信用证的区别

1）一般商业信用证仅在受益人提交有关单据证明其已履行基础交易义务时，开证行才支付信用证项下的款项；备用信用证则是在受益人提供单据证明债务人未履行基础交易的义务时，开证行方须支付信用证项下款项。

2）一般商业信用证开证行愿按信用证的规定向受益人开出的汇票及单据付款，因为这表明买卖双方的基础交易关系正常进行；备用信用证的开证行则不希望按信用证的规定向受益人开出的汇票及单据付款，因为这表明买卖双方的交易出现了问题。

3）一般商业信用证，总是货物的进口方为开证申请人，以出口方为受益人；而备用信用证的开证申请人与受益人既可以是进口方也可以是出口方。

### 8.1.4 备用信用证与银行保函的相同与区别

备用信用证与银行保函的相同之处在于：①两者都是备用性质的；②在要求提交的单据方面，均要求提交索偿声明。

不同之处有：①管辖二者的国际惯例不同。保函的国际惯例有《见索即付保函统一规则》（URDG758）；而备用证的国际惯例为《国际备用证惯例》（ISP98）。②URDG758 规定保函项下受益人索赔的权利不可转让；而《国际备用证惯例 ISP98》中订有备用证受益人的提款权利转让办法的有关条款，意味着备用证是允许转让的。③保函有反担保作保证；备用证则无此项目。④保函有负第一性付款责任的，也有负第二性付款责任的；而备用信用证总是负第一性付款责任的。

## 8.2 备用信用证的类型

根据在基础交易中备用信用证的不同作用主要可分为以下八类：

### 8.2.1 履约保证备用信用证

该备用信用证支持一项除支付金钱以外的义务的履行，包括对由于申请人在基础交易中违约所致损失的赔偿。

### 8.2.2 预付款保证备用信用证

该备用信用证用于担保申请人对受益人的预付款所应承担的义务和责任。这种备用信用证通常用于国际工程承包项目中业主向承包人支付的合同总价 10%～25% 的工程预付款，以及进出口贸易中进口商向出口商支付的预付款。

### 8.2.3 反担保备用信用证

反担保备用信用证又称对开备用信用证，它支持反担保备用信用证受益人所开立的另外的备用信用证或其他承诺。

### 8.2.4 融资保证备用信用证

该备用信用证支持付款义务，包括对借款的偿还义务的任何证明性文件。目前外商投资企业用以抵押人民币贷款的备用信用证就属于融资保证备用信用证。

### 8.2.5 投标备用信用证

它用于担保申请人中标后执行合同义务和责任，若投标人未能履行合同，开证人必须按备用信用证的规定向收益人履行赔款义务。投标备用信用证的金额一般为投保报价的1%～5%（具体比例视招标文件规定而定）。

### 8.2.6 直接付款备用信用证

直接付款备用信用证用于担保到期付款，尤指到期没有任何违约时支付本金和利息。其已经突破了备用信用证备而不用的传统担保性质，主要用于担保企业发行债券或订立债务契约时的到期支付本息义务。

### 8.2.7 保险备用信用证

保险备用信用证支持申请人的保险或再保险义务。

### 8.2.8 商业备用信用证

它是指如不能以其他方式付款，为申请人对货物或服务的付款义务进行保证。

## 8.3 备用信用证的运作原理

鉴于备用信用证"出身"于信用证家族，故其业务流程基本符合信用证运作原理，具体如下：

1）开证申请人（基础交易合同的债务人）向开证人（银行或非银行金融机构）申请开出备用信用证。

2）开证人严格审核开证申请人的资信能力、财务状况、交易项目的可行性与效益等重要事项，若同意受理，即开出备用信用证，并通过通知行将该备用信用证通知受益人（基础交易合同的债权人）。

3）若开证申请人按基础交易合同约定履行了义务，开证人不必因开出备用信用证而必须履行付款义务，其担保责任于信用证有效期满而解除；若开证申请人未能履约，备用信用证将发挥其支付担保功能。在后一种情形下，受益人可按照备用信用证的规定提交汇票、申请人违约证明和索赔文件等，向开证人索赔。

4）开证人审核并确认相关索赔文件符合备用信用证规定后，必须无条件地向受益人付款，履行其担保义务。

5）开证人对外付款后，向开证申请人索偿垫付的款项，后者有义务予以偿还。

## 8.4 备用信用证国际惯例

目前备用信用证适用的国际惯例主要包括两个，一个是《国际备用证惯例》（ISP98），另一个是 UCP600。本节介绍前者。

### 8.4.1 产生背景

《跟单信用证统一惯例》主要是为商业信用证制定的规则，因而备用信用证的诸多特点在其中无法充分体现，诸如涉及备用信用证的期限较长、自动展期、要求转让、请求受益人为另一受益人做出其自身承诺等，均未做具体规定，由此造成备用信用证解释上的不确定性，极易导致纠纷。针对上述背景，1998 年 4 月 6 日，在美国国际金融服务协会、国际银行法律与实务学会及国际商会银行技术与实务委员会的共同努力下，组织起草了《国际备用证惯例》，1998 年 12 月国际商会公布了《国际备用证惯例》，并于 1999 年 1 月 1 日起生效，并被定为国际商会第 590 号出版物，并在全世界推广使用。

### 8.4.2 主要内容

《国际备用证惯例》（ISP98）是根据《联合国关于独立保函和备用证的公约》，在参照国际商会《跟单信用证统一惯例》（UCP500）和《见索即付保函统一规则》（URDG758）的基础上根据备用信用证的特点制定的，它对常用的备用信用证，如履约备用信用证、预付备用信用证、投标备用信用证、反担保备用信用证、融资备用信用证、保险备用信用证、商业备用信用证和直接付款备用信用证等下了定义。

《国际备用证惯例》（ISP98）包括序言与十条正文，共 89 款。这十条分别为：总则；义务；提示；审核；单据的通知、排除和处理；转让、让渡及规定转让；撤销；偿付义务；时间安排；联合开证/权益份额等。

# 第9章

# 国际结算单据

## 9.1 国际结算单据概述

### 9.1.1 国际贸易结算单据的含义与作用

国际结算单据是指在国际贸易结算中使用的各种单据及凭证。国际商会《跟单信用证统一惯例》(2007年修订本)中规定:在信用证业务中,各有关方面处理的是单据,而不是可能与单据有关的货物、服务和/或其他行为。由此可见单据在跟单信用证业务中的作用,但单据的作用不仅在于此,从国际贸易的实践来看,单据具有极其重要的作用,主要体现在以下几方面:

**1. 单据是合同履行的重要依据**

单据工作是出口合同履行过程中最关键的环节。在备货、国外开证、审证、租船订舱、保险、报关、装运……中的任何一环发生问题,未能及时发现并纠正,最后都会在单据工作中暴露出来,这时有些问题还来得及补救。所以,单据工作在合同履行过程中还起到"把关"的作用。

**2. 单据是收取货款的重要工具**

出口贸易货款收取在采用托收、信用证或国际保理时,其付款的主要依据是单证,即使在采用汇付时,有时(如单到付现)单证也是付款的依据。随着国际贸易的发展,国际货物单据化,使得单证与货款的对流原则已成为国际贸易中的一般原则。

**3. 单据是发生纠纷时有关当事人处理纠纷的依据**

如买方提货时发现货物受损,如向保险公司索赔,保险单就是赔偿的凭证;如向承运人索赔,则提单或其他运输单据就是处理纠纷的依据。如关系到赔偿额计算的问题,发票则是依据。所以说出口单据又是涉外法律的文件。

此外,出口单据还具有政治意义。如海关发票或领事发票可供进口国海关考核该商品是否属于倾销的范围。而普惠制产地证则是供进口国家执行普遍优惠制及海关减免税的依据。故出口单据是体现一个国家方针政策的文件。

### 9.1.2 国际贸易结算单据的种类

国际贸易结算单据的类型很多,划分标准也很多,其中按单据本身的特性可将单据分为金融单据、商业单据及官方单据。

**1. 金融单据**

金融单据是指汇票、本票、支票等票据及其他代表一定货币债权的凭证如债券、息票及银行存单等。

**2. 商业单据**

商业单据是用来充当卖方已履约的证明及代表货物的凭证。

**3. 官方单据**

业务中对"Official"有两种理解：其一是将"Official"解释为"官方的""政府的"，认为"Official Bills"须是由政府机关签发的证件，如我国外经贸部、商检局等机构签发的单据。其二是将"Official"解释为"正式的""正规的"，认为除国家机关外，一些由民间组织如商会、工会等所签发的单据也是"Official Bills"。

## 9.2 国际贸易结算单据制作的基本要求

不管国际结算的单据种类如何，其制作均遵循"正确、完整、及时、简明、整洁"原则。

### 9.2.1 正确

单据的正确是出口单据工作的根本原则，是单据工作的前提和出发点。单据的正确性，具体表现在两个方面：

（1）单据必须与有关国际惯例和进出口国家的法规相符。

（2）信用证支付方式下的单据应保持"四个一致"。它们分别为：①单证一致：即单据与信用证一致，这是信用证支付方式本身对单据的要求，若单据与信用证有丝毫的不符，将可能遭到银行的拒付。②单单一致：就同一笔业务来讲，各种单据之间相应的项目要互相一致，决不能相互矛盾。这不仅要求大到每一个条款的内容，而且小到每一个字母的拼写都应完全相同。③单货一致：这是指单据上所记载的内容应与实际货物的情况一致，这实际上是要求卖方严格履行贸易合同。④单同一致：即单据内容与贸易合同的规定一致，否则进口方有权拒付货款。

### 9.2.2 完整

完整一般包括下列三层意义：

**1. 单据种类完整**

每一份跟单信用证都规定有各种不同的单据，如发票、提单、保险单、商检证等，遗漏任何一种单据，就是单证不完整。

**2. 单据内容完整**

每种单据由于各自的功能和作用不一样，所要求的内容也不一样。如提单须有发货人、收货人、通知人的名称、起运港、船名、件数、重量和品名等项目，遗漏一项内容即为不完整。即使信用证上未规定某项目，但该项目是本单据的必要项目时，也不得遗漏，遗漏者也算内容不完整。如对于提单，虽然信用证并未规定提单须列出货物件数（散装除外），但件数是提单必备的项目，如提单未列明件数，则为单据内容不完整。

**3. 单据份数完整**

信用证一般规定了向银行议付时须提交单据的份数，应如数提供，不能短缺。为此必须了解信用证中对单据份数的表示方法，一般有两种方式，具体情况如下：

1）一式二份：In Duplicate 或 In 2 folds。
2）一式三份：In Triplicate 或 In 3 folds。
3）一式四份：In Quadruplicate 或 In 4 folds。
4）一式五份：In Quintuplicate 或 In 5 folds。
5）一式六份：In Sextuplicate 或 In 6 folds。
6）一式七份：In Septuplicate 或 In 7 folds。
7）一式八份：In Octuplicate 或 In 8 folds。
8）一式九份：In Nonuplicate 或 In 9 folds。
9）一式十份：In Decuplicate 或 In 10 folds。

### 9.2.3 及时

单据工作的时间性很强，各类单据均有一个适当的出单日期。及时出单包括两方面含义：一是指各种单据的出单日期须合理、可行，如出单日期不能超过信用证规定的有效期或按贸易习惯形成的合理期限；CIF 价格术语下，保险单出单日期须早于或不迟于提单签发日期；提单签发日期则既不能早于也不能迟于信用证规定的装运期限。二是反映在交单议付上，这主要是指向银行交单议付的日期不能超过信用证规定的交单期，或未规定交单期时，不迟于运输单据出单后 21 天内交单。

### 9.2.4 简明

单据的内容应按信用证规定及国际惯例填制。单据的整洁，要求单据格式的设计和缮制力求标准化和规范化，单据内容的排列行次整齐、字迹清晰、重点项目突出、醒目。应尽量减少甚至不应该出现差错涂改的现象。

### 9.2.5 整洁

整洁的单据，其各项内容应当清楚、易认，表面应当清洁、美观、大方。

## 9.3 商业单据——发票

商业单据的种类很多，主要有发票、运输单据、保险单据、装箱单、重量单等。本节介绍发票的类型及其制作。

在国际贸易中，发票的种类很多，如商业发票、形式发票、银行发票、联合发票、厂商发票及海关发票、领事发票等。发票中，最常见的是商业发票，习惯上简称发票。它是全套单据的核心，也是出口商缮制其他单据的依据，因此这里着重对商业发票的缮制进行介绍。

发票是卖方开立的载有货物名称、数量、价格等内容的清单，既是买卖双方交接货物和结算货款的主要单据，也是进出口报关纳税的依据。

在出口贸易中，发票格式并不一致。我国各外贸企业的商业发票格式也不尽相同，但其主要项目和基本内容是一致的。

## 9.3.1 首文部分

**1. 发票名称**

这是采用发票还是商业发票的字样显示,应根据信用证或合同要求选择,并在显著位置标出。

**2. 发票号码、日期**

发票编号代表全套单据的号码,非常重要,不可遗漏,业务中汇票的号码也使用发票的号码。

**3. 信用证和合同号码**

信用证支付方式下的发票,一般都填列信用证号码。信用证未指明合同号者,可以不填。如果指明,则按原句说法照填,如:"As Per contract No..."或"Other terms as per contract No..."。托收方式下的发票则填制合同号。

**4. 收货人**

除非信用证有特别规定,发票都以信用证开证申请人为收货人名称。托收方式下发票的收货人名称按合同规定的买方名称填制。

**5. 运输工具及运输路线**

应严格与信用证一致,且必须和提单相符,此栏包括装运港、目的港及运输工具。若信用证规定起运地为"Any Chinese Port",则要打上某一中国装运港口;若只是"Chinese",则可打上中国任何内陆城市或港口。陆运显示"Per Rail",海运显示"Per Vessel"。

## 9.3.2 正文部分

**1. 唛头**

唛头又称运输标记,按国际标准化组织规定,它由买方简称或代号、参考号、目的港名称及件数四个部分组成,其作用在于便于货物的装卸、运输及存储。若信用证有关于唛头的规定,应严格逐字按信用证要求缮制。若信用证无唛头规定,可按照合同要求填制。

**2. 货物描述**

发票中货物描述一栏包括商品名称、规格、包装和数量。其中对商品品名及规格原则上应按信用证规定照样打出。

**3. 单价、总值及价格术语**

单价应按信用证规定照样打出,若来证未做具体规定,可不打制,或按合同缮制,但合计总数量和总金额必须与信用证相符。

**4. 其他内容**

若信用证有特殊条款,发票要加注某项内容或某种声明等,应照规定在发票上记载,不可遗漏。如要求加注生产单位、许可证号、其他参考号,或者对发票内容的正确性、真实性及货物原产地声明等。在缮制这类声明文句时要注意文句正确、通顺,有的且要注意此时应将发票末端印就的"E.O.E."(Errors & Omissions Excepted,有错或遗漏当查)划掉。

## 9.3.3 结尾

结尾的主要形式是由出口商加盖公司图章和签章,所有图章须与信用证受益人规定完全一致，且应与其他单据相同。目前不少公司都将公司名称及负责人签字印刷在发票右下角，但要注意若信用证要求手签，必须另加负责人的手签。

## 9.4 商业单据——运输单据

运输单据是指承运人或其代理签发给托运人的证明货物已经装船或发运已由承运人监管的单据，它是反映与货物有关的各种关系人的责任与权益的证件，也是交接货物、处理索赔、理赔以及银行结汇或议付的重要单据。按运输方式不同可将运输单据分为海洋运输单据、铁路运输单据、航空运单、邮包收据及多式联运单据等。其中海洋运输单据最为重要。

### 9.4.1 海洋运输单据

#### 9.4.1.1 海运提单

**1. 海运提单的定义**

海运提单简称提单（Bill of Landing，B/L），是货物的承运人或其代理人签发给托运人的，确认托运货物已经装上指定船舶，或者收到托运货物准备装上指定船舶运往指定目的港，并供有关当事人凭此在目的港提取货物的文件或凭证。

**2. 提单的作用**

（1）作为货物收据。承运人或其代理人签发了提单即表示承运人已按提单所载内容收到货物。它虽作为货物收据，并不以将货物装船为条件。通常是当货主将货物送交承运人指定的仓库或地点时，根据货主的要求，可先签发备运提单，待货物装船完毕后，再换发已装船提单。

（2）作为运输合同的证明。提单本身不是货物运输合同，因为在班轮运输中，船公司或其代理签发装货单，同意承运托运人的货物时，运输合同即告成立。租船运输时租船合同是运输合同，而提单是在此后才签发的，虽然如此，但提单上载明了通常运输合同所应具备的各项重要条件和条款，当承托双方发生纠纷时，往往仍以提单上载明的条款为依据。

（3）作为物权凭证。提单代表着提单上所记载的货物，提单的合法持有人可以凭提单请求承运人交付货物。

此外，提单还有作为收取运费的证明、凭以向银行办理抵押贷款等作用。

**3. 提单的当事人**

提单是运输合同的证明，从这一角度分析，B/L 的主要关系人有两个，分别为承运人和托运人。但从 B/L 的内容所涉及的有关人员来看，其关系人还包括收货人、被通知人；如是 B/L 被转让，还会出现受让人、持有人等。

（1）承运人。与托运人签订运输合同的船方，它对运送货物及货物在运送过程中的损坏与丢失负责，它既不是实际承运人，也不是船舶所有人（即船东或租船人）。

（2）托运人。托运人即货方，一般情况下托运人即是发货人，托运人有权指定收货人。当信用证规定"Buyer as shipper"时，托运人则是开证申请人。

（3）收货人。收货人是拥有在目的港凭 B/L 向承运人提取货物权利的当事人，通常是买卖合同的买方。但如何填制须根据具体情况而定。

（4）被通知人。这是承运人为方便货主提货的通知对象，可以不是与货权有关的当事人。

此外还有受让人、持有人等。

**4. 提单的内容**

一般情况下,提单的内容包括正面条款和背面条款。

(1) **提单正面条款**。提单正面条款包括两部分:第一部分为托运人提供并填制的部分,包括托运人、收货人、被通知人、货名、标志和号数、件数、毛重、尺码等项,如填写不正确,托运人要赔偿承运人由此引起或造成的一切灭失、损害和费用;第二部分为承运人印就与填写的部分。其中印就部分的内容主要有:外表情况良好条款,内容不知条款及承认接受条款。

(2) **提单背面条款**。提单背面印定的条款规定了承运人与货方之间的权利、义务和责任豁免,是双方处理争议时的主要法律依据。

**5. 提单的种类**

提单可以从不同的角度加以分类,主要有以下几种:

(1) **按货物是否装上船可划分为已装船提单和备运提单**。前者是指货物全部装上船后,由承运人签发的载明货物已由×××轮装运和装船日期的提单;后者也称收妥(讫)备运提单,它是承运人在货物已交其接管待运时签发的提单。鉴于这种提单无明确肯定的装运日期,且不注明装运船只的名称,将来货物能否装出无确切的保障,因而买方或提单的受让人一般都不愿意接受。在跟单信用证的支付方式下,银行一般也不予以接受。

(2) **按提单有无不良批注可划分为清洁提单和不清洁提单**。前者是指在装船时货物外表良好,承运人在签发提单时未加货损或包装不良等情况批注的提单;后者是指承运人在提单上对货物的表面状况或其他方面不良情况加以批注的提单,如批注标志不清、包装不固、货物表面污渍、漏损、破残等。对不清洁提单银行一般不予接受。

(3) **按运输方式可划分为直达提单、转船提单及联运提单**。直达提单是指货物由同一船只载运从装运港直接运达目的港,中途不经转船时签发的提单;转船提单是指船舶从装货港装船后,不直接驶往目的港而在中途港口换船把货物转往目的港(转船提单内一般注有"在××港转船"等字样);联运提单是当货物经水运与其他运输方式联合运输时由第一程承运人所签发的包括运输全程的提单。

(4) **按提单的格式可划分为简式提单和全式提单**。简式提单也称略式提单,是指提单上只有正面条款而无背面条款的提单;全式提单也称繁式提单,是指在提单背面列有承运人和托运人的权利、义务等详细条款的提单。

(5) **按提单收货人(又称"抬头")的不同可划分为记名提单、指示提单及不记名抬头提单**。记名提单又称"收货人抬头提单",是指在提单上收货人一栏内明确填明某一特定的人或公司名称的一种提单。使用这种提单时,承运人只能将货物交给提单上已指定的收货人。指示提单是指在提单上收货人一栏内只填写"凭指示"(To Order)或"凭××指示"(To Order of...)字样的一种提单,后者既可是凭托运人指示也可是凭进口方银行指示。而不记名提单又称来人抬头提单,是指提单上未指明具体收货人而采用留空或填上"To Bearer"字样的提单。承运人交付货物时凭提单而不凭人,谁持有提单,谁就可提货,转让时凭交付而转让,因而风险较大,在业务中极少使用。

(6) **按提单使用时的效用分为正本提单及副本提单**。正本提单是指在提单上有承运人、船长或其代理人签字盖章的提单，出口商提交银行凭以议付或进口商凭以提货的均应是正本提单。业务中提单正本可有两份或两份以上，但其中一份生效后其他的则自动失效。而副本提单是指提单上无承运人、船长或其代理人签字盖章，仅供工作参考之用，提单上一般有"Copy"或"Not Negotiable"字样，以与正本提单区别。

（7）迟期提单。这原指货物抵达目的港后收货人才收到的提单，主要发生于近洋航线。现在一般是指在信用证支付方式下迟于信用证规定的议付、付款、承兑有效期和/或装运期和/或交单期（未规定交单期时迟于提单签发后21天）向银行提交的提单，这会影响到有关当事人的利益，故根据国际商会《跟单信用证统一惯例》（2007年修订本）规定，银行不接受迟期提单。

（8）预借提单。这是指在合同规定的装运期或在信用证规定的装运期和/或有效期已到而货尚未装船或虽已装船但未装完时，承运人应托运人要求而预先签发给托运人的提单。这常常发生在船舶延迟到港或托运人未按期备货时，但如属于托运人责任，通常要向承运人出具"担保书"承担一切责任，但承运人仍需承担被指责签发假提单的风险。

（9）倒签提单。它是承运人应托运人要求在货物的实际装船日期迟于信用证或合同规定的装运期时，将装运期签成符合规定的装运期时的提单。承运人倒签提单的风险与预借提单相似，故一般不宜使用。

**6. 提单的制作**

（1）**托运人**。在信用证支付方式下，除非信用证另有规定，托运人一般为受益人。如是可转让信用证，则托运人可以是受让人（第二受益人）。托收方式下则把委托人当作托运人。

（2）**收货人**。信用证方式下此栏应严格按照信用证规定填制，因为它直接关系到提单能否转让及物权归属问题。一般提单多为指示式，其收货人应填"To Order"即空白抬头，或填为"To Order Of... Co."或"To Order of... Bank"（按开证行指示）或"To Order of Shipper"（按托运人指示）。托收方式下一般把收货人做成空白抬头。

（3）**被通知人**。信用证支付方式下提单上该栏须按信用证规定缮制。被通知人是收货人的代理人，货到目的港后承运人通知其办理提货前的有关事宜。故被通知人一定要有详细地址，以供承运人或其代理人通知。但当信用证未规定详细地址时，为保持单证一致，正本提单可留空不填。

（4）**船名**。该栏应填实际所装船的船名及航次。

（5）**装运港**。该栏填实际装货港名称，且要符合信用证要求。

（6）**卸货港**。该栏填写卸货港。若货物由装运港直达目的港，未经转船，则该栏填最后目的港；如在某港口转船，则填转船地。例如货在香港转船，则此栏应填"Hongkong (W/T)"，即"With Transhipment at Hong Kong"。

（7）**最后目的地**。该栏应按信用证规定的目的港填写，如遇同名港，还需要加打国名。

（8）**运费缴付地点**。若价格术语为FOB，该栏可填目的港；若价格术语为CFR或CIF，则本栏可填装运港。通常情况下此栏可留空。

（9）**件数和包装种类**。件数和包装单位都应与实际货物一致，并在"大写合计数"栏（Total Packages in Words）填列英文大写文字数目。如果货物包括两种以上不同包装单位（如铁桶、纸箱等），应分别填列不同包装单位的数量，然后再表示总合计件数。散装货物时，件数栏只填"In Bulk"，"大写合计数"栏可留空不填。

（10）**唛头**。信用证规定有唛头就按信用证填，且必须与其他单据上的唛头一致。

（11）**商品名称**。一般可简单表明，不必表明详细规格。

（12）**毛重和容积**。除非信用证有特别规定，提单可不填净重，只填毛重即可，以公斤表示，公斤以下按四舍五入处理；容积以立方米表示，立方米以下保留三位小数。

（13）**运费**。信用证方式下，提单的运费支付问题，要依据合同或按信用证规定的价格条款而定，以 FOB 成交时运费应注明"Freight to Collect"或"Freight payable at destination"或"Freight to be paid at destination"，以 CFR、CIF 成交时运费应注明"Freight Prepaid"或"Freight Paid"，不能注成"Freight Prepayable"或"Freight to be paid"。

（14）**签发地点与日期**。签发提单的地点应与装货港一致，其日期在国际惯例上视为装运日，所以提单签发日期不能晚于信用证规定的装运期。

（15）**提单签发份数**。信用证支付方式下正本提单签发的份数一定要按信用证规定的份数出具。如"Full set 3/3 original clean on board ocean B/L"。这样条款指定要出具三份正本。有些信用证在提单条款上没有规定签发正本份数，但在其他地方这样规定"... available by Beneficiary's drafts at sight drawn on us and accompanied by the following documents in duplicate"，即要求所有单据（包括提单）一式二份。

（16）**承运人签字**。该栏须由船公司或其代理人签字。

#### 9.4.1.2　海运单

海运单与海运提单一样也是在船公司或其代理人收到货物等待装船期间或将货装船之后签发给托运人的一份货物收据，也是运输合同的证明，所不同的是海运单不具备物权凭证的作用。一般而言，海运单仅签发一份正本。

### 9.4.2　铁路运输单据

铁路运输可分为国际铁路联运及供港货物铁路运输两种运输方式，并各自有自身的运输单据。国际铁路联运使用的是国际铁路联运运单，它是参加联运发送国铁路与发货人之间缔结的运输合同。合同中规定了参加联运的各国铁路和收、发货人在货物运送上的权利、义务和责任，对铁路和收、发货人都具有法律效力。凡快运货物，在运单正副本的正、背面的上下边，各加印一厘米宽的红线，以示与慢运运单区别。运单填写用发送国文字，但在每行下附上俄文（或德文）的译文。我国发送和到达货物运单除中朝、中越间不加译文外，其余均限用俄文。运单上除划粗线各栏由铁路填写外，其余由发货人填写。运单一批货物填写一份，一共有五联，分别为：运单正本、运行报单（参加联运的各铁路办理货物交接、划分运送责任、清算运送费用、统计运量和运输收入的原始凭证）、运单副本、货物交付单及货物到达通知单。

### 9.4.3　航空运单

航空运单是航空运输承运人接收货物的收据，它不具备物权凭证作用，也非可议付或转让的单据。每份航空运单有三份正本和至少六份副本。航空运单可分为两种：一种为航空运单，又叫主运单，由航空公司签发；另一种是航空分运单，又称小运单，由航空货运代理公司签发。航空代理经常将数批货物集中办理托运，航空公司仅签发一套运单，为便于工作，代理公司则另给委托人签发自己的分运单。分运单与主运单基本内容相同，其法律效果是相当的，只是前者由航空代理承担货物的全部运输责任。

### 9.4.4 邮包收据

邮包收据既是邮局收到寄件人的邮件后所签发的凭证，也是收件人凭以提取邮件的凭证。当邮件发生损坏或灭失时，可作为索赔和理赔的依据，但邮包收据不是物权凭证。

### 9.4.5 多式联运单据

多式联运单据是在多种运输方式联合运输货物时所使用的一种运输单据。它是由一种叫作"多式联运经营人"签发的证明货物已由他接管，他将对货物运输全程负责的单据。

## 9.5 商业单据——保险单据

### 9.5.1 保险单据的含义与作用

保险单据是保险公司与投保人之间的保险契约，详细规定了双方的权利和义务。保险单据是保险公司对承保人开出的承保证明。当被保险货物遭受保险责任范围内的损失时，保险单据是投保人向保险公司索赔的主要根据，也是保险公司理赔的依据。同时，保险单据还是全套货运单据的主要组成部分。

一般的财产保险其保险单不是保险标的的附属物，不能随保险标的所有权的转移而转移。但国际货物运输保险单有其特殊性，根据保险业的国际惯例，货物运输保险单由被保险人背书后，可随货物所有权的转移而转移，不必征得保险人的同意，也不必通知保险人。许多国家的保险法都有上述规定，中国人民保险集团股份有限公司也按国际惯例办理保险业务。

**保险单的当事人主要有：**①**保险人**，这是收取保险费并按海上保险合同的规定负责赔偿损失的人，也称承保人。②**被保险人**，也称投保人（Applicant）或要保人，是与保险人订立保险契约并交付保险费的人。在保险标的物遭受损失时，被保险人有权向保险人索赔，并接受保险利益的全部或一部分赔偿。③**保险代理人**，受保险人委托，在规定的授权范围内代保险人招揽保险业务出立暂保单或保险单，查勘损失及理算损失的中间商。保险公司对许多自己无法完成的业务与保险代理签订合约，保险代理人的代理费由保险公司支付，其代理行为所产生的权利义务的后果直接由保险公司承担。④**保险经纪人**，这是保险人与被保险人之间的中间人，专门代表被保险人同保险公司签订保险契约，而向保险公司收取佣金。

### 9.5.2 保险单的种类

保险单的种类很多，其中最主要的是保险单和保险凭证。

**（1）保险单俗称大保单，是一份正规的保险合同。**保险单用于承保某一指定航程内某一批货物发生的损失，对保险人和被保险人有法律约束力。其内容分为正面条款与背面条款两部分。其中正面条款的主要内容有：被保险人名称、地址；被保险货物名称、数量和标记；保险金额；装载运输工具、开船日期、装运港、目的港；承保险别；保险代理人名称、地址；赔款偿付地点；订立保险单的日期和地点及保险人签章等。背面条款则对保险人和被保险人的权利义务等方面做了详细规定。在以 CIF 或 CIP 价格条件订立的合同中，买方通常要求提供保险单。

**（2）保险凭证**俗称小保单。它不载明保险人与被保险人的权利义务等方面的详细条款，其他项目与保险单相同，并具有与保险单相同的法律效力，但若买方要求提交保险单时，不能以保险凭证代替。

保险单订立后，如果投保人需要补充或变更其内容，可向保险公司提出书面申请，经保险公司同意后，由保险公司订立注明更改或补充内容的凭证，这种凭证称为批单。批单与原保险单构成新的保险合同，对投保人与保险人有法律约束力。

### 9.5.3　保险单的制作

保险单（参见附录示样）由保险公司根据被保险人提供的投保单、商业发票、运输单据及信用证来缮制。通常情况下保险公司名称、地址及保险单名称的中英文名称已印就，下面仅就需要填写的栏目进行分析。

**（1）保险单号码**。一般由保险公司地区编号、年份及流水号三部分组成。

**（2）发票号码**。此栏习惯按商业发票号码填写。

**（3）被保险人**。被保险人填列在保险单上的"At the request of"后，习惯有以下三种方法：①若信用证未规定或要求"Endorsed in Blank"（空白背书），则填受益人名称，可不填详细地址，同时出口公司应在保险单上背书；②若来证规定保险单背书给××银行，如"Endorsed to the order of...Bank"，则仍填受益人名称，并在保险单背面填上"To order of...Bank"或"Claim if any pay to order of...Bank"类似文句，并由受益人签章；③若来证指定以××公司或××银行或某人为被保险人，则此栏可照办，且出口商不必背书。

**（4）标记**。此栏应与发票、提单保持一致，如来证无特殊规定，也可填成"As Per Invoice No...."。

**（5）包装与数量、保险货物项目**。此两栏应与发票保持一致。

**（6）保险金额**。来证一般规定按发票金额（CIF）110%填列，且此栏必须与大写的"总保险金额"（Total Amount Insured）保持一致。

**（7）保险费及保险费率**。此两栏一般为保险公司内部掌握，故保险单上已印就"按约定"（As Arranged）字样，可不填。但如来证规定须填写此两栏，须照办。

**（8）装载运输工具**。若是海运且为直达船，则在该栏直接填上船名、航次；若要中途转船，则应在填上第一程船名后再加上第二程船名并用"With Transshipment"连接两者；若为其他运输方式，也须相应填制，如"By Train, Wagon No..."（陆运）、"By Airplane"（空运）等。

**（9）开航日期**。按运输单据日期填写。

**（10）运输起讫地**。应参照运输单据填写，若需中途转船，则须填明，如从上海经香港转船至伦敦，应填为"From Shanghai to London W/T Hongkong"；若提单所载目的港为美国纽约，来证却规定投保至芝加哥，则保险单起讫地应填"From Shanghai to New York and thence to Chicago"。

**（11）承保险别**。信用证支付方式项下的保险单的险别按信用证规定办理。

**（12）保险公司代理人。** 应在空格处填上保险公司代理人的详细地址，如遇所保货物出险，收货人可立即与其联系。

**（13）赔款偿付地点。** 若来证未明确规定，该栏一般应填目的港。

**（14）签发日期及地点。** 保险单的签发日期应早于或等于运输单据的日期，但不得迟于运输单据的日期，签发地点应是受益人所在地，一般保险单上已印刷好。

**（15）保险公司签章。** 保险单经保险公司签章后方才有效，通常其签章已印刷在保险单上。

## 9.6　其他商业单据

### 9.6.1　装箱单和重量单

**1. 装箱单**

装箱单也称包装单、花色码单，它列明货物包装及每个包装单位内的详细内容，如每件货物的规格、花色、式样等，故也被称为内容明细表（Specification of Contents）。在国际贸易实务中，一般机器零件、服装、纺织品、工艺品和不定量包装的商品都要求出具这种单据，尤其是不定量包装的商品要逐件列出每件包装情况。进口地海关验货、公证行检验、进口商核对货物均以装箱单为依据。

**2. 重量单**

这是国际贸易中用来说明每个包装单位中重量情况的单据。按装箱重量（Shipping Weight）成交的货物，在装运时出口方须向进口方提供重量单，以供买方收货时核对用。业务中往往是粮食类商品或其他以重量为计价单位的商品要求出具此单，其内容偏重于该商品详细重量的记载和证明。重量单一般有以下内容：编号及日期、商品名称、唛头、毛重、净重、皮重、总件数等。

### 9.6.2　船公司证明

船公司证明是船公司出立的单据，是进口商为了满足政府要求或了解运输情况等要求出口商提交的单据。常见的船公司证明有：船籍证明、船龄证明、船级证明、黑名单据明、船行路线证明、转船通知证明及船长收据等。

### 9.6.3　受益人声明

该证明是信用证结算方式下，出口商按信用证要求出具的说明其已履行某种义务或办理某项工作的声明。实务中常见的有关于商品品质、包装、已发装船通知、已寄样品或副本单据等声明。受益人应根据信用证规定出立声明并正式签章。

红海和波斯湾一带的国家开来的信用证，一般要求受益人证明货物非以色列产品。这种受益人声明有时仅要求在发票中证明即可，其声明的文句可以是下述内容："This is to certify that the goods are not of Israeli origin and that on materials of Israeli origin have been used in their manufacture."

## 9.7 官方单据

官方单据在国际结算业务中是极为重要的单据种类之一。在业务中常见的官方单据有海关发票、领事发票、商检证书、原产地证明书等。

### 9.7.1 海关发票

海关发票是由一些国家的海关制定的一种固定格式的发票，要求国外出口商填写，这种发票有三种不同的叫法：①海关发票；②估价和原产地联合证明书；③根据××国海关法令的证实发票。进口国要求提供这种发票，主要是作为估价完税或征收差别待遇关税或征收反倾销税的依据，此外还可供编制统计资料之用，进口商进口报关时须向海关提交。

### 9.7.2 领事发票

领事发票是由进口国领事馆制定的一种固定格式的发票，要求卖方填写后由进口国驻出口国领事签证，但有时也可用商业发票代替，其作用与海关发票类同。各国领事签发领事发票时均收取一定的领事签证费。目前如国外来证规定要由我方提供领事发票，除北京地区的公司外一般不接受。

### 9.7.3 商检证书

**1. 商检证书的作用**

进出口贸易中，由国家/地区设置的检验机构或由经政府注册的、独立的，第三者身份的鉴定机构，对进出口商品的质量、规格、卫生、安全、检疫、包装、数量、重量、残损以及装运条件、装运技术等进行检验并出具的证书，称为商检证书。一般而言，进出口商品检验是货物交接过程中不可缺少的一个环节。

商检证书具有公正证明的作用，关系到有关各方的经济责任和权益，其作用表现为：作为卖方所交付货物的品质、重量、数量、包装及卫生条件等是否符合合同规定的依据；作为买方对品质、数量、重量、包装等提出异议、拒收货物、要求赔偿的凭证；作为卖方向银行议付货款的单据之一；作为出口国和进口国海关验放的有效证件；作为证明货物在装卸、运输中实际状况、结算运费及明确责任归属的依据。

**2. 商检证书的种类**

我国商检局对外签发的各种检验、鉴定证书、证明书较多，主要有：证明进（出）口商品的品质、规格或等级的品质检验证书；重量检验证书；数量检验证书；兽医检验证书；卫生（健康）检验证书；消毒检验证书；产地检验证书；验残检验证书；价值检验证书及证明所载货物的重量或体积的载衡量证书等。

### 9.7.4 原产地证明书

这是一种证明货物原产地或制造地的证件。在进出口贸易中是出口商应进口商的要求提供的，主要提供给进口国海关掌握货物的原产国别，以配合实施相应的贸易政策和措施。目前，我国出口公司在信用证项下提交的原产地证书包括一般原产地证书和普遍优惠制原产地证书。

**1. 一般原产地证明书**（即中国原产地证书）

一般原产地证明书共有十二栏（不包括在右上角的证书名称和证书号码栏，这两栏已印刷好）。其缮制要点如下：

1）第一栏，出口商名称及地址。若信用证无特殊规定，此栏一般填信用证受益人的名称、地址和国家，不得留空。地址要填详细地址，且与信用证一致。

2）第二栏，收货人名称及地址。若信用证有具体规定，应照填；若信用证无特殊要求，一般应填信用证上规定的提单通知人。习惯上此栏可加注"To Whom it May Concern"（致有关人）。

3）第三栏，运输方式和路线。此栏一般应填明装货港、卸货港及运输方式，如经转船则也应注明转运地，并与提单所列一致。例如"Shipment from Shanghai, China to London Per Vessel"。

4）第四栏，目的港。此栏填最终目的港。

5）第五栏，此栏为签证机构使用。申领出口原产地证的单位应将此栏留空，签证机构根据需要加注内容。例如证书丢失，重新补发，声明×××号证书作废等情况。

6）第六栏，唛头。此栏按信用证的规定填制，应与发票、提单上的唛头一致。

7）第七栏，商品名称、包装数量及种类。此栏的填制与提单同类栏的填法基本一致，且应符合信用证的规定，但商品名称要求填具体名称。有时国外来证要求加注信用证号码或某项声明时可加在此栏。

8）第八栏，商品 H. S. 税目号。

9）第九栏，商品的数量或重量。此栏应以商品的计量单位填制，通常以重量计算，须注明毛重或净重，一般填毛重，如"Gross Weight 12,500 kg"。

10）第十栏，发票号码和日期。此栏必须按照商业发票填制，为避免日期被误解，填制时日期一律用英文缩写，例如"2018 年 5 月 8 日"，应填"May 8th, 2018"。当第六、七、八、九、十栏填制完毕后，习惯上末尾加上表示结束的符号"＊＊＊＊＊＊"。

11）第十一栏，出口商声明、签字、盖章。出口商声明已印刷好，内容为："下列签署人在此声明，上述货物详细情况和声明是正确的，所有货物均在中国生产，完全符合中华人民共和国原产地规则。"

申请单位的证书手签人员应具有法人资格，且在签证机构进行过登记注册。申请单位在此栏盖章，手签人字迹清晰，签字与公章在证面上的位置不得重合。

此栏还须填制申报地点和时间，例如"Nanjing, China Feb. 25, 2014"。注意申报日期不得早于发票日期，且不得迟于提单日期。

12）第十二栏，签证机构证明、签字、盖章。签证机构证明内容为"兹证明出口商声明是正确的"。

**2. 普遍优惠制原产地证明书**

普遍优惠制原产地证明书简称普惠制证书，即 G. S. P. 证书。普惠制是发达国家对来自发展中国家工业制成品与半制成品普遍给予单方面减免关税的优惠制度。它的原则是普遍的、非歧视的、非互惠的。凡我国出口商品属于享受普惠制待遇的商品，一般应向给惠国提供原产地证书。

普惠制原产地证书种类很多，但用得最多的是普惠制原产地证。这种证书的填写方法为：证书第一、二、三栏内容及填法与一般原产地证第一、二、三栏相同，可参照填制；第四栏供官方使用，此栏出口商不填，与一般原产地证第五栏类似；第五栏，商品顺序号，在收货人、运输条件相同的情况下，如同批货物有不同品种，则可按不同品种、发票号等分列"1""2"……单项商品，此栏可填"1"或不填；第六、七栏内容及填法与一般原产地证书第六、七栏相同，可参照填制；第八栏为原产地标准，此栏是海关审证的核心项目，一般填法有：①填"P"，表示完全国产，无进口成分；②填"W"，表示含进口成分，但符合原产地标准；③填"F"，表示对加拿大出口产品，含进口成分（占产品出厂价的40%以下），但发往挪威、瑞士、瑞典、芬兰、奥地利、欧盟及日本时，均填"W"，且须在字母下标上该产品的 H.S. 税目号；第九、十栏内容及填制方法与一般原产地证第九、十栏相同；第十一栏，签证当局证明、签署地点、日期及授权签证人手签、商检机构印章；第十二栏，出口商申明。生产国横线上有"CHINA"字样，一般已印在证书上面，进口国横线上的国别应正确填写。若信用证有具体规定，则按规定填写，否则可以第三栏目的港国别为准。

申请单位在向商检局申请签单时还应提交一份普惠制产地证明书申请书和发票副本。

# 第10章

# 国际结算中的风险与防范

## 10.1 国际结算风险概述

### 10.1.1 风险与风险因素

**1. 风险的内涵**

企业的进出口贸易活动、收益的取得及其生存和发展，都是在克服各种风险，在有效管理各种风险的条件下取得的。

**2. 风险的特征**

尽管对风险的定义多种多样，但一般而言，风险具有以下三个基本特征：①客观性，因为风险无时不在，无处不在；②相对性，即风险可能会带来损失，也可能不会带来损失，甚至带来收益；③可控性，即随着人们识别和抵御风险的能力不断增强，风险可在一定程度上被降低，或使得风险的不确定性得到控制。

### 10.1.2 国际结算风险

国际结算风险是指在国际结算过程中，由于多种因素的影响而使国际结算过程中的有关当事人蒙受损失的不确定性。从不同角度，可对国际结算风险进行不同的分类。按产生的原因可分为自然风险和人为风险；按风险能否管理可分为可管理风险和不可管理风险；而按风险表现形式可将风险分为票据风险、结算方式风险及欺诈风险等。

## 10.2 票据风险与防范

票据作为国际结算中一种重要的支付凭证，在国际上使用十分广泛。由于票据种类繁多，性质各异，再加上大多数国内居民极少接触到国外票据，缺乏鉴别能力，因而在票据使用过程中，风险经常存在。

### 10.2.1 票据风险的含义与类型

**1. 票据风险的含义**

国际结算中的票据风险是指票据出具和/或流通过程中由于不确定性因素的存在而使有关当事人利益受损的风险。

**2. 票据风险的类型**

票据风险产生于与票据市场运行有关的不确定性或信息不完全。从票据风险的成因看，有经济因素，也有非经济因素；根据票据风险的表现形式可分为票据签发承兑风险、贴现风险、转让风险、再贴现风险、回购风险和收款风险等。而依据票据风险出现的形式，有短期的，也有长期的，有隐蔽性的，也有显现性的。

### 10.2.2　票据风险防范

对于票据风险，卖方和买方均可能有，这里以卖方为例，分析票据风险防范中应注意的要点。

**(1) 选择资信良好的客户进行交易。**在贸易成交以前，应通过各种途径调查客户的资信，与资信良好的客户进行交易。应特别注意那些资信不明的新客户及那些来自外汇紧张、经济落后、局势动荡国家（地区）的客户。

**(2) 认真签好外贸合同。**贸易成交前，买卖双方一定要签署稳妥、平等互利的销售合同。

**(3) 仔细审核票据。**对客商提交的票据一定要事先委托银行对外查实，以确保能安全收汇。

**(4) 尽量选择由对方在银行未收妥票款之前，不能过早发货，以免货款两空。**

**(5) 积累经验，以加强对伪造票据的防范。**

## 10.3　主要结算方式风险

在国际贸易结算过程中主要涉及出口商、进口商及银行三个方面的当事人，对于银行，因具体支付方式的不同又可能有不同的银行，如托收方式下至少会涉及托收行及代收行、信用证项下通常会涉及开证行、议付行。本节主要介绍托收及信用证两种常用国际结算方式下的风险。

### 10.3.1　托收方式下的风险及其管理对策

#### 10.3.1.1　风险因素

托收方式主要涉及出口商、进口商、托收行及代收行等四个当事人。不同的当事人面临的风险各不相同，相应地，其风险因素也不相同具体如表 10-1 所示。

表 10-1　托收方式下各当事人的风险因素

| | 外部环境 | 企业内部 |
|---|---|---|
| 出口商的风险 | ① 进口商拒付（如进口商信誉差、倒闭破产无力付款、行情发生不利于买方的变化、进口国贸易政策发生变化、申请不到外汇）<br>② 在途货物发生损失（在以 FOB、CFR 等由卖方承担运输风险的术语成交时），买方为避免资金占用或在途物未办理保险而不赎单/拖延赎单<br>③ 进口国对术语有特殊理解<br>④ 代收行与进口商勾结（如在远期 D/P 方式下，代收行自行允许买方凭 T/R 借单） | ① 对进口商资信不了解<br>② 单据不正确<br>③ 托收方式选择不当<br>④ 代收行选择不当<br>⑤ 价格术语选择不当<br>⑥ 未按合同规定履行交货义务<br>⑦ 对对方国家贸易法律/法规/惯例/贸易政策了解不透 |

（续）

| | 外部环境 | 企业内部 |
|---|---|---|
| 进口商的风险 | ① 出口商欺诈，如伪造提单骗取货款<br>② 出口商不按合同规定质量和/或数量履行交货义务<br>③ 出口商销售非己有而属于第三方所有的货物或通过"克隆"提单将同一批货物重复销售给多位买方 | ① 对出口商的资信及经营作风缺乏深刻了解<br>② 单据审核有误（如因对提单的真伪缺乏判断而收到假提单） |
| 托收行的风险 | ① 出口商资信不良（向资信不好的出口商提供了贸易融资，如出口押汇或汇票贴现等业务）<br>② 选择了信誉不良的代收行 | 未按托收指示书办理业务 |
| 代收行的风险 | ① 进口商凭信托收据（T/R）借单提货，但到期时拒不付款<br>② 承担远期 D/P 即期付款业务中进口商拒付的风险 | 未按托收指示书办理业务 |

#### 10.3.1.2 风险管理对策

**1. 出口商风险管理对策**

**（1）事前对策。** 在选择托收方式前，出口商在避免风险上是主动的，其可采用的方法包括：

1）提高业务人员素质，健全规章制度，严格按照 URC 办事，按授权办理业务。

2）只与资信及经营作风良好的进口商进行交易。

3）签好贸易合同。详细列明合同的各项条款，避免发生进口商不付款赎单或货物滞留目的港而被拍卖，出现货款两空的风险。

4）掌握授信额度。不宜在使用托收方式时进行大额交易。

5）仔细研究进口地的法律、外贸及外汇管理规定，对贸易和外汇管制较严的国家尽量不用或少用托收。

6）选择预付货款、信用证、国际保理等方式收取货款。

7）投保出口信用保险，以转嫁出口收汇风险。

**（2）事中对策。** 一旦被迫选择了托收方式，出口商面对风险将比较被动，但仍有很多好的方法来管理风险：①科学选择运输方式。应尽量避免使用铁路运输、内陆水运及空运。因为此时进口商凭有关运输部门在货物抵达目的地后发给其的到货通知提取货物，易造成买方在提货后找借口拒付或压价，使出口方陷于被动。②合理选择价格术语。尽可能采用 CIF 或 CIP 这类由卖方负责代办保险的价格术语成交，从而当发生进口商得知货物方式损失而拒付时可凭保险单向保险公司索赔来保障自身的利益。③控制好出口单据。④托收方式选择严格遵循两个优先原则。即在 D/P 及 D/A 中优先选择 D/P；在即期 D/P 与即期 D/P 中优先选择即期 D/P。⑤慎重选择代收行，加快收汇速度。⑥选择复合支付方式。如选择托收与汇付相结合或托收与信用证相结合的支付方式进行。使用后者时，建议选择跟单托收＋光票 L/C 方式，以保证单据不失控。

（3）事后对策。一旦风险发生，出口商将限于极为被动的局面，但仍有一些方法可减少损失的发生。只要出口商做到以下几点：①发现问题及时处理。如加强对收款时间的监控，及时催收货款，以防夜长梦多；在发生买方拒付货款时，及时委托需要时代理（Representative in-case-of-need）代为处理到达目的港的货物。此时还应注意必须选择我国驻当地的公司作为需要时代理。②诉诸法律保全。③及时索赔。

**2. 进口商风险管理措施**

（1）事前对策：①不选择托收方式。这种方式最简单，但国际市场上一些产品的卖方垄断的特点决定了买方有时无法回避。②选择资信良好的出口商进行交易。③合理选择价格术语。尽可能争取选择 FOB 等由买方自行派发运输工具的价格术语成交，避免卖方与船方勾结行为的发生。

（2）事中对策。在被迫选择托收方式时，进口商可通过以下途径来防范风险：①科学选择具体的托收方式。在具体托收方式的选择上，进口商也应遵循两个优先原则，即在 D/P 及 D/A 中优先选择 D/A；在即期 D/P 与远期 D/P 中优先选择即期 D/P。②认真审核单据。为防范出口商以虚假单据或发运残次货物的形式蒙骗进口商付款，进口商可以规定出口商必须提交商品质量检验证书，而且这些证书须由进口商在出口地的指定人或派出机构签发，或由出口地的公正检验机构签发，或由出口地的国际公认的权威检验机构签发，如瑞士的 SGS 检验机构等。

（3）事后对策。一旦进口商赎取了单据，但发现出口商未按合同规定交货，只能依据合同运用相关法律/惯例向卖方索赔；若出口商故意以假单据进行欺诈，虽然有时能通过法律途径获得赔偿，但更多的情况可能是进口方只能自认倒霉，从中吸取教训。

**3. 托收行风险管理对策**

对于托收行而言，其风险管理方法主要两条原则：①严格按照国际商会《托收统一规则》办理托收业务；②不向资信不良的出口商提供贸易融资。

**4. 代收行面临的风险**

对代收行而言，其风险管理方法也比较简单，只要遵循以下三条原则即可：①与托收行一样，严格按照《托收统一规则》办理托收业务；②加强对进口商的资信调查；③慎重对待"远期 D/P，即期付款"这一近年来产生的托收业务中新兴的融资业务，在此业务处理时，应仔细审核进口商的资信，以免陷自己于被动。

## 10.3.2　信用证方式下的风险及其防范

尽管信用证方式是建立在银行信用基础上的支付方式，但由于此方式下的出口商、各银行以及进口商等相关当事人在业务处理的过程中以信用证条款为基础，以出口商提交的单据为中心，而且信用证项下出口商提交的单据与实际发运的货物相分离，因此信用证项下各当事人可能面临更多、更复杂的风险。这些风险的防范将变得更加困难。

### 10.3.2.1　风险因素

信用证方式下的风险因素如表 10-2 所示。

表 10-2　信用证方式下各当事人的风险因素

| | 外 部 环 境 | 企 业 内 部 |
|---|---|---|
| 受益人的风险 | ① 进口商不按合同规定开立信用证<br>② 信用证对银行保证的有效期、对货物的装船日期以及对出口商的交单日期规定得比较短促<br>③ 信用证规定海运提单的收货人为开证申请人，造成出口商难于控制货物<br>④ 信用证规定 1/3 或 2/3 正本海运提单自寄开证申请人，不利于出口商控制货物<br>⑤ 信用证规定的有效日期及有效地点均在开证行所在地<br>⑥ 信用证方式下的银行费用均由出口商负担，加大出口商的成本<br>⑦ 软条款信用证<br>⑧ 开证行拒付，如因倒闭破产<br>⑨ 单证不符和/或单单不符 | ① 对进口商资信掌握不透<br>② 对信用证理解发生偏差<br>③ 未正确制单、交单<br>④ 对信用证欺诈行为的识别缺乏经验 |
| 开证申请人的风险 | ① 出口商伪造虚假单据来骗取信用证下开证行或其指定银行的付款<br>② 出口商巧妙利用信用证单据买卖特点，提交与合同规定不相符合的货物<br>③ 在预支信用证下，出口商获得预付款后延迟发货或携款潜逃<br>④ 对开信用证下货物或设备进口后对方迟迟不开证，使得进口商遭受损失 | ① 选择了信誉欠佳的出口商<br>② 对提交的单据未能充分验证 |
| 开证行的风险 | ① 开证申请人拒绝付款赎单/未完全支付信用证金额<br>② 受益人提交单据不正确<br>③ 预支信用证方式下，出口商不发货或延迟发货的风险<br>④ 假远期信用证方式下，进口商不付款 | ① 对开证申请人资信审查不严<br>② 对信用证项下单据审查不严 |
| 议付行的风险 | ① 受益人资信欠佳/或被追索时无支付能力<br>② 开证行拒付<br>③ 单证不一致和/或单单不一致 | ① 业务人员经验不丰富<br>② 对受益人资信审查不严 |
| 通知行的风险 | 信用证欺诈，如进口商杜撰信用证，或与银行勾结开立虚假信用证 | 不确定来证密押号码（Test No.）和/或预留印鉴（Signature）真伪时，将信用证通知给受益人但未告知不能确定真伪的事实 |
| 保兑行的风险 | ① 开证行资信欠佳<br>② 进口国发生政治风险<br>③ 受益人提交单据不正确 | 保兑资格审查不严格 |

#### 10.3.2.2　信用证项下的风险管理

**1. 受益人对风险的防范**

在信用证方式下，当接到进口商要求其银行开立的带有各种条款的信用证时，面对对方银行的付款保证，出口商应做到：①掌握开证行资信的真实状况，要求由资信良好的银行开立信用证。②应认真审核信用证中的各种条款。③应学会通过单据来控制货物。海运提单的抬头应做成对出口商比较有利的空白抬头形式，然后通过背书转让，出口商把单据交付其委托的银行，才能有效地操控货物。④出口商应向所在国保险机构投保出口信用保险。⑤在开证行拒付时，可研究拒付的理由并与往来银行商讨对策；或直接与买方或其代理商交涉；或对货运单据及货物进行保全；或转售或运回货物；或通过调解、仲裁解决纠纷。⑥针对开证行的破产，应选择恰当的措施加以防范。如在开立信用证前破产，买方可与银行解除开证契约，卖方也有权要求买方另选其他银行重开一张新的信用证；在信用证开立后破产时，如受益人尚未使用该证，一般就不会使用；如银行在对汇票进行承兑后破产，此时应根据情况灵活处理，以保障卖方利益。

**2. 进口商对风险的防范**

信用证方式下的进口商针对其面对的风险，应采取以下主要措施加以防范：①加强对出口商的资信调查，只与资信好的出口商进行交易；②在信用证中详细列明货物状况，解决信用证业务的单据买卖特点导致的单据与实际货物相脱离的问题；③对开信用证下应要求当收到对方银行开来信用证时，本方银行开出的信用证方可生效。

**3. 开证行对风险的防范**

针对信用证业务中存在的风险，可供开证行选择的避险措施主要有：①认真审核进口商的资信；②对预支信用证下的融资，开证行可要求出口地银行按照出口商备货以及发货的进度分批、分次发放，从而降低因一次预支而造成的款货尽失的风险。

**4. 通知行对风险的防范**

在提供通知服务时，通知行应严格按照UCP600的规定审核信用证的真伪。当不能确定信用证的真伪时，应及时通知有关当事人，避免由于自身原因而使虚假信用证过关并造成相关当事人的损失。

**5. 议付行对风险的防范**

在为受益人提供议付时，议付行应当：①加强自身人员业务训练，不断提高业务水平，严格审核出口商提交的单据，避免出现己方认为单证相符而开证行却发现不符点，进而造成拒付的情况；②仔细考核开证行的信用状况，避免由于开证行信誉不佳而造成己方替代付款而开证行却拒不履行偿付义务情况的出现；③加强对信用证业务中出口商的资信的了解，或要求出口商提供担保或抵押品以进一步减少可能遭遇到的损失；④在发现开证行面临较大的国内政治风险时，应学会拒绝接受议付以避免风险。

**6. 保兑行对风险的防范**

被指定银行提供保兑服务时，应审核开证行的信誉状况及所在国政治风险的大小，避免发生保兑付款后因开证行拒付而给自己带来损失。当面临风险较大时，保兑行可拒绝接受开证行的保兑邀请。另外，开证行要求某银行提供保兑服务时常常说明开证行在此银行开有账户并存有一定数额的资金。如无此种关系，被指定银行应审慎从事。

# 附　　录

## 附录 A　Bill of Exchange（汇票）

No. _____　　Date _____

Exchange for _____

At _____ days after sight of this FIRST of Exchange (Second of exchange being unpaid)

Pay to the Order of _____

The sum of _____

Drawn under L/C No. _____　Dated _____

Issued by _____

To _____

_____<br>AUTHORIZED SIGNATURE

# 附录 B  Remittance Application（汇款申请书）

## 境 外 汇 款 申 请 书
### APPLICATION FOR FUNDS TRANSFERS（OVERSEAS）

致：中国 ABC 银行×××分行
日期
TO：ABC BANK OF CHINA, _____  Branch   Date _____

□电汇 T/T   □票汇 D/D   □信汇 M/T    发电等级  □普通 NOMAL   □加急 Urgent

| | | | | |
|---|---|---|---|---|
| | 申报号码<br>BOP REPORTING NO. | | | |
| 20 | 银行业务编号<br>Bank Transac. Ref. No | | 收电行/付款行<br>Receiver/Drawn on | |
| 32A | 汇款币种及金额<br>currency & interbank settlement amount | | 金额大写<br>Amount in words | |
| 其中 | 现汇金额 Amount in FX | | 账号 Account no. | |
| | 购汇金额 Amount of purchase | | 账号 Account no. | |
| | 其他金额 Amount of others | | 账号 Account no. | |
| 50a | 汇款人名称及地址<br>Remitter's Name & address | | 对私 | 个人身份证件号码 individual ID NO. |
| | □对公  组织机构代码 Unit code | | | □中国居民个人  □中国非居民个人 |
| 54/56A | 收款银行之代理行名称及地址<br>Correspondent of beneficiary's Bank Name & Address | | | |
| 57a | 收款人开户银行名称及地址<br>Beneficiary's bank name & Address | 收款人开户银行在其代理行账号 Bene's bank a/c no. | | |
| 59a | 收款人名称及地址<br>Beneficiary's name & Address | 收款人账号 Bene's A/c NO. | | |
| 70 | 汇款附言<br>Remittance Information | 只限 140 个字位 Not exceeding 140 characters | 国内外费用承担<br>All bank's charges if any are to be borne by | |
| | | | □汇款人 our   □收款人 ben   □共同 sha | |

（续）

| 收款人常驻国家（地区）名称及代码 Resident country/region name & code | | | | | |
|---|---|---|---|---|---|
| 请选择： | □预付货款　□货到货款　□退款　□其他 | | | 最迟装运日期 | |
| 交易编码<br>BOP Transaction code | | | | 交易附言<br>Transac. remark | |
| 是否为进口核销项下付款 | | 合同号 | | 发票号 | |
| 外汇局批件/备案表号 | | 报关单经营单位代码 | | | |
| 报关单号 | | | | 本次核注金额 | |
| 银行专用栏<br>For Bank Use Only | | 申请人签章<br>Applicant's Signature | | 银行签章<br>Bank's Signature | |
| 购汇汇率<br>Rate @　　% | | 请按照贵行背页所列条款代办以上汇款并进行申报<br>Please Effect The Upwards Remittance, Subject To The Conditions Overleaf； | | 核准人签字<br>Authorized person | |
| | | | | 日期<br>Date | |
| 等值人民币<br>RMB Equivalent | | 申请人姓名 | | | |
| 手续费<br>Commission | | Name of Applicant | | | |
| 电报费<br>Cable charges | | 电话<br>Phone No. | | | |
| 合计<br>Total charges | | | | | |
| 支付费用方式<br>In Payment of<br>the Remittance | □现金 by cash | | | | |
| | □支票 by check | | | | |
| | □账户 from account | | 复核 Checker | | |

注：资料来源：https：//wenku.baidu.com/view/09421a659b89680202d82558.html.

# 附录 C  Documentary Collection Application（托收申请书）

## 中国 XY 银行
## XY Bank of China
### Documentary collection instruction

Office：XY Bank Of China，Jiangsu Branch

Address：

Date：

We enclose the following draft（s）/document which

Please collect in accordance with the instruct indicated herein.

This collection is subject to URC522.

| Principal（full name &address） | To：Collecting Bank（full name & address） | |
| --- | --- | --- |
| | Drawee（Full name & Address） | |
| Tenor： | Draft/Invoice NO.： | Amount： |

DOCUMENTS：

| Draft | Com. Inv. | Packing List | B/L | N/N B/L | Awb | C/O | GSP Form A | Insp. Cert | Cert |
| --- | --- | --- | --- | --- | --- | --- | --- | --- | --- |
|  |  |  |  |  |  |  |  |  |  |

Special instructions（mark "×"）

☐ please deliver document against ☐payment at sight/☐payment after _____sight ☐/acceptance

☐ all your charges are to be borne by ☐ the drawee / us

☐ in case of time bill，please advise us of acceptance giving maturity date.

☐ in case of dishonor，please do not protest but advise us of non-payment non-acceptance giving reason.

☐ please instruct the collecting bank to deliver documents only upon receipt of all their banking charges.

Disposal of  proceeds  upon  collection.

联系人：          电话：

江苏进出口有限公司

_____

（AUTHORIZED SIGNATURE（S）

# 附录 D　Letter of Credit（信用证）

| | | |
|---|---|---|
| 27 > | Sequence of Total | 1/2 |
| 40A > | Form of Documentary Credit | IRREVOCABLE |
| 20 > | Documentary Credit Number | 521010241936-A |
| 31C > | Date of Issue | 171118 |
| 40E > | Applicable Rules | UCP LATEST VERSION |
| 31D > | Date and Place of Expiry | 171215IN CHINA |
| 51D > | Applicant Bank | ABC COMMERCIAL BANK |
| | （DUBAI TRADE FINANCE） | |
| | LC REF.：188T1S4073220001 | |
| 50 > | Applicant | |
| | POWERFUL MACHINES LLC | |
| | PO BOX 12345 | |
| | DUBAI U. A. E | |
| 59 > | Beneficiary | |
| | XYZ GROWER INTERNATIONAL | |
| | TRADE CO., 9-10F-1002 | |
| | XIANQIANXIJIE MINGZHU PLAZA | |
| | MN, P. R. CHINA 214001 | |
| 32B > | Currency Code；Amount | USD3800， |
| 41D > | Available With...By... | ANY BANK |
| | | BY NEGOTIATION |
| 42C > | Drafts at... | DRAFT AT SIGHT IN DUPLICATE |
| 42D > | Drawee | |
| | STANDARD CHARTERED BANK (HK) LTD. HONG KONG | |
| 43P > | Partial Shipments | NOT PERMITTED |
| 43T > | Transhipment | NOT PERMITTED |
| 44E > | Port of Loading/Airport of Departure | ANY PORT IN CHINA |
| 44F > | Port of Discharge/Airport of Destination | DUBAI |
| 44C > | Latest Date of Shipment | 171130 |
| 45A > | Description of Goods and/or Services | |

　　ZLP 800 DIPPING ZINC PLATFORM 2M+2M+2M WITH 100M WIRE ROPE 8.6MM - 1 SET.

　　BENEFICIARY'S MUST CERTIFY ON INVOICE (S) THAT THE GOODS AND ALL OTHER DETAILS ARE EXACTLY AS PER PROFORMA INVOICE CONT. NO. 07JBE6345　DTD 24.10.2007.

　　INCOTERMS：CIF - DUBAI

46A > Documents Required

1. SIGNED COMMERCIAL INVOICE (S) IN 1 ORIGINAL PLUS 5 COPIES SHOWING THE NAME AND ADDRESS OF MANUFACTURERS OR PRODUCERS OR PROCESSORS OR EXPORTERS AND GOODS ARE OF CHINA ORIGIN (ORIGINAL OF WHICH MUST BE APPROVED BY CHINA COUNCIL FOR THE PROMOTION OF INTERNATIONAL TRADE)
2. FULL SET OF SHIPPED ON BOARD BILL OF LADING, (3 ORIGINALS PLUS 3 NON-NEGOTIABLE COPIES) DULY SIGNED BY THE ISSUER MADE OUT TO THE ORDER OF ABC COMMERCIAL BANK MARKED FREIGHT PREPAID AND MARKED NOTIFY: APPLICANT, (GIVING NAME AND FULL ADDRESS) SHOWING THE APPLICANT'S BANK L/C REF. 188T1S4073220001, NAME, ADDRESS, TELEPHONE AND FAX NOS. OF THE CARRYING VESSEL'S AGENT AT THE PORT OF DESTINATION.
3. CERTIFICATE OF ORIGIN IN 1 ORIGINAL PLUS 1 COPY ISSUED BY CHINA COUNCIL FOR THE PROMOTION OF INTERNATIONAL TRADE, CERTIFYING THAT GOODS ARE OF CHINA ORIGIN, SHOWING THE NAME AND ADDRESS OF THE MANUFACTURERS OR PRODUCERS OR PROCESSORS OR EXPORTERS
4. PACKING LIST: IN DUPLICATE
5. INSURANCE POLICY OR CERTIFICATE OF INSURANCE IN DUPLICATE, ISSUED TO THE ORDER OF ABU DHABI COMMERCIAL BANK, DUBAI FOR FULL CIF VALUE PLUS 10 PERCENT SHOWING APPLICANT'S BANK L/C REF. 188T1S4073220001, CLAIMS PAYABLE IN DUBAI IN THE CURRENCY OF THE CREDIT COVERING THE FOLLOWING RISKS. : ALL RISK. MARINE, WAR, INSTITUTE CARGO CLAUSES (A) .1.1.82 INSTITUTE WAR, STRIKE CLAUSES (CARGO) .1.1.82  RIOTS AND CIVIL COMMOTIONS INCLUDING TPND (THEFT, PILFERAGE AND NON DELIVERY) OF ENTIRE UNIT, PACKAGE, BUNDLE BAG OR PIECE, INSURANCE POLICY OR CERTIFICATE OF INSURANCE TO CERTIFY THAT COVER IS NOT SUBJECT TO A FRANCHISE OR AN EXCESS (DEDUCTIBLE)
6. DOCUMENTS TO INCLUDE A CERTIFICATE FROM THE OWNERS/AGENTS/MASTER OF VESSEL

　　A) CERTIFYING THAT THE GOODS HAVE BEEN SHIPPED BY CONFERENCE/REGULAR LINE VESSEL WHICH IS NOT OVER 15 YEARS OF AGE COVERED BY INSTITUTE CLASSIFICATION SOCIETY

　　B) STATING THAT THE CARRYING VESSEL IS PERMITTED TO ENTER ANY ARAB PORT IN ACCORDANCE WITH THEIR LOCAL LAWS AND REGULATIONS

　　C) CONFIRMING THAT THE CARRYING VESSEL/S. INDICATING THE NAME/S OF THE VESSEL/S HOLD (S) A VALID INTERNATIONAL SAFETY      MANAGEMENT CERTIFICATE (ISM CODE).

47A > Additional Conditions

1　BILL OF LADING AND PACKING LIST TO EVIDENCE SHIPPING MARKS AS: POWER MACHINES LLC.
2　ALL DOCUMENTS CALLED FOR IN THIS CREDIT SHOULD BE DATED, SHIPMENT OR

ANY DOCUMENT DATED PRIOR TO L/C ISSUANCE DATE NOT ACCEPTABLE.

3　ANY CORRECTION/ALTERATION ON DOCUMENTS CALLED FOR UNDER THIS L/CREDIT SHOULD BE SIGNED AND STAMPED BY THE ISSUING AUTHORITY.

4　ALL DOCUMENTS CALLED FOR UNDER THIS CREDIT SHOULD BE PRESENTED IN ENGLISH LANGUAGE, BILINGUAL DOCUMENTS ACCEPTABLE PROVIDED THEY BEAR THE TEXT IN ENGLISH LANGUAGE.

5　IN THE EVENT OF ANY DOCUMENTS AND OR UNDERLYING GOODS AND OR TRANSPORT EVIDENCING VIOLATION OF ANY LOCAL AND OR OFAC AND OR EUROPEAN LAWS/SANCTIONS, WE WILL NOT BE ABLE TO HANDLE THE DOCUMENT AND ANY PAYMENTS THERE UNDER MAY BE DELAYED AND OR NOT EFFECTED BY US.

6　APPLICANT'S BANK LC REF：299T1S4073220001 DTD 071118 MUST ALSO BE QUOTED ON ALL THE DOCUMENTS CALLED UNDER THIS CREDIT.

7　NEGOTIATION IS SUBJECT TO DEDUCTION OF USD. 151/-BEING CHARGES FOR THIS LC ISSUANCE.

/CONTINUATION OF FIELD 78

　　1) NEGOTIATION UNDER RESERVE OR GUARANTEE NOT PERMITTED.

　　2) THE NUMBER AND DATE OF THE CREDIT AND NAME OF OUR BANK MUST BE QUOTED ON ALL DRAFTS REQUIRED.

　　3) REIMBURSEMENT CHARGES USD65. 00 FOR THE ACCOUNT OF BENEFICIARY.

　　A DOCUMENT HANDLING FEE OF USD40. 00 PAYABLE BY THE BENEFICIARY.

　　A DISCREPANCY FEE OF USD65. 00 IS PAYABLE BY BENEFICIARY FOR EACH SET OF DOCUMENTS PRESENTED WHICH DOES NOT STRICTLY COMPLY WITH THE TERMS OF THIS LETTER OF CREDIT AND WHICH HAS TO BE REFERRED TO APPLICANT.

　　71B >　Charges

　　ALL BANK CHARGES ARE ON BENEFICIARY ACCOUNT

49 > Confirmation Instructions　　　WITHOUT

78 > Instructions to the Paying/Accepting/Negotiating Bank

　　DOCUMENTS TO BE DESPATCHED TO STANDARD CHARTERED BANK (HONG KONG) LIMITED, 7/F STANDARD CHARTERED TOWER, 388 KWUN TONG ROAD, KWUN TONG, HONG KONG IN ONE LOT BY COURIER SERVICES.

ON RECEIPT OF DOCUMENTS CONFORMING TO THE TERMS OF THIS DOCUMENTARY CREDIT, WE UNDERTAKE TO REIMBURSE YOU IN THE CURRENCY OF THIS DOCUMENTARY CREDIT IN ACCORDANCE WITH YOUR INSTRUCTIONS, WHICH SHOULD INCLUDE YOUR U. I. D. NUMBER AND THE A. B. A. CODE OF THE RECEIVING BANK IF THE CREDIT IS EXPRESSED IN U. S. DOLLAR.

EXCEPT AS OTHERWISE STATED, THIS CREDIT IS SUBJECT TO THE APPLICABLE RULES SPECIFIED IN FIELD 40E OF THIS MESSAGE.

57D >　'Advise Through' Bank

./80911421300016901
JIANGSU XYZ RURAL COMMERCIAL BANK CO. LTD., ABC,
CHINA SWIFT. L USRCCNSH

--------------------------------------------------------------------------------

MAC: Authentication Code
00000000
CHK: CheckSum
BF3631BD53EA

# 附录 E  Application for the L/C（开证申请书）

TO：BANK OF CHINA

| Beneficiary (full name and address) | L/C NO.<br>Contract No. |
|---|---|
| | Date and place of expiry of the credit |
| Partial shipments<br>○ allowed  ○ not allowed | Transshipment<br>○ allowed  ○ not allowed | ○ Issue by airmail<br>○ With brief advice by teletransmission<br>○ Issue by express delivery<br>○ Issue by teletransmission (which shall be the operative instrument) |
| Loading on board/dispatch/taking in charge at/from<br><br>for transportation to | Amount (both in figures and words) |
| Description of goods: | Credit available with<br>○ by sight payment ○ by acceptance ○ by negotiation<br>○ by deferred payment at<br>against the documents detailed herein<br>○ and beneficiary's draft for 100 % of the invoice value at after sight |
| | ○ FOB  ○ CFR  ○ CIF<br>○ other terms |
| Documents required: (marked with ×)<br>(　) Signed Commercial Invoice in 　 copies indicating invoice no., contract no.<br>(　) Full set of clean on board ocean Bills of Lading made out to order and blank endorsed, marked "freight (　) to collect/(　) prepaid (　) showing freight amount" notifying<br><br>(　) Air Waybills showing "freight (　) to collect/(　) prepaid (　) indicating freight amount" and consigned to _____.<br>(　) Memorandum issued by _____ consigned to _____<br>(　) Insurance Policy/Certificate in 　 copies for 110 % of the invoice value showing claims payable in China in currency of the draft, bank endorsed, covering (　) Ocean Marine Transportation/(　) Air Transportation/(　) Over Land Transportation) All Risks, War Risks.<br>(　) Packing List/Weight Memo in 4 copies indicating quantity/gross and net weights of each package and packing conditions as called for by the L/C.<br>(　) Certificate of Quantity/Weight in 　 copies issued an independent surveyor at the loading port, indicating the actual surveyed quantity/weight of shipped goods as well as the packing condition.<br>(　) Certificate of Quality in 　 copies issued by (　) manufacturer/(　) public recognized surveyor/(　)<br>(　) Beneficiary's certified copy of FAX dispatched to the accountees with 3 days after shipment advising (　) name of vessel/(　) date, quantity, weight and value of shipment.<br>(　) Beneficiary's Certificate certifying that extra copies of the documents have been dispatched according to the contract terms.<br>(　) Shipping Co's Certificate attesting that the carrying vessel is chartered or booked by accountee or their shipping agents: |

(　　) Other documents, if any:
a) Certificate of Origin in _____ copies issued by authorized institution.
b) Certificate of Health in _____ copies issued by authorized institution.

Additional instructions:

(　　) All banking charges outside the opening bank are for the beneficiary's account.

(　　) Documents must be presented with _____ days after the date of issuance of the transport documents but within the validity of this credit.

(　　) Third party as shipper is not acceptable. Short Form/Blank Back B/L is not acceptable.

(　　) Both quantity and amount _____ % more or less are allowed.

(　　) prepaid freight drawn in excess of the L/C amount is acceptable against presentation of original charges voucher issued by Shipping Co./Airline/or it's agent.

(　　) All documents to be forwarded in one cover, unless otherwise stated above.

(　　) Other terms, if any:

Advising bank:

Account No.:

Transacted by:

(Applicant: name, signature of authorized person)

# 附录 F　Standby Letter of Credit（备用信用证）

Date: 20 DECEMBER 2014

Standby Letter of Credit

With reference to the loan agreement no. 2014HN028 (hereinafter referred to as "the agreement") signed between Bank of Communications, SHENYANG Branch (hereinafter referred to as "the lender") and LIAONING ABC CO., LTD (hereinafter referred to as "the borrower") for a principal amount of RMB2,000,000 (in words), we hereby issue our irrevocable standby letter of credit no. 810LC040000027D in the lender' s favor for amount of the HONGKONG AABBCC CORPORATION which has its registered office at AS 8 FL. 2SEC. CHARACTER RD. HONGKONG for an amount up to UNITED STATES DOLLARS THREE MILLION ONLY. (USD3,000,000) which covers the principal amount of the agreement plus interest accrued from the aforesaid principal amount and other charges all of which the borrower has undertaken to pay the lender. The exchange rate will be the buying rate of USD/RMB quoted by Bank of Communications on the date of our payment. In the case that the guaranteed amount is not sufficient to satisfy your claim due to the exchange rate fluctuation between USD and RMB we hereby agree to increase the amount of this standby L/C accordingly.

Partial drawing and multiple drawing are allowed under this standby L/C.

This standby letter of credit is available by sight payment. We engage with you that upon receipt of your draft (s) and your signed statement or tested telex statement or SWIFT stating that the amount in USD represents the unpaid balance of indebtedness due to you by the borrower, we will pay you within 7 banking days the amount specified in your statement or SWIFT. All drafts drawn hereunder must be marked drawn under XYZ Bank standby letter of credit no. 810LC040000027D dated 20 DECEMBER 2014.

This standby letter of is credit will come into effect on 20 DECEMBER 2014 and expire on 09 DECEMBER 2005 at the counter of Bank of Communications, SHENYANG branch.

This standby letter of credit is subject to Uniform Customs and Practice for Document Credits (2007 revision) International Chamber of Commerce Publication No. 600.

Specimen of INTERNATIONAL FACTOR AGREEMENT

　　AGREEMENT made on _____ 20 _____ by and between these parties:
　　(1) _____ and

　　(2) _____

WHEREAS each party, from time to time, will engage the services of the other to act as an Import Factor with respect to the sale of goods or rendering of services to debtors located in the country (ies) where the Import Factor's services are to be performed. NOW, THEREFORE, in consideration of the mutual agreements herein contained, it is hereby agreed between the parties as follows:

Each of the parties hereby subscribes to and agrees to be bound by all of the terms and provisions of the General Rules for International Factoring ("GRIF"), the DEX and IFexchange Manuals and Rules between the Members and Partners, all promulgated by the International Factors Group ("IF-Group") and as formally revised from time to time.

The services to be performed by each party as an Import Factor shall be rendered with respect to all the receivables of each supplier designated by the parties from time to time. The indicative Import Factor's commissions and charges are contained in the Factor Information Sheet, as published on the IFG website in the Members section. The only binding rates are the ones indicated in the exchange, unless another compensation is agreed upon. Neither of the parties shall be obliged to engage the services of the other exclusively and each party shall be free to engage the services of any other service provider located in the country (ies) where the other performs its services.

This agreement shall take effect as of the date set out above and shall continue indefinitely, subject to termination by either party on 90 days' prior written notice to the other but such termination shall not apply to, modify or otherwise affect the obligations of the parties with respect to transactions occurring, accounts receivable transferred or indebtedness incurred prior to the effective date of such termination.

This Agreement contains all the matters agreed between the parties in relation to the receivables included by Article 3 of the GRIF and all agreements, warranties, representations and other statements made by the Import Factor or the Export Factor to the other before the making of this Agreement and the reliance on any usages or practices are excluded unless otherwise referred to herein.

Additional terms (if any) _____

_____

IN WITNESS WHEREOF, the parties have caused this instrument to be executed by their respective duly authorized corporate officers as of the date set out above.

For (insert full legal name of Factor) _____
Registered in (insert country and/or place of incorporation) _____

With official registration number _____

Signature

Full Names

Position:

Who by his/her signature (i) certifies that he/she is duly authorized to execute this document and (ii) undertakes to produce evidence of such authority if so requested.

For (insert full legal name of Factor) _____
Registered in (insert country and/or place of incorporation) _____

With official registration number _____

Signature

Full Names

Position:

Who by his/her signature (i) certifies that he/she is duly authorized to execute this document and (ii) undertakes to produce evidence of such authority if so requested

## 附录 G  Invoice（发票）

**江苏 XYZ 纺织品进出口公司**
**JIANGSU XYZ TEXTILES IMPORT & EXPORT CORP.**
**86，ZHUJIANG ROAD，HEXI DISTRICT，NANJING，CHINA**

发 票  S/C NO ＿＿＿＿＿＿
　　　　INVOICE INV. NO. ＿＿＿＿＿＿
　　　　Date：＿＿＿＿＿＿

From ＿＿＿＿＿ to ＿＿＿＿＿＿＿＿
For account and risk of ＿＿＿＿＿＿＿＿

| MARKS & NOS. | DESCRIPTION | AMOUNT |
|---|---|---|
|  |  |  |

**JIANGSU XYZ TEXTILES IMPORT & EXPORT CORP.**

# 附录 H  Bill of Lading（提单）

| Shipper | B/L NO. |
|---|---|

| Consignee | |
|---|---|

Notify Party

中国远洋运输（集团）总公司
CHINA OCEAN SHIPPING (GROUP) CO.
Combined Transport BILL OF LADING

| Pre-carriage by | Place of receipt |
|---|---|
| Ocean Vessel  Voy. No. | Port of Loading |

| Port of Discharge | Place of Delivery | | Final Destination | |
|---|---|---|---|---|
| Marks & Nos. container Seal No. | No. of Containers or Packages | Kind of Packages; Description of Goods | Gross Weight | Measurement |
| | | | | |

TOTAL NUMBER OF CONTAINERS OR PACKAGES (IN WORDS)

| FREIGHT & CHARGES | Revenue Tons | Rate | Per | Prepaid | Collect |
|---|---|---|---|---|---|
| Ex Rate | Prepaid at | Payable at | | Place and date of Issue | |
| | Total Prepaid | No. of Original B (S) /L | | Signed for the Carrier | |

LADEN ON BOARD THE VESSEL
DATE            BY (TERMS PLEASE FIND ON BACK OF ORIGINAL B/L)
(COSCO STANDARD FORM 11)

# 附录Ⅰ Insurance Policy（保险单）

**PICC 中国人民保险集团股份有限公司天津分公司**
The People's Insurance Company (Group) of China Limited, Tianjin Branch

货物运输保险单
**CARGO TRANSPORTATION INSURANCE POLICY**

发票号（INVOICE NO.）　　　　　　　保单号次
合同号（CONTRACT NO.）　　　　　　POLICY NO.
信用证号（L/C NO.）
被保险人：
Insured：_____

中国人民保险集团股份有限公司（以下简称本公司）根据被保险人的要求，由被保险人向本公司缴付约定的保险费，按照本保险单承保险别和背面所列条款与下列特агентство承保下述货物运输保险，特立本保险单。
THIS POLICY OF INSURANCE WITNESSES THAT THE PEOPLE'S INSURANCE COMPANY (GROUP) OF CHINA LIMITED (HEREINAFTER CALLED "THE COMPANY") AT THE REQUEST OF INSURED AND IN CONSIDERATION OF THE AGREED PREMIUM PAID TO THE COMPANY BY THE INSURED UNDERTAKES TO INSURE THE UNDERMENTIONED GOODS IN TRANSPORTATION SUBJECT TO THE CONDITIONS OF THIS POLICY AS PER THE CLAUSES PRINTED OVERLEAF AND OTHER SPECIAL CLAUSES ATTACHED HEREON.

| 标记<br>MARKS & NOS. | 数量及包装<br>QUANTITY | 保险货物项目<br>DESCRIPTION OF GOODS | 保险金额<br>AMOUNT INSURED |
|---|---|---|---|
|  |  |  |  |

总保险金额
TOTAL AMOUNT INSURED：_____

保费　　　　　　　　启运日期：　　　　　　　　装载运输工具：
PREMIUM____　　　　DATE OF COMMENCEMENT____　　PER CONVEYANCE：____
自　　　　　　　　　经　　　　　　　　　　至
FROM_____　　　　VIA_____　　　　TO_____

承保险别：
CONDITIONS：
所保货物，如发生保险单项下可能引起索赔的损失或损坏，应立即通知本公司下述代理人查勘。如有索赔应向本公司提交保险单正本（共2份正本）及有关文件。如一份正本已用于索赔，其余正本自动失效。
IN THE EVENT OF LOSS DAMAGE WHICH MAY RESULT IN A CLAIM UNDER THIS POLICY, IMMEDIATE NOTICE MUST BE GIVEN TO THE COMPANY AGENT AS MENTIONED HEREUNDER CLAIMS IF ANY, ONE OF THE ORIGINAL POLICY WHICH HAS BEEN ISSUED IN 2 ORIGINAL TOGETHER WITH RELEVANT DOCUMENTS SHALL BE SURRENDERED TO THE COMPANY IF THE ORIGINAL POLICY HAS BEEN ACCOMPLISHED, THE OTHERS TO BE VOID.

赔款偿付地点
CLAIM PAYABLE AT_____　　　　中国人民保险集团股份有限公司江苏分公司
出单日期_____　　　　　　　　The People's Insurance Company (Group) of China Limited
ISSUING DATE_____　　　　　　　　　　　　Tianjin Branch

# 附录 J  Packing List（装箱单）

**江苏 XYZ 纺织品进出口公司**
**JIANGSU XYZ TEXTILES IMPORT & EXPORT CORP.**
**86，ZHUJIANG ROAD, HEXI DISTRICT, NANJING, CHINA**

PACKING LIST　　　　INV. No. _____

　　　　　　　　　　　　Date: _____

| MARKS & NOS. | DESCRIPTION |
|---|---|
|  |  |

**JIANGSU XYZ TEXTILES IMPORT & EXPORT CORP.**

# 附录 K　Weight Memo（重量单）

| ISSUER | | | | | | |
|---|---|---|---|---|---|---|
| TO | | WEIGHT LIST | | | | |
| | | INVOICE NO. | | DATE | | |
| Marks and Numbers | Number and kind of package Description of goods | Quantity | Package | G. W | N. W | Meas. |
| | | | | | | |
| Total (in words) | | | | | | |

# 附录 L  Certificate of Origin（一般原产地证书）

ORIGINAL

| 1. Exporter | Certificate No. |
|---|---|
| 2. Consignee | CERTIFICATE OF ORIGIN OF THE PEOPLE'S REPUBLIC OF CHINA |
| 3. Means of transport and route | 5. For certifying authority use only |
| 4. Country/region of destination | |

| 6. Marks and number of goods | 7. Number and kind of packages; description | 8. H. S. Code | 9. Quantity | 10. Number and date of invoices |
|---|---|---|---|---|
| | | | | |

| 11. Declaration by the exporter | 12. Certification |
|---|---|
| The undersigned hereby declares that the above details and statements are correct, that all the goods were produced in China and that they comply with the Rules of Origin of the People's Republic of China.<br><br>_____<br>Place and date, signature and stamp of authorized signatory | It is hereby certified that the declaration by the export is correct.<br><br><br><br>_____<br>Place and date, signature and stamp of certifying authority |

# 参考文献

[1] 国际商会(ICC). 国际贸易术语解释通则2010 [M]. 北京：中国民主法制出版社，2011.
[2] 蒋琴儿，秦定. 国际结算：理论 实务 案例(双语) [M]. 北京：清华大学出版社，2007.
[3] 梁志坚. 国际结算 [M]. 北京：科学出版社，2008.
[4] 冷柏军. 国际贸易实务 [M]. 2版. 北京：北京大学出版社，2012.
[5] 邵新力. 国际结算(英文版) [M]. 北京：机械工业出版社，2012.
[6] 吴百福，徐小薇. 进出口贸易实务教程 [M]. 6版. 上海：格致出版社，上海人民出版社，2011.
[7] 徐进亮，张啸晨. 国际结算(双语版) [M]. 6版. 北京：对外经济贸易大学出版社，2016.
[8] 易露霞，方玲玲，陈原. 国际贸易实务双语教程 [M]. 3版. 北京：清华大学出版社，2011.
[9] 易露霞，陈新华，尤彧聪. 国际贸易实务双语教程 [M]. 4版. 北京：清华大学出版社，2016.
[10] 尤宏兵. 国际贸易实务 [M]. 北京：人民邮电出版社，2016.
[11] 岳华，杨来科. 国际结算双语教程 [M]. 上海：立信会计出版社，2007.
[12] 苏宗祥，徐捷. 国际结算 [M]. 6版. 北京：中国金融出版社，2015.
[13] 赵绩竹，熊涓. 国际结算(双语) [M]. 北京：人民邮电出版社，2015.
[14] 赵薇. 国际结算与融资(双语版) [M]. 2版. 南京：东南大学出版社，2015.
[15] 赵银德. 外贸函电 [M]. 2版. 北京：机械工业出版社，2010.
[16] 希尔. 国际商务 [M]. 9版. 王蒿，等译. 北京：中国人民大学出版社，2013.